The Making
of *Tombstone*

The Making
of *Tombstone*

*Behind the Scenes
of the Classic Modern Western*

JOHN FARKIS

McFarland & Company, Inc., Publishers

Jefferson, North Carolina

Photographs are from the collection
of the author unless credited otherwise.

LIBRARY OF CONGRESS CATALOGUING-IN-PUBLICATION DATA

Names: Farkis, John, author.
Title: The making of Tombstone : behind the scenes of the classic
modern western / John Farkis.
Description: Jefferson, North Carolina : McFarland & Company, Inc.,
Publishers, 2019. | Includes bibliographical references and index.
Identifiers: LCCN 2018049318 | ISBN 9781476675862
(softcover : acid free paper) ∞
Subjects: LCSH: Tombstone (Motion picture)
Classification: LCC PN1997.T59533 F37 2019 | DDC 791.43/72—dc23
LC record available at https://lccn.loc.gov/2018049318

BRITISH LIBRARY CATALOGUING DATA ARE AVAILABLE

ISBN (print) 978-1-4766-7586-2
ISBN (ebook) 978-1-4766-3503-3

Front cover image: Kurt Russell as Wyatt Earp in *Tombstone*
(Buena Vista Pictures/Photofest); *background:* A view from the front
of the O.K. Corral looking toward Fremont street. The two-story
Tombstone Epitaph building is on the far right
(photograph by Lee Gray/courtesy Catherine Hardwicke)

Printed in the United States of America

McFarland & Company, Inc., Publishers
Box 611, Jefferson, North Carolina 28640
www.mcfarlandpub.com

To Jean
You've supported me for so many years,
kept me on the right path,
and literally saved my life.
I love you more than life itself.
I know this sounds a bit corny, but it sure is appropriate:
"I promise to love you the rest of your life."

Acknowledgments

When I purchase a book of historical interest, the first thing I usually do is browse through the acknowledgments, bibliography and endnote sections, for it is there where one can determine the depth of the author's research. It is also where heretofore unknown manuscripts, letters, books and library collections are at your fingertips, if the author has cited his or her work properly. So once again, I thank my research assistant Leisa Johnson-Kalin for all her hard work and efforts. I owe you *big time*! Rick Hassler had filled the thankless role of correcting my grammatical and punctuation errors. After four books, you would think my writing would improve. As I told Rick, "They wouldn't put the keys on the keyboard unless they wanted you to use them." And I tried to use every stinkin' one!

In the bibliography, I've listed all the individuals I've interviewed, but there are several additional folks who need to be recognized for going above and beyond the call of duty: Jeff Morey, Sam Dolan, P.J. Lawton, John Peel, Peter Sherayko, Jerry and Judy Crandall, Jerry and Kathy Tarantino, Edie Fasano, Bob Boze Bell, Larry Zeug, Chris Swinney and particularly Anne Lockhart Taylor. Without Anne's encouragement and assistance, this project never would have gotten off the ground. The professionals at the Academy of Motion Pictures Arts & Sciences' Margaret Herrick Library, the Arizona State Library and Michigan State University were tireless in their efforts to assist, while members of the Tombstone Original Buckaroo Facebook webpage graciously welcomed me into their group. Virtually all the Buckaroo stories came from my contacts with them and, collectively, they significantly contributed to the quality of this book. Not only did I receive wonderful information, I also made some great new friends.

I also want to thank Joe Musso, Don Taylor, Tony Malowski, Myra MacKay, Frank Thompson and Allan Barra for their assistance in helping me contact many of the individuals whose interviews appear in this work. A special thanks goes out to Michael Blake, author of *Hollywood and the O.K. Corral: Portrayals of the Gunfight and Wyatt Earp*, who graciously allowed me the use of interviews he conducted for his wonderful book. In addition to some of the folks I have previously mentioned, I'd also like to thank Tom and Charley Ward, David Russell, Garrett Roberts, Wendy Wolverton, Billy Lang and Jake Johnson for allowing me to showcase their photographs. If I have failed to properly acknowledge or misidentified an individual's contribution, I sincerely apologize.

Once again, Mike Boldt has created a wonderfully creative book cover and I can't express my thanks enough for his efforts. Sorry we asked for so many changes, Miguel.

Table of Contents

Preface

This book is about the making of the film *Tombstone*, told in the words of those who were there. It is not supposed to be a detailed historical summation of what actually transpired in history; I suggest that those who are interested in an analysis of the story, browse through the bibliography section of this book. Authors Casey Tefertiller, Gary Roberts, Ben Traywick, Victoria Wilcox, Mary Dora Russell, Jeff Guinn, Paula Mitchell Marks, Bob Boze Bell and many others who are much more astute, informed and articulate than I, have delved into this story's minutiae. I have a very close friend who, when asked what time it is, will tell you how to build a watch. And that's great! For those who love history, that's the level of detail they desire. But for the casual fan, I instead chose to summarize the actual story and put it into some sort of historical context.

Tombstone is a classic tale of the Old West told in black and white and shades of gray. It is set in 1881 Arizona where former lawman Wyatt Earp, joined by his brothers and Doc Holliday, seek their fortune in a lawless silver-mining town. Their efforts are soon thwarted by a renegade band of outlaws know as "The Cowboys," who resent and resist any form of control. Forced to take matters into their own hands after the local sheriff is murdered, the Earps once again pin on badges and attempt to bring law and order to Tombstone. However, once one brother is ambushed and another murdered after the gunfight at the O.K. Corral, Wyatt forms a vigilante posse and vows to eliminate the outlaws.

It should come as no surprise that *Tombstone* itself is not 100 percent historically accurate because, after all, it's entertainment! Some events and the sequences in which they occurred have been condensed and modified for purposes of presentation. Historically, for example, Wyatt, Virgil and Morgan Earp did not accompany their "wives" to Tombstone. Rather, it was just Wyatt, James and Virgil; Morgan and Warren arrived later. Also, Wyatt and Virgil didn't take Morgan's coffin to Tucson, James did. Wyatt and his posse accompanied Virgil and Allie several days later. Similarly, Morgan and Virgil were not both attacked on the same night. And the list goes on and on. But for entertainment purposes, it's not that important, for a very simple reason: They only had two hours to tell a story.

Nor is this a book about why certain characters recite specific lines, how they react to others in a particular scene, or what their psychological makeup is *vis-à-vis* the surrounding environment. Again, there are a plethora of books out there that discuss film theory, scene development and the role of the auteur. This book addresses none of that but rather, how the film was actually made.

As readers are no doubt aware, films are not usually shot in sequential order. Actor

1

availability, weather, soundstage vs. locations, interior vs. exteriors shots, day vs. night and numerous other factors determine when a specific scene is filmed. To add to that complexity, there were two directors on *Tombstone*, Kevin Jarre and George Cosmatos, and the latter decided to use hardly any of the former's footage. Thus many scenes were filmed a second time. Dialogue was changed and, in some cases, a particular scene might have been filmed several times in different locations. Mid–1993 saw the Arizona production crew start filming on the Babocomari Ranch, move to Old Tucson Studios, then to Mescal, back to Old Tucson, and end up back at the Babocomari—and that was just the first unit. Throw in Mt. Lemon, Sabino Canyon and Douglas Dry Lake and, well, one can see just how difficult it was to detail what was what. As I have tried to determine day by day what occurred when, this also complicated matters, and the lack of a final shooting schedule only further exacerbated the situation. I have tried to put the shooting schedule in the proper order; any errors of date and content, while inadvertent, are solely mine.

This book is neither a tabloid-type exposé, nor an uber-fan hearts-and-flowers tribute. Rather, it's simply the story of how the movie was made as told to me. After the passage of so many years, it makes little sense to try and sully a person's reputation, although I have to admit in some instances some of the people in this book may not be presented in the most positive light. In many cases, I have been told the same story from several different people, so, even if the stories aren't true, maybe they should be, because they're funnier than hell.

There are those—and I am one—who love to pick out a film's inconsistencies and continuity errors. Not because I'm a perfectionist (which I am), but because I love films. You'll find many of those "errors" in the pages of this book.

So sit back, pour yourself some Red Eye and, if you love this film as much as I do, you should enjoy this book!

Prologue

"The researches of many commentators have already thrown much darkness on this subject, and it is probable that, if they continue, we shall soon know nothing at all about it."—Mark Twain

Wednesday, October 26, 1881. Tombstone, Arizona Territory. Four men—three peace officers and a deputized gambler-cum-dentist—walked defiantly up Fourth Street toward Fremont and a date with destiny. Awaiting them in a small lot next to the Fly house behind the O.K. Corral were two sets of brothers and two other individuals, collectively known as Cowboys. Little did any one of them realize that three of these outlaws would never see another sunrise.

Cowboys (or cow-boys as they were then derisively known) were little more than cattle rustlers and assorted lawbreakers ... a loose collection of semi-organized thieves. Robbing a stage or disturbing the peace were the types of activities in which they engaged. The tools of their trade: fear, intimidation and the frequent use of a six-gun. They resented any infringement of their personal freedom and generally were highly prejudiced against Mexicans. To them, stealing cattle south of the border and then selling them in southeast Arizona to local butchers, restaurants and even the military was not only proper, it was their birthright. The Tucson Citizen newspaper minced few words: "The cowboy is a name which has ceased in this Territory to be a term applied to cattle herders. The term is applied to thieves, robbers, cut-throats and the lawless class of the community generally. When a man follows as a legitimate occupation the tending of cattle or other stock he is called a herder and not a cowboy." The San Francisco Exchange told its readers, "Cowboys [are] the most reckless class of outlaws in that wild country. The cowboy is infinitely worse than the ordinary robber, who generally spares life if he can get money, in that he is utterly reckless of human life. He cares even less for it than money. He glories in being regarded a terror. He rarely cares to steal anything but cattle, but in the company of human beings his revolver is ever brandished, and on the slightest pretext, or fancied pretext, he sends a bullet into a victim's heart with as little compunction as he would kill a dog. He is worse than the Indians, in that he associates with whites and performs his reckless deeds amid peaceful surroundings." According to the detailed diary of George Parson, an early Tombstone resident and member of the Committee of Vigilance, "A cowboy is a rustler at times, and a rustler is a synonym for desperado—bandit, outlaw, and horse thief."[1]

Peace officers—whether they were U.S. marshals representing the laws of the federal government, local sheriffs protecting the rights of Tombstone's 2,100 citizens, or Cochise

County sheriffs who collected taxes from the mines and railroads—were obligated to follow the law, no matter what. Town ordinance No. 9, published effective April 14, 1880, spelled it out:

Be it ordained by the Common Council of the Village of Tombstone:

   Sec. 1: That it shall be unlawful for any person not an officer of the law to have or carry in the Village of Tombstone any fire-arms, knife or other dangerous weapon without a written permit from the Mayor, and anyone violating this provision shall be fined in the sum not to exceed fifty dollars ($50), or to be confined in the village jail for thirty days, or both, in the discretion of the court.

   Sec. 2: When travelers, prospectors, miners, or other strangers not resident of the Village of Tombstone enter the limits of the same with any dangerous weapon upon or about their person, it shall be the duty of the Village Marshal to notify them of this ordinance and request them to dispense with those weapons, and if any one so requested neglect to refuse to comply with the same, he shall be deemed guilty of a violation of this ordinance.

   This ordinance shall take effect and be in force from and after its passage and publication according to law. Passed by the Common Council of the Village of Tombstone, April 12, A.D. 1880.

This ordinance was revised on April 19, 1881:

   Section 1: It is hereby declared unlawful to carry in the hand or upon the person or otherwise any deadly weapon within the limits of said city of Tombstone, without first obtaining a permit in writing.

   Section 2: This prohibition does not extend to persons immediately leaving or entering the city, who, with good faith, and within reasonable time are proceeding to deposit, or take from the place of deposit such deadly weapon.

   Section 3: All fire-arms of every description, and bowie knives and dirks, are included within the prohibition of this ordinance.[2]

   The five Cowboys waiting next to the Fry house were said to be carrying the aforementioned "fire-arms" within the Tombstone city limits, had not obtained permits to do so, and were loitering on a vacant lot with little intention to leave the city. The peace officers knew this and were obligated to relieve the cowboys of their weapons.

   Conflict was inevitable.

   Tuesday, March 23, 1993. Hollywood, California. The Midwestern-born, 38-year-old screenwriter had finally completed the fourth revision of his proposed script. After almost 11 months, the first draft had been completed. Later that year, he'd finished the second revision, but it then took another five months before the third revision was wrapped up. The cuts had varied—a tweak here, elimination of a scene there, anything that didn't move the story forward, scenes that didn't have any relevance to the new draft. Character biographies were developed, backstories created. The basic premise of good vs. evil was well-developed, augmented with character development, strong motivation and a solid story structure. One hundred fifty-two solid scenes.

   The writer knew his craft; years earlier he had written a screenplay for a film that won three Academy Awards. *The New York Times* had praised it as a "good, lean screenplay." But this time, not only would he write the script, he'd also be the director. This newest work impressed one former child actor (Kurt Russell) in particular: "[This] screenplay was really the first time anyone has tried to present Wyatt Earp in his entirety. I mean, all of him: his relationship with his brothers, with his first wife, how he took up with Josephine Marcus, the traveling actress that he ended up spending nearly half a

Opposite: Framed Tombstone gun ordinance posted outside the Mescal set's Sheriff's office (courtesy Jerry Crandall).

THE MAYOR AND COMMON COUNCIL

OF THE

CITY of
TOMBSTONE

Territory of Arizona

Do Ordain as Follows.

1. It is hereby declared UNLAWFUL for any person to carry DEADLY WEAPONS, concealed or otherwise (except the same be carried openly in sight, and in the hand) within the limits of the City of Tombstone.

2. This prohibition does not extend to persons immediately leaving or entering the City, who, with good faith, and within reasonable time are proceeding to deposit, or to take such deadly weapons.

3. All fire-arms of every description, and bowie knifes and dirks, are included within the prohibition of this ordinance.

4. Any person or persons violating the provisions of this ordinance shall be deemed guilty of a misdemeanor, and, on conviction thereof, shall be fined in a sum not to exceed TWO HUNDRED and FIFTY dollars and costs, or imprisonment in the City Jail for a period not to exceed five months, or both at the discretion of the Court.

5. That this ordinance shall take effect and be in force from and after due publication.

Marcus P. Hayne,
City Attorney

John P. Clum,
Mayor

Seward B. Chapin,
Clerk, Common Council

APPROVED April 19, 1881.

century with. You could see the dark side of the man. This [script] is one brilliantly conceived piece…. [It] offers drama, comedy, action [and] romance, not only seen through the shots but told through the characters. There are some tough characterizations that have not been backed away from by anyone. [The writer's] understanding of the time period is remarkable."

Little did said writer realize he would develop just a handful of additional screenplays before his death.[3]

ONE

Discovery and Creation

In 1877, Pennsylvania-born Edward Lawrence Schieffelin, 29-year-old former U.S. Army scout, began his search for silver ore samples in a desolate and barren area east of the San Pedro River in southeast Arizona Territory. In 1876, he was described by David P. Lansing of Phoenix, Arizona, as "about the queerest specimen of human flesh I ever saw. He was six foot, two inches, and had black hair that hung several inches below his shoulders and a beard that had not been trimmed or combed for so long a time that it was a mass of unkempt knots and mats. He wore clothing pierced and patched from deerskins, corduroy and flannel, and his hat was originally a slouch hat that had been pierced with rabbit skin until very little of the original felt remained. I have never known a prospector more confident of finding a big mining proposition than he was, yet he told me that he has prospected a good part of 11 years with no results, while he had a frightening tough time of it. He was then 27 but he looked like 40."[1]

Prospecting in the 20-mile-wide valley at the base of the Huachuca and Dragoon mountains as well as the Mule and Whetstones, just 15 miles north of the Mexican border, was dangerous work for several reasons besides merely being the homeland of Geronimo and the Chiricahua Apaches. With little shelter from the elements, parts of the area were treeless. Opportunities for death were endless—excessive heat, wind, dust, starvation, disease, attack by wild animals, poisonous snakes, Indians ... and other prospectors. When fellow army scout Al Sieber heard what Schieffelin was doing, he cautioned his friend, "The only rock you will find out there will be your own tombstone." Others seconded that opinion: "Better take your coffin with you; you will find your tombstone there, and nothing else." And still others cautioned, "If you are determined to go, take along a chisel with you and when you get lost among the hills and come to die, chip your name on a stone and we'll stumble across it someday and put up a tombstone for you there."

But Schieffelin was nothing if not persistent. He had tried his luck in Coeur d'Alene, Idaho, after silver was discovered there when he was only 12. Then in 1869, he left his home in Oregon and traveled to Surprise Valley and Owens River in California, up to the Great Salt Lake, down to Death Valley, then on to Idaho, always looking for the next big strike. Nevada, Colorado and New Mexico and on and on, with nothing to show for his efforts. In January of '77, he even tried prospecting the Grand Canyon, but decided the "sedimentary strata and barren schists was enough to convince him to look elsewhere." When he wasn't allowed to purchase necessary supplies on credit from the Tucson freight and mercantile operation of Tully & Ochoa, he told a friend, "I am going back [to the San Pedro Valley]. It does not matter to me what these fellows say... I have seen enough to show me that there are mines there."[2]

Schieffelin's interest was understandable. In 1860, Prussian mining engineer Frederick Brunckow had discovered silver near the San Pedro River. Shortly thereafter, he built a cabin along its bank and began mining operations, but he and three other miners were murdered before they could take advantage of the find. It was a cursed site: "[Thirteen] more men were supposed to have been killed at the Brunckow Mine either in quarrels for possession of it or the ever lurking Apaches caught them with their heads in the hole." However, given the previous mining operations activity, Schieffelin felt there might be opportunity there so he set up operations in the old Brunckow cabin. Months went by with little to show for his efforts. But he found enough evidence of silver deposits to convince him that he wasn't on a wild goose chase this time. Covered by earth and vegetation, pockets of ore would have to be dug for or found in gullies that may contain "float," miles away from the mother lode. (Float is debris from an orebody washed downhill and found on the surface of the ground.)

Finally, on August 1, after several months of strenuous effort, he discovered silver ore in a dry wash on a high plateau called Goose Flats. "The [silver] ledges in [the area] were pretty hard to find," said Schieffelin. "They did not crop boldly out of the ground. All that summer I did not find anything of great importance; I found some good ores and good float

and found several croppings. I found enough, however, to satisfy myself that there were good ores there, or ought to be." Although his ore samples didn't really impress anyone, on September 3, 1877, a claim was recorded in Tucson by Schieffelin's fellow prospector William Griffith; it was named Tombstone. (Griffith was one of the men who earlier had employed Schieffelin to stand guard at the Brunckow Mine.)[3]

Despite being told his three samples were worthless, Schieffelin still sought out an assessor to evaluate the ore, and was told yet again that it was valueless. Schieffelin's brother Al eventually contacted Richard Gird, company assayer at McCracken Mines where both brothers worked, and requested an evaluation. Imagine their surprise when the samples were valued at $40 per ton, $600 per ton and $2,000 per ton! After looking at the first two samples, Gird supposedly said, "The best thing you can do is find out where that ore came from, and take me with you and start for the place." Gird, Al and Ed immediately formed a partnership and, five months later, went back to

Ed Schieffelin, long-haired and blue-eyed, was 29 when he discovered silver in Arizona. He named his first two claims "Graveyard" and "Tombstone." His usual appearance included a red flannel shirt and deerskin and corduroy work clothes. This photograph was taken in later years (sometime in the last two decades of the nineteenth century) when Schieffelin was flush with money.

Brunckow's cabin to continue prospecting. During the next five months, the trio discovered and filed 16 additional claims. Ed made his biggest strike, a silver vein so rich he would press a coin into it and leave an exact imprint. He later estimated the vein's dimensions at 50 feet long and 12 inches wide. Gird assayed the sample from this location at $15,000 to the ton, and said, "Ed, you lucky cuss—you have hit it." Appropriately, the mine was called the Lucky Cuss. Schieffelin later discovered the Tough Nut claim, so named as it took him several days to determine its exact dimensions. On April 5, 1878, the trio submitted bylaws to the Pima County recorder for the establishment of the Tombstone Mining District in the San Pedro Valley. Other prospectors quickly heard about this success and started prospecting for themselves. Wrote John Myers Myers, "Those were two of the three [largest] discoveries [in the area]. The third ... was found by another party. Hank Williams and John Oliver had moved into the district. Finding Gird on the scene, they made arrangements with him to assay their findings in return for a split in whatever claims they located. When Williams and Oliver did find something big ... they forgot about the agreement. Because of the agreement which took place before they got their rights, Gird and the Schieffelins called their share of the claim the Contention. The part Williams and Oliver kept they [named] the Grand Central."

Gird may have been his own worst enemy: He shared news of his find in a letter to some of his friends in Signal, over 300 miles away. Soon, most of Signal's population departed for the area. The race was on.[4]

Oh, no! Not again! It *couldn't* happen a second time. But it did. Screenwriter Kevin Jarre saw his project being sidelined by the influence and clout of another Hollywood wheeler-dealer.

Jarre was born August 6, 1954, in Grosse Point, Michigan, to actress Laura Devon (aka Mary Lou Briley). He moved with his mother to Los Angeles in the early 1960s as she began to pursue a career in films. After his parents divorced, the boy lived for a time in Wyoming with his father, a "Hemingwayesque [man] who combined ranching and fashion photography." It was there that Jarre developed his love of horseback riding. But like his mother, he too became involved in the entertainment industry: The young actor landed a small part in the television series *Flipper* starring Brian Kelly, who was married to Jarre's mother. Nothing lasts forever; in January 1966, Devon divorced Kelly. She married French

Tombstone's **first screenwriter and director, Kevin Jarre, in his usual black leather jacket.**

composer-conductor Maurice Alexis Jarre on December 30, 1967. His credentials were impressive: The Academy Award–winning maestro was best known for the classic film scores for *Lawrence of Arabia, Doctor Zhivago* and *Ryan's Daughter*, among many others. Maurice soon adopted Kevin and gave him the surname Jarre.

Artistic talent must have run in the family as Kevin eventually became a prolific writer. His first successful effort was in 1985 with the George Cosmatos–directed *Rambo: First Blood Part II*, screenplay by Sylvester Stallone and James Cameron from a story by Jarre. (Jarre said defensively that almost nothing of his original screenplay was left in the script.) The film won the Golden Raspberry Award for the year's worst screenplay, but Kevin Jarre continued to write. In 1988, his story *The Tracker* became a TV movie with Kris Kristofferson.[5]

During the 1960s, young boys used to play with model cars, rubber toy dinosaurs, cap-guns, electric trains, Play-Doh, Silly Putty and Frisbees, while devouring comic books and collecting baseball cards. They rode their bikes all day, in sunshine and rain, threw footballs and baseballs, and surfed on skateboards. They skated on ice and sledded on snow. Some played with toy soldiers and cowboys and Indians. Others, at least those who could afford them, had knights and horses made from lead. But not everyone. In 1961, the country began to celebrate the centennial of the nation's Civil War. Books were written, celebrations were held, re-enactments took place and monuments were raised. Kevin Jarre missed little of this. Steeped in American history anyway, he was a self-described "Civil War freak" who had received toy soldiers depicting that era as a Christmas present. Thus began his lifelong fascination with the War Between the States—its successes and failures, triumphs and tragedies. Dedication and sacrifice. Freedom and emancipation. Jarre would use this interest and passion to develop his next screenplay, one that would result in three Academy Awards.[6]

In 1986, Jarre was in Saratoga for the summer season of the New York City Ballet. Long-time friend Lincoln Kirstein saw a snapshot of Jarre on horseback and was struck by his friend's resemblance to the Augustus Saint-Gaudens equestrian statue of Col. Robert Gould Shaw, white commander of the all-black 54th Massachusetts Infantry regiment during the Civil War. The statue honoring the regiment had been paid for by public donations and erected opposite the Massachusetts State House in 1897. Stories differ on how Jarre became interested in this unique regiment. One said that his friend Kirstein later wrote the monograph *Lay This Laurel* (the title from an Emily Dickinson poem) about the regiment. Others said Jarre was inspired one day as he walked across Boston Common and noticed something unusual about a Civil War memorial that had escaped him in the past. The bronze relief sculpture was a "Memorial to Robert Gould Shaw and the Massachusetts Fifty-Fourth Regiment," and some of the soldiers represented on it were black. It had never occurred to him that blacks had even fought in that war. No matter what the motivation, Jarre and Kirstein subsequently met at Mother Goldsmith's restaurant ("a Saratoga tradition since 1939") and soon discovered this mutual interest.

"I knew about the 54th," Jarre admitted. "[But] Lincoln's interest was deeper. It related to his whole philosophy about surrendering yourself to something bigger, some larger cause. [I'd] always wanted to make a movie about the 54th." Encouraged by their conversation, Kevin began reading everything he could find about Shaw and his regiment. What he discovered amazed him. Once his research was complete, he "moved into Room 421 at the Gramercy Park Hotel in New York, opposite the Players Club, and wrote the script in four weeks, on spec. I never thought I could interest anybody in it. A Civil War epic, about black people? But I'd got really attached to the story. I had to kill everybody off [in it] and I'd end up in tears when I got through writing." In addition to Kirstein's monograph, Jarre incorporated into his screenplay material from Peter Burchard's novel *One Gallant Rush* and Shaw's personal letters.[7]

Using his connections, Kirstein brought Jarre's finished script to Merchant Ivory Productions, but the film company decided the project was way beyond its ability to produce. Jarre felt that Merchant "couldn't make head or tail of it." Undeterred, an agent sent it to director Bruce Beresford, who, along with producer Freddie Fields, took it to Columbia. But there it languished. Jarre's script was the story of one of the first Union regiments made up entirely of African-American enlisted men, led by white officers and told from Shaw's point of view. But the project quickly was attacked, both from inside and outside the studio. Jarre heard his work called "racist" and "inaccurate." And how did Jarre, a *white* historian, *dare* to have the audacity to write about *black* soldiers, complete with inappropriate language and non-stereotypical characterizations? A black historian from the University of Virginia "even denied some of the irrefutable facts about the regiment," complained Jarre. "I was able to punch holes in his attack." It didn't matter. Beresford left the project and it was dying a slow death as it remained in Developmental Hell.

But producer Fields finally stepped in and took it to Tri-Star, which had the courage and vision to bring it to fruition. Edward Zwick was named director. With an all-star cast that included Morgan Freeman, Denzel Washington, Matthew Broderick, Cary Elwes, Raymond St. Jacques and Jane Alexander, how could it fail? It didn't. Nominated for five Academy Awards in 1990, including Best Actor in a Supporting Role (Washington), Best Art Direction, Best Cinematography (Freddie Francis), Best Film Editing and Best Sound, *Glory* won three: Supporting Actor, Cinematography and Sound. Jarre had an unbilled part in the film as the soldier who picks a fight with Denzel Washington but later sparks the cheers for the black troops as they move to lead the attack on Fort Wagner when he yells, "Give 'em hell, 54th!" And Elwes (the fictional Cabot Forbes) absolutely loved the script: "Yeah, it is a beautiful story. History was one of my favorite subjects at school. Still is, really, so I am often drawn to historical films and scripts that are sent to me, that have historical value to them. I knew the writer … at least I got to know him … [and] when we met, it was like meeting a kindred spirit. He is an avid historian and his attention to detail is phenomenal."[8]

Critics were effusive in their praise. *Variety* wrote, "A stirring and long overdue tribute to the black soldiers who fought for the Union cause in the Civil War, *Glory* has the sweep and magnificence of a Tolstoy battle tale or a John Ford saga of American history…. Freddie Francis' masterful photography, eschewing the sepia haze that too often makes period films seem comfortably distant, plunges the audience into the battles with a vividness that is both spectacular and chilling." Vincent Canby of the *New York Times* called it a "beautifully acted, pageantlike movie…. [Broderick] gives his most mature and controlled performance to date…. [Washington is] an actor clearly on his way to a major screen career…. The movie unfolds in a succession of often brilliantly realized vignettes tracing the 54th's organization, training and first experiences below the Mason-Dixon line."[9]

Now on his way, Jarre followed *Glory* with *Navy Seals*, starring Charlie Sheen, and producer Larry Gordon acquired two more Jarre scripts, *Judgment Night* and *The Devil's Own*. Because of Jarre's success with *Glory*, Universal announced in January 1990 that he was working on another spec script he would also direct. By March 5, 1991, he had finished the first draft of a 113-page, 168-scene screenplay based on Bram Stoker's *Dracula*. Jarre sent it to author and cinema historian Philip Riley along with a cover letter. Apparently they had spoken previously as Jarre wrote, "Dear Phillip [sic], Here's the script as promised. Please look it over and let me know what you think. Call collect if you want to. It was a genuine thrill to speak with you on the phone as I've admired your work for a long time. The thoroughness and dedication you bring to your work together with your obvious zest and joy in classic pictures have been a source of inspiration to me. I can't wait until we meet face-to-face for a Chaney-Dracula consultation. Millionaire stuff, hardly seems like work."

A nice beginning to a tempting project, but unfortunately a common industry roadblock then appeared: another player with the same subject. Originally, Michael Apted was going to direct Stoker's vampire story as a TV film; actress Winona Ryder's agent gave her a stack of scripts, one of them entitled *Dracula—The Untold Story*. And since she'd never before read a Dracula

The Academy Award–winning *Glory* (1989) was nominated in five categories including Best Film Editing and Best Art Direction/Set Direction. It won for Best Sound, Best Cinematography and Best Actor in a Supporting Role (Denzel Washington).

script, she was immediately interested. Thus, after meeting with Francis Ford Coppola to discuss an adaptation of Jack Kerouac's *On the Road*, she mentioned the Dracula script in passing. Ryder had previously withdrawn from Coppola's *The Godfather: Part III* due to exhaustion and Francis, seeing this as a way to mend fences, so to speak, agreed to make the vampire film. Apted remained on board as the executive producer. Coppola's screenplay was completed on April 16, just 31 days after Jarre's. But once Universal learned of the rival version, it shelved Jarre's project.

Hollywood history is rife with dueling films, or "parallel development," as it's known: two motion pictures on the same subject from rival studios. Said former Tri-Star chairman Mike Medavoy, "These races are not always about quality. It's about getting the first picture out. The first film in the theaters does better at the box office, regardless of quality." MGM distribution president Larry Gleason agreed: "[T]here's only one rule to remember when you have competing films in production: Get finished and on screen first. The second film is often artistically superior, but there are very few instances when it out-grosses the first film that goes out in the marketplace." According to *Variety* writer John Brodie, "an earnest, well-meaning producer starts developing a tricky, high-concept project that happens to be in the public domain. Soon a rival shop swoops down, produces a knock-off, and takes his chances at the box office with a project based on a lesser script."

But not always. Witness the case of *Harlow*. In 1965, Paramount released a color film on the blonde bombshell, produced by Joseph E. Levine and starring Carroll Baker. Meanwhile, producer Bill Sargent and Electronovision, Inc., released a black-and-white *Harlow* that starred Carol Lynley. The two films opened within weeks of each other to less-than-stellar reactions. Lawsuits and counter-suits flew fast and furious; the only people who made money were the lawyers. Lesson learned? Well, briefly. In 1974, Warner Bros. bought the rights to Richard Martin Stern's book *The Tower*, while producer Irwin Allen purchased Thomas Scortia's and Frank Robinson's *The Glass Inferno* for 20th Century–Fox. Rather than produce two competing disaster films, the studios combined forces and jointly released *The Towering Inferno*, a tremendous success. This proved that studios could go into a partnership and make money. And in 1988, Universal and Warner Bros. agreed to split domestic and foreign receipts on Michael Apted's *Gorillas in the Mist* instead of mounting dueling Dian Fossey movies.

Cases of cooperation between studios were few and far between, though. Similar screenplays, hawking a script to several studios, and even industrial espionage produced comparable—and in some cases identical—films being released in the same year: *Fail-Safe* and *Dr. Strangelove* (1964), *Godspell* and *Jesus Christ Superstar* (1973), *The Howling* and *Wolfen* (1981), *Day of the Dead* and *The Return of the Living Dead* (1985), *The Abyss*, *Deep Star Six* and *Leviathan* (1989), to name just a few. After all, healthy potential box-office receipts have a way of swaying Hollywood's most firmly held opinions. But not this time. Universal and Coppola were eyeball to eyeball (on a Dracula film) and the studio blinked.[10]

The studio still owed Kevin a picture and gave him the option to come up with another project. It was Jarre's misfortune to actually develop the Dracula film idea, and he was understandably furious at the studio. "Universal didn't want to race [to bring it to the screen first] and dropped it," he said. "It was a huge blow." Others were disappointed as well. According to writer John Fasano, "Kevin Jarre had been screwed on *Dracula*. He had been working on a very [faithful to the book] script, and somebody mentioned it to Coppola, and they got theirs out first." Peter Sherayko, fellow actor, film armorer, weapons authority and friend of Jarre, says that Kevin was in Romania and Transylvania scouting locations when he learned that the studio had canceled his Dracula project. "[Kevin] was distraught," Sherayko recalls. "He paid so much attention to detail, so much attention to [the historical aspects of the story]. That's why he was over there, to do everything accurately. In my opinion, Kevin was destroyed. He disappeared from us, did not see us, did not answer phone calls for six months."

Given another chance by the studio, Jarre would do his damnedest to take advantage of it. And this time, he had a great idea of what he would try.[11]

Recalls Sherayko, "I met Kevin Jarre through [director] John Milius, Kevin's mentor. I met Kevin after they did *Glory*. I had been on [a hunting shoot] with John and with Cary Elwes. We were doing that ... and then shortly after that, John introduced me to Kevin. This is probably about 1990. Kevin is a great historian; knew his stuff. He had an extensive library on Western [history]. Loved the West ... collected Western artifacts. Kevin got a horse, he kept it out at Gary Gang's ranch and then once or twice a week we would go on our 'house of men ride.' So Frank [Trigani], Gary, Kevin, myself, once in a while one or two other people, we'd saddle up our horses about nine o'clock at night, everybody would have at least a pint of whiskey, and everybody would have about a hundred rounds of ammunition, of live ammunition. We'd leave Gary's ranch and go much into the hills ... and we would not come back until all the ammunition or whiskey was gone. We were shooting off horseback, live rounds; ten, eleven o'clock at night and we all had a great time together."[12]

Jarre was starting to slowly pull an idea together for a Western—a genre that had been written off, left for dead. It had been over two decades since Westerns ruled the screen. For those enamored with the horse and six-gun, 1969–70 were banner years: *The Wild Bunch, True Grit, The Undefeated, 100 Rifles, Once Upon a Time in the West, Support Your Local Sheriff, Little Big Man, Two Mules for Sister Sara, Rio Lobo* and *The Ballad of Cable Hogue* were just a few of the oaters gracing the screen. And according to *Variety*, Clint Eastwood "deserve[d] a special award for the man who picked up John Wayne's mantle and kept the Western alive when all others were moving into science-fiction and buddy-cop movies." *Joe Kidd, High Plains Drifter, The Outlaw Josey Wales* and *Pale Rider* were Eastwood's brilliant efforts to keep the Western on the silver screen.

But in the '80s, other than the underappreciated *Heaven's Gate*, only *Silverado, Young Guns, Lonesome Dove* and a handful of others attempted to resuscitate this type of entertainment.

However after *Young Guns II* was released on August 1, 1990, quickly followed by *Quigley Down Under* on October 17 and *Dances with Wolves* just two weeks later, Hollywood, as always, was quick to jump on the trend. Nominated for 12 Academy Awards, Kevin Costner's *Dances with Wolves* won seven, including Best Picture and Best Director; the only other Western ever to win Best Picture was *Cimarron* (1931). Said writer-director Burt Kennedy, "What's important is what happens to the next one. If the first one made without Clint Eastwood made money, then there will be a trend. If the next one goes into the toilet, then there goes the trend. Clint has brought it all around. At least now you can talk [to film executives] about a Western. For a while you'd get thrown out of the office." Maybe the moviegoing public was ready for another one! And, if you'd ask anyone what major events they recall about the West, inevitably, they would say, "The Alamo, Custer's Last Stand and the Gunfight at the O.K. Corral."[13]

Wyatt Earp historian Jeff Morey says he met Jarre at an Alamo gathering given by famed production illustrator and collector Joe Musso in July 1991. "Someone told me that they'd invited Kevin Jarre," explained Morey, "and I'd admired [him]. I first noticed his name on the credits on *The Tracker*.... There was more historical understanding there than usual with movies like that. I had a photograph of a group of men standing in front of the old Tombstone firehouse, and I believed one of the men was Wyatt Earp. So I took a copy of it and Kevin came in. He was only there for maybe 15 minutes and I handed him the photo and that was that." Jarre later told Morey that he was sitting in his office and looked up and saw the picture, and that is what gave him the idea to do a film on Earp. Morey adds, "[Jarre's] real dream was to do the [Wild Bill] Hickok story. Earp was just a prelude to doing that."

Predictably, if Kevin was going to do it, it would be done right. He would be very specific—no glamour, no glitter, with authentic costumes, weapons, scenery. And by doing so, he would correct the inaccuracies of John Ford's *My Darling Clementine* and the Hollywoodization of John Sturges' *Gunfight at the O.K. Corral* with its larger-than-life superheroes.

Baseball, hot dogs and apple pie. What could be more American than Westerns? Actor Powers Boothe, who eventually played Curly Bill Brocius in Jarre's film, said it best: "Thematically, men standing up for themselves and making their way in the world is a theme that's been in movies throughout the world. But it's particularly an American genre, and it has to do, in my mind, with the development of our nation: You can do anything you're strong enough to do; right is right, and wrong is wrong. And at least in the movies, right wins out."[14]

An avid historian, Jarre defined the original parameters of the project. It must be accurate and it must explain the reasons behind the conflict between the Earps and the Cowboys. To do so, he threw out all the myths and legends from past movies about this shootout, although he would pay homage to some of those older films in his script. He tapped whatever resources he could to assure that what he wrote was correct, constantly asking questions, always trying to correctly interpret facts. Morey didn't know this, but the Earp historian played an integral part in Jarre's understanding and development of the story. Following their meeting at the party, the two met again at director John Milius' Culver City office and spent almost 90 minutes discussing Wyatt Earp and the gunfight with the Cowboys. Morey did not realize he was actually being interviewed for a job; the next day, though, Jarre phoned to say he wanted to hire him as historical consultant: "Kevin contacted me … because he was told I was well-informed about Wyatt Earp. [When informed he wanted to hire me, I was] flabbergasted. I recommended he talk to some other Earp researchers before deciding on a historical advisor. But Kevin wanted me, so I agreed to work with him. He told me that my take on Earp (that Wyatt's problem in Tombstone actually was that he was very naïve and unaware of the evil around him) was so close to his own that it gave him the shudders. He was surprised by how much my slant on Earp fit in with his own. That became a focal point in Kevin's script."

On a trip to Arizona that fall, Jarre and Morey visited historian Jim Dunham in Phoenix. During a four-hour breakfast, Jarre asked Dunham, "Why should I do a Wyatt Earp movie?" Replied the historian, "One of the reasons is that there are five good women's roles in the story and no one has ever really fleshed out their roles. I don't know how good the movie's script is but I bet you could get financing." Jarre and Morey then continued on to Tombstone. Jeff and Kevin became fast friends. Jarre would invite Morey over for dinner and then use him as a sounding board. "He never had a list of questions, he never took notes, he never worked in a linear or chronological fashion," says Morey. "He studied enough and read enough of the Old West and Earp literature. He was interested in questions of motivation. 'Why did the men who went on Wyatt's vendetta ride take the risk of siding with Earp?' I told him I didn't have a ready answer for such a question. They may have been close to Morgan Earp. On the other hand, they may have been paid gunmen. As a historian, I could tell him what happened, but getting into the hearts and minds of those men was his job as a screenwriter. Once, out of the clear blue, I said, 'I don't know if you are going to cover the confrontation between Doc Holliday and Johnny Ringo, but if you do, be sure to use the line from Walter Noble Burns' book *Tombstone*: 'I'm [your] huckleberry. That's just my game.'"

In a January 1992 phone call, Jarre asked Morey why he thought Earp liked Holliday. Explained Jeff, "I believe it was because Doc could make Wyatt laugh." Through their research, the two discovered "unknown facts" about Earp. "I was never convinced the books and movies told what really happened at the O.K. Corral," confessed Jarre. "The real truth is far, far, far more romantic than the fiction. It's almost Biblical, what happened."

Morey wasn't the only one Jarre contacted for input. "As Kevin was writing the script," explained Dunham, "he would mail pages for me to read and then we talked on the phone. One of the things I said was I thought that Ike Clanton was more important and less of an idiot than portrayed in the script. Kevin asked me, 'At what time does Wyatt Earp kill Ike Clanton?' I told him that Ike was killed much later by circumstances totally unrelated to the Earp story. Kevin said, 'That's right, and the audience will not like it if the main bad guy gets away at the end. Curly Bill and Ringo have to be the heavies.' Then I called Kevin and said, 'You have Wyatt upset that Curly Bill was not charged with killing Marshal Fred White. You know from the material Jeff gave you to read that both the dying marshal and Wyatt said it was an accident and that Curly's gun went off when Fred grabbed it.' Kevin said, 'I can't make Curly Bill a sympathetic figure and then have Wyatt later kill him at Iron Springs. He must stay evil throughout.' Then we talked about the timing of Virgil's wounding and the death of Morgan. I said it certainly was not on the same night! The gunfight is in October, the hearing takes all of November, and Virgil gets shot in December and Morgan is killed just before Wyatt's birthday in March of '82. Kevin sighed and said, 'Jim, we're just making a movie.'"[15]

Sherayko also remembers Jarre's effort: "It took him about a year to write the script and during that time, he swore us all to secrecy. [The story is in public domain and Jarre didn't want anyone to steal it. This was six months after losing the *Dracula* opportunity.] He said, 'Okay, I'm back. I'm better now. Now, we're going to do another movie.' Well, he

Buckaroo Garrett Roberts and Peter Sherayko, who played Texas Jack Vermillion (courtesy Garrett Roberts).

took Frank and Gary and me, individually, and said, 'I want to swear you to secrecy. I'm going to let you know what's going on but you do not tell anybody else.' So, all that time, neither Frank or Gary or I spoke to each other what we were doing. We all knew but we would not divulge that.

"Now, he also knows that I'm a blabbermouth and can't keep a secret. What he told us was, 'We're going to do a movie on the California Gold Rush of 1850.' I started getting every book I could on the [subject] and started making my notes and figuring out what to do, what type of guns to have, what the saddles looked like and everything. Well, it was about six or eight months later and I had done all this research. [Then] he took us all on one of the 'house of men' rides, swore us to secrecy, [and] said, 'What we're doing is, we're doing Wyatt Earp, we're doing the O.K. Corral. We're making the vendetta ride the premise of the whole movie.'" Gary was going to be the head wrangler, Frank was in charge of the saddles, Peter would be in charge of the guns.[16]

"As Kevin started writing *Tombstone*, [Frank, Gary and I] never talked to each other [about the script] but every ... at least once a week ... we were still going on our 'house of men' ride. We would never talk about the movie ... because all of us were together. Once a week Kevin would call me up and I'd go down to his house around 11 o'clock at night and he'd give me four or five pages of his script. And he'd say, 'Okay, look at these characters that are in there and design your guns.' So I would go home and do that, talk to him the next day or the day after and tell him what I'm thinking about [the] character(s). That's why I tried to have every character have the exact same type of gun that the real guy had. Kevin would override me on a few things. Doc Holliday had a seven-and-a-half-inch Colt which I wanted him to have but [Jarre] wanted him to do the gun twirling, thinking it would be very good with a four-and-three-quarter-inch gun. Same thing with Johnny Ringo. Johnny Ringo, when he was found dead, he had a seven-and-a-half-inch Colt. And that's what I wanted but Kevin said, 'No, I want both he and Doc to have the same type of guns so they could be evenly matched.' And he wanted the four-and-three-quarters; those are guns that are literally designed for twirling. They're the best-balanced gun around. So that's how he overrode me on those things.

"Another time I said, 'You know, I think [Sheriff Behan] should have a four-inch Sheriff's model,' 'cause they just came out on the market. He's a dapper guy, he has a walking stick, he doesn't really shoot but he has.... I'd like to give him that. So I went down to Kevin's house, after he gave me the pages with Behan in it, and he said, 'No, no, no, no, no. I think he should have a dainty gun or a smaller gun.' And I said, 'Okay, no problem.' So that day I left Kevin, I went down to a place in Orange called Little John's. They have these gun auctions on all high-end stuff. I went down there purposely to buy a '76 Winchester, which is the one that Jason Priestley used. So I bought the Winchester and John said to me, 'Hey. I got an auction coming up in about a month. You ought to come down to it. I've got some interesting guns in there.' So he gave me the catalogue and in there was Johnny Behan's gun. The original gun. Four-inch Sheriff's model, the same that I told Kevin that I think he should have. So as soon as I saw that, I immediately drove back to Kevin's house, knocked on the door, and just held the catalogue open to that page. He looked and he read it and he said, 'Okay, you can get the four-inch sheriff's model.' Kevin knew exactly what he wanted in the film, and I tried my damnedest to give him what he wanted."[17]

Eventually, Jarre's script came together. Future producer Bob Misiorowski recalled that Jarre's dialogue was quite accurate for the period: "The F bomb word wasn't used back then (despite how frequently it was used in *Deadwood*). Kevin researched letters and newspapers. The writing is in the vernacular. He took his language from his sources for very authentic language." Jarre finalized the first draft of his script on January 22, 1992, but knew it wasn't quite ready. He continued to work but already was thinking about who should play the lead role of Wyatt Earp.

His first choice was always Kevin Costner. By then, the 37-year-old, married Costner was a powerful Hollywood force, a major star. The one-time truck driver, deep-sea fisherman, Hollywood tour guide bus driver, and Disneyland Jungle Cruise operator had even made a soft-core porn film (*Malibu Hot Summer*) but had vowed never to work in films again if that was the only work he could get. Costner had appeared in several forgettable films (*Frances*, *Table for Five*, *Fandango* and *Stacy's Knights*) but gotten his big break when he portrayed Alex, the corpse in *The Big Chill* (his scenes were later left on the cutting room floor). But director and friend Lawrence Kasdan never forgot the decision to eliminate him from that film, and eventually included Costner in the cast for *Silverado* (1985), where Costner played his break-out role. It was quickly followed by *The Untouchables, No Way Out, Bull Durham, Field of Dreams, Dances with Wolves, Robin Hood: Prince of Thieves* and *JFK*. His résumé could have been even more impressive: He turned down roles in *WarGames, Platoon* and *The Hunt for Red October*.

In July 1992, Jarre, working with Alphaville film producers Sean Daniel and James Jacks at Universal, decided to send a copy of his Earp script to Costner for consideration. According to John Fasano, when Jarre asked Costner to play Earp, Costner told director-writer Kevin Reynolds, "'Yes, I've just read a great script. I'm going to play Wyatt Earp.' But Reynolds apparently warned him off, saying, 'Don't do that one. I'm developing Wyatt Earp as a mini-series. Let's make that into a movie.'" However, in the October 1994 issue of *Film Review*, Costner said he'd never even looked at Jarre's script "because I had worked on my own version of the story for four years. I didn't even want to look at it. I said [to Jarre], 'Look, I don't want to. I have my own. I had it before yours. Mine's good, yours is okay.'" We thus must wonder ... how would Costner know that if he didn't read the Jarre script? Given that the Earp–O.K. Corral tale already had been told numerous times on screen—*Frontier Marshal* (1939), *Tombstone: The Town Too Tough to Die* (1942), *My Darling Clementine* (1946), *Gunfight at the O.K. Corral* (1957), *Hour of the Gun* (1967) and *Doc* (1971)—it seems logical that Costner was naturally reluctant to tell the story once again. Maybe. But Costner still sounded a bit interested, saying he'd do it "if we can make this thing on the level of complication of *The Godfather*, if we can realize that his life is interesting before the O.K. Corral." Apparently writer Dan Gordon was able to accommodate that protracted-version direction: "Kevin [Costner] is the only person I've turned a script in to that has one note: 'Make it longer.' His original idea was to do two three-hour movies, one for summer and the other for winter, and end the first with a cliffhanger." And that was after Costner abandoned the idea of making the Wyatt Earp biography into a six-hour major pay-per-view mini-series for cable television. In the fall of 1990, Gordon contacted Jeff Morey about a proposed Wyatt Earp mini-series. According to Morey, "Gordon and I flew out to Arizona, where I introduced him to Bob Palmquist." Palmquist later recalled that once, "Kevin showed up wearing a bomber jacket, ball cap and carrying a bottle of Stoli's. And after the 'Pleased to meet yous,' were over, the first words out of his mouth were, 'Gee, I hope you got some orange juice.' Which we did; screwdriver was his drink of choice. We settled down over one of those and I showed him my library. We sat and talked, not only Earp but I had a bunch of books on the Civil War, and, of course, he authored *Glory*. Talked quite a bit about that."

After meeting Gordon, according to Morey, "We spent the day driving around the Tombstone area. While Gordon drove, he had Palmquist and me verbally review the Earp story. At the end of the day, Gordon asked [us] to write a short chronology of Earp's Dodge City and Tombstone years. Palmquist covered Kansas and I covered Arizona. We only had a few weeks to do this."

"I committed to television first," says Costner, "but I soon realized that the anger and violence associated with the story couldn't be told in an effective way on TV because of the [TV censors] ... the ridiculous codes of what you can't do on TV vs. what you can do." According to Gordon, Costner's mandate was to ensure that every part in the picture was so strong that he would have difficulty deciding which one to play.[18]

Costner's claims are interesting, but Jarre begged to differ. "[Costner] was the first person I thought of [to play Earp]. After he read the script, he called and respectfully declined. He said he had a mini-series he was developing for pay-per-view on the whole life of Earp and we left it at that." Apparently, Jarre's script focused mainly on the O.K. Corral incident and its aftermath, and also surrounded Earp with a wide cast of colorful characters, while Costner wanted a much-expanded version of the lawman's career, one that followed Earp through the years of his life, rather than centering on his brief, tumultuous time in Tombstone. Says Morey, "Costner took the Stuart Lake slant and Jarre took the Walter Noble Burns slant. He saw that's where the story was. The problem with [Costner's approach] is that he has too many people and too many characters. By the time he gets to Tombstone, he doesn't have enough time to tell the story. Because Costner's picture was so much bigger, you could argue that it was more accurate. But, if you look at *Tombstone*, *Tombstone*'s more authentic because you've got the period vernacular; you've got the period clothing. You've got a time and place that is depicted in the film in a way that is totally missing from the Costner film." Supposedly, Kasdan subsequently contacted Costner and volunteered to rewrite Gordon's 500-page script and turn it into a three-hour feature film. Rationalized Costner, "To take something from six hours to three is a terribly difficult job and I was way too close to it.... Larry, in his own way, knew how to go in there and construct the man's life. What is important is the formation of this man. Larry makes movies about relationships, about people. It stood to reason that's what was going to happen to [Earp]."[19]

Disappointed by Costner's rejection but not dejected, Jarre continued working on his script and early that summer, he invited Jeff Morey to read it. "As I read it, he hovered over me like a nervous and expectant father," Morey said. "What I read amazed me. It was personal, yet epic. It captured the historical period without losing a contemporary audience. And it had a remarkable driving energy. When I finished reading it, I told Kevin that he had redefined the Western film. While I supplied Kevin with a good deal of information for the film, I never could have [fit] that data into the script that he created. He had the rare power of an alchemist who could transform the harsh noise of life into pure music." Buoyed by this praise, Jarre was pleased but knew he could do even better. And so, over the summer, he revised his work and finalized the second draft on November 5. And what a marvelous draft it was! Many of the film's most memorable scenes and dialogue appeared in this draft. Jarre began with a collage of historical photographs and illustrations mixed with silent live-action vignettes, all dark and heavily shadowed. An overly long voiceover narration addressed "the economic explosion that followed the Civil War, which created an unprecedented nationwide market for beef" and its ensuing ramifications. The voiceover then introduced red-sashed Wild Bill Hickok, complete with flowing locks, Prince Albert coat and flashing pistols as he shoots three barroom patrons, quickly followed by Bill's subsequent demise at the hands of a drifter while playing poker. Earp and Bat Masterson are seen in Dodge City as they face down a group of carousing cowhands by clubbing them with pistols, aka "buffaloing" them. Unaware there was yet another armed drover sneaking up behind, the duo is saved by Doc Holliday (announced as Wyatt's guardian angel), who thwarts the ambush.

The scene then shifted to the interior of an elegant Victorian home where Josephine Marcus is introduced. The narration continued as Texas Rangers are seen driving out "the absolute dregs of the Texas underworld to the most dangerous, uncivilized ... southeast corner of the Arizona Territory." Next, prospector Ed Schieff[e]lin discovers silver and the founding of Tombstone begins. Although this was a unique, informative way to introduce the plot and characters, none of the preceding narration had appeared in the script's initial draft. Finally, with "pounding hooves [and] flowing manes, a pack of night-riding horsemen kicking hell-for-leather [ride] across the desert moonscape." The narrator simply states, "They called themselves the Cowboys." What a powerful way to start the film![20]

Following are just some of the scenes that appeared in that version of the script but aren't necessarily included in the film in their entirety[21]:

Scenes 1–7: The film opens with a shot of a squad of Mexican Federales as they come upon a massacre in a small house near the border. Vowing revenge, the soldiers ride across the border and into a dark canyon. Sensing an ambush, they attempt to turn back but are attacked and slaughtered by the Cowboys, including Old Man Clanton, Curley Bill Brocius, Ike and Billy

TOMBSTONE

an original screenplay

by

Kevin Jarre

June 25, 1992

The cover page of Kevin Jarre's *Tombstone* draft, dated June 25, 1992. He followed with additional drafts on November 5, 1992, and January 30, March 15 and March 18, 1993 (courtesy Jeff Morey).

Clanton, Florentino and Johnny Ringo. Only three soldiers survive. The Federale captain warns the Cowboys in Spanish that a rider on a pale horse will seek revenge. Ringo kills the captain and Bill asks what the captain meant; Ringo replies, "It's from the Bible. Revelations: '...behold a pale horse and the one that sat on him was Death and Hell followed with him.'" (This last bit of dialogue was inserted into the film in a different scene.)[22]

Scenes 11–12: After the Earp brothers and their wives leave Tucson, they embark on a 70-mile trip to Tombstone. While in their wagon, the women engage in jovial banter, with a few semi-risqué comments. Mattie's issue with laudanum is also touched on. While camped that evening, Morgan turns philosophical and discusses the stars, Heaven and Hell. The dialogue from this conversation was used in a different scene.[23]

Scene 24: The Earps, their wives, Doc Holliday and his paramour Kate Horony, Mayor John Clum and his wife Mary and Marshal Fred White sit in the upper balcony of Shieffelin Hall. (In the film, this scene takes place in the Bird Cage Theatre, which didn't actually open until December 1881, two months after the gunfight. Shieffelin Hall, an opera house-theater-recital hall-meeting place, was built by William Harwood and Albert Schieffelin, the brother of the town's founder. The two-story, 60 × 120-foot adobe structure contained four rooms, a 29 × 61-foot auditorium, a 28 × 59 stage and a 19-foot gallery that ran around the interior of the auditorium. With a 24-foot-high ceiling, the seating area was comprised of "well built back-rest benches 20-feet long," with a total capacity of 700 patrons. Shieffelin Hall opened on June 8, 1881, six months before the Bird Cage. The main floor of the Bird Cage contained three sections: a saloon, an auditorium and a performance stage, with a basement beneath the stage and auditorium for storage and private card games. A 14-compartment, drapery-enclosed balcony extended along two sides of the auditorium.)[24]

Scenes 31–37: In the next scene in Jarre's script, Ike Clanton, Ringo and Curley Bill exit the Oriental Saloon. Curley Bill spots a Chinaman and follows him down the street into an opium den. Later, Morgan and Josephine walk together toward the Grand Hotel as Morgan spouts spiritualism. This whole sequence, albeit in a slightly modified format with different characters, occurs later in the film.

The Oriental, described as "the most elegantly furnished salon this side of the favored city of the Golden Gate," was established on July 22, 1880, by Milton Joyce, with gambling concessions run by Lou Rickenbaugh. When it opened, the *Epitaph* wrote, "[T]wenty burners suspended in chandeliers afford illumination of brilliance and the bright rays reflected from the many colored crystals on the bar which is beautifully carved, furnished in white and gilt capped with a handsomely polished mahogany top. The floor is covered with a brilliant body Brussels carpet and suitably furnished in the style of a grand club-room, with conveniences for the dealers in polished ivory. Milt Joyce displays an exquisite taste in the selection of the furniture and fixtures in his establishment." The theater burned in the June 22, 1881, fire but was rebuilt by Vizina and Cook. When state prohibition came to Tombstone in 1914, the Oriental became a drug store and remained so for several years. Since then it has had many tenants and purposes but still stands in its original historic location. Currently there are two stores in the old saloon building.

According to the September 9, 1880, edition of *The Tombstone Epitaph*, the Grand Hotel was "luxuriously furnished, provided thick carpeting and its walls were adorned with costly oil paintings. Providing 16 bedrooms, each with a 'view,' they were fitted with solid walnut furnishings, toilet stands, fine fixtures and wallpaper. The lobby was equipped with three elegant chandeliers and more luxurious furnishings, while the kitchen boasted hot and cold running water and facilities to serve some 500 people in the span of a couple of hours." It was destroyed by a May 25, 1882, fire that left only the adobe walls standing. A new building was then erected; it housed three businesses, two on the first floor and one in the basement. In May 1924, a fire wiped out most of the structure. When it was rebuilt, the old adobe facade became a functional part of the structure. In the 1970s, it became Big Nose Kate's Saloon.[25]

Scene 38: In a scene written but not used, Wyatt testifies in court before Judge Spicer: "Then you actually didn't see it… Can't have a murder without a witness. Case dismissed for lack of evidence." This dialogue is referred to in a subsequent scene in the Campbell & Hatch Billiard Hall where the Earps again decline Mayor Clum's offer to be the town marshal.

The Campbell & Hatch Billiard Hall was opened in 1880 by Bob Hatch and John Campbell. The saloon and billiard parlor burned in the 1882 fire and was one of the first to rebuild. Prohibition closed all the saloons in 1914. As with many other structures, Jarre used the names of the actual 1881 buildings in his script.[26]

Scenes 44–48: Virgil tells Wyatt that Wyatt's black stallion was stolen from the O.K. Corral. Wyatt mounts one of his other horses, borrows Virgil's gun and starts tracking the outlaw. The hoof prints run past Henry Hooker's ranch where Earp confronts the owner and asks if he's seen anything. Hooker refuses to identify anyone, saying, "You're just passing through. Us cattlemen gotta live here. Best I can do is to point you to Galeyville. That's their roost." (Galeyville, founded in 1880, was a small mining town about 60 miles due east of Tombstone on the eastern side of the Chiricahua Mountains. Founder John Galey, a Pennsylvania oil man and president of the Texas Consolidated Mining and Smelting Company, had found silver on the site. The town had 30 various establishments and 11 saloons, but like many local mining towns, its tenure was short-lived. Galeyville was completely shut down in 1888 and its buildings reassembled in Paradise, just a short distance to the south.)

In Galeyville, Sherman McMasters tells Wyatt Billy Clanton took the horse. The two ride together as McMasters explains the Cowboy creed. Wyatt enters the Cowboys' camp, Rustler's Park, and confronts Clanton. Before the argument can escalate into conflict, Curley Bill intervenes and orders Billy to give the horse back. As Earp rides away, Curley Bill is alongside and they agree to stay out of each other's way. Again, Brocius reiterates the Cowboy creed: "We all go on one, one on all. Fight one of us, you fight us all."[27]

Scenes 50–51: Mexican Federales ambush Old Man Clanton and four cowboys in the Guadaloupe Canyon area of the southern Peloncillo Mountains. (The canyon straddles the modern Arizona–New Mexico state line and connects New Mexico's Animas Valley with Arizona's San Bernardino Valley.) All five are killed. Frank Stillwell notifies the Cowboys at Rustler's Park. Brocius takes command of the outlaws and vows revenge. A humiliated Ike Clanton, denied the leadership role, rides away.[28]

Scenes 52–55: A shorter version of this scene appears much earlier in the film than it does in the script. Looking to avoid Josephine riding sidesaddle through a cut, Wyatt unsuccessfully attempts to find a shortcut. After their ride, they dismount, Wyatt spreads his duster on the ground and they talk. This romantic interlude is much more passionate than what appears in the film. After they kiss, Wyatt falls to his knees, arms wrapped around her legs, face pressed into the folds of her skirt. "You know this is adultery," she says. "You burn in Hell for that."

"Then, let's make sure we get our money's worth," he replies.

Afterwards, Josephine visits Fly's Photographic Studio and, naked beneath a diaphanous veil that shrouds her from head to toe, she has her picture taken as "I want to remember how I looked this day." (Camillus Sydney Fly was one of the earliest photographers of the Old West. His first Tombstone studio was in a tent, but in 1880, he built the 12-room boarding house at 312 Fremont Street that housed his studio and gallery in the back. The latter portion of this scene sequence implies that the famous Kaloma veiled photograph, so named because it appeared on the cover of a composition piece titled "Kaloma Valse Hesitante," is, in fact, Josephine Marcus.)[29]

Scenes 69–74: The Earps and Holliday head toward the O.K. Corral. Various characters, including Milton Joyce, Frank and Tom McLaury, and Billy and Ike Clanton, all have dialogue. These scenes switch back and forth between the street and the corral. The Cowboys pass a liquor bottle around as Behan notifies them that the Earps are on their way. Several townsfolk have conversations as the lawmen pass. As they walk, the Earps discuss their plans for the arrests and approach the intersection of Fourth and Fremont. Behan tells the Earps that the Cowboys are unarmed, then enters Fly's gallery. Once the quartet reaches the corral, Wes Fuller and Billy Claiborne also dash into Fly's gallery. Frank and Billy jerk their pistols and the gunfight begins. Shots are fired, participants are hit. Ike dives toward Wyatt, claims he is unarmed and then flees to the gallery. The fight continues: Virgil, Morgan, Frank, Tom and Billy are all wounded. Inside the gallery, Ike grabs Fuller's gun and fires at Wyatt through the window. Doc fires toward the shattered window to defend Wyatt. Behan grabs Ike and, along with Fuller and Claiborne, dashes out the gallery's back door. Outside, Billy and Frank are again hit. Morgan and Doc kill Frank. Billy Clanton, the last Cowboy still alive, leans against the Harwood house. Pistol empty, he piteously asks for someone to load his gun. Fly bends down and takes his gun. The fight is over. Behan unsuccessfully attempts to arrest everyone. Josephine and Wyatt smile at each other as Behan and Mattie fume. The other Earp wives hug their husbands. In the script, the fight lasted 20 seconds and on film, 97 seconds. In reality, it lasted 30 seconds.[30]

Scene 78: The script then shifts to Rustler's Park as Curley Bill gives a poetic eulogy for Clanton and the McLaurys, demands Fuller and Claiborne's red sashes (they ran from the fight) and then counsels the rest of the Cowboys to bide their time. Revenge is best served cold.[31]

Scenes 82–86: These next several scenes take place in Galeyville, the Sonora desert, Tombstone and Rustler's Park. A drunken Ringo offers to buy a prospector some gin in a Galeyville saloon. When the old man refuses and asks for a beer instead, Ringo kills him. Curley Bill's original follow-up line ("I tell you, boys, even I'm worried what'll happen when Ringo runs this outfit") is still used in the film but moved to a different scene. The scene switches to an adobe house in the desert. A Mexican family is gathered for dinner when Ringo and Curley Bill burst in with guns drawn. Bill looks at the radiant young wife, licks his lips and nods at Ringo: "Look, son, there is a God after all!" We then quickly switch to Tombstone where lightning flashes across the evening sky as the wind howls. Florentino is inside the Oriental Saloon nursing a drink. We cut to Rustler's Park where Curley Bill tells the Cowboys, "It's time to get wooly."[32]

Scene 89: After the scene of the attack at Virgil's house, we switch to Mayor Clum's house. A shotgun pierces the parlor window and fires at the mayor's wife Mary, who is sitting in a rocking chair. The mayor dives to protect her.[33]

Scenes 102–05: In an extended sequence, Wyatt, astride his horse Dick Nailor, and leading four other stallions, rides into a wagon train camp. After a short scene around the campfire, where Wyatt and the wagonmaster discuss the concept of revenge, we next see Holliday, McMasters, Texas Jack Vermillion and Turkey Creek Jack Johnson riding into camp the next morning. Earp throws a wad of money at them, and after some discussion, all agree to form a posse and eliminate the Cowboys. They prepare to leave that evening, each horse saddled and waiting with a rifle in a scabbard and a double-barreled shotgun across each saddle fork. Wyatt swears each one in as a federal deputy. Doc reluctantly agrees but won't wear a badge. Lucinda, a scarred pioneer woman, runs up to Wyatt and ties a blue and gold silk scarf around his neck. As Wyatt and his posse leave the wagon train's camp, a young lad jumps up on a wagon and gives a wordy, loquacious and entirely out-of-character toast. Wyatt turns in the saddle and waves his hat in a cavalier's flourish.[34]

Scenes 107–21: In the script, Wyatt's Vendetta Ride is captured through a series of vignettes: Wyatt and the posse ride into Galeyville and burn it to the ground. Wyatt throttles Indian Hank Swilling to within an inch of his life. Then on to Pete Spence's camp: Florentino attempts to escape, his horse is shot by McMasters, and Florentino is killed by Wyatt after admitting he was paid $15 to be a lookout to Earp's brother's murder.

Wyatt ropes the dead Cowboy and drags the body back to Spence's camp. In the next scene, the posse ambushes the Cowboys as they emerge from a cut in a canyon, the same cut that Wyatt and Josephine rode through weeks earlier. The last scene is at Iron Springs, where the posse is ambushed by Curley Bill and 17 Cowboys. Almost surrounded, Wyatt grabs a shotgun and advances on the outlaws. With bullets whizzing around him, he calmly shoots and kills Brocius and several other Cowboys before they scatter.[35]

Scenes 123–26: In another series of scenes not included in the film, the two lone survivors of the battle at Iron Springs ride into the Cowboys' camp and describe Wyatt's superhuman effort. Ringo calmly kills them for their cowardice. Later that evening, while the rest of the Cowboys are asleep, Billy Grounds and Zwing Hunt quit the group and sneak away into the night. The following morning, Ringo meets with Behan in the sheriff's office. The two then ride back to camp where they are joined by Deputy Breakenridge. Ringo deputizes the Cowboys.[36]

Scene 132: Several scenes later, while resting atop a hill, Hunt and Grounds spy a stagecoach: "Just what we need. Travelin' money."[37]

Scenes 135–40: The next few scenes, though scripted, are not in the film in any form whatsoever. As Doc lies in bed, Wyatt professes his love for Josephine and tells Doc he'll love her when he's dust. Then we switch to Hunt and Grounds' camp. Deputy Breakenridge walks in to arrest the duo. As Grounds raises his pistol, the deputy stumbles backward in fear and his rifle accidentally fires, killing the outlaw. Hunt draws his weapon but this time the lawman's aim is true. Another Cowboy is dead. Hooker tells Wyatt that they took a vote: The posse can stay at the ranch as long it wants, Cowboys or not. Ringo and his posse ride up and stop atop a hill overlooking Hooker's ranch. Hooker and six ranch hands ride out to meet them. After Hooker tells Ringo to get off his property, another five ranch hands arrive. Ringo smiles and tells Hooker he'll be back.

Scene 144: After a Cowboy brings back McMasters' body and Wyatt accepts Ringo's challenge, Vermillion and Johnson discuss with Wyatt his odds of beating Ringo.[38]

Scenes 157–60: In the film, immediately after Ringo's death, Wyatt's Vendetta ride continues. In the script there are several quick cuts. As Wyatt and Doc emerge from a thicket, Vermillion and Johnson almost jump for joy. Texas Jack yells, "Praise Jesus!" Turkey Creek follows with "I'll be dipped in shit. I will, too." On the other side of the thicket, Ike and Behan hear the gunshot and believe Ringo has killed Earp. After Doc mounts his horse, they decide to leave Arizona as the Cowboys are waiting to ambush them. Vermillion wants to finish them off, Johnson agrees. Wyatt looks at Doc, who shrugs. Off they go, the last charge of Wyatt Earp and his immortals. As they ride into the Cowboys' camp, the outlaws panic and scatter. Only Ike remains, then he, too, cuts and runs. As they approach, Deputy Breakenridge remains. As Wyatt passes, he points his finger and gives the deputy a salute.[39]

Scene 161: Father Feeney, a priest, discusses the mysteries of the Catholic church with an emaciated Doc, who lies in a Denver hospital bed. (The use of the surname "Feeney" is a possible homage to the great Western director John Martin Feeney, aka John Ford. Of course "Pappy," as he was affectionately known, often gave his name as Sean Aloysius O'Feeny or O'Fearna, so, who knows?) Wyatt visits; he and Doc have an extended conversation. During their talk, Wyatt confesses, "All I wanted was to live a normal life." Doc replies, "When will you wake up? You wouldn't know a normal life if it bit you in the ass." This is a great line, derived from a conversation between Kevin Jarre and Jeff Morey. According to Jeff, while at the writer's house one day, Jarre asked what

Morey wanted out of life. "I just want a normal life," replied Jeff. Kevin was quick to reply, "There's no such thing as a normal life." Morey was just as quick to reply, "Kevin, you live in Hollywood. You wouldn't know a normal life if it bit you in the ass." Luckily, this humorous real-life conversation found its way into the scene.[40]

Scenes 162–65: The script's four scenes are condensed into just two in the film. We first see the Palace Theater in Denver where *H.M.S. Pinafore* is being performed. Cut to the stage where Josephine and three chorus girls dance the seaman's hornpipe. After the performance, the chorines are backstage, chatting and removing makeup. As the door bursts open, the girls scream and Wyatt enters. He falls to his knees and grabs Josephine's robe. They kiss. In the next scene, a train rushes through a mountain pass as the couple navigates their way through a swarm of reporters in the parlor car. Outside, Wyatt and Josephine, bathed in sunlight, hang onto the rail. The screen turns white. The epilogue, like the prologue, is a series of photos and live-action vignettes. The narrator gives a lengthy explanation of the demise of the Cowboys and Tombstone. Ike Clanton and Behan are seen as well as Wyatt and Josephine, now an elderly couple. Flickering images of actors Tom Mix and William S. Hart appear on the screen and the narrator continues. The images fade to black.[41]

Most of the above-referenced scenes appeared in all subsequent script revisions in some fashion or another, albeit with slightly different dialogue or characters. Jarre had told a wonderful story full of action, romance, heartbreak, comedy, heroism and atmospheric richness. Those who read the first draft versions were impressed by his storytelling ability, colorful though somewhat anachronistic dialogue, and authentic and accurate historical detail with carefully crafted logic and *mise en scène*. Morey recalled, "I read it … and was very impressed with it. [Kevin] always said that he wanted to do a period movie and this script had all the period vernacular. I thought it had the potential to be one of the great classic Westerns." Sherayko loved it, too: "I got home around four o'clock in the morning and literally couldn't put it down. It's what we call a page-turner. You wanted to see what was happening next. And I read the whole script. I was done about 5:30, 6:00 in the morning. I really enjoyed it."

According to Kurt Russell, "Jarre's screenplay was really the first time anyone has tried to present Wyatt Earp in his entirety. I mean, all of him: his relationship with his brothers, with his first wife, how he took up with Josephine Marcus, the traveling actress that he ended up spending nearly half a century with. You could see the dark side of the man. There's stuff in that original script that if you were ever to read it, you'd go, 'Oh ho ho.'" Val Kilmer called it "one of the greatest that he'd ever read." According to Val, the film's authenticity came from Jarre's attention to "how everyone wore their wealth on their bodies. They said who they were by how they turned their hats and what colors they wore." Dana Delany had an unusual take on the subject, noting, "[Kevin's] attention to detail was what attracted the wonderful cast of actors. He wanted to tell the true version story of what happened in Tombstone. I certainly didn't know that ladies wore fashions from Paris at the time."

Eventual producer Bob Misiorowski was awed: "The original screenplay opposed to the final film was a work of art that leapt off the page. The strength of the script was the relationships between the brothers and Doc. The Earps were vagabonds. The entire family was a family in motion. Wyatt wanted to settle down and have a family in Tombstone and he'd had all sorts of trouble in Dodge. At the same time, I was made an offer to produce *Color of Night* or do *Tombstone*. Once I read the first ten pages, I'd made my decision and went with *Tombstone*." Writer Henry Cabot Beck may have expressed it best when he wrote, "Jarre was able to reach deep inside that story and turn it into an operatic epic, more colorful and grander than anyone before him, including John Ford. He did it by recognizing and respecting the facts with uncanny accuracy. Like Coppola's *The Godfather*, (his script) colors a routine genre with wit and brilliantly realized characters to the extent that it made people who knew the story care about it anew, and attracted those who had never heard of it. His script helped people not only appreciate the history, but also the era, when greed and ambition, chaos and character were intertwined. [But] Jarre's script does contain a great deal of exposition. Fans of history would have loved it, but filmmakers ... who are schooled in disciplined productions can't help but see such expositions as either indulgent or unnecessary. Determining what should be kept or cut is a thorny issue, because the decision can mean the difference between art and commercial success."

Makeup artist David Atherton felt that some of the scenes were "too poetic," in particular the Wagonmaster scene: "I don't think it would have worked in this movie anyway. I think if we did keep that scene in, people would have just rolled their eyes.... It was, to me, a little over the top ... you had this little kid making this speech just coming out of left field, and as Wyatt Earp is riding away, he's standing on top of a wagon waving at him saying this flowery passage.... It was better they cut those scenes out." But that was okay. Scenes could be modified, dialogue changed.[42]

And then, probably predictably, it all hit the fan. Kevin Costner already had rejected Jarre's request to play Wyatt Earp in this film because the actor was working on his own pay-per-view Earp project. On December 7, Costner and Lawrence Kasdan announced they would do back-to-back Westerns at Warner Bros. once Kasdan finished re-writing Dan Gordon's script. Paragon Entertainment, a Canadian film and television production company, had originally developed the Earp project through its exclusive arrangement with writer Gordon. Paragon chairman–CEO Jon Slan presented a nine-page outline to the producers that "became a 300-page script." Explains Gordon, "It was to be two movies, in fact, centering on three families: the Earps and two organized crime families. Kevin and I were visualizing a Western *Godfather*. Mike Gray, a bizarre image of Earp, managed to get Tombstone, the richest town west of the Mississippi, deeded to his private company. It was a land-grab worth $10 million to $20 million in 1880 dollars—and the only thing between him and that money was Wyatt Earp. That's what our story was about. Our version put the whole story into the realm of classic tragedy. Earp realized that he had become that which he had been fighting against. And there's no sign of China Mary, who served as the Greek chorus of the piece, or the whole Tombstone Chinese community."

Gordon added that Kasdan's rewrite not only eliminated the villains but tacked on a lengthy, superfluous opening sequence, diluting the love story and substituted an inconclusive flashback for the more satisfying original ending: "[Kasdan] had to put his fingerprints on [the script], and he dicked up a good movie.... They just ruined it. It was boring. He cut out the bad guys. How do you have a Western without villains?" Kasdan wasn't any more complimentary about Gordon's work: "I used some elements from that other script, but only the things I really loved, and there weren't that many."[43]

Jim Wilson, partner with Costner in Tig Prods. (Costner's production company, named after his grandmother), said that while the Earp project came to Tig as a TV long form, "we tossed it back and forth [between TV and feature]. Clearly, you couldn't do the whole Wyatt Earp biography in a short picture, and pay-per-view was very attractive to us. But, ultimately, our bread and butter at Tig is movies. When Kasdan entered the mix, clearly it became a feature." Whether it would be one film or a two-part film series would be decided when he finished rewriting and revising the script. Later it was decided when shooting was complete on the first script, production would immediately begin on the second. At the time, the specific format hadn't yet been decided, but it didn't take long to figure that out. Four days later, Jarre learned of Tig's decision: "I got wind that Costner and Kasdan were doing (the Earp project) as a feature. Costner called me … and said, 'Look, I hope you don't think we're trying to squeeze you out. There is room for both movies.' I said, 'Would you tell that to [Universal head of production] Casey Silver?'" Jarre said the suddenness with which a TV project became a film project—as Costner read Jarre's script—"struck me as very odd."

By that time, studio executive James Jacks and Jarre were already discussing potential casting and filming locations. And what an interesting cast it would have been. After Costner's rejection, Jarre wanted Liam Neeson to play Wyatt Earp, with David Bowie as a potential Doc Holliday. (In an early version of the script, Wyatt's love interest Josephine commented on his broken nose. While neither the historical Wyatt nor Kurt Russell sported a broken nose, Liam indeed had had his nose broken.) Jeremy Irons and even the 49-year old Michael Douglas were considered. According to Morey, "[Kevin] liked the idea of echoing or referencing earlier Earp movies and thought Douglas might be intrigued to take a role his father once played." In fact, *The Hollywood Reporter* claimed, "Jarre also tried to snare Kirk Douglas for a cameo but that didn't pan out, so he's now hoping to lasso Oscar-show ham Jack Palance for it." Some may recall Palance once performed one-arm pushups on the Academy stage to the amazement of the audience. (Once the film was officially announced, stars such as Brendan Fraser, Timothy Hutton and Michael Madsen were also said to have expressed interest. Jarre once mentioned that Hutton and Tommy Lee Jones were his choices to play the roles of Johnny Behan and Curly Bill, respectively.) One actor who desperately wanted to play Wyatt was Richard Gere who, according to Jarre, just about pestered him to death.

On December 16, a Warner Bros. press release announced that Wilson, Costner and Kasdan would produce their film, which would start shooting in May 1993. "We're not looking to make one four-hour movie," explained Wilson, "but we'd love to make two two-hour movies." This release started a war of words between the two studios. A Universal spokesperson said that the announcement would have "absolutely no impact on our project. They haven't written theirs and we have a script. We will be tracking it closely." Replied Wilson, "This is nothing like that. You could do five pictures about Wyatt Earp. Ours is vastly different. It's not a competitive thing. Whatever time it takes to make our film a good film is what we'll do." Other industry insiders weren't so sure. "I don't think [Tig] can start in May," said one. "[The announcement] is just a bluff to try to kill off the Universal project."[44]

The whole situation sounded suspiciously like another episode that had occurred just the previous year, and Costner was involved in that one as well. Joe Roth, president of Morgan Creek Productions, had supposedly begun developing a script based on the story of Robin Hood. When he left Morgan Creek and became head of 20th Century–Fox, he took the project along with him and approached Mel Gibson about the starring role. In the wake of Roth's departure, Morgan Creek then suddenly began looking for its own Robin Hood project. Coincidentally, Tri-Star also entered the fray with yet a third Robin Hood film with Marshall Herskovitz (*thirtysomething*) directing and Kevin Kline or Alec Baldwin as Robin. Fox bought Mark Allen Smith's script and John McTiernan (*Die Hard*) was set to start to direct *The Adventures of Robin Hood* starting October 22, 1990. Roth was furious, claiming that Morgan and Tri-Star "acted unjustly, if not immorally" by rushing competing projects into production as Fox was "first" to develop such a product. In fact, both of the other two studio planned to begin filming on September 3, almost two months before Fox, even though neither had any commitments for the starring role. According McTiernan, "We finished the script two years ago and made the mistake of letting people know about it." One of Roth's major issues was that the William Morris Agency, which represented McTiernan and Smith, also handled *Prince of Thieves* screenwriters Pen Densham and John Watson, who along with Richard B. Lewis would produce the Morgan Creek project. Clearly, it appeared that the agency knew what it was doing when it engineered the sale of Mike Simpson's Robin Hood script to Morgan Creek for the tidy sum of $1.2 million. Roth felt Morgan Creek was well aware of the project even before he left the studio for Fox. Tri-Star claimed they had started work on its script in 1985 and it was only a huge coincidence that three studios were developing the same project, although they admitted, "We were aware [of the other projects] but proceeded believing ours is the best." McTiernan said he had pitched *Robin Hood* to Warners, Disney and MGM way back in 1983 before "Fox stepped up to it." And, John Watson claimed, "We initiated the idea out of our own heads. We heard of one other project in the works [at Fox] but we decided to go ahead with ours.... When you're writing, and you get into the creative process, sometimes you just can't stop."[45]

Hollywood tradition holds that when competing studios try to bring the same story to the screen, the first one out forces stragglers to drop out. Despite the daunting rate of failure, no studio wants to drop out of a race that could yield huge profits at the finish line. "The trouble with racing to get things out," said one executive, "is that between deal-making and picture-making, picture-making always suffers. It's physics. No matter how much you scream at the airport or yell at the pilot, you still can't fly [from LA] to New York in two hours. You have to be a lot better than the other guy if you come in second.... The way we operate between agents, studios and talent, everybody is either so afraid or so full of shit that artists lose perspective and think they don't need any assistance."[46]

Two weeks after Roth's outburst, Morgan Creek announced that Costner would star in *Prince of Thieves,* and the ballgame was all but over. (Interestingly, Roth, McTiernan and Costner previously had had several conversations about the Fox project but nothing came of it. Sean Connery was also approached but passed on the project.) Although Roth had previously stated that they would go forward with production "no matter what, and we're not going to stop until we get this picture made," they now were rethinking their position. Gibson didn't want to make the picture and the script's rewrite wasn't even ready yet, although Roth disputed that fact. Tri-Star also believed the fate of its project was unclear and that it hinged on retaining an appropriate cast. "We're proceeding prudently," admitted producer Mike Medavoy, "and trying to figure out whether we should make it." And, to pour salt into the wound, Morgan Creek also announced they were moving up its film's release date from the next summer to spring, in an attempt to beat the other two projects to the theaters. When the dust settled, Fox bowed out and decided that *The Adventures of Robin Hood* starring Patrick Bergin would be produced as a three-hour telepic for Fox TV as well as be released overseas. Tri-Star dropped out of the picture entirely.[47]

Now this was happening all over again: rival studios with the same Earp project and Costner in the starring role. If the Tig announcement was a bluff, it surely made Universal and Jarre nervous. They knew the only way to beat Costner to the punch was to start filming their project first. So Jarre continued tweaking—eliminating scenes and characters, consolidating dialogue. The script thus shrunk in both content and size: 165 scenes down to 152, 135 pages reduced to 122. Excluding atmospheric background players (they *hate* to be called extras), Jarre reduced the number of roles from 88 to 81 and speaking parts from 65 to 64. He also eliminated a potentially controversial rape and murder scene that would show up again in his next draft. But it was to no avail. Explained James Jacks, "Kevin Jarre came to me and said he wanted to make a movie about the real story of Wyatt Earp and Doc Holliday. So we got financing from Universal for him to write the script, but when Kevin Costner announced that he was gonna do *Wyatt Earp*, Universal decided they did not want to race or get into any kind of battle with Costner and Warner Brothers." No wonder. Not only was Costner a major star with a proven track record, Universal had its future tied up in Costner's latest project, *Waterworld*. (Written in the late '80s by recent Harvard grad Peter Rader, *Waterworld* was originally bought by New World Pictures and budgeted at $3 million. In 1993 when Universal took on the project from Largo Entertainment, it was budgeted at $64 million, almost $10 million more than *Jurassic Park*. Largo's Japanese joint-venture partner JVC wasn't willing to commit more than $25 million per film and was fearful of budget over-runs. By the time production started, the cost had risen to nearly $100 million, and with a final cost of over $175 million, the project, known as "Kevin-Gate" and "Fishtar" at the time, was the most expensive film ever made ... until *Titanic* came along in 1997.[48])

While Jarre continued working on his Earp script, Universal debated the project's feasibility and eventually decided the risk was just too great. Why alienate a studio breadwinner, especially one named Costner? Jarre passed the bad news along to his horseback-riding buddies. "We're not doing this at Universal any more," he told Sherayko. "They threw us out." Peter was distraught but even though Jarre felt Costner's untitled film was "an attempt to crush my picture," Kevin consoled his friend: "No, no. We have a lot of people backing us and we know it's going to be good." Costner maintained "that he personally went to Universal and asked them to release the Jarre version into turnaround and let another studio pick up the project but Jacks said, no, that was incorrect." The studio cancelled the project after the announcement and would not release it to be shopped around.[49]

Now the question one must ask is, why would a major movie star, on the top of his game, ask his home studio to put a project into turnaround? Was he fearful of the competition? Turnaround is studio-speak for development purgatory—the place where scripts go when studios want to dump them. There are different reasons why turnaround–development purgatory exists. For instance, a reshuffling of top production executives may spur the desire to start with a clean slate. Or scripts may come in at too high a budget. Or a top actor or director may decide to pull out of the project during pre-production. Genre gridlock can doom a picture or a studio can sour on a particular star. In many instances, the project comes with a unique demand; for example, a screenwriter may want to direct. In any case, when studios place a project "on the shelf," they might still look for a buyer who is willing to pay the studio all the costs they've already incurred, including overhead and interest. In the case of *Tombstone*, none of the above was applicable: Costner just didn't want the film to be made.[50]

Of course, one major issue in getting Jarre's project off the ground was fairly obvious: Who would appear in it? Costner was represented by Michael Ovitz's powerful Creative Artists Agency (CAA) and with Ovitz's backing, Jacks and Daniel couldn't get a decent-sized studio interested in backing Jarre. Jacks even accused CAA of "telling people our movie won't happen." Even Brad Pitt, who at one time agreed to play Earp with Johnny Depp as Doc Holliday, backed out after the rival project was announced. Pitt, also represented by CAA, was dissuaded by his agent. Fortunately, Kurt Russell's ex-agent at William Morris surreptitiously gave the actor (another CAA client) a copy of the script. Russell, a long-time friend of Cinergi Production's Andy Vajna, contacted him as Vajna had a distribution deal with Hollywood Pictures, a division of Disney.

"Andy and I had been on a bicycle trip," explained Russell, "that's where the relationship came from. A bicycle trip we did a couple of years earlier. He said, 'If you ever have a project...' I said, 'Fine.' I left my old agent [at William Morris]. I was the last one to leave, actually. My old agent called up one day: 'There's a script that I'm aware of, that you should do. But, there's a lot of politics involved.' I thought it was a phenomenal script, and I called and said I wanted to do it, and they said 'Ooh,' because Costner was at CAA. I went to [Cinergi] and got the money. I went to my brother-in-law Larry Franco, who produced a thousand movies, and I asked, 'Larry, can I do this for $25 million dollars?' He looked at it, went through it, semi-budgeted it, and said, 'Sheee—Just.' I remember when I read *Tombstone* and I remember feeling that it was quite unique and I loved the dialogue and I loved the feeling that [Kevin Jarre] just had a style and a complete approach to the western that I had never really read before. I liked it! It was fantastic. It was a movie that needed to be made and I would love to do it." According to Russell, Costner exerted his influence to try and have *Tombstone* frozen out: "I got a phone call and it was just before Val was going to come on—we had to have a release. Costner had shut down all avenues of release for the picture except Disney, except for Buena Vista. He was powerful enough at the time, which I always respected. I thought it was good hardball. I was told that by Kevin Jarre. Jarre said, 'We're dead in the water any place but Buena Vista.'"[51]

Universal eventually relented and put the Jim Jacks–Sean Daniel Western *Tombstone* into turnaround on February 5, 1993. William Morris, which represented Jarre, immediately tried to find the project another home. Once Russell became involved, Cinergi Prods., in competition for the project with Inter-scope Communications and Carolco Pictures, agreed to purchase the package. On February 12, 1993, two days after this announcement, sources indicated that Cinergi was willing to commit $20 to $25 million to the project.[52]

TWO

Only the Beginning

Once word of Schieffelin's claims became widely known, it was only a matter of time before the area was inundated with swarms of would-be prospectors. Cowboys, homesteaders, lawyers, speculators and even "ladies of the night" flocked to the area in droves. Soon, a quasi-collection of canvas tents and ramshackle dwellings materialized on the landscape near Schieffelin's Lucky Cuss mine. Initially known as Watervale, or Waterville, this odd collection of souls numbered almost 100. The first man earning the distinction of meeting his death by violence after the Tombstone silver rush was Watervale resident John Hicks, shot during a card game in the fall of '78. Despite the fact that the presence of water was the only thing to recommend the area, neighboring communities with names like Richmond, Austin City, Stinkem, Fairbank (initially called Junction City, then Kendall), Millville and Contention quickly popped up. Their creations were identical: First came the prospectors, both professional and amateur. Those who knew what they were doing knew what to look for—surface outcrops of rocks with black lines of silver-bearing ore. Others with no experience, no training and no knowledge of geology just hoped to trip and fall into a strike. They came by horseback, they came by wagon. Others defied the odds and walked into the valley with a pack burro. But come they did. Claims were filed: 600 × 1500 feet. All it took was a few piles of rocks and a stake. Find a likely spot, swing a pick and dig a hole. If you were unsuccessful, you could always jump a neighbor's claim.

Tucson merchant John Vosburg described a typical settlement: "By this time lots of people, mostly men had come, and things were getting lively. There were lots of miners and prospectors with their attendant burros. A town of tents and hastily made adobes had sprung up like magic on the bottom land along the side of the mill site. They named it Charleston.... Ike Clanton started and ran our first boarding house in a tent and he soon had plenty of boarders."

Predictably, after the prospectors came the merchants and drummers (salesmen) as miners needed food, clothing, tools, something to drink. Why break your back looking for silver when you could make your fortune off of those who did? Restaurants and saloons popped up like prairie dogs. Boards and wooden barrels served as tables, rotgut whiskey quenched thirsts while professional gamblers did their best to part miners from their hard-earned wealth. Dirty? If you were of a mind, bath houses and tents served to wash off the dirt. Then came female entrepreneurs; makeshift tents, saloons and dance halls served as their places of work. Most of the prospectors were bachelors, alone for weeks or months at a time, with little to entertain them. The women were ladies of easy virtue. As Chicago reporter A.H. Noon wrote, "The atmosphere is dirty and abominable, but they dance away, nevertheless—the men inanely grinning, the women evidently dancing as a matter

31

of business." Others didn't bother to dance. Slowly but surely, these little camps began to expand.[1]

Still, it took quite a bit of financial wherewithal to be a successful miner. Anyone could dig a hole, but to be profitable, you had to dig deep, which meant equipment and manpower. Silver mining was a long, arduous, labor-intensive, time-consuming process; assay works, smelters, refineries and stamping mills all took funding. Rare were the individuals who could finance all this on their own. Due to the success of Gird and the Schieffelin brothers, the trio, along with Arizona's third Territorial Governor Anson Safford and John Vosburg, pooled their resources to create the Tombstone Gold and Silver Mill and Mining Company. A stamp mill to process the silver ore soon followed. The people from all of the towns (actually, these "towns" were little more than camps) floated back and forth between them. But, as the mill was being constructed, residents from the outlying shantytowns began relocating into the area. Other conglomerates soon formed the Western Mining Company (later to be the Contention Consolidated Mining Company) and the Grand Central Mining Company. Means of transportation were required, so stage, freight and express lines soon started serving the needs of the newly established mining district. In October 1878, 38-year-old J.D. Kinnear pioneered the first once-a-week, 95-mile stagecoach service between Tucson and Tombstone. The one-way trip cost $10 and took 17 hours. Ten weeks later, Kinnear's Express had become so successful that he found it necessary to implement twice-weekly runs. The following year Kinnear changed its name to Tucson & Tombstone Mail and Express. As early as September, a Tucson correspondent reported that "the new townsite is progressing finely; two stores, one barber shop and a restaurant underway already." By December 2, a post office had been established. On March 5, 1879, U.S. Deputy Mineral Surveyor Solon M. Allis laid out a town on a mesa above the Tough Nut Mine in a place called Goose Flats, the nearest level spot closest to the mine. In honor of Schieffelin's claim, the town was called Tombstone. Buildings were relocated from other sites, and by mid-summer correspondents reported houses were being started almost every day and "seemed to grow like mushrooms" with temporary canvas structures giving way to more substantial materials.[2]

Allis's 320-acre townsite was laid out in a typical Western town pattern, with streets running at right angles to each other, thus forming a grid. This orderly design supposedly was advertised as a safeguard against overcrowding, disease and fire, but sadly, future events would show this not to be the case. Streets in a grid are numbered, lettered or arranged in alphabetical order—this was the case in Tombstone, where streets ran the length of the three-quarter-mile–long by quarter-mile–wide mesa. The numbered streets, First through Fifteenth, ran at right angles to the others, pointing north and west. The named streets were as follows: North, Fitch, Fulton, Bruce, Safford, Fremont, Allen and Toughnut. Toughnut was named after Schieffelin's claim, Fremont for Arizona's fifth territorial governor John C. Frémont, and Allen for John Brackett "Pie" Allen, an enterprising capitalist who sold apple pies to the soldiers at Fort Lowell and Huachuca. The resulting grid consisted of 98 individual full-lots available for $5 each with seven additional quarter-lots. Since Fremont Street, named after the famed explorer and current governor, would be the main thoroughfare, it was laid out five feet wider than the other streets. Shortly thereafter, the town's first house was built and in October 1879, the Cosmopolitan Hotel was in full operation. Built by Carl Bilicke, the two-story building contained 50 beds, elegant black walnut and rosewood furnishings, a restaurant, bar, ladies sitting room, general merchandise outlet, cement sidewalk and Tombstone's first piano. Prior to its construction, Bilicke's "hotel" had consisted of a mere tent, albeit with beds, not cots—functional but not very fashionable. But he did offer *his guests fresh milk from his own cow. Bilicke spared no expense in his new hotel—his hand-carved, rosewood grand piano had been shipped around South America's Cape Horn and finally transported to Tombstone from San Francisco via mule train.*[3]

That same year, Jim Vogan and Jim Flynn opened a wholesale liquor store, sample room and ten-pin bowling alley. The Golden Eagle Brewery, later known as the Crystal Palace and ultimately the most imposing building in town, was constructed by Frederick Wehrfritz; it quickly became the town's social center. Its second-floor offices were occupied by coroner Dr. Harry Matthews, Cochise County Sheriff John Behan, former army surgeon Dr. George Goodfellow, attorney George Berry, justice of the peace Wells Spicer et al. (After the Earps arrived in Tombstone, town marshal Virgil Earp maintained a second-floor office.) In December 1879, photographer Camillus "Buck" Sydney Fly and wife Mary arrived in Tombstone and shortly thereafter established Fly's Studio, first in a tent and then later in a more substantial structure on the south side of Fremont, between Third and Fourth Streets. (The next year, the Flys opened a 12-bedroom boarding house and studio called Fly's Gallery.) Earlier in 1879, Quong Kee had opened the Can Can restaurant; the prior owner was Ah Lum, whose wife was known as "China Mary," the absolute ruler of Tombstone's Oriental population. Proprietor of one of the town's better-known establishments, Kee was later buried in Boot Hill, along with the famous and infamous: outlaws, gamblers, miners, prostitutes, cowboys, storeowners and housewives. The Boot Hill property originally had been laid out as a burial plot in 1878 and bore the name "Tombstone Cemetery." Miner John Hicks, the first person to be buried in Boot Hill, was shot down in front of Sam Danner's saloon in 1879. Since Tombstone was home to a sizable Chinese population, Kee's funeral procession included flying dragon kites and exploding firecrackers. The town's Chinese district, bordered by Second, Third, Fremont and Toughnut and derisively known as "Hop Town," contained several hundred residents and covered two square blocks. ("Hop" was slang for opium.) Selling general merchandise and lumber, M. Calisher, a California company, also opened for business that year, as did Vizina & Cook's Saloon and Mary King's boarding house.[4]

Tombstone was a most picturesque place as one visitor described its character: "On the principal street, lined with adobe buildings, large tents and frame structures, we find nearly every other building is a saloon.... Some are filled with rough-looking men, miners and others with quite a sprinkling of red-nosed bloated looking gentry, plainly belonging to the ancient order of the mining camp bummer.... Gambling is in full blast ... in a stifling atmosphere of stove-heat, unwashed humanity, whisky fumes and the cloud of tobacco-smoke...." Tents and adobe buildings were followed by bare-bones wooden buildings. But nothing fancy because miners were too busy digging for precious metals to worry about lavish ornamentation. In the evenings, residents might attend the local "theater," a rickety frame shack with a badly torn canvas roof. The surrounding mountains were heavily laden with pine and oak "in great abundance and fine growth," while newspapers reported that numerous canyons "are often almost impenetrable with heavy growth."

Soon, the sounds of additional hammering of nails and sawing of wood filled the air. Merchants naturally wanted something a bit more substantial than canvas and mud. Windows to keep out flies and doors to keep out the dust were a necessity. Predating the film-set industry, false-fronts were added to give the imposing appearance of stability.

One reporter observed that by early the following year, "the upper town is now growing daily and is now a town of some importance there are three restaurants now, so that one stands a chance of getting a square meal." Gen. J.B. Allen set up a general store and nearby

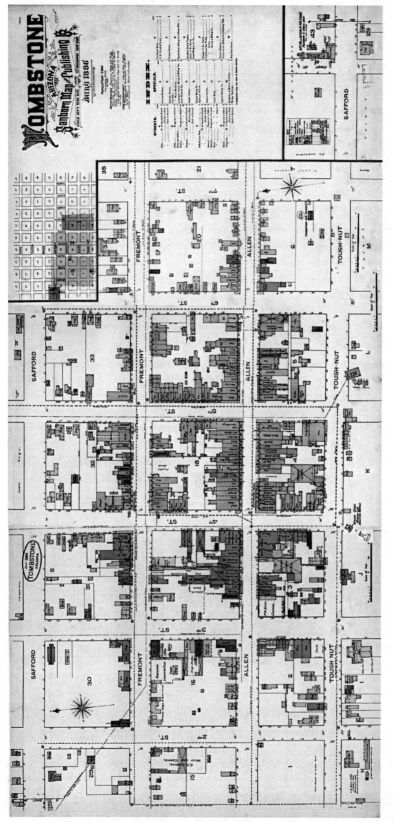

Sanborn Fire Insurance Company map of Tombstone, Arizona, July 1886. The O.K. Corral is located in the block bordered by Third and Fourth streets and Fremont and Allen streets.

restaurant to take advantage of the situation: "To supply it with eggs and milk he has sent out a lot of chickens and cows, fresh butter is a regular thing there. Behind the store he has a stable well supplied with forage. In fact, the General has fixed himself to meet every want of visitors." George Parson described Tombstone's atmosphere in his diary: "Stores set up shop in tents, and restaurants were similarly housed." With a rapidly increasing population, shanties and jacals housed several new families. Even the fourth estate became firmly established that fall with the publication of The Nugget. *(Its better-known rival,* The Epitaph, *came onto the scene the following May.) Businesses of all kinds were well represented since the two lines of daily stagecoaches were always full of passengers. Kinnear's line left Tucson on Mondays, Wednesdays and Fridays; the Tucson and Tombstone Stage Company, owned by William Ohnesorgen and H.C. Walker, Kinnear's former agent, ran on Tuesdays, Thursdays and Saturdays.* The Arizona Daily Star *reported, "An enterprising sportsman has just exported a complete outfit of 'Keno' from Tucson to Tombstone. This indicates that money is beginning to circulate out there...."*

The growth continued. The tent occupied by Sam Danner's saloon provided the setting for the community's first religious service. On December 14, 1879, A.W. Stowe opened a general store. One week earlier, the Pima County board of supervisors had officially declared the town of Tombstone incorporated; a mayor and common council were elected the following January. Tombstone's first public school opened a month later. There even were those who wanted to change the town's name but wiser heads prevailed. Shortly thereafter, Fred White was elected city marshal—his tenure would last less than a year.

Early in 1879, the town had 40 cabins and about 100 residents. The population swelled from 474 residents in September to 900 in October and over 1500 one month later. By February 1880, over 2000 residents called Tombstone home. (The official U.S. Census taken on June 1, 1880, tabulated 2170 individuals.) But unemployment was rampant. The Arizonian *reported that Tombstone was overrun with "destitute, helpless men seeking employment and finding none. The mines are said to be good enough, but they can give work to only a few persons."* The Daily Arizona Citizen *seconded that opinion: "Saloons of the lowest class and dance houses where men and women of the vilest sort herd together and make the night hideous are becoming well-settled institutions, and unless suppressed or regulated they will breed crime and death. Shooting has been a frequent thing, though happily the marksmanship has been very bad and but little damage has [been] done." Labor crowded into the area faster than capital developments. As a result, criminal elements began to take hold of the town. By the end of 1879, there were two drugstores, three or four doctors, two lawyers, eight desperados and one genuine Western celebrity.... Wyatt Earp.*[5]

The following year saw no decline in the expansion frenzy. Buildings were constructed as fast as material became available: "One lawyer ordered a house built and the carpenters began on a Friday. On Sunday, the lawyer moved in his library and hung out a sign." Reporters were effusive in their praise of civic improvements: "We now have three two-story buildings in the course of construction, two of which have frontage of 60 feet, and we hear of others that are soon to be commenced, together with additional stories on buildings now in use." The town's improvements were rapid. By late spring, 40 brick buildings for businesses were in the works, with new stores established daily, and families were finally setting up permanent residence. Houses 40 × 80 rented for $500 per month. Schools and churches were in session and there was even talk of a permanent theater. In July, the Western Union telegraph line from Tucson to Tombstone was finally completed and a local office opened. July also saw the formation of a glee club. In direct competition to the Cosmopolitan, the

Grand Hotel opened with an invitation-only ball on September 9, 1880. Later that month, the 60-member Tombstone Club opened on the second floor of the Ritchie Building. "Tastefully furnished with writing and card tables, easy chairs and reading tables," this gentlemen's club included "more than 70 publications comprising all of the leading American and foreign newspapers, magazines and periodicals" along with "a magnificent sideboard, well ladened with choice liquors and cigars." The Alhambra Saloon reopened that same month with a new black walnut bar, elegant paintings and engravings in the reading room, gold and bronze chandeliers, gambling tables and a three-piece orchestra.[6]

By 1880, the following Tombstone businesses were well established: The Agency Pima County Bank; Arizona Trading Co.; U.S. Meat Market; Bland Livery & Feed Stable; Delmonico Restaurant; Bourland's cigar shop; Brown, Taylor & Co, Livery Stable; Brown's Hotel (on the second level of Hafford's saloon); Coffee & Acker Meat Market; Dauner & Owens Saloon; Davis & Uplinger carpenters & cabinet makers; Diana Lodgings and Saloon; Eaton & Rice, druggists; Eswch & Hotz Saloon; Fry & Ackerson Saloon; H.L. Gehman, shoemaker; O.W. Greisenhofer, baker; Gray & Gray Real estate; Nevada Boot and Shoe store; W.A. Harwood, lumber dealer; Haynes, Lucas & Street, attorneys at law; Rural House; McKean & Knight, groceries; G.A. Millard, dentist; Montgomery & Benson Livery & Feed Stable & O.K. Corral; Pasquale & Co. Saloon; Ravel Robinson, tailor; Safford, Hudson & Co. bankers; Cochise Hardware & Trading Co.; Taker & Hoke, liquor and general merchandise; Walker House; Waterman & Goodrich, stoves & tinware; Rockway Oyster House & Restaurant; Seamans Watchmakers, Jewelers and Opticians, and on and on. By the end of 1880, it was estimated that 75 of Tombstone's businesses were saloons. More than 510 building were now erected, all but one in the past 12 months. The town was booming.[7]

Once Kurt Russell was on board, word spread like wildfire and even though casting wasn't yet set, the project generated interest all over Hollywood. Billy Zane, his sister Lisa and Jarre were friends at the time and endlessly discussed who should play each role. The trio put together a list of their actor friends and Jarre tried to include as many as possible in the project, including Dana Wheeler-Nicholson, Jon Tenney, Lisa Collins and Paula Malcomson. In fact, Kevin wrote the part of Josephine Marcus with former sweetheart and still close friend Lisa Zane in mind, and to a certain extent even modeled it after her by playing to her artistic strengths. In earlier drafts, Lisa's small American Eskimo dog, Bintar, was also added as an accessory for Marcus. Powers Boothe, later cast as Curly Bill Brocius, said, "It was such a great script that, as I understand it, everyone pretty much cut their money to do it. All of the better folks in Hollywood were tripping over themselves trying to get in the film. Kevin Jarre … at that period of time was certainly one of the best writers around. The research he did, every character, right down to the color of the horse you rode, your wardrobe and all that stuff, was just [perfect]."

It is little wonder Kurt wanted to be involved: "Movies start with a screenplay, and this one is brilliantly conceived. The characters are well drawn. It's a great story and not weighed down by what I consider a 1950s sort of mentality of what the Old West was like. There are some tough characterizations that have not been backed away from by anyone on this film. This is a script that offers drama, comedy, action and romance. A lot of people, a lot of studios, wished *Tombstone* would just die. Kevin Costner was gearing up his film *Wyatt Earp* at the same time, and it would have been easier if we had just gone away. But *Tombstone* had a lot of things going for it. First and foremost, it had me."

Names of those interested in the film were bantered about willy-nilly; in some cases the interest was genuine, in others, their persona just fed the publicity mill. Some actors asked to be in the film, others were asked to be involved. And, some didn't even know they were being considered. In late February 1993, it was announced that Billy Baldwin, who had tested very well, would play the role of Doc Holliday. Baldwin had worked with Russell in the 1991 movie *Backdraft* in a role supposedly turned down by Tom Cruise, Johnny Depp, Matt Dillon and ... Val Kilmer. Less than a week after the announcement, Kilmer replaced Baldwin as Doc. Kilmer noted, "Kevin Jarre did a great job. The character was already there, ready for me to more or less step into. He's never been portrayed as three-dimensionally as this. I liked being Doc Holliday. It's fun to be insightful and aristocratic, to stand up for your friend and make sacrifices for him. It was fun to be arrogant like he was and have the goods to back it up. Although, let's not forget that he did kill a lot of people." According to screenwriter John Fasano, "Everyone thinks they said, 'Go get Kurt Russell,' because [his] son is named Wyatt. But actually Andy Vajna said, 'Can you get Val Kilmer to be in it?' Val was cast first as Doc Holliday. Sherayko said Jarre told him Cinergi told him they would put up the money if they could get Kilmer to play Holliday. But they didn't have a distributer so Disney said they would distribute it if they could get Russell to play Earp." According to Russell, the person Jarre really wanted to play Holliday was Willem Dafoe. Kurt admitted he would have been phenomenal but Disney wouldn't go for it. Due to the controversy associated with *The Last Temptation of Christ* (1988), the studio wouldn't release the film with Dafoe playing Holliday, telling Jarre, "You can go with Val Kilmer, but not Dafoe."

Kilmer wasn't the only one who wanted to play Doc. "It was in the spring of '93," recalls Thomas Haden Church, "and both *Wyatt Earp* and *Tombstone* were being cast at the exact same time and [were] sought after by most of the young actors in town. I read the script and met with the head of casting who thought that I was authentic enough to be cast in the film. At the time, I was doing a small-budget detective movie with Sam Elliott [*Fugitive Nights: Danger in the Desert*] and he asked me one day if I had met the casting director for *Tombstone*. I told him I had and that I wanted to be cast as Doc Holliday. Sam told me that that was not going to happen as Val Kilmer had the part. He started going through a murderer's row of actors who I really admired, and I thought, 'Shit, I'm not going to get cast in this movie.'" But Elliott suggested Church go back and read for one of the smaller parts. So Church returned, spoke again with the casting director and suggested that maybe he could play Billy Clanton. Although another actor had already been selected, they were having second thoughts about him. "A week later," Church adds, "Sam and I had just driven to a small location in Palm Desert, California, where we were filming the detective movie. I got to the set for the first night shoot and Sam came over to me and asked me how I was doing. Then he said, 'Well, we're going to have to get you on a horse,' and that was how I found out I was cast as Billy Clanton."

Elliott had already been cast as Virgil Earp. According to Sam, Jarre handpicked the cast. "I remember going and having lunch with him at a place on the Sunset Strip in Los Angeles," recalled the actor. "Kevin said he was having all these meetings there, like he was holding court. I think Kevin's the one who really controlled this thing creatively before it got off the ground. The dialogue was there. Kevin Jarre wrote a brilliant script. I think across the board, every character there was well drawn. And he brought actors you normally wouldn't associate with Westerns. I would have done any role in this film. But what I really liked about Virgil was the fact that he was about what I consider to be a kind of moral core of this story. I'm not sure how set in reality that is, but it's always a nice kind of character to play within the context of the film you're doing."[8]

Jarre already had decided which actors he wanted for specific parts; now he just needed to ask them. "I got a phone call," remembers Chris Mitchum. "[Kevin and I] had never met. He said, 'Chris, I love Westerns. And I love the stuff that you have been in. I really like the picture that you and Heston did [*The Last Hard Men*]. I'm doing a film called *Tombstone*. We've hired Heston, I would love it if you would come and work for me about a week. I'd love to put you on film with him together again.' So, he sent me the script."

According to Stephen Lang, "I received the script along with an offer to play Ike Clanton. No meeting, no audition. I was surprised and pretty thrilled to be asked. Surprised because I had no expectation of being offered anything at that point in my career without having to audition. Which, by the way, I would gladly have done. When we met, I asked him why [Jarre] saw me as Ike. At the time Kevin was involved with the lovely Lisa Zane, and he had cast her as Big Nose Kate. Lisa is a terrific actress: She had played the love of my life when I played Babe Ruth for NBC. Kevin and Lisa had attended a screening of the film at the DGA. Kevin had seen me in *Death of a Salesman* on Broadway, and had said to Lisa, 'There is no way Lang can play Babe Ruth!' Well, he changed his mind when he saw the movie. So when we met, he told me, 'I figured if you could play the Babe, you could play anything.' That's why he offered me Ike."

Frank Stallone was another actor who had a role in the film even before he knew there was a role to be had: "I was at Billy Zane's house, and he was having a big party. At that time, my hair was real long, I had a beard. I didn't look like the Hollywood set–type guy. There was another guy who looked exactly like me there. We

Kurt Russell as Wyatt Earp and Val Kilmer as Doc Holliday (www. moviestillsdb.com).

were in the huge kitchen, drinking, having a cigarette and all this bullshit, talking. All of a sudden I just got on the subject of gunfighters 'cause I've already had a huge library of Western folklore and I love it. I'm enamored by it. He started talking about Ed Thompson, Doc Holliday, John Wesley Hardin, Dallas Stoudenmire, all these other gunfighters, Long Haired Jim Courtright, and he was keeping up with me the whole time we were talking. We were having a good old time. I realized that three hours had passed and we were still talking. People were even staring at us … at a party talking about cowboys. Everyone around us didn't know what the hell we were talking about. I didn't even get the guy's name.

"A year and a half later, I got a call from my agent, who said, 'Listen, they're doing this movie about Wyatt Earp, and they want you in it. All you have to do is to say "yes," and the part is yours.' I said, 'Sure. When do I read for the role?' She replied I didn't have to. It was already mine. I couldn't believe it. Then my agent wanted to talk money. I told her, 'Forget it. I'll just do it.'"

It turned out the fellow at Zane's house was Jarre, who never forgot Frank's interest and passion. Jarre also waged a war to get his girlfriend Lisa the role of Josephine Marcus but the studio, in particular Andy Vajna, preferred Dana Delany, who narrowly beat out Jennifer Connelly in a last-minute screen test. Zane was then asked if she would play Holliday's significant other, Big Nose Kate Horony. (Kate was born Marie Katherine Horony. At some point, other members of the family began to use the spelling Haroney.) Confesses Zane, "[It] left me cold, but I agreed because I believed in the greatness of [Jarre's] script and in what the movie could become. I wanted to be a part of it, beyond just in its inspirational phase." Professional that she is, she did a camera test and began to search for Kate's props, including a Gladstone bag and bullwhip. (Zane's brother Billy would later be cast in the small but memorable role of the devil-may-care stage actor Mr. Fabian.[9])

John Philbin, who was cast as Tom McLaury, won his part without any tryout: "I didn't have to read or audition or anything. Kevin Jarre saw my picture and he cast me based on my résumé and my picture and made the offer. I think I was in Hawaii at the time I received the offer. I came home, I was like, 'Yeah, I'll just do it.' My agent called and said, 'Listen. This is who is doing this movie,' and I said, 'Oh, my God. Yes.' I wanted to do it, totally. Kurt Russell was already involved. Val Kilmer, Sam Elliott and Bill Paxton [were] involved. Maybe Charlton Heston and Powers Boothe; some of those other actors were already involved already. I never met [Jarre] before we did the movie. There may have been a movie I had done that he liked or he had seen my work in something and trusted his instincts enough based on his impression of that role to give me that part."[10]

El Paso resident Nathan Simmons was in the area looking for an acting job and happened to luck out: "Actually, I've been in the film industry since 1987 and I was going out there for *Unforgiven II*, which they never made. But the lady at the casting director's said, 'You know, we've got a movie called *Tombstone*.' I said, 'That sounds good, I'm in the area already.'" Meanwhile, Wyatt Earp's real-life fifth cousin also was interested. Born in Perkins, Oklahoma, the 6'4", 200-pound Glen Wyatt Earp was struggling to start an acting career despite his leading man looks and famous name. "Actually, there has been greater skepticism of me as an actor because of my name," admits Glen. "Casting directors would call up my agent and say, 'Is this guy for real?'" Once Earp heard that the two films were being cast, he contacted both. He claimed that through informal negotiations he was going to play an "unnamed role" in Costner's film but as the script wasn't ready and

They called them "The Cowboys": Front row: John Philbin (as Tom McLaury), Michael Biehn (Johnny Ringo), Powers Boothe (Curly Bill Brocius), Jason Priestley (Billy Breckinridge), Stephen Lang (Ike Clanton), Thomas Haden Church (Billy Clanton), Tomas Arana (Frank Stillwell). Back row: Stephen Foster (Hank Swilling), Robert Burke (Frank McLaury), John Corbett (Johnny Barnes), Bo Gray (Wes Fuller), Forrie Smith (Pony Deal), Paul Ben-Victor (Florentino), Glen Wyatt Earp (Billy Claiborne) (courtesy Larry Zeug).

he had a chance to read Jarre's script, he instead cast his lot with Cinergi. Producer Jacks didn't mind: "We were very interested to see what he thought about the screenplay because of his family. It also helped the actors to be able to talk with him since, obviously, he had been researching this story for most of his life."[11]

While potential cast members were identified, tested and selected, other pre-production activities were already underway. Visual artists began conceptualizing the script on storyboards and a detailed schedule was created to accommodate the proposed availability and arrival timing of all the elements required for filming. Department heads—cinematographer, casting director, editor and costume designers, for example—were brought on board. Locations were scouted, props and wardrobe requirements were identified, equipment vendors were selected, and materials were rented. These and a myriad of other tasks, including the key areas of financing and budget preparation, were identified and assigned.

While actors supply a character's appearance and personality, directors create and execute the vision, and producers pull the whole project together, it's still the craftsmen listed in the closing credits who are critical to a film's success. And since this was a Western, it was especially critical to create a historically authentic set that would establish and graphically depict the mood and tone of the story. Not only should size, lighting and camera placement be taken into consideration, but the set's overall visual look should inspire both actors and audience. The "look" of a set or location is vital: It draws the audience into the story and makes a film convincing. A great deal of work and imagination goes into constructing the backdrop to any story and choosing or building locations and/or sets. Therefore, production designers are critical because they are responsible for the visual concept of a film. How better to do that than to create an exact replication of 1881 Tombstone? Enter Catherine Hardwicke.[12]

The 37-year-old Hardwicke was trained as an architect at the University of Texas in Austin. She designed and built townhouses, subdivisions, office buildings and low-income housing projects before entering graduate school at UCLA. "I designed and built a bunch of houses in Texas before deciding that real architecture might be a bit of a creativity sti-fler," she recounted. "I applied to grad school in Film at UCLA and people said, 'You're an architect, why don't you design my movie?'" While there, she won two major student film awards. An artist-animator, her first job was with Tim Burton "making little sculp-tures and things."[13]

The typical movie set Western town is almost iconic. If you've seen one, you've seen a million: a broad, smooth, well-graded main street bordered on each side by two-story, false-front, splintered wooden structures. Saloons with bat-wing doors, wooden side-walks, banks, a boarding house, sheriff's office and jail, livery stable, school, hotel and perhaps even a restaurant. These were the typical features of a Western whether filmed at the Melody, Corriganville, RKO Encino, Iverson, Jauregui, Walker or Paramount movie ranches or in Kanab, Lone Pine, Red Rock Canyon, Kernville, the Alabama Hills, Moab, Monument Valley, Sedona, Apache Junction, Mexican Hat and dozens of other locations.

But Jarre demanded more. Why not show Tombstone the way it had really looked? If it was a newly constructed town, it should look new. Not gray and weathered, but alive and vibrant with period buildings and features, which was almost impossible to depict accurately because of the town's rapid, explosive expansion. Adobe huts, canvas tents and wooden structures of variable size and shape had dotted the town's ever-changing landscape. And Jarre insisted on accuracy. But as large as Tombstone actually was, it was physically impractical to replicate the town's every nook and cranny. In fact, most of the historical action took place in a six-block area: Lot 2, blocks 17 through 19 (each 300 × 300 feet) and blocks 3, 4 and 5 (each 300 × 228 feet). Not only did this confined section contain hotels, cigar stores, billiard parlors and general stores, it also included 20 saloons: Tomlinson's, Bonanza, John Lang's, Keefe & Co., Tivoli, King & Moore, Old Palace, Pat/Lynch, Gruner & Schmidt's, Headquarters, Hafford's, Oriental, Arcade, Rafferty's, J.A. Miley, Brown's, Bank Exchange, Capital, Campbell and the Crystal Palace. No wonder that part of the West was so wild! With an initial construction budget of only $641,607, it was necessary to stretch every dollar. Hardwicke's budget included $26,200 to recreate the interior of the Oriental, $40,000 to build Hooker's ranch building (which was sub-sequently left for the owners of the ranch where the scenes were filmed), $12,000 for sig-nage, $40,400 for general street construction and enhancements, $40,000 to recreate the O.K. Corral, $1800 to create Boot Hill and $34,000 for the interior set of the Bird Cage Theater, even though this building wasn't in full operation at the time of the shootout. Initially, Jarre had scripted a scene for Schieffelin Hall, but after he and Morey visited Tombstone, Jarre decided the Bird Cage worked better.

The production company later increased the construction budget by an additional $140,000. (Actual costs eventually ballooned to $931,000.) Since two Western sets were already located in the immediate area, Tucson, Arizona, seemed the logical choice. While a few scenes were filmed at Old Tucson Studios (Kansas Street, Mexican Plaza and the Reno train depot; the soundstage also was used), most of the action was filmed at the standing Western town set of Mescal, located about 50 miles from Old Tucson. The Mescal set had been constructed in 1969 for *Monte Walsh* and, at the time, the location was known as Happy Valley. Property for the 2400-acre, $200,000 set was purchased from the Double X Ranch. A sister set of Old Tucson, the town had appeared in such films and television shows as *Dirty Dingus Magee, The Life and Times of Judge Roy Bean, The Outlaw Josey Wales, Little House on the Prairie, The Sacketts, The Buffalo Soldiers, Frisco Kid, Tom Horn, The Young Riders I, I Married Wyatt Earp* and many more. But by the time the *Tombstone* crew showed up in February 1993, the town set was in pretty rough shape and the crew only had two months to correct and dress it. "We rebuilt much of Mescal," said Hardwicke. "Tombstone was a boom town and we wanted it vibrant and full of life. Saloons seemed to spring up almost overnight, each more gaudy and outrageous than the last, and homes were more excessive than one might expect. We often think of the West as black and white but actually the colors were wild and garish. It may have been the Wild West, but women at least tried to tame their homes. They took great pride in getting the perfect wallpaper, trim and curtains. They were very vain and conscious about their homes and décor. I took the script and did a breakdown of all the sets and I went and visited the real Tombstone and I looked at tons of research from the archives, the Arizona Historical Society and all over and then came out to this town, which we were going to convert into Tombstone, and tried to figure out how to overlay the matrix of the two and turn them into the same thing for the least amount of money and the most dazzle. I read a lot of [historical documents] from that time period and I started finding out that they really wanted to make it look upscale and flashy. In the saloon, it turns out there was some imported wallpaper and I read there were some glass-front bookcases. That they were really going for a level of elegance. The Bird Cage Theater had all these chandeliers in it. [They were] really trying to attract an upscale patron to some of these establishments."[14]

The Mescal set was in such bad shape that they first had to address all the clean-up and safety issues to bring the buildings up to a workable standard. Then they could start to renovate them. They took a photo of every existing building—all the way down one side and then back up the other. They took the photos back to the art department—long shots of every existing building. Utilizing tracing paper or re-drawing it, they then created the new set the way they wanted to see it. "We worked for a couple months with my crew, constructing, building, researching, drafting, designing everything," says Catherine. "Looking for antiques. We made everything in this room from scratch. We built the building from the ground up, built the bar and all the molding and everything we made in the shop. A lot of the wallpaper is reproductions of historic wallpaper and the light fixtures are authentic old light fixtures that we recreated just for this from a photograph. That's why we made the town really colorful and very elegant. We wanted to give that feeling of vitality and exuberance to the town." But sometimes you can't win for losing: One oblivious critic wrote that "[the town] looks like it was built yesterday." Exactly!

A professional sign painter was brought in from Budweiser to hand-paint over 300 signs that appeared in the film. Hardwicke also made incredible drawings of every building, hand-colored to show how the structures should look. "The art department shrieked at first because it looked odd because they didn't have any aging on them. But once the

Allen Street on the Mescal Tombstone set. Left to right: Oriental Saloon, Campbell & Hatch Billiards, Telegraph/Assay office, Town Marshal's office (courtesy Larry Zeug).

whole thing meshed together, it was really very well done." Old Tucson Studios agreed that the corner building in Mescal, known as the Saloon, would be torn down and completely rebuilt as the Oriental Saloon. Tombstone Productions had permission to leave the new building in place at the conclusion of filming without having to rebuild the old saloon as long as the new building's exterior was "aged down with paint to fit into the look of Mescal."[15]

The re-enactors also helped Hardwicke achieve the richness of depth and texture that she desired. "I remember one day we were doing the O.K. Corral," she recalls, "and I had gone to all the prop houses in LA and [got] all the period saddles, and [did] everything we could. A couple re-enactors came up to me and said, 'You can do a lot better than that. We have the real stuff because we made it ourselves, and we're going to lend it to you. The right kind of leather and the right design that we copied from a photograph.' They just brought their stuff and put it in there which just elevated it so much to have somebody that cared that much. And they really did it right and they let us use it."[16]

Meanwhile, back in Old Tucson, another crew worked to adapt the soundstage to accommodate all necessary interior filming. Built in 1967, the 80 × 160-foot, $190,000 facility was air-conditioned, had a 50-ton capacity electrical heating and cooling system, and housed wardrobe, production offices and general office space. The soundstage floor even had six inches of concrete under a layer of 1⅛ inch plywood. An inch-thick, hard surfaced, sound-deadening board had been laid atop that so that dollies could noiselessly roll. There was even a special power hookup to shut off all electric motors and still all telephones when the director called for quiet on the set. Any of this soundstage's existing sets, staging and light fixtures that interfered with *Tombstone* sets had to be moved to another location. The catwalk was raised and both the Bird Cage Theater and Denver Stage dressing room were constructed. To accommodate shows once the initial build period was completed, space on the Bird Cage set was left for two rows of seats for park visitors.[17]

Located at the corner of Front Street and Columbia (later renamed Kansas Street), the Red Dog Saloon had been one of the first buildings added after Bob Shelton took over the Old Tucson property's lease in 1959. To replicate the Prescott, Arizona, saloon where the script depicted the knifing of Ed Bailey by Doc Holliday, the Red Dog was modified by replacing its chair rails and baseboards, adding valances, a removable stage floor, luan flooring and bases for the arch columns.[18]

Cinergi entered into a contract with Old Tucson Studios to rent both locations (Tucson and Mescal) used in filming: Ten weeks' preparation work at Mescal totaled $18,000; six weeks of filming at Mescal, $46,000; ten days at Old Tucson Studios, $15,000; four days of prep and strike work at Old Tucson Studios, $2400; six days' strike work at Mescal, $1800, for a grand total of $84,000. Strike and restoration alone was estimated to be almost $40,000. Periodic payments would be made by Cinergi, based on timing and deliverables.

Tombstone Productions began its preparation activities on April 26, 1993, and agreed to a complete restoration of Mescal by August 1 and Old Tucson within three days from completion of filming. Construction and scenic activity on the Old Tucson Studios soundstage was scheduled between April 27 and May 8; creation of the Prescott Saloon took place between April 28 and May 8; the train station and exteriors were completed by May 12, and re-decoration of all studio sets occurred between June 11 and June 16. As Old Tucson Studios already had other productions scheduled that summer as well as standard walk-through tours on the soundstage, the production company agreed to accommodate those activities while filming. Film department manager Nicola Hartmann said, "It will be a great boon for the community during what has traditionally been its slower season." Seconded spokesperson Ann McBride, "Any time a film of this size comes to town, they typically use many local goods and specialty services that may be needed for production. The final result is a very, very positive economic impact in the community and surrounding area."[19]

As the town of Mescal was being rebuilt, set dressers searched for period fixtures. Not only do these individuals select the items that decorate the set, they must make the scene look convincing. You're always going to have wagon wheels, rope, barrels and crates, burlap bags, water troughs and other items typically found in a Western. But when you look at individual scenes, the set dresser's creed is that you never want to repeat the same prop, whether it's a chair or pot-bellied stove. So before any item is ever purchased, a great deal of historical research is conducted. They confer with the director to understand the visual style and look of the film. According to set dresser Matt Marich, "You have to make it feel like it's a lived-in experience. Or, you're making that set unique to that actor. When you go into Wyatt's house, what things would Wyatt have in his house that are significant to him? There might be pictures of him and his first wife or whatever. So we

Doc Holliday's room, located on the second floor of Mescal's Grand Hotel. Though the room appears on-screen for just a single minute, note the set-dressing detail (photograph by Lee Gray/courtesy Catherine Hardwicke).

have to get into the characters a lot. That is very significant when you do contemporary movies. We have to make it feel, we're not just putting furniture in. It's figuring out, how does that shopkeeper make his shop look. How does that hotel differ from that hotel? What makes it look lived in and real? What lighting is practical that we are adding for the cinematographer? Because he can come in and light it all day long but if the movie had oil-fired lamps, we need to put oil-fired lamps on that set so that it seems like the motion picture lighting is coming from that direction. We're heavily involved in [tone and atmosphere]. Everything from posters printed and handbills and things that were in the Bird Cage, all that printing that was around there."

So the dressers hit every antiques shop in Phoenix and Tucson where they obtained western trucks, easy chairs, roll top desks, spittoons, lariats, etc. They rented a vintage billiard table from Arizona Pool Tables along with a felter who could repair the table if necessary. Some items were obtained from International Antiques in Tempe, Modern Props in Los Angeles and from studios, including Paramount. Usually the dressers would get a list of items needed, then look for things that caught their eye. Once these items were rented (for 20 percent of the face value), Polaroid photographs were taken and then hung from a large chain, with details of the item's appropriate cost, description and where it was used in the film written on the back of each photo. This is important because actors sometimes get rambunctious and furniture often is moved in and out of sets, often when cameras are set up to film different shooting angles. So if something gets damaged, the film company ends up buying it. Propmaker Brian Stewart recalls, "We received a walnut dresser back that was missing the mirror, which is attached to the top. The mirror was not returned and, consequently, we had the option to file an insurance claim. However, because of the great number of prop furniture pieces that were used, we let it go. While watching one of the second floor gunfights, I saw the dresser mirror hit with gunfire and realized that it was blown up to make the film more authentic." Old Tucson Studios had a huge prop and costume department, including many items previously purchased from MGM or physically created on-site. So, the dressers put together their list and Old Tucson Studios attempted to fill it: Flags and bunting, washboards, icebox, books, fabric and porcelain dolls, candelabra, maps, desk chairs, ledger books, barber pole and chair, wheelbarrows and carts, shot glasses, beer mugs, poker chips, roulette wheel, scales, baskets, cash registers, tables and chairs, wagons, tents and on and on. Each item was rented on a daily and/or weekly basis with an appropriate loss-damage value assigned. And a good thing it was as numerous items were damaged or destroyed during filming. Jay and Joanne Gammon, owners of Gammon's Gulch in Benson, rented over 500 items to the production, including many of the items used on the O.K. Corral set.[20]

As items were obtained, they were stored in a large two-story industrial warehouse off Grande and St. Mary's in downtown Tucson. The front of the building included Hardwicke's office, several drafting stations and a large open lobby; the remainder of the floor housed the construction department and set dressing storage. Various sections of the warehouse were taped off, each identified with a scene's storyboard. The sections stored all items necessary for a specific scene while the storyboard identified what was there and where it would be placed on the set. For example, Wyatt's room inside his house would have a bed, dresser, basin on a stand, pictures for the wall, coat rack, etc. All of those items would be stored in their proper position in the warehouse so everyone knew where they should be placed when the set was dressed.[21]

Not all items were rented or purchased; the creative dressers sometimes had to fabricate what they needed. For example, the Earp cabins and Bird Cage Theater all were built onsite by Billy Holmquist. Henry Hooker's ranch house was made from real adobe supplied by a Tucson company, while structures that neighbored the O.K. Corral were built with fiberglass adobe brick. The Oriental's ceiling was salvaged from a building in Nogales, Mexico—stamped, metal, turn-of-the-century, embossed and very accurate. The saloon's floor is fairly unique: luan plywood stained three different colors, cut into strips and randomly installed. As Ida Random, Catherine's counterpart on Costner's *Wyatt Earp,* said, "When you're building sets and shooting in such a wide [anamorphic] format, you find elements that fill the frame and make it more interesting. You become very conscious of the details—door frames, door jambs, fireplace lines, how high, how low, etc. I think designers have to pay a lot of attention to what is in the camera's eye, what the camera sees. Because that's all there is."

On *Tombstone,* there were 72 individual sets and over 70 dressers. Lights handcrafted with filigree while brass fittings were purchased from a Chicago antique lamp store. Other lamps appeared to be gas-fired, which might prove to be a safety hazard, so wires were run through the gas lines so they could be dimmed or flickered. Door hinges and hardware were resin-cast plastic. Of course, everything didn't always go as planned. Marich

Interior of Mescal's Oriental Saloon. Note the stamped-metal ceiling and the ornate light fixtures. Billy Bob Thornton's (Johnny Tyler) altercation with Kurt Russell (Wyatt Earp) occurred near the faro table in the far back left-hand corner of the room. The Campbell & Hatch Billiard Parlor was constructed on the right side of the bar on the far right of the photograph. Note the stuffed animals on the wall (photograph by Lee Gray/courtesy Catherine Hardwicke).

recalled, "One of the guys on the construction crew came to us at Mescal and said, 'I'm going to Home Depot. What do you guys need?' We gave him a list of what we needed and off he went. He showed up three days later with the stuff. And we're like, 'Uh, we needed this stuff three days ago,' and he goes, 'Well, yeah, I know. But I met this girl.' Later, the same guy had an accident and almost sawed his leg off."[22]

Russell summed up all of this prep work perfectly: "I love some of the old Wyatt Earp movies, but in some of them, when you saw what a bleak, depressing place Tombstone is, you [would] say, 'Why would Wyatt Earp or anyone else ever want to come here?' What we wanted to do was to show people why so many wanted to come to Tombstone during the silver rush. It was a sprawling, bustling frontier town, spilling over with energy. We didn't design this town to look like the Old West—we designed it the way people saw it in 1879, as the New West." Buckaroo John Peel summed up the atmosphere correctly: "[In] so many of the Hollywood westerns we grew up watching, everybody in town is sort of just hanging around. Nobody's working or doing anything. They're either sitting in a saloon all day or sitting on a sidewalk doing nothing. [Kevin] wanted activity;

it was a big, bustling, booming mining town. There were miners and whores, bars running, everything's going on."[23]

According to Robert Burke, those very factors helped the actors to get into their characters. "No refrigeration, drinking hot whiskey, 110° in Tombstone," Burke points out. "Of course they're out of their minds. Pulling guns on each other. Opium influence, Chinese building railroads. The rotgut they were putting in their bodies, wearing wool because polyester wasn't invented yet. A lot of these elements were brought home to you as a modern-day person who could go back to an air-conditioned trailer after riding a horse for six hours. The elements: the heat and the sand and the dust. Kevin brought a whole bunch of actors there to have this experience. You wouldn't otherwise have it to that degree. It really put you in a mind [of] who these people were. The flavor, the layers—that was a tribute to Kevin to his artistry."[24]

You can't have an authentic set without authentic costumes. But even though *Tombstone* would begin filming more than two months before the start of *Wyatt Earp*, both productions were still competing for the same wardrobes ... and Costner's film had already usurped all of Hollywood's available Western costumes; and *Tombstone*'s producers were forced to look elsewhere. Russell wasn't overly bothered: "It forced us to go to Europe, which in fact is where the nouveau riche of Tombstone bought their clothes in the first place." Jarre's attention to detail was paying off in atmospheric richness but at what expense? The original wardrobe budget was $402,692, but due to availability issues, it was increased to $544,286. Several costume designer applicants submitted their portfolios and were interviewed—but they failed to realize Jarre's envisioned concept. Brown, beige and earth tones were not what Kevin wanted. Hardwicke: "If you look at clothes left from that period, if you look at wallpaper samples and paint samples and books, people have very wild use of color, they use lime green and purples and very jarring color schemes and this director really wanted to see that because a lot of westerns they do go for that sepia tone brown amber gold."

Costume designer Joseph Porro had never worked on a Western before: *The Blob*, *Fright Night Part II*, *Death Warrant*, *Kickboxer II*, *Universal Soldier* and many others, but no Westerns or period films. "Actually, I did a Western-style vampire film in the '80s before *Tombstone*," admits Porro. "It was called *Near Dark*. But it was modern day, so that probably even wouldn't count. ... I really didn't have much period experience on my résumé or any Westerns but I went to the interview dressed in vintage Western clothing and [Jarre] just loved it. That had a lot to do with me getting [the job], and I brought a lot of research and information with me." It turned out he desperately needed such material because there were at least four Westerns in simultaneous pre-production: *Tombstone*, *Wyatt Earp*, *Geronimo* and *Geronimo: An American Legend*. "It made it really, really tough," Porro admits. "There wasn't even a cowboy hat left [to rent] anywhere at any of the studios. And I freaked out. I went to the places.... American [Costume] wouldn't let me rent from them. Kevin was going to use Luster Bayless. Then he heard of some problems with Luster, so he passed on him and he ended up with me. And then I stupidly go to [American] and [Luster's] angry because he just got fired from *Tombstone*. I had no idea that he even had been involved with it and he sits there and berates me for 15 minutes and tells me to leave his costume house. So the only other costume houses are Warner Bros. and Western, and their stuff was all cleaned out by the three other movies that were shooting at the same time. So I had no choice but to make everything, which I did." And that's where Sherayko and the Buckaroos came in.[25]

Peter had created Caravans West Productions several years before the start of *Tombstone*. Manned by period-authentic re-enactors, Sherayko's group helped out filmmakers by providing casting services, wardrobe, guns, ammo, technical advice, horses and special effects. Each Buckaroo would provide his own costume, be it cowboy, soldier or townsperson. Most were members of the Single Action Shooters Society and carried at least three weapons, including a rifle, shotgun and pistol. Excellent riders with period saddles and well-trained horses, they had to be able to handle their weapons with safety and skill. According to Peter, Jarre "knew his saddles, and he wanted exact period stuff. He knew the look he wanted and that look made the film." Sherayko even had a huge collection of artifacts and a library of over 5000 Western books. "I visited the set of *Wildside* in 1985 and noticed all the guns and rigs were wrong for the timeframe," Peter says. "When I mentioned that to Monte Laird, the technical advisor, he said, 'A gun is a gun. The audience is stupid, they don't know any better.' That planted a seed in my head. I started around 1987 or '88 [by] bringing my own [historically correct] guns into movies. [I told producers,] 'Let me bring these guns in, I'm not going to charge you for them.' I started doing that and by 1990 word got out and I started renting stuff out and people [began to call me] to do guns on the set. Act in a role, that was my ploy. Getting acting jobs by renting stuff. That's how Caravans West was born."[26]

Porro then worked with Sherayko and the Buckaroos to farm out the wardrobe requirements. "Since this was a non-union film…. I had most of the stuff manufactured in downtown LA [in the garment district]. I had a Filipino shirt-maker who worked out of her house, and she made all the shirts. Preparation was nasty. I think I had four weeks at the most, and we were [making costumes] through the whole shoot. Long six-day weeks, 16 to 18 hours a day. Everything was being manufactured at all these different places. Nothing was made in a costume house. I think I may have rented, all together, a rack of clothing. I did rent for the ladies' background. I did some rentals in England and some derbies and suits." However, because of his lack of "period" experience, Porro somehow had to translate historical research into reality. Jarre wanted something different as he was determined to avoid the Stereotypical Western Look. *Tombstone* would be the first Western film to be authentic in all departments. According to Sherayko, "Jarre wanted to capture the Victorian look of the cosmopolitan boom town of 1881–1882. He wanted a very clean, colorful, affluent look around Tombstone as was the fashion of the day. Joe would send his people out to my house. I said, 'Joe, come out. Go through my books, go through my stuff. Look at that.' And then he designed everything. He designed all the outfits but I had the people make stuff for him. He would buy the material and they would make it." According to Buck Taylor, who played Turkey Creek Jack Johnson in the film, "A lot of the shirts and hats were based on clothes depicted in paintings by [Frederic] Remington and Charley Russell."[27]

The first staff meeting between the director, writer and department heads set the tone and direction Jarre wanted to take. Sherayko: "We had the prop guys and the set guys and Joe and I'm there, of course. [Kevin] said, 'Peter, bring in the Buckaroos, let me see what these guys look like. I haven't seen anything yet.' Well, I put them in alphabetical order and the first guy…. There's a famous photo of a guy from the Hashnut cowboy outfit in northern Arizona in 1880. What he did was recreate that guy's outfit and he modeled the picture in the same way that the original photo was done. He did it in sepia. So, I gave him the picture. Well, Kevin looked at the first picture and said, 'That is an 1880s Arizona cowboy. That's what I want the Red Sash gang to look like! This is it. Joe, take a look at this picture.' Joe looked at the picture and said, 'Okay, fine,' and then he looked at the pictures of the other guys I brought in. When the meeting was over, [Porro] came up to me and said, 'What book did you get this picture out of?' I said, 'Joe, that's not a picture from a book, that's one of my Buckaroos I'm bringing in.' He stopped, his jaw opened and he said, 'Oh, my God. I can't have the extras looking better than the principals.' And I said, 'We can help you.'"

A variety of suppliers fulfilled Porro's requirements: Island Girl Clothes, using material supplied by Porro, manufactured over 300 shirts, while the Stetson Hat Company provided 100 hats. "We gave them an original of the period," said Porro. "They copied it, they did the block, we did it in different colors. Just made a slew of them and then by shaping them and having different bands, ... each one [was given] a little bit of character." Island Girl was the nickname of Lanier Clark, the wife of Logan, one of the Buckaroos. The Montana Boot Company supplied 20 pairs of Stovepipe and Coffeyville boots while R. Gang made a majority of the gun belts. "[The playing card] boots was Kevin's idea," explained Boothe, "but I just thought they fit so well with the character. One of the things about the cowboys of that era was that they enjoyed dressing up, especially when they came to town. It was really the only chance they got." The Tucson Opera Company made all the women's costumes, including Dana Delany's. Most of the men's suits were made by a Korean Hollywood tailor, Mr. Oh. Kurt Russell's long coat "was based on actual clothing," said Porro. "That coat exists, absolutely. No one ever used it in a movie before. It was probably a little more full and I might have thinned it out for him. That coat is in one of my tailor books, those giant tailor books with swatches from the 1870s. I have two tailor books from that period. You would go into a tailor shop and they would have a book, and they would have pictures of the style and then they would have fabrics, wools and stuff that you could pick from. That coat was in a tailor book of the period and we had it copied."

Even so, Porro wasn't entirely satisfied with his results: "It's not 100 percent period when I look at it now. My eye has changed. There was too much padding in the shoulders. That was my tailor. Another part of that was the help of the actor's shape. Today, I would have had no shoulders pads at all. It would have been all much softer. But that's really the only thing, otherwise the clothes were pretty accurate. I used a lot of clothing of the period, original pieces, and had them copied. The only thing that bothers me now to look at it is the shoulders didn't fit quite right."[28]

Although some claimed that Jarre added the red sashes as "gang colors" or to merely identify the outlaws, Porro says the sashes were period-correct. Period pants normally didn't contain belt loops, and braces, galluses and suspenders always got in the way, so sashes often were used as belts on high-waisted trousers. They also protected fabric from gun oil. Porro: "I don't know where it's written but somewhere historically it says that they wore this red sash. [It was Kevin's direction.] We had to make those. I had those made at the Opera company." It could also be that Jarre's hero was Bill Hickok. Jeff Morey indicated that the source for Kevin's sashes idea was Tombstone resident John Pleasant Gray as quoted by Paula Mitchell Marks in her book *And Die in the West*. "Gray remembered [Billy] Leonard as 'a man much above his fellow rustlers in intellect and education.' Leonard performed a service for [Gray] and received in payment a copy of a book chronicling the life of Wild Bill Hickok. The delighted Leonard gathered his fellow rustlers around 'and then spent the rest of the day reading to them,' with the result that Hickok was 'the hero, henceforth, of the rustlers.'" The obvious connection was that as Hickok

Members of the Red Sash gang pose inside Fly's Studio with Peter Sherayko (middle row, far left). Seated in front is Larry Zeug. Middle row: Sherayko, Reggie Byrum, Logan Clark. Back row: Rick Malone, Garrett Roberts, and Jeff Dolan (courtesy Larry Zeug).

wore a sash, so should the rustlers. One day, future director George Cosmatos told the various Cowboys why *he* thought they wore the sashes. Says stuntman Dickie Stanley, "He explained it as the Batman bad guys. In the *Batman* series, all the bad guys wear the bubblegum shirts so you knew who the bad guys were. He used that as an example. That was so the audience could tell who the bad guys were."[29]

"The Tombstone wives, a couple of their dresses were rentals," adds Porro. "I did make all of the female leads, Dana Delany, all her dresses I made. But some of the lesser female characters were rentals from England. And they were good, they were quite accurate, they were just so much better quality than the few that were left in America. I was at least able to do all of Dana's stuff, which was fun." When Porro couldn't manufacture everything, Old Tucson Studios once again came to the rescue and met the designer's requirements, providing moccasins, concho and beaded-belts with knife holder, a vintage Prince Albert frock coat, vests, pants, robes and skirts, corsets, handbags, pinafores, long johns, socks, shirts, boots and sombreros. If Old Tucson had it, it rented it out, usually for anywhere from $1 to $5 per day.[30]

Frank Castanza, a saddle-maker from Montana, was brought in to help the actors with their chaps. Buckaroo Rick Terry describes Frank's approach: "[The chaps] were brand new and they needed somebody to help make them look antique, or make them look used and worn. Frank ... grabbed all their chaps and threw them out on the parking lot there and had them pick up certain chemicals and some brushes and other things, and in 15 minutes they had worked-over chaps. If they would have done it by hand it would have taken hours, but the way Frank had them do it, it took just a very short period of time." Many of the clothes were worked over as well-washed and rewashed and rewashed yet again to give them that worn feeling.[31]

As for historically correct hats, that's where Tom Hirt came in. Hirt had worked with Sam Elliott on *Conagher* and other films, so it was no surprise that Hirt received a call asking if he was available to help out. According to Tom, he was hired four or five months before the start of production and "most of the wardrobe people in town were booked to do [Costner's movie], so they were a little bit behind on people that were capable of doing [*Tombstone*]. People like Sam ... kind of pulled these [specialists] out of the woodwork." Hirt then met with Jarre and discussed the style of each character's hat. They needed to be consistent with the era and of a style that would have been available in Tombstone at that time. All the Earp brothers wore the same style of hat, consisting of a 75 percent beaver and 25 percent rabbit blend, and Russell's hat had a low, open crown, derby-style, with flat brim showing a southwestern influence. Most of the actors either came in, or contacted Hirt and/or Jarre, to discuss what they wanted to see. Buck Taylor designed the hat he wanted to wear, the actor deciding everything from style to color to type of brim. It usually took about ten days to hand-make each hat, including time to block and shape. Each character had at least three duplicates of his hat in case one was damaged.[32]

As for Holliday's hat, Kilmer was one of the few people who never made contact with Hirt. Says Tom, "Kevin and I were sitting in wardrobe talking about Doc. We had a black hat just sitting there. I picked it up and took the edge of my hand and hit it like a karate chop and creased it in the front. As I was holding it, my hand was rolling the brim up on that one side, but not to a big degree. Kevin said, 'Hey, that looks pretty cool just the way you did that.' So I steamed it a little bit, and it worked out really good. The hat only had a little three-eighths inch ribbon band on it with the tails hanging loose off the side. We just left it like that without any type of formal bow on the side, or any formal type of hat band. Val Kilmer put it on and it just seemed right."

As for Johnny Ringo's chapeau, he had a "horse-haired hat band with the bow on the left side. The brim curled up on the right side, the opposite side of the other hats, to add a little individuality." Hirt admits that it drives him nuts when he sees Biehn in the shootout scene with Kilmer: "I wasn't on the set the day they filmed the shootout set. If you look closely, you will see the hatband is on backwards with the bow on the right hand side. The hatband must have fallen off and somebody must have put it on backwards."[33]

Initially, Jarre checked out everyone's wardrobe but soon, given all his other responsibilities, turned that job over to Hirt. He told him, "Tom, I don't have the time to critique everybody as they come out here. I want you to be my eyes. I want all the wardrobe, all the costumes, I just want you to look at it. And if you see something out of place that doesn't look right, doesn't look historical, doesn't look like it belongs, tell me about it and I'll take care of it." Porro was irritated, but two weeks into filming, the costume designer approached Hirt. "Tom, I came out here and I had some ideas what I wanted to do," confessed Porro, "and you were out here and it irritated me. But we've been getting our dailies and getting really, really great reviews and saying how well the costuming is.

I just wanted to thank you for your input because you're making me look really good." Tom shook his hand as that meant a lot to him.[34]

Peter Sherayko and Porro had a handshake agreement that for $5000 Sherayko would buy all the costumes for Caravan West Productions after filming was complete. "Well, Joe left the movie about two weeks before we were finished," recalls Peter, "because he had another job. We went over. We were only supposed to film 10 or 12 weeks, and we ended up going 17 weeks. He had already booked another job, so he left. After the movie, I went up to the line producer who was in charge of everything and I said, 'Joe and I made a deal for buying all the costumes.' And he said, 'Yeah, yeah. I want to sell them but [someone else] offered me $25,000 for them. If you can match $25,000, you can have them.' I said, 'Joe and I made a deal for $5000.' He said, 'No, no, no. I can't do that. I need to get some money back.'" Although many of the principals and Cowboys still have their own costumes (Russell, Kilmer, Taylor, Rooker, Sherayko, etc.), all the rest were purchased by ... American Costume.[35]

Renee Clothier was in charge of the wardrobe, art, scenic and prop departments at Old Tucson Studios. "[The costume department] was housed up in the *High Chaparral* [building]," recalls Renee. "They had a workshop set up there where they had stitching equipment. We had a lot of [items from] Western Costume, MGM, Warner Bros. We had big bins of shoes and boots and all of Barbara Stanwyck's stuff. We had so much stuff. [The studios] would have come in and selected pieces that they wanted to rent. We would just write up the rental agreement and usually I would let them take whatever they wanted. If it didn't work, they could bring it back so we could charge them for the actual used pieces. Either they would come to me and say, 'These are my people. Can you dress them up?' Or they would be a movie company like *Tombstone* that already has crew people and they have stitchers and so forth and they would get supplementary pieces from us for the extras. They would use some stuff, not the whole thing. Because we didn't have tons and tons of stuff, but we had a good amount they could use. It varied. They had some stitchers. One of the gals they had on stitching was Maggie McFarland."[36]

THREE

Here We Go!

In 1803, the Louisiana Purchase opened 828,000 western square miles and stretched the boundaries of the United States from the Mississippi River to the Rockies, from Canada to New Orleans—virtually doubling the size of the country. Encouraged by the concept of Manifest Destiny, migration to the western edge of the continent was deemed essential— both justified and inevitable with the unintended consequences of assimilation and accul- turation. Fur traders and mountain men crossed the Rockies into Great Britain's Oregon Territory while pioneers and adventures went south and west into Mexican territory. In 1836, Texas won independence from Mexico and nine years later joined the Union. The 1848 Treaty of Guadalupe Hidalgo ended the Mexican War; a million square miles were added to the county. Included were California, half of New Mexico, most of Arizona, Nevada and Utah, and parts of Colorado and Wyoming. The 1846 Oregon Treaty had already added Oregon, Idaho, Washington and parts of Wyoming and Montana, and in 1853 the Gadsden Purchase brought in an additional 30,000 square miles of Mexican territory—southern Arizona and southwest New Mexico. These actions effectively defined the current borders of the continental United States. Migration into these new territories implied annexation and occupation. As Jeff Guinn noted in The Last Gunfight: The Real Story of the Shootout at the O.K. Corral—And How It Changed the American West, *initially, these hardy souls only wanted to grow enough produce to feed their families, and hunt enough game to survive in minimal comfort. But expansion meant increased population and opportunities. Soon "subsistence farming was no longer the main goal for some of these frontier landowners; capitalism became primary. Settlers needed manufactured goods, markets back east needed raw materials."[1]*

At the end of the Civil War (or the War of the Rebellion, or the War Between the States, or the War of Northern Aggression, or whatever one chooses to call it), Confederate veterans, wearing little more than the tattered remains of their ragged uniforms, returned to villages and farms only to find their homes destroyed, crops razed, livestock stolen or killed, their families destitute. Given one last chance, some decided to repair what was broken, turn over the soil anew, plant whatever crops they could and pray that they would somehow sur- vive. Others returned to the cities and looked for new opportunities: telegraphists, railroad men, lumber mill workers, schoolteachers, hotel employees and storekeepers. Still others decided to pack up their families and belongings and move west, filled with the frontier spirit of adventure; to plant roots in another state where land was more favorable, climate more temperate and opportunity boundless. "Where all men were equal," wrote Western novelist Louis L'Amour, "where each had his right to his own. The open land beckoned, offered the vastest empire man could desire, providing the space and riches needed for the accomplishment of the nation's manifest destiny." A place where a man could change his identify, forget who he was or what his problems were. A popular period song asked, "Oh, what was your name in the States? Was it Thompson, or Johnson or Bates? Did you murder your wife and fly for your life? Say, what was your name in the States?" It was a place where one could ignore Yankee occupationists and the Federal government, a place where people could do as they pleased with minimal interference. Expansion was an opportunity for anyone, honest man or fugitive, to make a new life for himself. Said noted author, historian and professor Paul Hutton, "The victory of the Union in the American Civil War is a victory for the forces of incorporation for the West. But what happens after the Civil War surprises even those that dreamed of settling the West because it happened so rapidly. What had taken 300 years to accomplish now is wrapped up in a generation." Before the war, most Western migrants originated from Northern and Midwestern states; after the war, Southern states were more than well-represented. And along with their presence, these hearty adventurers brought along their values and beliefs: independence, loyalty, self-reliance, dedication and responsibility. Most Southerners were Democrats and opposed both the anti-slavery Republican Party and the Federal government. "Support and defend me when necessary. Otherwise, stay the hell out of my business!" These beliefs permeated wherever the pioneers choose to settle: Topeka, Laramie, Deadwood, Wichita, Dodge City, Abilene. Wide-open and lawless. Anything goes, 24 hours a day!

And, in the entire West, what greater riches could be found than those in Texas! Just the word brings to mind land speculators and cattle ranches, railroads and wagon trains. Mountains and canyons, deserts and rivers. Cotton and bluebonnet, Longhorns and sheep, barbed wire and open range. Cowboys and Indians. And outlaws![2]

And it was a dangerous time. Gunfights, murder and robbery were commonplace among these ruffians and scoundrels. Ravaging and plundering, they took what was not theirs, they gambled, they drank, they stole horses and cattle. Robbers of both trains and banks, they also ambushed and murdered innocent farmers, ranchers and townsfolk, showing contempt for both people and the law. They arrived from all over the country: James Brown Miller and John Selman from Arkansas, Sam Bass and Sherman McMaster from Illinois, William "Curly Bill" Brocius and John Peters Ringo from Indiana, Elliot Larkin Ferguson (aka Pete Spence) from Louisiana, and a thousand others like them. They were the law when the law was the man whose gun was fastest and true. And Texas was enormous! For miles and miles, all one could see was miles and miles. Endless prairies, hardwood forests and rolling hills, desert grasslands and valleys, mountains, hills and swamps. It was just impossible to maintain order over this vast area when all one was concerned about was the threat of Indians. And the outlaws had an infinite number of places to hide. As Jeff Guinn wrote, "Texas became a magnet for fugitives from every other part of the country. All across Texas, towns and ranches were terrorized by packs of armed thugs who broke laws with impunity because there was no one to stop them." But time was running out for these desperados as more and more townsfolk demanded respect for the law and would do whatever they could to assure it was upheld. But first things first.[3]

During the early 1800s, there were over 50 Indian "nations" who roamed the prairies of Texas, among them the Cherokee, Apache, Tonkawas, Wichitas, Kiowa, Caddo and the Comanche. The latter had a ruthless, well-earned reputation as the most relentless and feared war machine in the Southwest—great warriors and masters of cavalry tactics and horsemanship. With an intense brutality, they butchered their prisoners for entertainment and prestige. Some tribes were indigenous, others migratory. A few tribes were agriculturists who lived in permanent dwellings, others were fishermen, still others survived on buffalo, deer and small game. They were skilled traders, extraordinary artisans. Over time, some tribes were ravaged by cholera and smallpox epidemics and virtually ceased to exist while others were decimated by the advance of civilization. Many tribes resisted this invasion into their land and occupation of their hunting grounds, responding with devastating settlement raids, murdering pioneers and their families, stealing horses, cattle and in some cases women and children. Settlers lived in constant fear of attack. In December 1838, the Republic of Texas' second president, Mirabeau Lamar, stated in his opening Congressional address, "If the wild cannibals of the woods will not desist from their massacres, if they continue to war upon us with the ferocity of tigers and hyenas, it is time that we should retaliate their warfare." And so they did, for the next 40 years. Since these Native Americans hindered American advancement and settlement into Texas and threatened the lives of newly arrived families, extermination of their race was the only solution. Campaigns were waged against all Native Americans, peaceful or otherwise. As villages were burned, the defeated tribes moved to other areas and settlers quickly took their place. While the intent was never to commit cultural genocide, by removing these indigenous peoples from their hunting grounds and overland trade routes, and slaughtering buffalo, the effect was just that.

A complement of 10 "rangers," so called as their duties required them to range over the entire country, had been formed by Stephen F. Austin in 1823 to protect Texan colonists from the Indians. Over the next several decades, this organization increased in both size and responsibility, and operated under varied conditions and demands for service. Its numbers rose and fell, influenced by threats to the Texas Republic. In 1835 the legislature created three 56-man companies known as Texas Rangers. Lamar added eight more companies in 1838. Known as guardians of the frontier, they were said to "ride like Mexicans, shoot like Tennesseans, and fight like the very devil." During the Revolution, they served as scouts and guerrilla fighters; during the 1840s and '50s, they pacified the Mexican border and stopped feuds in the state. But always, they addressed the Indian issue; numerous battles occurred from the Red River to Brownsville. At the end of Reconstruction, the Texas legislature met again to reorganize the Ranger outfits. Two 500-man units were created, one led by Major John B. Jones to assist the U.S. Cavalry in fighting Comanches and Kiowas, the other led by Capt. Leander H. McNelly to address the ever-increasing criminal activities of outlaws who had virtually overrun the Western frontier. McNelly was given specific responsibility to restore order out of chaos along the Nueces Strip, a portion of land between the Rio Grande and the Nueces where the two rivers run parallel to each other. Texas claimed the Rio Grande as its southern border; Mexico claimed the Nueces as its northern boundary. Here, cattle-rustling was rampant, not only on local farms and ranches, but across the border in Mexico as well. Bands of outlaws would cross the Rio Grande, liberate foreign cattle, re-cross the border, and then sell these freed bovines to legitimate ranchers in Texas. Mexican bandits would respond by conducting guerrilla operations against local Texas ranchers. So severe was this issue that McNelly's Special Forces were financed by the very ranchers whose cattle were stolen.

Over a two-year period, Jones' Frontier Battalion engaged in numerous major battles (15 in 1874 alone) and by 1875 finally eliminated the Indian threat. McNelly was equally successful and when the two units joined forces, it was only a matter of time before over 3,000 outlaws were killed, jailed or forced to relocate to more favorable climes.[4]

The bad men moved further west, first into New Mexico and then into Arizona. Its rugged mountains and virtually inaccessible canyons provided the last refuge for outlaws on the run. As Marshal Trimble, Arizona's official state historian, wrote in Arizona Outlaws and Lawmen: Gunslingers, Bandits, Heroes and Peacekeepers, *"its wild, untamed country, lack of good roads and proximity to the Mexican border made it ideally suited to men riding the 'Owl Hoot Trail.' The rich boom towns, stagecoaches and railroads carrying express boxes loaded with gold coins, along with large herds of cattle, were easy pickings in the remote regions by bands of outlaws and cow thieves."* [5]

By the late 1880s, the Southwest territories had become very well-established. The first to arrive in the area were Spanish explorers and conquistadores in search of riches and glory. In 1541, Francisco Vázquez de Coronado failed in his quest to discover the legendary Seven Golden Cities of Cibola but he brought with him the first domestic livestock, horses and churro sheep, which significantly changed the way of life for the natives. These intrepid adventurers were quickly followed by the Spanish clergy seeking to convert native Apache, Navajo and other indigenous tribes to the ways of Christianity. As the Spanish military presence increased, settlers soon arrived and established permanent communities such as Santa Fe, Taos, Albuquerque, Las Cruces and Tucson. French-Canadian and American trappers and traders arrived in the late 1700s, and commerce began to expand. Pottery and baskets, jewelry and weavings, woodwork and religious icons were transported to eastern markets via the Santa Fe Trail. The 1846 California gold rush turned the Southwest into a major thoroughfare for prospectors on their way to the West Coast. The Butterfield Overland Stage Line crossed the territories in 1858 and the coming of the railroad in 1879 provided easy access to full-scale trade and migration. The mid-century saw an extensive growth in the Southwest; its land and people were a primary destination for businessmen looking for opportunities to sell or manufacture their goods, adventurers and gold prospectors, lawyers and politicians hoping to provide a legal and political system for the lawless territory, and ranchers and homesteaders looking for cheap land. Due to the arid nature of the country, cattlemen could more easily use the land than farmers could. [6]

Most of the cattle herds were driven in from Texas and California to supply federal troops and Indians with beef. Wrote J.J. Wagoner in the Arizoniana *journal, "Hundreds of emigrants were coming into the new cow country to begin an experimental exploitation of the luxuriant grasslands. They settled along the rivers where there was water and an abundance of native forage. They ran their cattle on the unfenced and unregulated public domain. Though they did not own the grass or land, it was understood among neighbors that the appropriation of water entailed the possession of certain range rights." From what was once a meager 20 to 75 head of cattle on a handful of scattered Mexican ranchos, now came an industry of tens of thousands of cattle in the Santa Cruz, Rillito and San Pedro valleys of Arizona. Among them were the "English boys" Empire Ranch of Vail; Hislop and Harvey, which grazed 5000 head; the Cienega Ranch, which had 1000 cattle and 23,000 sheep; and the Babocomari with 3600 head. Most other holdings were 50 to 250 head each, with virtually every water claim adaptable to the cattle business holding livestock. (By 1880, New Mexico supported three to four million sheep and over 130,000 head of cattle; in 1891, there were nearly 721,000 head of cattle on the Arizona tax roles.)*

And along with all the cattle came cattle rustlers—the Clantons and McLaurys. [7]

As costumes were sewn and buildings constructed, actors were still needed to round out the *Tombstone* cast. Whether you were a main character or a background extra, the role still required someone. And that's where Holly Hire came in. Wife of actor-stuntman Don Collier, she had started out as a casting agent in Los Angeles. Collier joked he married

Holly to advance his career. According to Collier, they met in L.A. when he was auditioning for a chili commercial. "I went in for an audition and got the job. I got a couple of more jobs and figured the best way to get more work was to marry her." Holly had a Hollywood background and had lived there for years (she began working in casting in 1968) before the two married. The Colliers later moved to Tucson where, due to her local connections as well as those in Los Angles, she continued to work in casting. It was an ideal situation: She knew who was available and what they could bring to a production and, as a result, many Tucson extras just called in and had a job. Naturally, Collier was cast in the film.

Said extra Glen Gold, "I had been doing films [and] I've done some things for Holly and other stuff in *Young Riders*, so when they started *Tombstone* I got a spot on there…. There was a bunch of us around here and she knew she could count on us if she needed us." Extra Eddie Perez said, "Holly contacted me and said [she needed] some people who understood the ropes." Other actors had a somewhat indirect connection to Kevin Jarre, which didn't hurt. Charles Schneider got involved because he was fortunate enough to be at a dinner party with Lisa Zane, whom he had gone to school with in Chicago. "At this dinner party was Kevin Jarre, who Lisa Zane was dating," explained Charles. "He and I instantly hit it off. Throughout the evening he kept looking at me with a certain fascination as if he had something in his mind. At this point, of course, he was set to direct the film. He came up to me towards the end of the dinner party and said, 'Charles, do you know how to juggle?' and I said, 'No, but I can learn.' He said, 'I think you would be just perfect for this character, Prof. Gillman. You've got about six months to learn.'"[8]

Others, such as Montana cowboy Forrie Smith, had to work a little harder. "They were looking for Pony Deal, and I'm a half-breed Indian from Montana," said Smith. "I had to go to, I don't know how many times, I had to audition for the local casting lady. Then the casting people from L.A. came out and then I got to go in front of Kevin Jarre…." Smith finally got the role and Jarre even escorted him to wardrobe to pick out a costume.

But Smith wasn't the only one who had to audition; even Sherayko's Buckaroos had to prove they could fit the bill. Jerry Crandall explains. "In early 1993, I received a call from longtime friend Peter Sherayko. In the past we had worked together in Wild West shows and other similar projects. He asked if I wanted to be in a major Western movie. He explained that the writer and director, Kevin Jarre, was a collector of Western history, including memorabilia and art. As a result, he knew of my paintings and interest in the history of the Old West. They put out this bulletin that they needed 30 cowboy-type guys for extras for *Tombstone*. (Actually, 50 Buckaroos were required, but due to budget constraints, the number was reduced to 30.) From what I understand, about 300 guys applied, 'cause everybody wanted to be a cowboy in the movie. But the problem was you had to furnish your own horse, guns, saddle, bit, everything, hats, and they had to be authentic to the period. Well, 90 percent of the guys that do this have no real clue what the stuff should really look like. They all have modern or semi-modern chaps and hats and all that. So, right away, Kevin Jarre … rejected most of them. But it came down to about 30 guys that they needed so we had to send in photos of our outfits, saddles and our horses. (Applicants and Buckaroos Kane Rubalcaba, Jake Johnson, Reggie Byrum and Curt Stokes were from California, Frank Castanza, Montana, Jerry Brown and Tom, Paul and Charley Ward, Oklahoma, and John Peel, Garrett Roberts, Rick Terry, Jerry Crandall, Jeff and Sam Dolan and many others were from Arizona.) We had to get our stuff ready and report down to the location on the Babocomari Ranch in southern Arizona. We got down there (May 6) and they announced they were going to have a test for all of us to see our ability; see how our horses do under gunfire and all."

An embarrassed Tom Ward relates, "Well, we were all out there: Terry Leonard, Terry's wife (Teri Garland), one of the producers, [director of photography William] Fraker, [Kim Burke and Kevin Jarre]. I'm sitting there on my horse and it bucks me off right in the middle of the crowd. Right there in front of everybody. First thing you do is jump off and look around to see if anybody saw it. Everybody saw it! Well, that's a good way to start."

Kane Rubalcaba: "And then we had the shakedown ... we rode around. We did drills 'cause a lot of us were military, Civil War re-enactors. We did military-type drills on horseback, kinda get everybody tuned up. And then by the time it went down to the *horsemanship* test ... we're all laughing. We're like, 'You got to be freaking kidding me.'" Crandall continues, "Thirty of us were there in a field and we had to mount up, lope down to the end of the field, fire a pistol, come around a barrel, kick the horse into a full-gear run and fire again and then come to right where the judges were and skid the horse to a stop. Spin him to the left, spin him to the right and drop the reins to see if he would stand still. Unfortunately, some of the guys, they looked good, they knew their dress and all but they weren't real great horsemen. So a couple of guys fell off their horse, and the horse didn't perform well." Buckaroo John Peel explains the evaluation system: "They gave everybody a score; five being the best, one being the poorest. Most of the guys were threes and fours, there were a couple of twos and a couple of fives. The better horsemen were fours and fives, the guys that were a little less so were threes and twos, and there might have even been a couple of guys that were ones. Some of the guys literally bought a horse and a gun to work on the film. Other guys already had wardrobes of historical clothing and lots of guns, horses and saddles." And they were well-paid for their time: $350 a week for their work and another $450 a week to rent their horses, guns, saddles and gear. Not bad for ten weeks' work. (One evening several years later, Tom Ward visited the Leonards, and Teri asked Tom if he ever was a Buckaroo in *Tombstone*. "Yes, I was," Ward replied. She continued, "I remember at the riding audition there was one of the Buckaroos that got bucked off." Tom, thinking he'd better end this conversation before someone got too embarrassed, admitted, "Well, that was me." Teri laughed and said, "Well, I thought it probably was somebody who didn't know how to ride a horse." All Tom could do was confess, "At that particular time, I guess I didn't."[9])

Four of the Buckaroos were upgraded to Screen Actors Guild members and given speaking roles; along with Charley Ward, Jake Johnson and Frank Costanza, Jerry was one of the lucky ones. He knew it was going to be a tough shoot. Wrote Sherayko in an instruction letter to all Buckaroos, "We're all in this together. This will be a lot of fun and a good time but also hot, hard, long work. But you know what you're in for. When you sign on, you sign on so no bellyaching." Unfortunately, if you were upgraded, it was both good news and bad as once you were in SAG you were paid a higher wage and as the production crew didn't want to incur extra costs, your tenure on the film was short-lived. Jarre was so impressed with Charley Ward's natural ability that he asked the lad to audition again. Afterward, Jarre told Charley, "Listen, I don't have a part for you right now. But I'm going to write a part for you tonight." Kevin later told Charley's father Tom that he did so because Charley "reminded him of himself when he was 15." Charley, so excited after he saw what they were going to pay him, didn't even read the rest of the contract—he just signed it. Five weeks' work and 25 to 30 lines—not bad for a 15-year-old.

Buckaroo members line up at the horsemanship tryout on the Babocomari Ranch (courtesy Jerry Crandall).

After the test, Jarre evaluated each Buckaroo costume and made the necessary suggestions. Larry Zeug recalls, "We got a call one day—they wanted to see us down in Tucson at the Holiday Inn, dressed in costume. Kevin Jarre came by and he looked at everybody and he said, 'Okay, you with the long hair, go get your hair cut or put it under your hat.' Five or six had long hair. He looked at everybody's costume and okayed it or didn't okay it. The only thing he changed on me, he gave me a scarf." Jarre reached the end of the line of candidates and then addressed everyone: "My name is Kevin Jarre and I'm the director. I just want you all to know if you ever have any questions or problems, come look for me. I'm the guy wearing the black hat." After Jarre walked away, the AD spoke up. "Yeah, what he just said," they were told. "If you ever have any problems, come to *me,* not the director. He's the boss of everybody, but I'm *your* boss."

Sherayko previously had run into Zeug at a parade in Palm Springs. As Larry recalls the encounter, "Peter comes riding up to me and saw that I had a '76 Winchester and he goes, 'Hey, you want to sell that?' I said, 'No. I got three of them.' 'Well, do you want to do a movie?' I said, 'Sure,' and that was how we met. After the parade, he learned that I did gunsmith work … and we started getting together. He said he was supplying the guns for this movie and he wanted somebody working on the guns that knew what they were doing."[10]

Production was originally set to begin on March 29 but due to Costner's involvement or lack thereof, the turnaround issue, finances and Russell's late acceptance, it had to be delayed until April 26. In the meantime, the Hollywood publicity mill continued to churn out obligatory announcements: April 5, David Strathairn signed on to play Johnny Behan. At that time, Bill Paxton, Powers Boothe, Michael Biehn, Sam Elliott, Jason Priestley, Michael Rooker, Stephen Lang, Billy Zane and Glenn Ford were already on board; April 29, *Variety* belatedly announced that Ford would join Robert Mitchum and Charlton Heston on *Tombstone*; May 5, Dana Delany was hired and flew immediately to Tucson for rehearsals. One week later, *Variety* announced that Frank Stallone was added to the cast. Even though filming had not yet started, Disney, determined to get their film out before Costner's, had already announced its release was scheduled for the next spring or early the next summer. And, just to show you can't believe everything you read, *The Hollywood Reporter* stated on August 3, 84 days *after* filming started, that William Baldwin was in the film.[11]

Jarre worked on additional script development: additions, deletions, modifications. Dialogue was moved from scene to scene and, in some cases, given to different characters. Extraneous lines were eliminated, others consolidated and still others expanded. He continued to revise his previous draft, which was completed on January 30, 1993. The opening sequence of photos, historical prints, silent live-action vignettes and voiceover narration remained unchanged. However, rather than show the aftermath of a border family massacre in the first scene, the event is now merely mentioned in conversation between the Mexican Rurale and his captain. This was a typical change—entire scenes being consolidated or eliminated, but with their context only being referred to in passing. As a result, the third draft was reduced from 165 scenes, 135 pages and 88 characters, to 152 scenes, 123 pages and 81 characters. The script now was tighter, the flow improved.

The ambush of the Mexican patrol and murder of its captain remained in the script. Wyatt Earp's arrival in Tucson, his refusal of U.S. Marshal Crawley Dake's offer, and Earp's subsequent greeting from his brothers and their wives, remained unchanged although the role of the young boy who commented on Wyatt's horses was eliminated. (That role, albeit without dialogue, was re-added in later revisions.) As the Earps and their wives camp for the evening on their way to Tombstone, a scripted risqué conversation about Wyatt's horse Dick Nailor was also dropped. The next several scenes, including the Earps' arrival in Tombstone, their introduction to Cochise Country, John Behan and Marshal Fred White, and the rental of three small cottages on the edge of town, didn't change, but White's explanation of local politics and graft was shortened. The memorable dialogue from Wyatt's confrontation with Johnny Tyler and subsequent meeting with Doc Holliday and Behan didn't change from the prior draft. Similarly, the next 11 scenes, which included the introductions of Turkey Creek Jack Johnson and Texas Jack Vermillion, the stagecoach arrival of a theatrical acting troupe, Marshal White's identification of numerous Cowboys at Shieffelin Hall, the stage performances, the six-gun-tin cup-Latin duel between Ringo and Holliday, and Curly Bill's sojourn to the opium den, are identical to the previous script.

Marshal White's murder scene is modified to include Wyatt's subsequent confrontation with Ike, Billy Clanton and six other cowboys. This confrontation is important because it inflames and enhances the antagonism between the two factions. In the tightened script, the next 30 scenes remained relatively unchanged although the murder of Old Man Clanton is now just referenced rather than shown. The remainder of the script was almost identical in content to the second draft although Scene 83 (the implied rape at a Mexican wedding) is gone, as is Scene 89, the attempted assassination of Mayor Clum and his wife. Also eliminated is Scene 98, the sale of Wyatt's holdings in Tombstone to a high-roller.

The epilogue voiceover narration is modified to eliminate any reference to Tombstone, the Cowboys, John Behan and Ike Clanton:

EPILOGUE, like the prologue, v.o. narration over a series of images and live-action vignettes. First, pictures of Tombstone in various stages of development followed by scenes of dust and desolation giving way to tourist events....

After the famous gunfight, the power of the Cowboy Gang was broken forever but it hardly mattered in the end. In 1886, the mines flooded out and Tombstone was a boom town no more, by the end of the century dwindling into just another dusty small town in the Arizona desert. But the immense fame it gained during its lawless era left an enduring legacy of myth and legend and Tombstone was reborn in the 20th century as a tourist attraction. It remains so to this day, the big draw its annual 'Helldorado Days' celebration, the highlight of which takes place at the O.K. Corral with a highly fanciful re-enactment of the famous gunfight.

But Jarre wasn't satisfied, making subsequent changes on March 18 and 29 as well. When completed, the 128-page script consisted of 158 well-defined, relatively accurate and emotionally charged scenes. Jarre's final version also eliminated Prof. Gillman's cigar boxes, Morgan and Josephine's discussion of the hereafter, Judge Spicer's trial scene, and Ringo's murder of an old prospector in Galeyville. Jarre also re-inserted the ambush and death of Old Man Clanton in addition to the implied rape of a young Mexican woman.

While Jarre fine-tuned his script, location manager Lauren Ross and unit production manager Terry Collis scouted potential locations. Ross was charged with finding sites that would meet both the script's requirements and the director's creative vision. Once the appropriate locations were identified, Jarre flew in to check out their feasibility, transportation captain Billy Getzwiller having picked him up at the Tucson airport. Ross also negotiated the terms of use and secured the necessary permits. Several factors are considered when searching for a viable location: logistical feasibility and distance from base camp, sources of daylight, lighting requirements and time of day when used, electrical sources, ambient noise limitations, evaluation of surrounding geography, budget restrictions, availability of parking, housing requirements, local weather conditions, and a myriad of other issues. (Base camp is an area, as near as practical to the set, where the actors' trailers, food facility, honey wagons, main equipment trucks and crew cars, etc., are assembled.[12])

Naturally, Old Tucson and Mescal were at the top of her list. Other Arizona filming locations included the Babocomari Ranch, Fort Crittenden and the Empire Ranch (all located in Sonoita), Patagonia, Elgin, Texas Canyon, Little Dragoon Mountains, San Simon Valley, Sonoran Desert, Skeleton Canyon and Harshaw.

It was rumored that Costner wanted to shoot his Earp film in modern-day Tombstone and had offered the city $9 million if it would allow him to construct period-correct store fronts along Allen and Fremont Streets. After the town council voted down his proposal, he decided to shoot the film at various New Mexico locations including the Santa Fe area's Cook, Ghost and Eaves movie ranches where portions of *Silverado* had been filmed. However, a search of the Tombstone town council records failed to show any discussion regarding this proposal. And, as the various buildings fronting Allen and Fremont are owned by individuals and not the town, the council would not have any authority to accept the proposal anyway. In any case, Costner would have had to contact each owner for specific approval, no doubt a cumbersome task. Failure to receive approval from just a handful of owners would have doomed the concept. (Ironically, while filming *Tin Cup* in Tucson, Sonoita and Nogales, Costner returned to Tombstone in the fall of 1995 with his kids. As nobody would leave him alone long enough to eat, he once again left town.) Catherine Hardwicke says that she, too, looked to see if the real city of Tombstone could be used, but quickly decided it was impractical: "When I went there, I saw that it was super-touristy. It accommodated tourists and it just wouldn't work at all. We couldn't have done it because we would have to take over the town. I was [at Mescal] for over six months building the set, changing the set and shooting and transforming everything. We just couldn't demolish the whole tourist industry of Tombstone. We would have to have access to everything, take out all the modern elements. When I looked at all the things that would have to be changed, including the street itself ... this would never fit in our budget."[13]

Local resident Victoria McLaren didn't mind that the town wasn't used. "It's just too modern here," she explained. "It would have been too difficult to film the way the town is now.

They would have had to change too much. We have paved streets, and cars, and it would have disrupted business."[14]

Dressed in his black leather jacket, Jarre, along with Ross, Collis and Getzwiller, drove all over the countryside and scouted pre-selected locations. According to Getzwiller, "When we were scouting, we would look at locations and he would say, 'I'd like to put an insert car in here.' 'And then I'd like to have a nice rising shot coming over the hill with cranes.' [But the powers that be] said, 'No. No insert car. No cranes.' They just really cut him back and wouldn't let him do what he wanted to do. And as soon as [the replacement director] came in, my [transportation] crew was another third bigger just in special equipment. They gave [Cosmatos] everything he wanted. They had an insert car on the set all the time. They had cranes on the set all the time. Special effects water."[15]

Most of the Buckaroos arrived on the Arizona location in mid–May and set up a base camp on the Babocomari Ranch. Sherayko had purchased a few military-style tents and even though they were erected, no one really used them. Most brought their own accommodations: horse trailers, campers, pup tents, bedrolls, even a wigwam. Several chain-link fences were set up as corrals for the horses, the corrals adorned with green and blue plastic tarps for shade. Recalls Larry Zeug, "There were squares where you had your horses. We had to get up, clean them every day, clean out the stalls, haul it out. We lived like real cowboys with our horses. They brought in a shower trailer so we could get a shower every morning and night. Sometimes that didn't work, either. They didn't have gas for it and we'd all be raising hell. When I was out there with my two horses, you lose track of everything. No worries. We rode them to the set every day. If you went to craft services, you got something for your horse, too. You rode your horse, took off his saddle, brushed him down and then went to sleep. Sometimes you even slept with your horse. Take care of your horses, live like a cowboy. And that's what we did. They said, 'Just stay [in the camp] until you get a call to go to work.'"

Alhambra Saloon, Can Can Restaurant, and the Sheriff's Office—Mescal.

Buckaroo base camp, Babocomari ranch. Horses are housed in chain-linked corrals, Buckaroos in tents and trailers (courtesy Larry Zeug).

While the Buckaroos were setting up camp, the production company staked out the Tucson Holiday Inn on Palo Verde Boulevard. More than 150 rooms were rented, including rooms for production offices. According to Holiday Inn executive Elly McFadden, the hotel had 300 rooms and half of them were suites: "They took over half the hotel. We couldn't close it to the general public but, especially back then, if you had ten percent occupancy, you'd be lucky. So I was a real hero, booking in that many rooms for the whole summer. I gave them a really good deal; I gave them what they wanted and then some, [so] they accepted the bid."

Terry Collis coordinated the rentals with McFadden, but Terry's secretary handled all the arrangements. "Terry Collis' secretary … she was kind of crazy-busy all the time with details," says McFadden. "She would call me up on a Friday afternoon just before I'm ready to go home and say, 'We need another suite for tomorrow. We have another star coming in.' And I'd say, 'Well, you know what? You have all my suites already. You already have them all.' 'No. We have to have one per contract.' I said, 'Okay, I'll try to build one by tomorrow.' What could I do … kick somebody out? She was so frantic all the time [that] we gave her a little basket from the front desk." Later, when production ran longer than scheduled, it became an even bigger problem for McFadden. Other guests had reservations for that same time period but once someone is in a hotel room, you literally can't evict them. Fortunately, while houses were on loan for many of the principal actors, others stayed in the Freedom Park apartments as well as at the Rancho Mirage, Silverado and the Los Portales.[16]

Several Buckaroos arrived a day early and it's fortunate they did, as a member of the production team drove out to the Babocomari and said, "Hey, I need four or five guys by the hotel at five o'clock tomorrow morning." So Bob Vincent, Jemison Beshears, Garrett Roberts and John Peel got up at an ungodly hour, piled into Peel's pickup and drove about one hour to Tucson. Jarre walked out of the hotel, looked at their clothing and, after approving them with some modifications, drove west of the city where they were filming trailers with Kurt Russell. According to Peel, "This is before any of the other guys showed up or real production even started. We got out there ... and Thell Reed was there. They just shot some stuff, four cowboys coming up over a hill drawing their guns. Sort of like shadows, silhouette. They shot some scenes with Kurt flipping a silver dollar in the air and when [it] lands on the ground, it's a U.S. marshal's badge. Kurt picks it up and pins it on. Teasers they call [them]."[17]

Many filmgoers believe that the lightning seen in the movie was the result of special effects, but that wasn't always the case. The lightning often was real and it was constant, which impressed many. Some called it unnerving, amazing, and that they'd never seen it as intense as it was on that movie set. It put on quite a show the day after most of the Buckaroos had arrived at the Babocomari: There was a huge storm and one gigantic lightning strike only 300 yards from where they had camped. Seeing the subsequent flames, one fellow got in a truck and called the fire department. They were told, "Let it burn." And so they did. Eventually, a fire marshal came out and told the Buckaroos they had to move out due to the danger.[18]

Actors and crew members were given an hour-by-hour schedule that detailed all the various activities for that particular pre-production day. For instance, the schedule for Saturday, May 15, 1993, was as follows:

> 7:00A to 11:30A and 12:00P to 1:15P, Hair and Makeup session in the MKUP/HAIR trailer.
> 7:00A to 11:00A, Buckaroo riding/Weapons rehearsal at the Main ranch house on the BABOCO-MARI ranch.
> 9:00A to 11:00a and 3:00P to 7:00P, Wardrobe fittings in the WARDROBE trailer.
> 9:30A to 10:30A, Choreography session in the DIRECTOR'S office. [In addition to filling the role of Big Nose Kate, Lisa Zane was also budgeted as the dance director and was given an allocated portion of both Alphaville's production fee and Jarre's directorial earnings.]
> 9:30A to 1:00P and 2:30P to 6:30P, RIDING rehearsals at the BABOCOMARI corral. Conducted by Kim Burke, riding rehearsal participants included Dana Delany, Michael Rooker, Buck Taylor, Glen Wyatt Earp, Jon Tenney, Jason Priestley, John Philbin, Powers Boothe, Michael Biehn, Stephen Lang and Robert Burke.

The day finished with a pool party that was scheduled to run from seven to ten p.m.[19]

"Kevin Jarre wrote a brilliant script," says Michael Biehn. "And everyone flocked to it—you can tell by the cast. I immediately was interested in who they were going to cast as Curly Bill because we'd be working together. I knew Powers from his Jim Jones performance, which was incredible. Powers was always a real presence on film. There are certain people—like Lee Marvin—who just have character in their face, in them. You just know that they've lived a life and it's been an interesting one. Before we went to Tucson, [Boothe and I] went out to dinner. I said, 'I'm going to take my car out there. It's only going to be a seven- or eight-hour drive. Why don't you come along with me?' So, we drove to Tucson together."[20]

Robert Burke was excited to be a part of the project. "[I was offered the role] pretty early on. [Jarre and I] hit it off. [Kevin] called my guys the same day [of the interview] and said, 'It'll be Ringo if Biehn isn't settled in, it'll be [Mayor Clum] if Jon Tenney's pilot gets picked up, or Frank McLaury. One of the three.'" Burke was very agreeable to coming on board and said, "Hey, listen, pal. This script is so strong, you give me a spear and tell me what corner to stand in and I'll be there." According to Burke, "I really wanted to be a part of the show."[21]

But before filming began, several days of rehearsals were required. "I arrived in Arizona for a read-through and rehearsal with Kevin Jarre," John Philbin recalls. "When I got there, the whole cast was there: Jason Priestley, Stephen Lang, Billy Bob Thornton, Sam Elliott. We did a read-through and it was fucking great and hysterical with Kevin and he was really nice, people asking questions and it was super cool and we were all so excited to be a part of this. I think the reason all those actors agreed to do the movie was because of the script that Kevin Jarre wrote. And I think the reason the movie got funded was because Kevin Jarre was able to get all those actors who loved Westerns and the history of Westerns and identified with Westerns and wanted to play a real-life cowboy from that time with such a historic event like the O.K. Corral and law enforcement and Wyatt Earp and Doc Holliday. It's a dream come true for an actor. A lot of those guys ride horses; shooting guns is always fun for an actor. So Kevin Jarre, based on his script, got all those huge actors together, because they had juicy, juicy roles, almost all of them."[22]

Prior to rehearsals, several actors did their own in-depth research of their characters. "Sure, I did the research," said Stephen Lang. "Read the transcript of the inquest, which I've always felt would be the basis for a good piece of theater—kind of a *Rashomon*. Also histories and newspaper stuff—lot of rehashing. Mostly I just cowboy-ed up—roping, shooting, riding, and lots of drinking."

The veteran stage actor continues, "In the end, after the research, I let the script fire my imagination. I used the facts, the historical record, in a Shakespearean way, which is to say that Julius Caesar or Henry V were resource material, points of entry (or departure) for Shakespeare. He shaped history to his own ends, so his histories are historical fiction. That is a fair characterization of my approach. I felt that Ike could occupy a singular and colorful niche in the saga."

Fellow actors Sam Elliott and Bill Paxton took it to another level, as resident Tombstone historian Ben Traywick recalls: "What they did, they came out and asked me how [their characters] cut their hair, what their mustaches looked like, where they wore their guns. Sam borrowed an old pickup truck from Old Tucson and spent the whole afternoon with me.

"I had never seen Bill Paxton before," admits Traywick, "and Sam says, 'You know who we are?' I said, 'I know who *you* are but I don't know the gentleman with you.' [Paxton said,] 'It won't be long before you know who I am.' My wife [was] upstairs and she can hear us talking through the ventilator, and we talked quite a while. When she came down, she had her hair in those big tin can rollers and she said, 'Who are those people?' And I said, 'That's Sam Elliott.'

"'Oh my God!'

"Said Sam, smoothingly, 'Marie, don't worry about it because I see Katherine like that most every morning.'"[23]

Michael Biehn took a slightly different approach to his research. "Any time I do a role for a film, and certainly if it's based on a real character, I read as much literature as I possibly can on the subject. There is a lot of literature about Wyatt Earp and about the shootout at the O.K. Corral, and some out there about Johnny Ringo, too. The stuff about Johnny Ringo, about the way people remembered him, and what kind of guy he was, actually and realistically intrigued me. So what I originally did was read as much as I could about not only Johnny Ringo, but Tombstone in general, and also about the Earps and Curly Bill Brocius. I wanted to know what people thought about them back then and back there. When an actor plays a historical man, it serves him well to take a look at what was written about that person by people alive at the same time, not just the scholars who wrote about him later on, in a different time period than Ringo's."[24]

In addition to rehearsing their lines, several actors needed to hone their riding skills. Some were skilled horsemen, others (like Powers Boothe) brought their trainers along with them. Still others looked like a monkey on a football. Wrangler Gary Gang was assigned the task of training them while Frank Trigani provided saddles they were comfortable with. "I had all the actors at my stable one day," admits Gang. "It was a fricking zoo. It was a testosterone day. Everybody was there—Kurt, Val, Jon Tenney, every actor. Michael Rooker. Michael had his horse with me, too. All these guys and half of them were trying to out-macho each other. I'd been working with quite a few of them for riding, like Michael Biehn. He wasn't afraid of horses, he just wasn't comfortable on them. Trying to get these guys to look like they were 1800s riders. To have the look that Kevin wanted as far as horsemanship. I took Val for a ride and prior to that, I kinda thought he was a dick. I didn't realize he was a method actor. And he was [in character as] Doc Holliday. I took him for a ride, and we're talking and he suddenly became this guy from San Fernando Valley: 'You're kinda cool. I'll hang out with you.'"

Others, like Robert Burke, were experienced horsemen: According to Burke, "Kevin Jarre said, 'Can you ride a horse?' [I replied,] 'Like the fucking wind.' My whole family in Ireland are horse people: trainers, vets, so I knew how to ride. One day, the guys are coming out of the jail, my horse is fucking around ... how the hell do I ... Terry [Leonard] said, 'Come on, Robert. You're a cowboy. Just throw yourself up there.' I ran beside my horse and threw myself up there and I landed on my you-know-whats. And I had to ride out of town. I don't think it made the picture but we did that scene seven or eight times because my horse kept shying. There were some guys who told Kevin they could ride but they were found out very quickly in an embarrassing, almost hazardous type of way. Kurt had this goddamn stallion—two of them I think. And this horse was piss and vinegar. Kurt is a horseman through and through. And that horse didn't give him an ounce of grief. There were some fellas who just didn't like riding. You can't blame them if you're not used to it."

In some scenes, the less-skilled riders needed a little assistance. Says Larry Zeug, "I'm the guy that runs into the scene and holds the horses for Jon Tenney and Jason Priestley [after the death of Romulus Fabian]. Priestley and Tenney didn't know how to ride a horse. They couldn't jump on a horse and go off riding. So what I did, I turned around and slipped the stirrup over Jason Priestley's foot so that he could turn and ride out of the scene. And the same thing with Jon Tenney. If I remember right, the only one they pick up on the scene is Jason Priestley, but that's just so he can ride out of the scene."[25]

Gang was also involved in acquiring horses for the production. Although the Buckaroos brought their own mounts, several horses were rented from Red Wolverton in Phoenix. Gang recalls, "We looked at horses for production and were primarily looking for black horses for Wyatt Earp. We had this guy bring over his stallion. Beautiful black stallion had some white on him [and] was one of the nicest horses ever, well mannered, just perfect. I told Kurt about him and they didn't want to use him because he was a stallion and you can't have a stallion on the set. I showed Kurt the video and said, 'This horse is perfect. You couldn't ask for a nicer horse. He models everything Kevin envisioned with his horses.' [Kurt] said, 'Well, we can do whatever I want.' I said, 'They don't want to use this horse.' He said, 'I'll buy the fucking horse. That's the horse I really want. If I want that horse in the movie, that horse will be in the movie.' Kurt didn't buy him but that horse was in the movie." Many of the horses were short-term rentals and, of course, the Buckaroos bringing their own horses kept the costs down. Jarre even had two horses there—Brocius and Jake. Jake was a bay horse but wasn't used much as he was there for Kevin. Brocius was a big black thoroughbred. According to Gang, "You couldn't buy any black hair dye in Tucson because I bought every bit of [it]. Half those black horses were chestnut horses that we dyed black." Lisa Zane also trained for months at Gang's ranch, learning to ride sidesaddle on her horse Phoenix while Michael Rooker rode one of Gang's two palominos, Topper or Sargent. These two horses were both full brothers and wound up doubling each other. Rooker rode Sargent because he was a golden palomino and a little flashier than Topper but also was a bit more of a handful.

Due to the extreme heat, many horses lost a great amount of weight and became ill. According to Robert Burke, "My horse was named Chaisey and [she had] bronchitis." He mentioned it to head wrangler Kim Burke, but was told, "No, no, no. She's already established. We can't switch her out." Robert adds, "So one day we were walking into town and [my horse] collapsed. As it went down, it went to the left side so I was able to step off. I told Kim, 'Do you believe me now? The damn thing's dead.' It had bronchitis so they switched it out. The horse was snorting and green was coming out of its nose and I'd wipe it but they did change the horse out for another shot we were doing." Jarre's horse had an issue with a cactus needle but Gang was able to treat it with Bute (an anti-inflammatory for horses), poultice and rest, and soon it was right as rain again.[26]

While looking for horses, they also kept their eyes open for wagons and carriages. On a trip to the Tombstone Western Heritage Museum, Gang saw and rented several carriages as well as a large ore wagon. Hauled by a team of four draft horses, the wagon was ten feet tall but its size and difficult handling nature made it something you rarely see on film. Although interested, production didn't want to spend the money. Instead, they obtained a replica 12-passenger stagecoach from rancher Red Wolverton. Red explains its construction: "Buffalo Bill Cody had a 12-passenger coach that he wrecked up around Cheyenne in 1882, and somehow or another, the wreck was in a barn for a long time. (Eventually, the owner sold the wreckage to someone in Oklahoma.) [The buyer] didn't have any blueprints so he took all the broken parts and pieced them together on a big table … in the middle of his shop and laid all the pieces out there. When we went to build the coach—people were much smaller back then—we made the coach six inches longer, three inches higher and three inches wider than it was originally. It's a brand-new coach; they just used the metal parts out of the old coach. None of the wood was usable. [It took about] six months and 3000 man-hours of labor [to build] a coach like that." Built in Oklahoma City in 1975, the stagecoach appears thrice in the film. It is seen first in scene #18 when the theatrical troupe arrives in Tombstone. It next appears in scene #121 when the Cowboys and Behan stop the coach on the road to Hooker's ranch with passenger Mr. Fabian lying dead in Josephine's arms. In scene #122 it's outside of Hooker's ranch house when Wyatt bids goodbye to Josephine. While Red drove the stage in the first scene, his son Kip commanded it in the other two. The stagecoach was pulled by a six-horse "hitch," or team, consisting of three pair of horses: the wheelers, which were next to the coach; the swing team in the second row; and the leaders in the front row, which actually led the team. Pairs of horses often worked together and they also may be hitched the same way as well—each animal always placed on the right-hand or "off-side," or the left-hand side or "near-side." For *Tombstone*, Wolverton used six pairs of Morgans: Breeze and Gandy Dancer, Sherwood Roulette and Royal Brightstar, Bandido and Houlihan, Guidon and Sherwood Drifter, Singleshot and Sherwood Hondo, and Sherwood Gambler and Cisco.

Driving a stagecoach is a particularly demanding challenge but the Wolvertons are experienced horsemen and expert drivers. Stagecoaches were built to go straight down a road as hard as the horses could run, turning no more than a few degrees either way. If turned too sharply, the coach rolls up on the wheel and tips over. Red and Kip made sure theirs didn't. In the scene when the stagecoach arrives at Hooker's ranch house, Kip was driving with Red as the outrider. However, one of the grips felt the coach was coming in at too fast a clip and would hit a cable coiled on the ground. So he reached out and pushed one of the horses as it went by. Red went into action and reminded the grip, in no uncertain terms, *never* to touch his horse ever again. The grip didn't.[27]

After several delays, filming began on Monday, May 17. But even before the first frame of film was exposed, an amusing incident occurred. Traditionally, canvas-, vinyl- or leather-backed deck chairs are provided for the director and principal actors to use

Red Wolverton's Wolverton Mountain stagecoach. The extras prepare for their wild ride. Kathy Tarantino is Dana Delany's stand-in (courtesy Jerry Tarantino).

The *Tombstone* director's chair of Charley Ward. The main actors had their own chairs; the remaining players sat in "Cast" chairs. Makeup artists Cheryl Nick and Patricia Androff pooled their resources and bought Ward a personalized chair for his 16th birthday. Ward said, "It was the most kind thing that ever happened to me in the business" (courtesy Charley Ward).

between takes. It is customary that the film's title and actor's name are lettered or embossed on the back of each chair. So, on the first day of filming, the prop master carefully unfolded the chairs and set them up for Jarre, Russell et al. As he stood back to admire his work, a Buckaroo stepped up and said, "I hate to tell you this, bub, but the name of the film is 'TOMBSTONE,' not 'TOMSTONE.'" "Oh, my God! I'm going to be fired!" yelled the crew member as he hurriedly grabbed the chairs. The backs were quickly replaced with the title properly spelled and no one was the wiser. (The chairs were sold at auction after the filming for a pretty penny.[28])

Jarre Initially planned for a six-day work week, 62-day filming schedule. The Memorial Day and July 4 holidays would be observed on Mondays with no work scheduled those days. Movies are not usually filmed in chronological or script order. The weather, day vs. night, interior vs. exterior, soundstage vs. location, and most importantly, actor availability—these all determine the sequence in which scenes are filmed. The first series of scenes were shot in the Los Encinos area of the Babocomari Ranch, west of Hwy. 83, just south of Elgin. Located 65 miles from Tucson, the area was known for its rich savanna rangelands, lush native grasslands and wetlands, desert and mountains, and cottonwood-lined Babocomari Creek—a perfect location for Henry Hooker's ranch as well as the

At Babocomari Ranch, Kevin Jarre directs the scene in which the Earp posse surprises the Cowboys (courtesy Larry Zeug).

Cowboy and wagon train camps. The Buckaroos would either ride or tow their horses to the site while a caravan of vehicles brought actors and crew members from Tucson. Budget Rent a Car mini- and maxi-vans, props and FX vans traveled, in order: ADs and makeup-hair, cameramen and wardrobe, grips and electrical, cast and finally, a white Lincoln with the director of photography and producer.[29]

The first scene Jarre filmed on May 17 was #105 (partial), "Wyatt and his men trap the Cowboys." As originally written, Pony Deal and a party of ten Cowboys are pushing a herd of stolen cattle. They spy Earp and his posse and start to chase them. Turning the tables, Earp and his men eventually ambush the Cowboys, killing all save one. Said Buckaroo Larry Zeug, "It was a bowl area and that's where Jon Tenney and Jason Priestley and Stephen Lang [were] supposed to ride in and tell us we can no longer be rustling cattle because of the Earps. Then they turn around and see the Earp posse riding towards us and one of the actors hollers out, 'Now it's time to get a working job.' And we all turn and scatter. You see all these Cowboys going out in every different direction riding balls-out over this hill and that was the way the end of this movie was supposed to go. It was like bees out of a bee's nest and it's kind of a neat scene, 'cause … it looked like everybody was scattering." That scene, along with many others filmed during the first several weeks of shooting, was reshot later in production.[30]

Later that day, scene #44, the horse race between Wyatt and Josephine, was filmed. Although Delany had learned to ride sidesaddle, in several shots in this sequence, you can see her legs astride the saddle in a standard fashion. Stuntwoman Teri Garland doubled in the scene in which Josephine gallops downhill. In one shot, you can clearly see Delany's right leg on the off-side of the saddle. The saddle actually had stirrups on each side and sported a fake leg attached to the camera side, simulating a sidesaddle approach. Dana freely admits her greatest challenge was "wearing an authentic corset under period costumes and pretending to ride sidesaddle in 114° in Tucson in August. And I'm not good with horses. It was kind of a tough one. I wish I could say they paid me lots of money. Actually, I had met the director on Monday, I was cast Wednesday, I was in Tucson on Thursday, and I had to learn to ride in five days—sidesaddle! That was really hard for me." She added, "[The funniest moment in the film for me was] seeing my fake sidesaddle leg flap as I rode. [The saddles used by Delany and her double were provided by the Davis Leather Company.] But I got to learn how to ride horses, I got to sing and dance, and I got to act like I was in 1880 and kiss Wyatt Earp. I mean, that's pretty great."[31]

Jarre continued to shoot portions of scene #105 the following two days as well as on May 29 and June 4. Numerous stunts and gags were required, many of which appeared in the final cut, albeit in a different sequence: horse drags, falls and a scene where Wyatt hangs along the side of his galloping horse and shoots at Pony Deal from under the horse's neck. Although Kurt Russell is an excellent horseman, Cliff McLaughlin doubled him in this stunt, and Clint Lilley stood in for Pony Deal. Close-ups with Russell were later filmed to complete the gag. Jarre also filmed one of the scenes he wrote for young Charley Ward. Charley's father Tom describes it as follows: "There was a kind of wash, gulley there. You could tell where the flash floods had come through but it was dry [and] had six-foot walls. Kevin wanted Charley to see the Earps [posse] coming, and he's scared. He twirls his horse around, goes up this little ravine, an arroyo that has lots of flat river rocks in it, mesquite trees on either side and a [fairly steep] rise. We're all going up there to watch and Sam Elliott [is right next to me]. As they set up the camera, Kevin tells Charley what to do and then tells [D.P. William] Fraker what he wants to see. [While] Charley is sitting on his horse, Kevin has his back to him, so I walk over to him. I said, 'Listen, son. Let's make this look good. They don't know what they want. Let's make this good.' He said, 'What do you mean, Dad?' Charley carries a quirt like I do. I said, 'They don't know what little old Dish (Charley's horse) can do. I tell you what: When all this happens, you whirl your horse around and take off in a wide-open gallop. Turn around when you get about a hundred feet, look over your shoulder and you whop that horse with your quirt, except don't hit your horse. Hit your leg, hit your chaps. I think it'd look pretty neat.' So, Kevin comes over, talks to him again. Of course, Kevin doesn't know I talked to [Charley]. 'Action!' Charley pursues this routine, turns this horse around, 'Whap!' As he goes up this ravine, it's river rocks and it sounds like a machine gun going off. When he gets to the top of the arroyo, there's a tall yucca plant and doggone it if the kid don't jump that plant with his horse. Kevin was excited, 'I had no idea [he could do that]. I just wanted him to walk up there, trot.' Sam turns and says to me, 'I tell you what. If we had 12 more guys like that, we could make a Western.'"[32]

The first scene in which Charley had lines involved Powers Boothe, which must have been a bit daunting. Curly Bill was in a train car and Ward's character was supposed to report to Earp and his posse. "Powers Boothe was really helpful," remembers Charley. "I was pretty nervous. Kevin Jarre had said to me, 'Just do your deal. Don't worry about it. Don't act. Just be you. And you're okay. I don't need you to act like something. Just you be you and you'll be fine.' Powers Boothe said, 'Hey, will you do me a favor? I'd like to go over these lines. I just feel like I'm missing something. I'd appreciate it if you'd do them with me and do yours and maybe I can get a better feel for it.' We went through it several times, there really wasn't anybody around, just me and him. The whole time, all he was doing was helping me and coaching me, but saying it was [for] him. It really loosened me up a little bit." Unfortunately, this was yet another one of Charley's scenes that ended up on the cutting room floor.[33]

On Thursday, May 20, the wagon camp sequence was filmed. The camp was located in the same general area as the Buckaroo base camp on Gas Line road, west of the Elgin-Canelo road. Extra Nikki Pelley recalls, "When I first arrived there, you're going on this road and you're just driving and there's a little sign on the side of the road. You go up the dirt road for three or four miles and I was pretty sure it was the wrong place, a little dirt road out in the middle of nowhere. It opens up to this valley and then you saw it—a huge encampment. It didn't matter what end of the encampment you went to.

"I was looking for newcomers coming on set. They took me to where I was supposed to be. I was just looking around because there were so many people there, asking people, 'Oh, what are you doing on the show?' Some people were just there. One gentleman said, 'Oh, I just took off from work so I could be here.' 'What's your part?' I asked. 'I'm just going to be here in case they need me.' There was someone sketching pictures. It was surrealistic when you saw it. They were all camped up. It was cowboy cooking, everybody outside with chuck wagon cooking. I've never seen anything like it. It was just amazing." Nikki played the part of a pregnant pioneer woman and was filmed walking around the encampment and climbing into horseless wagons.[34]

In these scenes, Wyatt rides into a camp and meets the wagon master, played by a leather-fringed Hugh O'Brian. Later, Holliday, McMasters, Vermillion and Johnson arrive and are deputized. Years earlier, Russell's father Bing had appeared in two episodes of O'Brian's television series *The Life and Legend of Wyatt Earp*. Bing also played a deputy in 1957's *Gunfight at the O.K. Corral*. Said publicist Patti Hawn, Goldie's sister, "It was a wonderful opportunity to have the older Wyatt and the younger Wyatt meet." Added Sherayko, "The scene called for Wyatt coming in and talking to Hugh O'Brian. Doc goes and gets Turkey Creek and my character and we ride in. Wyatt wants us to become his deputies. Mike Rooker rides in, and that's when he throws down the sash and says he'll join them. The five of us go riding out from the wagon train. Hugh O'Brian literally handed Kurt Russell something. The feeling of it was the old Wyatt Earp ... now giving his blessing to the new Wyatt Earp. As we ride out, the wagon train is behind us, O'Brian is watching us ride off, this little kid gives this speech, waving his fist in the air [and] the five of us simultaneously make a jump over a fallen tree. It was just a great shot." Unfortunately, neither the camp scenes nor the jump would appear in the final version.[35]

Dana Loraine Goodge, another extra in this scene, had an entirely different experience than Nikki Pelley: "The wagons were all in a circle. They had me come stand in the middle of the circle—I had no idea what I was doing. All of a sudden, Val Kilmer comes on horseback, leans over the horn of the saddle, points his gun at me and says, 'Take off your clothes.' I was like, 'What?' (He was either playing his sarcastic self or he was flirting.) Later, it was so hot we were sitting by the trailers trying to keep cool and we had these bonnets on that covered some of your face. Kurt Russell, Val Kilmer and the other guys were standing in a circle in the middle of this wagon train circle and Kurt kept looking over at me. Then you would see him look around everywhere else. He kind of walked up [to me] and then turned around and came back. I didn't find out until later what was going on: Somebody told me that when they were over in the circle, he thought there were hidden cameras on him and that they had snuck Goldie Hawn on the set. [Everyone thought Dana looked like Goldie.] When he came over to get a cigarette, he wanted to see what I looked like up close." For the rest of the summer, Goodge was known as either Dana #3 (Delany was Dana #1 while Wheeler-Nicholson was Dana #2), or Goldie.[36]

While Jarre filmed the wagon camp scene, Terry Leonard continued to film horse drags, saddle falls and other stunts. Usually, they first break down the script into action sequences and then assign them to a second unit director. Leonard had an added advantage: Not only was he a director, he was also the film's stunt coordinator. Explains Leonard, "We do all the action sequences in harmony with the first unit director, the producer and the writer. It's an amalgamation of putting the action sequences in the proper perspective on the film. The quickest way to lose a job as a fledgling director is to start shooting stuff that you think is right, even though it might be, and you're not adhering to the wishes of what was laid prior to you going in and shooting it. We don't go out there without weeks and weeks of preparation. I hire [all the stuntmen, and] I don't tell a stuntman how to do his stunts. That's the way I work. It's just stupid. I'm not the guy to be telling people how to do stunts. I've done them all and I know when it's a good piece of business or when a guy doesn't have the moxie to get it done. Everybody talks about the [stunt] and the horses we're going to use and how we're going to lay it out. I'm going to tell them where I'm going to put the cameras and what I need to see; it's all a composite effort, everybody putting in their two cents worth. But the final say-so is me. And if it doesn't work, they all turn and look at me. And if it works, everybody gives the guys a cheer, and that's what it's supposed to be.

"I never like to do a stunt more than once, ever. Because that's like putting another bullet in the gun: Russian roulette. I want to make sure we rehearse the daylights out of

Kurt Russell (Wyatt Earp), Michael Rooker (Sherm McMasters) and Peter Sherayko (Texas Jack Vermillion) chase the Red Sash gang. Second unit director Terry Leonard stands behind the camera in a white shirt (courtesy Jerry Crandall).

Top: Cowboys begin to scatter on the Babocomari as Cliff McLaughlin, stunting for the character Wyatt Earp, shoots a red-sash–wearing Cowboy. The members of the posse are stunt doubles; the sequence was directed by Terry Leonard. *Bottom:* Gunsmoke fills the air as the Earp posse attacks the Red Sash gang on the Babocomari Ranch (both courtesy Jerry Crandall).

it, and if something goes really wrong, yeah, we gotta reshoot it. But I hate to reshoot stunts. I have an incredibly vivid imagination. When I sit down with the director, I need to look at the storyboards because I need to see what he wants to shoot and how he wants to shoot it. But I read the script, I see the scenes unfold in front of him; and when we're talking about action sequences, I can visualize it and go to the director. I can see it all. I don't mean to sound overbearing but I grew up with imagination, so … I lay it out and talk to the director about it. I come in harmony with the concept. So when I'm laying out the stuff for stuntmen, I see exactly what it's supposed to be and what it's supposed to look like. And we talk about it. I don't hire guys the first year in the business, I hire guys who have done their stuff. So they know what I'm talking about."[37]

Recalls Jerry Crandall, "One day we did some wild things: galloping across rivers, skidding down mountains. One of the mountain things we did was pretty scary. We were way up on top of this ridge and [they] had us come, almost at a run, skidding down this rough mountain, bouncing over rocks and stuff. It's dangerous but it's real flashy and looked great, I'm sure. We were doing our stuff with the stunt guys who were dressed like Wyatt Earp and his posse. I was with the bad guys. Horses rearing up, horses falling over. One of the stunt guys broke his jaw. There were about eight or ten of us in this mêlée of horse action. That was when the Wyatt Earp posse caught the bad guys and we had a big shootout but, unfortunately, it was all cut when the new director came in."[38]

But even the best-laid plans of mice and men often go awry. Leonard told Buckaroo Jerry Crandall that his character would be killed in a specific scene. Crandall, 58 at the time, was asked if he preferred that a professional stuntman perform the saddle fall during which Crandall would be shot off his horse. Having performed this gag numerous times in the past, Jerry felt confident he could do it again. His main concern was his gun. Jarre had told him they might want to take some close-ups of Jerry firing a Colt Single-Action revolver, so the weapon had to be the correct version for 1881. Explains Crandall, "Guns that were made before 1898 have a different configuration than the later Colts. You can still buy a single-action but they have a little different [appearance] and Kevin was aware of that. [Said Jarre,] 'I want you to have a black powder frame single action,' so I went out and bought a nice [custom-made] replica [from Cimarron Arms], and had it nickel-plated." His concerns were swayed when Leonard told him not to worry as rubber guns were available for the gag. However, when Leonard called for the stunt gun, none of the rubber guns were available right then so Jerry had to use his own expensive pistol. "Terry told me not to land on my feet," said Crandall, "as they would be filming the entire fall all the way to the ground. No problem, I thought. When Terry clapped his hands, this would be the signal for me to take a dive off my horse, Apache. They stripped my saddle down, took one of my stirrups off and put an angle iron [bracket] on it so I could get a better way to [leap] off the horse. 'Action!' He clapped his hands and, throwing my pistol way up in the air, I took off. Unfortunately, I put out my right arm to soften my fall and, as a result, my rotator cuff cracked and my upper arm snapped. I continued to work for another few days but my arm kept slipping out of the socket, so I was told to leave and seek medical attention. Regrettably, I was unable to return to the set." Meanwhile, Crandall's revolver landed in soft ground and came through unscathed. Jarre considered the fall so unique and different from what a professional would do, they decided to leave it in the film.[39]

Leonard filmed a variety of memorable stunts: "Oh, we did a bunch of stuff. I designed a shot where Bobby McLaughlin gets knocked off of the back [of] the horse—

Buckaroo Jerry Crandall is shot off his horse Apache. This second unit scene was filmed by Terry Leonard on May 25, 1993. Jerry broke his arm and was later forced to leave the production (courtesy Jerry Crandall).

he does a backover. We put the blood bag in the stock of the rifle and Tony Boggs comes through and hits him in the face and he turns over backwards. You see [Bobby] bleed; a really neat shot from them galloping away from the town."[40]

Crandall's incident wasn't the only accident. On June 2, Teri Garland (Terry Leonard's wife at the time) was injured when her saddle broke while she was riding sidesaddle.

Since most of the saddles were authentic, the leather on them was quite old. She was examined by the set medic Chris Swinney and released back to production. The scene was re-filmed and she used a new saddle. In another stunt, Mark Warrick did a saddle fall into a drag, but the horse ran so fast and Mark bounced so hard that he couldn't get his hand on the release cable. It was only through the quick reactions of Leonard, Swinney and a few horse wranglers that the horse was stopped and Warrick saved.[41]

At the end of the first week, Kevin filmed scenes #116 and 117. In this sequence, Earp and his posse, atop a plateau, watch a Ringo-led, badge-wearing posse of outlaws. The very sick Holliday suddenly faints and is caught as he falls. Kilmer wasn't the only one to fall off his horse during these scenes. Billy Lang recalls that one of the *outlaws* accidentally fell off his horse as they were filming the posse galloping in the distance. Obviously, it put a damper on filming.[42]

On May 26, Jarre moved his operation to the Hooker ranch set. Henry Clay Hooker, a wealthy and influential cattleman, had owned the Sierra Bonita, a 250,000-acre ranch in the Arizona Territory, located in what was later known as Sulphur Springs Valley. A friend and supporter of Earp, Hooker also aided the lawman's posse during the Vendetta ride after the Iron Springs shootout. The film's three-sided "Hooker ranch house" was built about two miles east of the wagon camp site on the Babocomari and constructed with adobe provided by a Tucson supply company. Although interior scenes were filmed inside the building, there wasn't an actual rear wall. Most of the hardware seen inside the house (hinges, etc.) were resin-cast plastic provided by set dresser Matt Marich. After filming was completed, the building was disassembled and all the adobe blocks were taken to the Babocomari ranch house where they still lay, unused and crumbling.

Not surprisingly, the Hooker character's persona significantly changed once veteran actor and screen legend Charlton Heston took on the role. Jarre had initially described Hooker as hesitant, unwilling and reluctant to be involved in the Earp-Cowboy conflict. When asked by Wyatt for information about the Cowboys, Hooker declines and hangs his head in shame. Naturally, the actor's resonating, distinctive voice, chiseled jaw, broad shoulders and larger-than-life, commanding appearances in such films as *The Ten Commandments*, *El Cid*, *Ben-Hur* and *Khartoum* wouldn't jive with Jarre's description. As a result, Heston played the role as ... Heston. Seventy years old at the time, his stooped, hunched-over, frail appearance fooled the other actors. They may have thought him tired and weakened by age and injuries, but when the bell sounded, Heston, the total pro, stormed from the gate in full stride, his six-foot, two-and-a-half-inch frame ramrod-straight. When the director yelled, "Cut," he would collapse. Several extras commented that they couldn't believe this change in appearance. Said Buckaroo Zeug, "The breakfast wagon was out there and Heston was over at the wagon. He stooped over, fixing coffee. We're sitting there watching him and thinking, 'How's he going to shoot this scene?' And as soon as they said 'Action!' he stood up, rigid as hell and he was ready to go." Between takes, Heston would sit on the ranch porch, regaling extras with stories from his fabled life and sharing pearls of wisdom. Several extras were waiting with bated breath for the next scene, chomping at the bit, as it were, to act with Heston. One observed, "How cool is this? We're hanging out with Moses. How freaking cool is that?" Moses then spoke unto the assembled multitude: "Guys, just remember. They pay you to wait. Your acting is for free." When asked if he wanted to go to his trailer, he would say, "No. I'm holding court here." An Arizona monsoon rolled in with a tremendous crack of thunder and a

At Babocomari Ranch, Henry Hooker's Sierra Bonita ranch house. This adobe building was later torn down and the blocks moved to the Babocomari main house where they remain today (courtesy Garrett Roberts).

crew member exclaimed, "Oh my God! Look at that!" He then felt a hand on his shoulder and The Voice intoned, "Boy. Fetch me my staff."

Surprisingly, Heston had a wicked sense of humor. After filming a scene with Russell, Kilmer, Taylor, Sherayko and Rooker, Heston and assistant director John Cameron walked behind the camera. Hat maker Tom Hirt was sitting in Heston's chair and was told to move by Cameron. Heston said, "No, that's Tom. That's okay. You go ahead and sit there, Tom. I'm going to sit in Kurt Russell's chair. It'll drive him crazy."[43]

During one such session, while Heston held court on the porch with Sherayko, Buck Taylor, Chris Mitchum, Michael Rooker and a handful of extras, Russell and Kilmer were inside the ranch house filming a scene. And it was literally taking all day. Kurt wasn't happy with it: "We gotta do it again. We gotta do it again." Several additional scenes were scheduled to be filmed that day as well, and Rooker got tired of waiting. One observer noted that Rooker eventually stormed into the room where they were filming and yelled at Russell, "Goddammit. ... I'm not on this movie to be sitting around outside while you're fucking with these lines. Now, get this scene over with because I want to do [my] scene!" Whatever Russell replied apparently wasn't satisfactory because Rooker stomped out of the building, slammed the door, got in his car and roared off to the hotel. Whether this incident actually occurred is debatable but it is a fact that several actors, including Rooker, had their parts significantly reduced in subsequent drafts.

Despite his prestige and mystique, Heston, from his very first day on the set, just wanted to be one of the guys. While other folks used the honey wagon—a mobile multi-stalled rest room with washrooms—Heston preferred to wander in the desert and commune with nature. One time, Buck Taylor, Forrie Smith and several other actors were standing in the Holiday Inn parking lot, waiting for the van that would take them to the set. Smith had already agreed to ride with Taylor. A large black limousine rounded the corner. It stopped, out stepped Heston, and an aide directed him to his own van. "Oh, hell," Heston said. "I'm going to ride with these boys right here, by God. I'd rather ride with Buck Taylor and … who's this guy?" From then on, Smith rode in a different van.

Heston also was extremely courteous while on location. When he arrived at the set, he would go to the first PA. "What do you want me to do? What do you need? What do you want? I'm here to work. Do you want me to go to wardrobe, makeup?" Recalls Smith, "Everybody was the same [to him]. It didn't matter if you were the lowest PA on the show or whatever. Heston treated everyone as human beings and that energy carries over to the film." During lunch hour, he would go through the line, get a tray for his wife Lydia and himself, and carry them back to his trailer. When asked, "Can I help you, Mr. Heston?" he would invariably reply, "No, no. Thank you. I've got it."[44]

Asked why he accepted the cameo role, Heston didn't hesitate: "The character … intrigued me. And, like most actors, I like doing Westerns. I hadn't done one for a while, so it was a welcome thing for me." He was impressed by his real-life character's strength: "In the case of Henry Hooker, though he is not central to the action in the film, he is crucial to it. Hooker was a historical figure. He was indeed the largest rancher in the area. And his concern was not who was right or who was wrong in these conflicts, which to him was not important. But he knew that the area had to be stable and was determined to make a personal stand if necessary—in essence, when he says, 'Not on my land, not in my house.'"[45]

But not all the scenes Heston appears in actually feature Heston, who was on location for just three days. It was only after his departure that the filmmakers realized they had a major problem on their hands; in all of Heston's over-the-shoulder shots, his hairpiece was crooked. (In an over-the-shoulder shot, the camera is placed behind the shoulder of a character whose head and shoulders are seen in the foreground and are used as a framing device for the shot. Most often, a second character is the subject of interest.)[46]

What to do? Fortunately, Jeff Dolan, one of the Buckaroos, bore an uncanny resemblance to Heston. After a change of wardrobe, Jeff was taken to makeup and given a haircut, yak-hair mustache and sideburns so he could stand in for the departed actor. After his hair was grayed, the first AD took Dolan over to the director for approval: "Yeah, sure. We'll give it a whirl." Dolan was more than a Buckaroo, he was also a professional actor; earlier in his career, he had studied under Marie Dent at the Palos Verde Playhouse in Los Angeles (Marie was part of Lee Strasberg's Actors Studio). But according to Dolan, "Nobody knew that. I was just some dumb cowboy from Arizona. And Sherayko's a wreck. So, they were afraid. 'Oh, Jesus. He'll screw up the lines.' The initial stuff was an over-the-shoulder where I was doing a scene with Michael Biehn. And Biehn was doing his mean [persona], and he truly was, too. A mean, evil-looking appearing Johnny Ringo. Very intimidating, especially to a novice. So, all I had to do is stand there and react to his dialogue. Sherayko was off-camera reading Heston's dialogue because they didn't know if I could do it. Basically, I just had to react."[47]

Chris Mitchum vividly recalls being on the set with Heston. "People said, 'Chris, why did you do that movie?' I said, 'It's a nice little part.' I had scenes with Val, I had scenes with Kurt. Every time there was a scene at the [Hooker] ranch, [Jarre] would give me dialogue and he would work me into [it]. It was a nice little cameo appearance. I'm in the movie on the porch [but] you can't see me because I'm in the shadows. In the script there was the killing of Rooker's character where they throw him into the fire. Everything was different. Rooker comes riding in. I say, 'Rider coming in.' He comes in [and] there's a whole lot of dialogue. There was so much stuff. There was a lot of dialogue in the bedroom with Val recuperating in bed. There's a big scene in there with Chuck, Kurt and myself talking with Val. There's a lot of stuff in there that was cut. There's a scene outside with Kurt on horseback and I was standing there with Chuck. Because my character was not scripted, [Kevin] wanted to make me the foreman of the ranch. So every time Chuck was in the scene, I was standing next to Chuck and we were doing dialogue. Chuck and I were very good friends and [they'd] say, 'Chris, I want you to do that line instead of you, Chuck,' and Chuck would say, 'Great,

Jeff Dolan, a Buckaroo and Charlton Heston's double (courtesy Jeff Dolan).

give it to Chris.' I was like splitting dialogue with Chuck. It was the best script I've ever read. Kevin would throw in an added line for me to come in to say something. I'd say, 'Kevin, this is so beautifully written. Please don't spoil it just to give me a line.' I would talk myself out of dialogue.[48]

Jeff Dolan: "When you see all of the guys standing on the porch at Hooker's ranch, it's a shot from the distance. Chris Mitchum, Heston and Buck Taylor, all the guys standing there on the porch. That's actually me, not Heston. He was long gone [by then]. The sunset scene at Hooker's ranch when the stagecoach shows up and Dana Delany's all upset because her friend the actor is dead, and she says goodbye to Kurt Russell, that's Chris Mitchum and me in that scene, too, not Heston. They used me a lot. The close-ups where you can see his face are the only ones he's actually in. I'm a lot cheaper than Heston. They had me for $750."

Pickup shots were later filmed during the time the crew was located at Mescal. Although the adobe house had long since been dismantled, Jeff also was featured in wide master shots of Hooker riding up to meet Wyatt, and in a reshoot of the Cowboys riding up the ranch to call on McMasters for a parley. So, if you see Hooker from behind, or if his face is seen in the distance in profile, chances are it's really Dolan.[49]

Michael Biehn also had a few scenes with Heston that didn't make the final cut. "I had a couple of great scenes with Charlton Heston where I am nose to nose with him," Biehn told an interviewer. "I wish I had those scenes. You know? Just for my grandchildren.

Or my grandchildren's grandchildren. Where they could see me going nose to nose with Charlton Heston on this porch. At one point, the Cowboys ride out and try to break into his house. Charlton Heston says, 'You guys aren't coming in here!' I go up on the porch and have a conversation with him. This guy is such a big name actor, like playing opposite Sean Connery. It's something I would really liked to have had in the film. I wanted to have that in my library. It's gone."[50]

Of course, some folks couldn't tell the difference between the real Heston and the screen Heston. Eddie Perez recalls sitting and chatting with Sam Elliott one day, having sneaked over to where the stars were eating. "I figured I was hungry and didn't want to sit and wait," says Perez. "I was actually sitting across from Heston as he was having a conversation with Elliott [and] I didn't know who he (Heston) was. When the movie came out, my wife's grandmother said, 'Oh, yeah. That's Charlton Heston.' 'Yeah, I sat across from him for lunch,' said I. 'And you didn't get his autograph?' cried the lady. 'That's the man who parted the Red Sea.'" Perez sheepishly adds, "I never heard the end of it until the day she died."

Heston stayed with the rest of the cast and crew at the Tucson Holiday Inn. The Phoenix Suns and Chicago Bulls were playing in the NBA finals that year so the lounge was fairly busy. Heston would come down, have three Scotches and go back to his room: very nonchalant, very unpretentious. Supporting actor Grant James (Dr. Goodfellow) said, "Some wag from the crew went around and put the word 'Doc' in front of every Holiday that was there. It soon became the Doc Holiday Inn."

At the time, the hotel was quite the place to be. Stingray's lounge was known as a real trendy place: sunken bar, dance floor, DJ booth, pool tables, dart boards and disco glitter balls. Cast and crew would congregate there after a hard day's shoot for rest, relaxation and drinks. Jarre said that every Saturday night was a "Mandatory party. I buy the first round." Peter Sherayko recalls, "Every night, we'd come back from the set, and when you walked in the bar, there were always two or three tables with the Cowboys—Powers, Michael Biehn, Thomas Haden Church, all those guys were sitting there. And way at the other end of the room it was Bill Paxton, Sam Elliott, myself, and Buck [Taylor]." Remembers employee Victor Vizcarra, "[Stingray's] was a humongous lounge … a happening place. It was really popular, a real hot spot." Evening manager Brett Hust recalls, "About every three weeks, they throw a party at the bar. They do drink quite a bit." The gatherings hadn't attracted much interest but according to Hust, "Quite a few teenagers are bopping around here trying to find Jason Priestley." Next to the lounge was John Q's Hammons Fine Dining Restaurant, a full-service establishment offering a complete complement of meals throughout the day. As production sometimes required filming at night, the hotel kept room service open from 2:30 p.m. to 5:30 p.m.—times when it was normally closed—to accommodate the variable schedule. Housekeeping didn't begin until after the normal 5:00 p.m. call time.[51]

Both Vizcarra and James Brooks, another hotel employee, recall that the actors pretty much stayed by themselves: "[They] were generally pretty nice. They were able to mingle. I didn't see any fans going into the restaurant asking for autographs. Nobody bothered them and they were decent tippers. We automatically [got] a built-in tip and then they gave us money on top of that. That was always a plus. [They chose our] hotel because they had over a dozen hotels out at the airport. They get all the fanfare [but] celebrities want to get away from all that—have some peace and quiet. They were isolated enough that they knew the hotel wasn't around anybody else that would be a threat. They could let their hair down but, [we] did have security." As a small perk, "They gave us a chance before they got started to be a part of the cast," said Brooks. "They needed a piano player [and some employees auditioned]. I didn't make it."[52]

When a pre-production party was scheduled in the hotel's upper and lower terrace, ropes and stanchions were set up to segregate the actors and crew from other hotel guests. A Weight Watchers convention was being held in one of the rear ballrooms, and when the meeting was over, the participants departed past the terraces, with predictable results: Once they recognized Sam Elliott, the place went crazy. Ladies rushed the ropes, guards tried to hold them back. One lady negotiated the obstacles and boogied with the actors. A good time was had by all. Robert Burke remembers another incident: "We were there one week and there were quilters—big old gals in their 50s, 60s and 70s. Sam [Elliott] came through the lobby and he found himself in the middle of a pack. We were over in the corner and somebody said, 'Look at Sam. He's too much of a gentleman to go out of his way.' He signed everything, he did pictures, tipping his hat. Later that afternoon, we saw him run through a doorway. They were on his tail again and he was trying to duck away from them. [But] he made time for everybody."

But some hotel patrons found the celebrities ... *weird*. One guest told storyboard artist Donna Cline, "Wow! The actors, they're just [always] in character. The never get out of character even when they talk to us. Sometimes the actors come up to the front desk and they act like they're still cowboys."[53]

Cast and crew members availed themselves of the hotel's amenities, which included the swimming pool and Jacuzzi. After filming was done for the day, you typically could find Kilmer, Priestley, Delany, Boothe and numerous others hanging around the pool, many partaking in alcoholic libations and chemical substances—sometimes to the point of excess. One wasted actor, holding a long box, was seen stumbling around the pool's edge, barely keeping his balance. He suddenly lost his equilibrium and the box, containing an eight-foot party sub, sailed into the pool, where it floated for the rest of the evening, a long Italian submarine. On another occasion, Kane Rubalcaba recalls, "One night we were sitting there with Peter [Sherayko] in the hot tub, me and Kurt and him. And of course, Peter had a bottle of Jim Beam, just sitting there B.S.ing. I don't know how he got it but Powers Boothe got a big box of roses from somewhere, somebody must have left it. [There was] Powers Boothe, lit off his ass, dancing around the pool, singing to the roses. I said, 'That dude's going to fall in and drown.' It was just insane."[54]

On another occasion, Dana Delany went swimming "bare-assed naked" in the pool which naturally resulted in several guys standing around the pool's edge watching her swim. Unaware, Chris Swinney walked up and asked, "What are you guys looking for?" Swinney ruefully adds, "Right then, [Dana] swam up and put on an earring. And I look at these two guys like ... 'Yeah, right. That's exactly what you're looking at.' So I go, 'Oops,' and *accidentally* knock both of them in ... [actor] Terry O'Quinn and another guy. Monday I show up for work and they're all like, 'Do you still have a job?' 'Why?' 'Do you know the guy on the right that you pushed in the pool?' 'No. They were staring at the boobs and the butt and I got them.' 'That was [producer] Jim Jacks.'" Not a wise career decision.[55]

Jarre insisted upon absolute authenticity in his characters' appearances, so his actors were encouraged to work on their tans to produce darkened, healthy glows. No man-tan or QT for this director. Naturally, some took his recommendation to an extreme, as Sherayko wryly recalls. "I had to fire three guys because they were idiots," he admits. "I

The infamous Holiday Inn swimming pool where an Italian submarine protected the occupants. Many wild nights were spent around the pool.

wouldn't have fired them, I kept on trying to tell them what to do. Kevin hired one to be Ringo's right-hand man. He was supposed to be a Buckaroo in the morning, and in the afternoon after lunch he was supposed to go down to do this other scene with Ringo. And he got there an hour late because he fell in the water on his horse, riding over to the new set. Got all dirty, went back to the Buckaroo camp, took a shower, changed his clothes and went back and he was late. They already replaced him. They said, 'Where the hell were you?' 'Oh, I got muddy.' That's how stupid he was. Some of the Buckaroos had never worked on movies before. They were good cowboys, they were good shooters, they were good horsemen, and I brought them on, but they were idiots. [The aforementioned Buckaroo] actually got sunburned feet at the pool and then went to the medic because he couldn't put his boots on. He told the medic a horse stepped on his foot. So the medic let him have a couple of days off. So what the idiot does, [he] sits down at the pool during the day while all the production officers were there. One producer came up to me and said, 'This guy's getting paid to sit down at the pool because he can't ride? Send him home.'"

Sherayko recalls another scene where they wanted four Red Sash gang Cowboys to ride over a hill and down toward the camera. Three of them rode down the hill; the fourth rode around it. The director screamed, "What the hell are you doing?" The Buckaroo said, "Well, it was easier to ride around." "I don't give a damn if it's easier going around. I need you to ride down in the shot." Needless to say, the horseman was let go.[56]

On May 28, Jarre filmed the scene in which Ringo becomes head of the outlaw gang after Curly Bill is killed. Sheriff Behan and Deputy Breakenridge both look on as Ringo says, "Now, gather 'round, children. Gather 'round and raise up your right hand." After the gang is sworn in, all received badges. Unfortunately, the prop department later ran out of badges as these particularly popular items had a tendency to walk off the set. Confesses Greg Poulos, "One day the Buckaroos were not playing in our unit, so we gave the badges to the second unit who was using it that day. It turned out [first unit] wanted the Buckaroos there so we quickly made some badges out of cardboard, which from ten feet away, you wouldn't have known. And these people are further away from that. It just so happened that one of the Buckaroos rode by the camera and [the director] saw this cardboard. 'What the heck is this? You were my favorite department,' [he yelled]. 'What kind of a cheap production is this? Now, why are you ruining this movie with these horrible cardboard badges?' [A chagrinned Poulos could only reply,] 'It was offsetting unit. It wasn't on the list.'"[57]

Forrie Smith remembers one of the many scenes that didn't make the final cut: "There's a scene where me and Michael Rooker are in a camp and I'm sitting there cooking at a fire with my knife out, stirring whatever I had in the frying pan. When [Wyatt Earp] came riding into camp, I gave him a look. [My character] hated everything about him, everything he represented. Kurt Russell fell apart. 'Why are you looking at me like that? [Your character] wouldn't do that... My God, Pony Deal would think I was special when I walked into a room.' I said, 'No. I'm a killer and you're nobody to me. You're nothing. All I've heard about you is whacking people with your pistol. I'm a true-blue killer and I'll kill you before I let you come in here and disband the Cowboys and put me back on the reservation.' And Kurt was upset. 'No, you don't look at me like that.' Kevin took me aside and said, 'Yeah, you are right.' Bob Misirowski tried to settle Kurt down. He threw a fit, then we did it a couple more takes."[58]

The telephone rang early one afternoon. Just shy of his twenty-seventh birthday, Adam Taylor was taking a siesta; his young wife Anne answered the phone. "Hello. This is the production office in Tucson. The AD has been fired and we'd like to speak to Adam Taylor." She said he'd call right back and quickly ran into the bedroom to wake her husband. "Get your ass out of bed," yelled Anne. "They just called from *Tombstone* and you need to call them back!"

Apparently, AD John Cameron was a Directors Guild of America union member, and DGA bylaws specifically state that members cannot work on non-union projects. "The DGA tracks all non-union ... productions, investigates any situation in which a member is suspected of working on a non–Guild–covered project and takes disciplinary action as appropriate," said DGA spokeswoman Sahar Moridani. "In no way do we allow members to work non-union." Someone must have called the union about it because once it was determined he was working illegally, Cameron was fired. Enter Adam Taylor. Adam had been a production assistant and first AD on numerous low-budget movies for first-time directors but now he had a chance to work on a major project. He had previously submitted his résumé to the production office and never received a reply. His father Buck was already on the film and may have said, "Oh, my son's an AD. Why don't you talk to him?"

Adam took about 20 minutes to wake up and compose himself before he returned the call. Negotiations continued throughout the day; he then packed a bag, flew out of Burbank the next morning and was hired. (Cameron stayed on location for an additional 48 hours to facilitate the change.)[59]

The first AD is critical to the success of a film. He is in charge of scheduling each

At Babocomari Ranch, Kevin Jarre discusses a scene with (left to right) Thomas Haden Church (Billy Clanton), Stephen Lang (Ike Clanton), Powers Boothe (Curly Bill Brocius) and Michael Biehn (Johnny Ringo) (courtesy Christian Ramirez).

day's shoot and decides which actors will be called at what time. On a Western such as this, the first AD is an extremely busy person, scheduling the horses, wranglers, gunsmith, paramedic, etc., planning how many extras are needed. He also tracks the daily progress against the production schedule, prepares call sheets, maintains safety, security and order on the set and, at the end of each day, signs off on time sheets to assure each actor's time is properly recorded. When all was said and done, the first AD provides the key link between the director and cast and crew. Adam fit this role to a T. According to his wife Anne, as well as numerous other actors and crew members, "Everybody adored him. He could make people do anything he wanted because he treated them all with respect. He could say to someone, 'Hi. You see that port-a-potty there? I want you to go over and dive in head first.' And he could make them think they thought of it first. He had an artistic eye for setting up shots and he knew how to manage disputes between people." Taylor was a valuable, much-needed asset for the production team.[60]

And they desperately needed it. A dark cloud was building on the horizon, one that would soon come down on Jarre with its full wrath and fury.

FOUR

Lights! Camera! Action! What?

In 1873, Newman Haynes Clanton arrived in the Arizona Territory and settled in the Gila Valley near Camp Goodwin. Born in Davidson County, Tennessee, Clanton, like many pioneers, lived a nomadic existence, traveling from state to state looking for a pot of gold at the end of the rainbow. In 1840, he was married in Missouri; ten years later he left his wife and three sons for one year—an unsuccessful California sojourn in search of gold. Upon his return, he moved to Illinois; two years later he moved to Texas. After the Civil War, Clanton traveled to Fort Bowie, Arizona; a year later, after his wife passed away, his family of four boys and two girls left for California. Some time between 1869 and 1873, he returned once again to Arizona, settled on the Gila River and claimed a desert water hole on the trail between Yuma and Phoenix.

In 1877, he moved first to the San Pedro River and then to Lewis Springs, four miles south of Charleston, where he built a large adobe house known as Clanton Ranch. Known either affectionately, or derisively, as "Old Man," Clanton brought along his sons Joseph Isaac (Ike), Phineas Fay (Phin) and William Harrison (Billy). Given the vast number of cattle in the area, and the increased need for beef, it only seemed natural that Clanton— rancher, farmer, businessman—would provide needed supplies to miners, soldiers and farmers. Entrepreneurship must have run in the family as in 1878, son Ike opened the short-lived "lunch counter" Star Restaurant in nearby Watervale, this after his father had previously operated an inn at Fort Thomas in the mid–1870s. Neither was very successful. But they were undeterred in their efforts as the June 16, 1880, census humorously listed the family occupations as "keeping dairy" and "freighter."[1]

The local demand for beef was overwhelming; for example, the San Carlos Reservation alone required over 3.5 million pounds annually! If you raised cattle, you had a willing market, but you also needed to have a herd. Those who did were flush; those who didn't either let the opportunity pass by or became cattle rustlers. The Clantons chose the latter. Mexican cattle, American cattle, it didn't matter. "Obtain" what you need, change the brand and sell it to the highest bidder. As a result of overgrazing, drought and an abundance of cattle, many herds were driven from Texas into New Mexico and Arizona. J.J. Wagoner wrote in Arizoniana *that shipments "were especially numerous because of the passage of the Texas land law of 1879 … which initiated a mandatory leasing system providing for the payment of nominal fees. Texas ranchers objected to the new system and many of them moved their herds to Arizona where they found unrestricted grazing."*

Along with these herds came drovers, wranglers, cowpokes, buckaroos and, more than likely, Tom and Frank McLaury and Curly Bill Brocius.[2]

Although some documents stated that they were born in Mississippi, both Thomas and

Robert Findley "Frank" McLaury were actually from Courtright Center, New York, at the foot of the Catskills. The family was educated and relatively prosperous: father Robert was an attorney and brother Will was a successful judge in Fort Worth, Texas. Ironically, while the family was living in Belle Plaine, Iowa, some even said the brothers studied pre-law at a local academy although there isn't any evidence to support that contention. Upon the death of their mother during a typhoid epidemic, their father married a woman only slightly older than the brothers. Upset by her young age and the lack of time their father had spent grieving, the two brothers abandoned their studies and traveled west to seek their fortunes. They eventually settled along the Babocomari River in Hereford, Arizona, where they built a windowless, doorless shelter. Since no paperwork exists to determine the legitimacy of their claim, they could have been either actual homesteaders or mere squatters. No matter: They purchased a herd of Mexican cattle with money they brought from Iowa and sold it for a good profit. They also grew alfalfa hay and developed a herd of horses. It was at this time that they became associated with the Clantons.[3]

Very little is known about the Arizona origins of Curly Bill Brocius aka Curly Bill aka Brocious. In reality, his name may have been an alias. Some said he actually was one William B. Graham from Kansas although historians tend to discount that claim, He could have arrived from Texas, Missouri or even Mexico in 1878 with a herd of cattle for the San Carlos reservation. How he obtained them is unknown. In 1880, during conversations with the murderer while Wyatt Earp transported him to Tucson for the death of Marshal Fred White, Earp got the impression Brocius was an escaped outlaw from Texas. Bill admitted that years earlier he had been convicted of a crime in which a man had been killed in El Paso during an attempted robbery. According to comments made by Earp to the Tombstone Epitaph, *"we learn that the man who killed Marshal White is an old offender against the law. Within the past few years he stopped a stage in El Paso County, Texas, killing one man and dangerously wounding another. He was tried and sentenced to the penitentiary, but managed to make his escape shortly after being incarcerated. The facts leaked out in this way: On the road to Tucson, Byoscins [sic] asked Earp where he could get a good lawyer. Earp suggested that Hereford & Zabriskie were considered a good firm. Broscins [sic] said that he didn't want [James] Zabriskie, as he had prosecuted him once in Texas."*

Further research suggests that Brocius was really William "Curly Bill" Bresnaham, who was convicted in a U.S. Army robbery attempt in Texas in 1878 along with another Tombstone area cowboy, Robert Martin. The men were convicted and sentenced to five years in prison, but both escaped, presumably to the southwest Arizona Territory. Since both Martin and Curly Bill became known as leaders of the rustlers in Arizona Territory, they are likely the same Robert Martin and Curly Bill of the Texas crime.[4]

Along with assorted cattle rustlers, horse thieves and road agents, Martin and Brocius were based in Arizona's San Simon Valley. Among those included in this semi-organized band of outlaws were Charles Ray (Pony) Diehl, Charley Snow, Dick Lloyd, Johnny Oliver, Jim Wallace, Jerry Barton, Billy Leonard, Johnny Ringo, Joe Hill, Tom Harper, Pete Spence and Jim "Six-Shooter" Smith.[5]

Little is known of Johnny Ringo that isn't questioned. Born in Missouri, "one of the West's deadliest pistoleros," was fluent in Latin and knowledgeable about Shakespearean literature—or so they said. All untrue. Born May 3, 1850, in Washington, Wayne County, Indiana, John Peters Ringo did go to school in Gallatin, Missouri, but only received an elementary education. Distantly related to the infamous Younger clan, Ringo and his mother lived for a year on the Younger ranch near San Jose, California, before he returned to Missouri in 1870. He later moved to Texas, and after a series of misadventures that included murder and vengeance, ended up in an Austin prison where he met the notorious John Wesley Hardin. Ironically, after Ringo was released, he won an election as constable in Loyal Valley, Texas, and served for almost a year before he left for the Arizona Territory. It was rumored that while in New Mexico, he murdered two brothers in a saloon and escaped to Arizona where, after shooting a bar patron for his choice of liquor, he joined Robert Martin and Curly Bill Brocius.

In 1880, Ringo became a delegate to the Pima County Democratic Convention and served as an election official in San Simon, located in southern Arizona near the New Mexico border. Deserved or not, Ringo's reputation always preceded him. Claimed the Grant County Herald, *"During the past few years 32 men have dared to doubt his honor. They now fill 32 graves.... [A]lthough he had many competitors in his line, he had no true rivals, and Curly Bill and Billy the Kid will not bear comparison with him."*[6]

Some say Ringo was silent, dour and but they really didn't know him. In reality, he was ... well ... silent, dour and severe with a no-nonsense attitude, similar to a man named Wyatt Earp.

Wyatt Berry Stapp Earp was born March 19, 1848, to Virginia Ann Cooksey and the prolific Nicholas Porter Earp. The sixth of nine children, Wyatt was preceded by brothers Newton, James and Virgil, and by sisters Martha Elizabeth (who died when she was ten) and Mariah Ann (who died when she was two months old). Over the next 16 years, the Earp family moved back and forth between Monmouth, Illinois, and Pella, Iowa, before traveling to the San Bernardino Valley in California. At 17, Wyatt was employed as a stage-coach swamper, and worked with his brother Virgil, who drove a stagecoach between the Valley and Los Angeles. Eventually, the brothers were hired to drive a ten-animal, mule-and-oxen freight team between San Pedro and Prescott, Arizona. The next year, Wyatt drove a 16-animal team between San Bernardino and Salt Lake City. From 1868 to 1869, Wyatt held such occupations as railroad grader, boxer, promoter, gambler and referee.

In 1869, the family moved to Lamar, Missouri. Wyatt's father Nicholas was named justice of the peace while Wyatt replaced him as the town's constable. In Lamar, Wyatt married Urilla (Aurilla) Sutherland, who died while giving birth nine months later. In early 1871, still in grief over the death of his wife and child, Earp began a downward spiral when he was accused of not repaying a $20 debt and then later, along with Ed Kennedy and John Shown, of stealing two horses in the Indian Territory. The trio was eventually caught, arrested and jailed. Kennedy was later acquitted, and although some say Earp was let go after Kennedy's acquittal, in fact, Earp and Shown escaped.

In 1872, while buffalo-hunting along the Arkansas River, Wyatt met Bat Masterson, who invited him to join his hunting party. Earp declined, left for Peoria, Illinois, and worked in a brothel as a bouncer. While there, he may have "married" 16-year-old Sarah Haspel, who worked in the same house of ill repute. After a short stint in Ellsworth, Kansas, the Earps moved to Wichita, where, falling back on his experience as a peace officer, Wyatt became a deputy marshal in 1874, albeit not a full-time position ... and, once again, a bordello bouncer. In April 1875, he was appointed a regular member of the police department, reporting to Marshal Mike Meagher. At some point during this time in Wichita, Sarah departed for parts unknown and Wyatt "married" his third wife, Celia Ann "Mattie" Blaylock, who may have followed him from Peoria. Earp's tenure in Wichita ended after he assaulted Bill Smith, Meagher's opponent in the 1876 election. Shortly thereafter, Earp was fired for conduct unbecoming an officer and even though Meagher was re-elected, a Wichita commission voted against re-hiring Earp. Fed up with local politics, Wyatt packed his bags and he and Mattie left for Dodge City.[7]

Founded in 1872, this western Kansas cow town was originally named Buffalo City before the name changed to the legendary Dodge City. It was known as the buffalo capital of the west, so it was only natural that the railroad would establish a line to haul all the hides east. Once the Atchison, Topeka & Santa Fe Railroad arrived that September, the town was never the same. Frame structures, tents, saloons, grocery stores and restaurants sprang up overnight and the stench of slaughtered buffalos filled the air. Wrote Robert Wright, one of the directors of the Dodge City Town Company, "Hardly had the railroad reached there, long before a depot could be built ... business began; and such a business! Dozens of cars a day were loaded with hides and meat, and dozens of carloads of grain, flour and provisions arrived each day. The streets of Dodge were lined with wagons, bringing in hides and meat and getting supplies from early morning to late at night.... I have been to several mining camps where rich strikes had been made, but I never saw any town to equal Dodge." Along with the railroad came buffalo hunters and traders, drifters and drovers, gamblers and gunfighters. Although by 1876, over 1.5 million hides had been shipped from Dodge City alone, the buffalo trade was short-lived, and the great herds that had roamed the west were no more. But they were replaced by cattle. Earlier that year, the cattle trade had shifted from Ellsworth and Wichita to Dodge, and with it came the cowboys. That year, over 250,000 head of cattle traveled through the city. Eager to blow off steam after long, hard cattle drives, the drovers were rowdy and flush with cash—prime ingredients for disorder. The town needed a police force to curb this lawlessness, so in 1876, Earp was contacted by Dodge City's mayor and asked to leave Wichita to help rein in this chaos. Upon his arrival in May, Wyatt was appointed deputy marshal. His first duty was to fill out the police force, which he did with the addition of the Masterson brothers, Bat and James. Along with Ford County sheriff Charlie Bassett and his undersheriff Bill Tilghman, the lawmen were charged with taming the town.

Supposedly, it was also during this time that one Edward Zane Carroll Judson, aka Ned Buntline, commissioned five custom-built, single-action, long-barreled Colt revolvers, and presented them to Wyatt, Bat, Bassett, Tilghman and Neal Brown for their peacekeeping efforts. The fact that Judson wasn't anywhere near Kansas that year, or that Colt has no records of the custom-made weapons, or that Wyatt and Bat weren't yet famous, is irrelevant. When fact becomes legend, print the legend. Later that year, when Bat Masterson left Dodge to search for gold, Wyatt's younger brother Morgan was appointed to replace him. Once the cattle drives had ended for the year, Wyatt's meager salary, augmented by an additional $2.50 per arrest, took a significant hit as there were fewer cowboys around to cause trouble. As a result, in early 1877, he and Mattie took a short sojourn to Deadwood, South Dakota, where Earp removed his badge and fell back on his earlier professions: freight hauler and stagecoach guard.

As usual, that didn't last long. The allure of Dodge was too strong and once again, Wyatt was back to peacekeeping. Masterson had also returned and was now an undersheriff reporting to Bassett. After the election of 1878, both Masterson brothers held positions of authority: Bat was elected Ford County sheriff and Ed was the Dodge City marshal. But after Ed was murdered by Jack Wagner on April 9, Bassett took over as marshal and Wyatt was named deputy marshal, so once again, Wyatt had an air of respectability. Due to his several years of capturing desperados and defusing difficult situations, Earp's reputation had traveled far and wide. And, through timely information provided by one Doc Holliday,

Wyatt notified Bat Masterson, who was able to capture the outlaw Dirty Dave Rudabaugh. That spring, Holliday and his paramour, Kate Elder, arrived in Dodge, and later that year he literally saved Wyatt's life. In subsequent years, Earp described the incident: He was out in the street, surrounded by a crowd of desperados. Holliday, seated inside at a monte table, noticed the confrontation, borrowed a revolver, burst out through the saloon doors and yelled to the crowd, "Throw up your hands!" This sufficiently distracted members of the crowd and gave Earp the opportunity to draw his weapons and arrest them. Said Earp, "On such incidents as that are built the friendships of the frontier." Earp's subsequent relationship with Doc lasted to the latter's dying days. Wyatt called Doc "a loyal friend and good company. He was a dentist whom necessity had made a gambler; a gentleman who disease had made a vagabond; a philosopher whom life had made a caustic wit; a long, lean blond fellow nearly dead with consumption and at the same time the most skillful gambler and nerviest, speediest, deadliest man with a six-gun I ever knew."

Kevin Jarre was a marvelous writer—historically knowledgeable, extremely well-researched and effective, terribly creative and brilliant. His prose was smooth with memorable dialogue that almost flew off the page. And he was really into both his characters and the West; he'd walk around the set in boots, spurs—the exact same pair that Kurt wore—and an old-time cowboy hat.

As talented as he was as a writer, that's just as bad as he was as a director … at least according to several actors on the set. *But*, to give him his due, he had never before directed any film although he may have fancied himself a modern-day John Ford. Ford had a distinctive style that Jarre tried to emulate. Film journalist Ephraim Katz described it as follows: "Of all American directors, Ford probably had the clearest personal vision and the most consistent visual style. His ideas and his characters are, like many things branded 'American,' deceptively simple. His heroes … may appear simply to be loners, outsiders to established society, who generally speak through action rather than words. But their conflict with society embodies larger themes in the American experience. Ford's films, particularly the Westerns, express a deep aesthetic sensibility for the American past and the spirit of the frontier…. [H]is compositions have a classic strength in which masses of people and their natural surroundings are beautifully juxtaposed, often in breathtaking long shots. The movement of men and horses in his Westerns has rarely been surpassed for regal serenity and evocative power. Ford also championed the value and force of the group, as evidenced in his many military dramas…. [He] expressed a similar sentiment for camaraderie."

With more than 46 years in the film and television industry, working with directors such as Alfred Hitchcock, Blake Edwards, Clint Eastwood, Norman Jewison and Steven Spielberg, storyboard artist and senior illustrator Joseph Musso unfolds the Ford mystique even further. "How many Westerns are out there that look like they've been made by John Ford?" asks Musso. "That's what makes John Ford, John Ford. Everybody wants to make a [John Ford] movie. Shots like Alfred Hitchcock or John Ford. Ford just knew when to shoot master shots and then cut in the camera. He would do a master shot and then he'd have the actors leave out a key line of dialogue and he'd put it in the close-up. He forced the producer or studio to cut it the way [Ford] wanted to cut it. He'd cut in the camera. He knew what he was doing."

Actor Harry Carey, Jr., further details Ford's technique: "It was the simplicity. He didn't waste time doing close-up, close-up, close-up. What they do now is just big heads of everybody all the time. Very few of the modern directors do it the old way. Ford loved the country more than the actors. In those days they staged a scene, as a group shot, and you could see the interplay between the actors, and for a key line they would have a close-up. It's harder to do it that way. It takes more knowledge of what you're doing to get the looks right; that's why directors duck it now."[8]

A master shot, filmed from an angle that keeps all the actors in view, contains most or all of the action for a given scene. Often a long shot, it can also function as an establishing shot. Generally, all other shots in a given scene are related to what happens in the master shot. The master shot is then augmented by additional coverage: other camera set-ups that help shape the film's story. Experienced storytellers compose scenes using multiple shots that allow them to change camera angle and framing for both practical and cinematic purposes. From a practical perspective, it's simply easier to capture each element separately, particularly with live actors. From a cinematic perspective, moving between close-up shots of each character and other kinds of shots helps keep the viewers interested.[9]

Jarre valiantly tried to copy that style but didn't really understand the underlying foundation of the concept. Or maybe he did but struggled with its execution. Or perhaps it was even deliberate. Even the actors knew something just didn't feel right about the way Jarre was directing. The general mood on location was upbeat and expectant, but strong opinions and gossip filled the air regarding the progress of things. One concern was, were the dailies capturing what was on the page? "I stayed aloof of the politics," says Lisa Zane, "but I had this sense of a slow-motion train wreck." Producer Buzz Feitshans told Jarre he couldn't shoot only master shots. Replied Kevin, "If I shoot coverage, then [the studio] can cut my vision." Countered Feitshans, "Kid, you can't keep directing this movie if you only shoot master shots." Nevertheless, he sadly failed in his efforts. He knew exactly what he wanted, though, almost to the point of being obsessive. As he was responsible for the overall vision of the film, he felt he could micromanage, as it were, and tell the actors how to walk, how to move, where to place their hands, how to *act*. There are few things actors hate more than being told exactly how to deliver a line. Part of an actor's character development is figuring out what tone, emphasis and inflection a particular line may need or works best. Experiment, and through repetition and change, make the final decision. One never, ever, tells the actor how say a line in a specific way. This *faux pas* is called line reading.[10]

Sherayko offers a typical example of Jarre's obsessiveness: "There was a scene between Kurt and I where I'm telling Kurt that he had no chance against Ringo, Ringo's going to kill him. So we did a take of that. 'Cut.' Kevin comes over to me and gives me a line reading and tells me, 'I want you to say it this way.' So, I went back, I did the scene again. 'Cut.' Kevin grabbed me again, pulled me on the side and tells me, 'I want you to move your hand this way. I want you to do that.' Okay, I go back, do the scene again. 'Cut. Okay, I want you to do this.' Then he grabbed Kurt and he walked Kurt away. [I'm thinking] 'Oh my God, he's telling Kurt there's something the guy doesn't know what he's doing.' Comical. That's how I was feeling. Every week we would have an actors meeting with Kevin … we're at the actors meeting and we're all sitting there. And Michael Biehn raises his hand and says, 'Kevin, please. I cannot do a line reading for you. Let me act. Let me do what I have to do. Do not tell me how to move and how to talk and how to do every little nuance.' Dana Delany was sitting three feet away from me and I looked over and had a surprised look on my face. I said to her, 'Oh my gosh. I thought it was just me.' Dana looked at me and said, 'No, Peter. It's all of us.' That's what he was doing, whether it was Val or Kurt or Michael or Powers Boothe or Dana or Mike Rooker, or anybody. He was giving them line readings, he was telling them how to move. When you walked into a doorway, into a room, he wanted you to put your hand in a certain way on the door jamb. If you're sitting down at the faro table, he wanted you to have this posture, and he would tell you how to do that. 'Cut.' It finally got to all the actors, because when you're acting, you create your own character.

"Now, my belief is that when Kevin wrote the script, he envisioned every scene, every nuance, every way that a person would stand, would walk, would talk, would handle a gun. He would picture how Doc is going to hit Big Nose Kate on the ass, 'You're not wearing a bustle.' He would picture that. He would say, he's directing, you would have to do it the way he envisioned it. But you don't know what he envisioned, so it's impossible for you to do that. That's what took so long. He would do a scene over and over again. There were a lot of takes with Kevin telling people what to do and he was getting frustrated. Everybody was getting frustrated by it."[11]

This frustration also boiled over to Cinergi in Tucson. Filming had begun on May 17; two weeks later Jarre was already behind schedule. But it wasn't for a lack of effort. By June 2, Jarre and Leonard had filmed 27 scenes, 18¾ pages of script, 45 minutes of coverage and 272 set-ups in just 14 work days, an average of almost 20 per day. Not great but acceptable, though it wasn't what the studio wanted. According to producer Jim Jacks, "[Kevin] wasn't getting a lot of support from [executive producer] Andy Vajna. Andy had no real confidence in Kevin. At one point the actors began to have less confidence in him. When that happened, the flame was burning out."

Although action films were always popular, this genre really came into its own in the 1970s and '80s with films such as *Dirty Harry*, *The Poseidon Adventure*, *Earthquake*, *The Towering Inferno*, *Star Wars*, *Raiders of the Lost Ark*, *Superman*, *Beverly Hills Cop*, *The Terminator*, *Death Wish*, *Rambo*, *Lethal Weapon*, *RoboCop*, *Die Hard* and on and on. That's what the studios wanted, that's what they expected. Computer-Generated Imagery (CGI), special effects and unlimited, non-stop action. Granted, although a bit more difficult, Westerns could still fulfill that requirement. In fact, cinema viewers experienced the first 2-D animated effect in *Westworld* (1973) as well as 2-D digital compositing and 3-D CGI in *Futureworld* (1976).[12]

Featuring heroes, villains, magnificent landscapes and good over evil, Westerns explored our history and reflected our current politics and self-image, i.e., *The Wild Bunch*, *Butch Cassidy and the Sundance Kid*, *McCabe & Mrs. Miller* and *Heaven's Gate*. But a review of Jarre's early dailies revealed a failure to provide that type of action. According to those present, the first-time director wasn't getting nearly enough coverage and was shooting nothing but master shots. He struggled with composition and many of the scenes he did shoot couldn't be cut into other footage. Scene composition is the invisible structure that organizes shot elements into the imagery needed to tell a story. Consisting of point-of-view, focal point, paths of motion and the illusion of depth, a three-minute, wide-angle shot of four horsemen equally spaced across the screen and riding toward the camera, for example, can be excruciatingly boring without close-ups, framing angles, reaction shots, sound effects and music. Film editing is the art of assembling these various shots and scenes into a cohesive whole. Jarre was a marvelous writer, both energetic and forceful as evidenced by his insistence on period costumes and authentic saddles and firearms. But he didn't have the necessary directorial experience to bring his vision to fruition. Dialogue that had leapt off the page in the script now sounded wooden and artificial when filmed, and many actors' performances seemed forced and pedestrian, without emotion or flair. Experienced directors can evoke a unique atmosphere and even provoke heretofore unknown actor characterizations. With some exceptions, first-time directors can rarely do so as well. Jarre seemed oblivious to all this.

And to make matters worse, by June 5, Jarre was already $398,983 over budget. Executives viewing these dailies weren't pleased with what they saw and communications began to fly back and forth among the various parties. Producer Bob Misiorowski and unit production manager Terry Collis reviewed the script and eventually pulled five days out of the schedule and reduced the page count on other days to make filming more practical. Misiorowski knew the cast loved the script and feared they'd be upset at a point in production when unity was paramount. Nevertheless, executive producers Vajna and Feitshans told Jarre the cuts were required in order to meet the 62-day shooting schedule. However, they did offer an alternative: "If you disagree with these cuts—you are welcome to make your own cuts which will have the same result—but as of now—I have instructed Bob Misiorowski that the following scenes must be removed from the schedule—or be altered to make the schedule work."[13]

Entire scenes were cut and the roles of Kilmer, Boothe, Jon Tenney and Liza Zane were affected. Eliminated scenes included:

Scene #10: Doc Holliday and Kate Horony escape town after Prescott saloon incident.

Scene #13: Sheriff Behan shows Earps three cottages in Tombstone.

Scene #18: Josephine Marcus and actress discuss tall man.

Scene #19: Sherman McMasters helps Josephine in the Grand Hotel lobby.

Scene #21: Mr. Fabian and actress conversation backstage Shieffelin Hall.

Scene #27: Curly Bill Brocius, Ike Clanton and Johnny Ringo go after a Chinaman.

Scene #27B: Curly Bill full of hop outside opium den.

Scene #29: Wyatt and Virgil Earp outside of jail after Wyatt locks up Curly Bill.

Scene #42: Wyatt misjudges Cowboys, wants to go into the cattle business.

Scene #42A: Old Man Clanton and four others ambushed in Guadaloupe Canyon by Rurales.

Scene #47: Josephine is photographed inside C.S. Fly's studio.

Scene #57: Ike sends a telegram.

Scene #62: Ike, Billy Clanton, Frank and Tom McLaury have conversation in lot behind O.K. Corral.

Scene #64: Behan warns Cowboys that the Earps and Holliday are coming.

Scene #72: Behan confronts Josephine outside of Nellie Cashman's, Morgan Earp defends her while Curly Bill watches.

Scene #73A: Curly Bill and Ringo burst in on Mexican family in their adobe house.

Scene #75: Nightfall on Allen Street.

Scene #76: Interior of Oriental during storm.

Scene #77: Curly Bill gathers Cowboys at Rustler's Park.

Scene #78: Behan enters Josephine's hotel room.

Scene #90: Doc leaves Kate at Tucson train station.

Scene #103A: Wyatt and posse ride through blazing Cowboy camp.

Scene #107: Curly Bill plans ambush.

Scene #108: Wyatt plans to go to Iron Springs.

Scene #111: Turkey Creek Johnson and Texas Jack Vermillion give back money to Wyatt.

Scene #113: Billy Grounds and Zwing Hunt desert Cowboy camp.

Scene #114: Ringo faces Behan with newspaper.

Scene #115: Ringo, Behan and Billy Breakenridge ride into Cowboy camp.

Scene #120: Grounds and Hunt rob stagecoach.

Scene #121: Cowboy camp, Josephine speech regarding Mr. Fabian's death.

Some of these scenes had already been filmed but wouldn't be included in the film while others would subsequently be added back with different dialogue and/or characters.[14]

Aware that the young director was struggling, the studio even offered the assistance of award-winning writer-director John Milius. Known for *Dirty Harry*, *Jeremiah Johnson*, *Magnum Force*, *The Wind and the Lion*, *Apocalypse Now*, *Red Dawn* and other films, Milius volunteered to assist his friend without screen credit, but the offer was rejected. "They wanted me to come out there," admitted Milius. "I offered. I said, 'Yes, I will come out there. I will help Kevin. I will do everything.'" (However, according to author Michael Blake, *Hollywood and the O.K. Corral: Portrayals of the Gunfight and Wyatt Earp*, Jim Jacks told him that Milius declined the offer and claimed Jarre was okay.) Jarre would do it his way without any help whatsoever. This stubborn, my-way-or-the-highway attitude was doomed to fail.

"If we weren't afraid with a first-time director," says Vajna, "we'd all be nuts." By the first week in June, the studio executives were so concerned with what was being filmed, they inquired whether director John McTiernan was interested in taking over. McTiernan, known for *Die Hard*, *Predator* and *The Hunt for Red October*, had previously directed Cinergi's first production, *Medicine Man*, starring Sean Connery. Although attractive, the offer was rescinded when McTiernan requested a two-week shutdown to prepare and to review existing footage. An *Entertainment Weekly* article stated that according to sources on the set, Jarre wasn't thinking visually and even shunned advice from his own cinematographer, six-time Oscar nominee William Fraker (*WarGames*). According to remote head technician James Danicic, "One thing that drove Fraker absolutely nuts [was that] he wanted to shoot establishing shots last and do coverage first. But, wherever he wanted to do coverage, there was always shit in the background."

One episode in particular typifies Jarre's inexperience. Before a scene is filmed, it must be blocked. Blocking refers to the preparation activities that occur before the camera rolls. These activities include but are not limited to: determination of camera position and placement of actors on the set; lighting of the set; rehearsal of crew and actors; adjustments based on rehearsal; filming of the scene. This particular scene was filmed outdoors and as it was being blocked, Jarre insisted on moving the camera position. However, in doing so, the camera now faced the base camp. Advised Fraker, "Well, we can shoot here while they move the base camp a little bit at a time and then we can shoot there. The light's better this way; you don't have all the trucks." Jarre was adamant, "No!" So they would sit and wait while they moved the entire camp, then shoot that particular angle, and then turn the camera around. But now, the base camp was in view again so they had to wait once again to move it. Naturally, Fraker informed the director that wasn't practical:

"Let's do a big establishing shot and we can see what we're going to see." Jarre wouldn't have any of it and demanded that the base camp be moved—a time-consuming and very expensive undertaking. The end result was a day's lost efforts.[15]

There were numerous rumors on the set: Jarre was out riding his horse all day, he was drinking, he was going too slow, he was doing drugs and one even said he was deliberately being sabotaged: "[A crew member] had the shot list and [Kevin] would say, 'Did we get everything we need for this scene?' They'd say, 'Yes.' And he was missing two close-ups." One on-set rumor said that the only reason Jarre was directing was because the studio wanted his script; once they got that, they found a reason to get rid of him. Sam Elliott said, "A week into the fucking thing—a day if you were really watching—you knew this kid couldn't direct. It was shocking and, at the same time, it was heartbreaking, because he was a real nice-looking guy and a soft-spoken kid, and you just wanted him to fucking succeed because of the thing that he put together. If he had *any* talent—he could've sat back and had conversations; none of us were inexperienced actors at that point, and he had one of the best DP's in the business in Bill Fraker—he could've gotten through it. But he didn't. And what he was turning in was no good. A guy named Jim Jacks was producing that movie, and he was a very close friend of Kevin's. I think he's probably the one that got him the job directing it. He convinced the studio to stick with him." Fraker confided in one actor, "I keep telling [Kevin], I can't cut this." Added Jacks, "Kevin was shooting in an unconventional, old-fashioned, John Ford style, with very few close-ups, [and] Andy Vajna and others finally felt that when Kevin was finished, the movie wouldn't work."

Other actors were also worried, as Michael Biehn noticed: "[Jarre] wanted everything in this long master shot. That's the way they used to shoot in the '40s, and that's the way he wanted to shoot his movie. Val and Kurt and Jim Jacks were looking at dailies, thinking, 'This is not a modern telling of an old story. This looks like an old Western that is being shot back in the '40s.'" Added Biehn, "I had a conversation with Kevin … and said, 'Listen, Kevin. It's collaborative. Kurt's been doing this since he was three years old. He knows what he's doing. Listen to him. Or listen to Frank [Urioste, the editor]. Listen to Val. These guys are smart, they're filmmakers. They know what they're doing. Listen to them. Don't just turn your back on them like their suggestions don't mean anything.'" Russell himself even warned Jarre, "It's not working, and they're going to come in here and can you." "I was very disappointed with Kevin," admitted Biehn. "I told him he was going to get fired."[16]

Seconded Stephen Lang, "[Jarre] didn't know what he was doing. It was pretty demoralizing being on set with him as he sabotaged his own fine script, making it static and lifeless. He didn't create master shots so much as [he created] tableaux that didn't really have a start or a finish, just a frozen picture in the middle of something. That's fine if you are a painter or photographer, but it don't play in the movies." Catherine Hardwicke agrees: "It was interesting because [Jarre] had such a great knowledge of history and the period and his screenplay is fantastic. It's so detailed…. [But] I realized he didn't have pre-visualization skills, and most writers don't. He couldn't make the leap even though he had beautifully described it. He had a very limited view and he'd watched a lot of John Ford Westerns that were static camera and simpler. He wouldn't collaborate with his production designer and cinematographer. He was very stubborn; maybe he'd done too much research … and he wasn't open and spontaneous and creative."[17]

Over the next few weeks, Jarre continued to film such scenes as Hunt and Grounds preparing to rob a stagecoach, various vignettes at the Cowboy camp, the arrival of Fabian's dead body in a stagecoach, Ringo's death, and Wyatt's and Josephine's wild ride and subsequent kiss. Virtually all of this footage was either re-shot and/or eliminated from the final cut. Buckaroo Jake Johnson recalls a scene he filmed *twice*: "It was during the Vendetta ride. The Earps' posse was chasing the Cowboys. Stephen Lang turns to me and says, 'Kill 'em. Kill 'em. There's only four of them.' And I look at him and say, 'I think it time to start working for a living,' and I spur my horse and ride out of the scene. They shot my scene again at the end of the movie. I don't know what the situation was but [they] felt the line needed to be in it, so they shot the scene again. Knowing what the SAG day rate was, I did everything I could to get myself connected to the right people and have an opportunity to do that again before they found somebody else. I got in costume again, showed up with my horse and I got a second try at it but they still didn't use it."[18]

On Monday, June 7, Kevin filmed the scene where Wyatt rides to Rustler's Park and retrieves his stolen horse from Billy Clanton. Curly Bill avoids a confrontation and insists Clanton return the horse. After Earp asks, "How come you call yourselves Cowboys? Cowhands ride for the brand," Curly Bill replies, "Oh, we ride for a brand, all right," and gives Earp the finger. Naturally, this scene wasn't used.

Some cast and crew members believed that *Tombstone*'s too-tight shooting schedule stacked the deck against Jarre. "From the beginning they allotted too little time to do this movie," says Michael Rooker (*Cliffhanger*). "Kevin was trying to do it in the amount of time contracted for, which was way underestimated. No way in hell." Key Grip Mark Rainsford agrees: "I remember sitting down at one point before we shot the movie, because the schedule, it was 69 or 70 days. It was a pretty tough schedule and the first AD told us, 'You're not going to get this done.' They wanted to cut it to 63 days. He said, 'You're going to cut days from it and you going to need at least a week more to do this show.'"

After four weeks during which he says he gave Jarre every chance to improve, Vajna finally fired Jarre. "There was no goodbye," said Powers Boothe. "Kevin was incredibly crushed." *True West* magazine executive editor Bob Boze Bell was present when Jarre may have filmed one of his last scenes: "They were filming [the] scene of Earp rid[ing] into the cowboy camp [during the Vendetta ride,] on the Research Ranch property near Elgin. When [we arrived], several people wanted to kick us off the set ... it was like, 'What are you doing here?' and that kind of thing. I had a Canon camera ... and [the AD] turns to me, 'Hey, no pictures.' Very intimidating. There was a scene where ... Val Kilmer, Kurt Russell, Buck Taylor and Peter Sherayko ... have ridden across [a] wash and they [ride up in] sight of [the Cowboy] camp, and ... exchange words. Russell and Kilmer start improvising a scene where the posse rides up and over several rustlers and confronts them. Russell quirts one of the bad guys, tosses his hat to Kilmer and gets down to beat the daylight out of [the rustler.] (The hat takes off in the wind on the fifth take.) This seems totally made-up on the spot. When Russell punches, he actually says, 'Pow!' and 'Bam!' So Kevin comes up; 'No, no, no.' You can see he didn't like it and [Jarre] came in and model[ed] a Queensbury rules kind of fistfight where you had to use your fights in that exaggerated kind of old-timey kind of thing. Then Kevin backed away and said, 'Action!' Kurt would go into this really typical Hollywood kind of blocking the blow, it's like kids in the backyard to me. [Then, Jarre] said, 'Cut.'"

Jeff Dolan remembers, "Kevin had Kurt Russell punch a guy out. And the way he

In one of the last scenes Kevin Jarre directed, Sherm McMasters and Turkey Creek Jack Johnson get the drop on several Cowboys (courtesy Bob Boze Bell)

wanted him to punch him … it might have looked good for [the] camera, or he might have thought it looked good for [the] camera but it just wasn't a good solid guy punch. They almost argued over it. 'No, I want you to do it this way.'"[19]

Billy Lang is the Cowboy that Russell fights with. "Rick Terry and I had a really good scene that was cut out," says Billy. "We were just shooting the breeze at the campfire. You hear a gunshot, Rick and I walked out, and there's a riderless horse come running to us—it was amazing how the wrangler got it to do that. We walked out to get him, 'Oh oh. There's blood on the saddle.' We turn around and here comes the posse and Kurt gets off his horse and he and I get into a fistfight. He threw some pretty good punches."[20]

Jeff Dolan was also a part of this sequence: "I rode my horse over and showed up early that day. Adam Taylor, the first AD, called over because he knew who I was and said, 'I got a job for you. I want you to be a Cowboy riding into camp and we're going to do a POV.' I ride into camp past a bunch of guys and the camera films me doing that. Then they turn around and put the camera on a dolly and the camera becomes me. So basically, they're using me as a vehicle to show the different characters that are in the camp. It's my POV of the camp as I'm riding in but it was cut."[21]

"At the end of the scene," continues Bell, "Turkey Creek Johnson remarks that Florentino is getting away and turns to fire a Winchester at him. The first time he does this, he pulls, cocks and aims right at the gunsmith. Being a bevy of gun-savvy extras, they all dive out of the way. Turkey is oblivious to their very existence. In fact, each time this is re-enacted, Turkey's horse starts walking and he has to rein in and aim, several times per take. [After about 45 minutes,] Jarre walked towards us [and] sat down next to Jeff [who] was the historical consultant on the movie. [Kevin] was very slight, very small, almost fragile looking."

Constantly smoking, Jarre looked like he'd lost 15 or 20 pounds. One week earlier, scene #105 was filmed in which Earp and his posse attacks the Cowboy camp. Morey stated, "Every time I was on the set, Kurt Russell was at a distance from Kevin and I could hear him complaining about Jarre. I never saw [Russell and Jarre] together. I saw them once when they were filming a scene when the [posse] ride to the Cowboy camp when Wyatt [kills] Florentino. [The camp] was fairly large, almost 25 people. Russell was complaining to the producers that it didn't make any sense that the Cowboys wouldn't just shoot Earp as he came into view. He was very bothered by this and I remember him talking to Jacks about it. And I can't argue that point but that's not the way it's in the script. Kevin was adamant and he was going to do the script that he wrote."[22]

Several scenes were filmed the day before Jarre's dismissal. Bob Palmquist remembers, "My wife Laurie and I went out there the day before and we watched [Jarre] shooting

Historical consultant Jeff Morey (left) and director Kevin Jarre during a break on the Babocomari Ranch. Days after this photograph was taken, Jarre was fired and George Cosmatos was brought on to direct (courtesy Bob Boze Bell).

a couple of scenes. A bunch of cowboys are sitting around the campfire, one guy doing a dance on top of a beer keg. And Stillwell comes roaring in and yells that Old Man Clanton has been killed at Guadeloupe Canyon. [Stephen Lang] says, 'I guess that makes me leader of the gang.' And Powers Boothe says, 'You ain't got enough in your britches, boy.' That never made the cut. And the other one was the death of Indian Charlie (Paul Ben-Victor). He was killed by Wyatt and the posse. They ride up to the Cowboy camp and gun him down. In the version that Kevin shot, that's where Wyatt gives the famous, 'The Cowboys are finished in Cochise County and Hell's coming with me' speech. That occurs here rather than at the killing of Stillwell in Tucson. I got a chance to talk to Paul Van Victor a little bit after that scene was shot and actually gave him a copy of the coroner's inquest into Florentino's death. The next time I saw him, I said, 'How'd you liked that transcript?' 'Oh, it's great stuff.' Then he looked kind of sad and said, 'But I don't think my death is going to wind up in the picture after all.'"

Adds Palmquist, "[We] were behind Michael Rooker and Val Kilmer and Russell as those couple of scenes were [filmed]. Kilmer was very, very silent, Russell was doing a lot of complaining about Kevin Jarre and his direction of the picture. Michael Rooker was spewing forth some sort of obscenity-laden discussion about this and that and the other thing."[23]

The dancing Cowboy Palmquist was referring to is Jerry Tarantino, who was very impressed by Stephen Lang's horsemanship: "They had a camp setup, it was during the day and they had a small campfire going. They had me doing a kind of Irish jig around this campfire and [Curly Bill and Ike] were shooting at my feet, making me dance. [Jarre] asked all of the Buckaroos if they could [do an Irish jig]. I was the only one that came forward. I'd never done one before but they taught me how to do it. I got the nickname Dancing Jerry. We were drinking and falling and laughing. I filled the whole frame and they cut it. We were so disappointed. A Cowboy comes into this scene, pushes me aside and he went to Curly Bill and said Old Man Clanton has been killed. So Curly Bill and Ike have this close-up where they're having this conflict where Bill says, 'Okay, boys. This is what we're going to do.' [But] Ike says, 'Wait a minute. I'm the next in line. I'm the son. That was my dad.' Ike gets mad, runs and jumps on a horse, puts his foot in the stirrup, hikes his leg over the saddle and rides out of the camp. That was the end of the scene. They did that like 20 times, I am not kidding you. And every single time, Stephen Lang hit that stirrup, put his butt into the saddle and went out of the camp perfectly. It wasn't uncommon, at least in *Tombstone,* to do 10 to 15 to 20 takes. It was mind-numbing. But these guys would do it over and over and over and every single time it was perfect."[24]

In the Indian Charlie death scene, Russell and the posse ride in and Buckaroo Jemison Beshears was so keyed up, he bit his pipe in half. Reggie Byrum explains, "It was [Jemison's] birthday, they came right at him and he got so excited he bit his pipe in half. They were trying to get Buck Taylor's horse to run into a guy and the horse wouldn't do it, so the guy had to bounce off the horse himself."[25]

According to Rick Terry, "The last scene Kevin directed before he got fired was a night shot at the Babocomari. There was a hillside, kind of a steep hillside, almost a cliff, and they positioned a lot of the Buckaroos on their horses on this hill. And then Curly Bill comes and stands on the top of this hill and gives this speech, 'It's time to get wooly, boys...' and that was the last time I saw Kevin Jarre. In fact, when we finished shooting that, it was really late, Kevin Jarre was shaking all of our hands as we rode past him.

In this behind-the-scenes shot, Cowboys meet with Wyatt Earp at Rustler's Park on the Babocomari Ranch, near Sonoita, Canelo and Elgin (courtesy Larry Zeug).

Thanking us for the work that we did and making it look great and patting us on the back. Little did we know. That was the last time I saw Kevin."[26]

Jeff Dolan may have witnessed Jarre's actual dismissal: "At the end of the day, everybody's leaving, and we're all riding our horses back to the camp. I saw [Jarre] talking to Jim Jacks a couple of times, just standing in the pasture, the two of them talking. And the conversation seemed kind of intense and it wasn't like it was a fun conversation. I thought, 'Oh boy. Something's up. This is not good.' And then I heard that they just weren't happy with his work. They weren't happy at all with how the film was coming out."

But Jacks told Morey that he fought to keep Jarre. He thought the film could still be salvaged even if Jarre was the director and pushed the studio to keep Jarre right up to the very end. Nevertheless, it was Jacks who gave Jarre the word he was let go because in Jacks' words, "I knew [Kevin] best. [The conversation] wasn't pleasant." In retrospect, Jacks regretted not insisting Jarre direct a couple of smaller films before "attempting something as demanding and complicated as a big western."[27]

Continues Bell, "Jeff [Morey] called the next day and was very upset. He said, 'Kevin Jarre just got fired. I want my name taken off the movie.'" Morey said, "I didn't like the way things were going. I heard Curly Bill was killed in the river and Hugh O'Brian's scenes were cut. After I learned that the scene with the wagon master was eliminated, I told Jim Jacks that I wanted my name removed from the credits. That scene was important to me because it clearly indicated when Wyatt Earp first started to become mythologized. I worked for Kevin and was very unhappy how things transpired." Bell later interviewed

Michael Biehn, who said that Jarre wanted to do a different fight scene than Russell wanted and it pissed him off, so the producers fired Jarre. Word quickly spread around the set that the director was dismissed. Many were very surprised and angry, others expected it and still others thought their days were numbered. They expected the new regime would clean house and that those too close to Kevin would be gone. Sherayko felt the only reason he was kept was because of the Buckaroos: "Due to my relationship with Kevin, I probably would have been fired if I hadn't supplied the guns, saddles and re-enactors. I couldn't believe it." Buck Taylor noted that for all his years in the business, he'd never experienced anything like it. Parties were usually held every Saturday night in the hotel's bar and Kevin always insisted on buying the first round. But that day, after everyone heard the news, "it was like a morgue … everyone was walking around in shock." No one knew who would be fired next.[28]

Jarre took it like a gentleman, and insisted that those associated with him should carry on. The next day, Biehn ran into Kevin settling up his bill at the hotel front desk and thought that was a touching, classy gesture: "If that would have been me," admitted Biehn, "I would have driven away and never even done anything."[29]

It is not known if Russell was involved in Jarre's dismissal, but Kurt was fairly blunt in his opinion of the situation: "I had backed [Jarre] as the director. The biggest surprise was, he was as lost as a director as he was found as a writer. He was a brilliant writer, but it's a different job. Bringing it to life is a different job. He was really in trouble there. I told him early on, 'It's a shame you can't do *Tombstone* after you've had ten movies under your belt."

Production ground to a halt during the search for a new director. According to Stephen Lang, "Disney was going to pull the plug on that movie because it wasn't going well [but] Kurt Russell flew back to Hollywood and convinced these guys to not shut us down and that we could make a really great movie if we could bring in a shooter." In a 2006 *True West* interview, Kurt stated that the studio asked him to take over the project. "I said, 'I'll do it but I don't want to put my name on it. I don't want to be the guy.'" Russell had previously worked with Sylvester Stallone on *Tango and Cash* and knew that Sly had ghost-directed *Rambo: First Blood Part II* with George Cosmatos. Cosmatos followed that up with another Stallone flick, *Cobra*, and there were rumors Stallone ghosted that as well. So Sly not only knew what Cosmatos was capable of, he knew George could be controlled. Kurt called up Stallone and said he needed a guy. How about George? Russell must have convinced the studio of the practicality of this decision as just a few days later, both Cosmatos and John Fasano were assigned to the project. "I was in the [Cinergi Productions office] developing a script for *Die Hard 3*," said Fasano, "and [Cosmatos] was developing a Washington mystery, *The Shadow Conspiracy*. [We were talking in the hallway] when Andy Vajna opened the door to his office, saw us standing there and said, 'You. You. Come here. You are going to direct *Tombstone*. You are going to re-write it.' Before we knew it, George and I were on Andy's [Gulfstream GV] private jet headed for the set." Fasano received $40,000 for services rendered, including 11 revisions, all looping dialogue, and several rewritten opening narrations. (According to Fasano's widow Edie, John was supposed to receive writing credit but Jarre objected. The dispute either went into negotiation and/or WGA arbitration, and Fasano was awarded an associate producer's credit. As he didn't own the script's copyright, he never received any residuals. At the time that he worked on *Tombstone*, Fasano had already signed a deal with New Line to write and direct the movie *Battle Tech* which never materialized due to his efforts for Cinergi.) Cosmatos, who died in 2005 of lung cancer, recalled that the transition was quick, to say the least. "It was very tough. It's tough enough to prepare for any movie, so to be ready in three days and move in…. I read the script on a Wednesday, we made the deal on Thursday, and I was on a plane on Friday. Saturday, I changed some locations, some of the sets, some of the costumes. I changed some of the actors on Sunday, and on Monday we had a production meeting. By Tuesday we were shooting. So there was a kind of psychological turmoil on the set."

Stephen Lang was convinced that it was the right decision: "George knows how to swing a lens real good. When it came to the visuals, George was as good as anybody. Remember, he was working with no prep time and while George, I believe, loved and appreciated westerns, but he wasn't a student of western culture. But he was fortunate: He had Val and Sam and Kurt and myself and Paxton. He had a lot of actors who knew what they were doing and so, in a way, it was a little bit [of] 'Stand back and you let us do what we're doing and you capture it.' There's a lot of truth in that, but it's also slightly unfair because George does bring a very strong point of view to everything."[30]

However … if one analyzes various internal Cinergi documents, it's clear that Cosmatos was hired *before* Jarre was fired. In the director's aforementioned comment, he states that he finalized a deal with Cinergi on Thursday. The call sheets for Thursday (June 10) through Saturday (June 12) still listed Jarre as the director, which should not be a surprise—why announce the change before Jarre was notified? (Utilizing the director's shot list, a call sheet is distributed to cast and crew to notify them when and where they should report for the next day's filming. Usually developed by the second AD, then reviewed by the first AD and/or unit production manager, the final call sheet then is circulated around ten p.m. to all pertinent parties.) Virtually all of the film's principal actors were involved in scenes #43, #44 (partial), #77, #102–03 and #121 (partial). The second unit filmed that Friday as well. Kevin was even scheduled to direct scenes #102–03, and partial scenes #116, #121 and #146 on that Saturday. Cosmatos' name doesn't appear on any daily production report until Tuesday, June 15. So, if he was on location as he stated, he must have been ensconced somewhere out of sight. Having Kevin's name on Saturday's call sheet is not unusual. Even though many actors and crew members had a hunch Jarre might be dismissed, call sheets with his name still on them preserved the illusion that all was under control. And, although Cosmatos was already signed, something still could have changed that. Better safe than sorry.[31]

Known as a savior of troubled productions, Cosmatos was the beneficiary of an extremely lucrative contract to take *Tombstone's* reins. While Jarre received $200,000 for the script and $150,000 as a director, $7500 of which would be given to Lisa Zane, Cosmatos received $1 million, $250,000 of which would be deferred until the adjusted gross receipts equaled cash breakeven. In addition, he also had back-end participation: ten percent of 100 percent of the production's adjusted gross receipts in excess of cash breakeven until second breakeven was achieved at which time he would receive 15 percent of 100 percent. After filming was complete, he received an office in Los Angeles for one year from the commencement of post-production, a shared secretary, and two round-trip business tickets from his home in Vancouver to Los Angeles.

Tombstone was initially a non-union project. But once Cosmatos came aboard, it fell under the auspices of Director Guild of America (DGA) guidelines. To determine their eligibility to continue working on the film, a list of all assistant directors and other personnel under DGA jurisdiction was developed. Further, a schedule was provided that detailed the number of days each individual had with the DGA for purposes of working on the production, and all pay scales had to be brought up to minimum requirements. And, as mentioned previously, since it had been necessary to reshoot numerous scenes, each actor and his/her agent was contacted so that appropriate pay arrangements could be made for additional time, if necessary. The net effect was a significant increase in the film's revised budget—an additional $3.547 million that included $760,000 of current overage. The film's budget had now swelled to $25.333 million.[32]

With the production in a state of complete turmoil, in order not to lose their completion bond, some sort of filming was necessary. Among other activities, a completion bond guarantees the actors that their salaries will be paid in the event of project cancellation. So, as shooting had already been scheduled for Saturday, June 12, up stepped first AD Adam Taylor. Relates Buckaroo Reggie Byrum, "When they fired Kevin, the next morning we're on the set and here's Adam Taylor wearing a [white shirt and a] tie, and he announces to us that Kevin has left the film. He didn't use the word *fired*, but Kevin had been let go and left the film. [Adam] said, 'I'm first AD today and I just want to make sure they understand I'm serious about this because I want to be here until the picture is over. For the time being, I am the director of the film and hopefully in a few days another director will show up and I can take this tie off.'" According to Taylor's wife Anne, "That was his thing—a tie on Friday. He did wear the tie while directing and every Friday thereafter." It's likely Taylor shot some stock footage during this period; the producers knew nothing may be used but at least it showed the cameras were rolling.[33]

The production meeting mentioned by Cosmatos was held on Monday, June 14. As expected, many of the participants were less than supportive because most had been hired by Kevin or had joined due to the nature of his script. "If you think about it logically, there had to be something special about the particular project," mused Boothe, "or they never would have attracted the cast that they did. That, in my opinion, was extraordinary writing. Every character was a principal; every character had a beginning, middle and end that reflected the life of Tombstone in that era. No one was written as a typical good guy or bad guy, they were written as human beings." With Jarre now gone, many feared the quality of the production would severely suffer and that their roles would be diminished. As a general rule, production meetings are typically held to address concerns, discuss resolutions, share ideas and suggestions, explore new developments, insure that everybody is on the same page, and—a key element—inform cast and crew of sensitive issues and topics. Entering this meeting in the hotel, Fasano admitted he felt like a Christian entering the Coliseum. (Numerous little casitas on the hotel's grounds housed various production offices, including Accounting, Editing, Transportation and Production.) "Everyone in that room was angry, they want[ed] to kill each other," said Fasano, "and their dream project was on the verge of falling apart. Some wanted to know why I was needed. Andy [Vajna] says, 'Here's your new director, and your new writer.' Everyone was arguing against us, and it was huge." The hotel pool had been drained for re-plastering, so the various hotheads had nowhere to cool their tempers. Vajna told the group there was no way the current script could be finished in the time budgeted. (And if it *could*, the resultant film would be over four hours!) According to Fasano, "It wasn't enough to cut the script. [By the time Fasano released his first set of revisions on June 24, he had already cut 70 scenes and added 29 more.] Scenes would have to be conflated so that many of the great moments that got these actors to commit to the movie would not be lost." The actors were still unconvinced. "We didn't hire George because we wanted an action movie," says Vajna. "We're certainly not saying it hurt, because George made the action scenes crackle, but he also helped supply a visual element that we felt was badly needed. A lot of recent Westerns have deliberately gone for a drab, colorless look. I think people were ready for a truly gorgeous-looking Western." After Vajna said he supported Cosmatos, Russell stepped up and said he believed George could do it. That seemed to calm the waters a bit and the meeting concluded.[34]

In a January 1994 interview, Russell explained, "When we ran into the situation where Kevin was having problems, there were feelings that the script could provide an opportunity to make a better movie than was being made. It was also becoming apparent that we weren't moving fast enough. Because I spent so much time with Kevin and Jim Jacks on the screenplay, and because of my position in the movie, it was my position as well to make sure that this thing didn't fall apart. I wanted to give George all the help he had to have. Somebody had to step up and say, 'We're going to get this movie made, but it's not going to be easy.' It wasn't Powers Boothe's position, it wasn't Val Kilmer's position. It was mine. I had gotten the movie financed. I could not shirk that responsibility. So I banded the actors together and I explained to them that we had to make this thing happen—it was too good a project to give up on. And they did. They were champs, every one of them, and George was a champ as well. We all worked together from that moment on to do something that we felt was important—that was, bring Kevin Jarre's screenplay to the theaters."

Continues Russell, "There was no way George could have withstood the onslaught from everybody—wardrobe, props, action. He needed lots of time and help. I spent 20 hours dealing with *Tombstone* the movie in every other sense than my role. I didn't have a chance to play Wyatt Earp."[35]

Added Powers Boothe, "Kurt was our leader. He's been in the business all his life. But he's a team player all the way, and, in this case, he had to be. Because we got behind a bit with Kevin, when George came in, the first thing the producers did was rip out 20 to 25 pages of the script. And to Kurt's credit and Val's credit, they fought to put a lot of that stuff back in, even though a lot of it didn't have anything to do with their characters on the page. It's because, in my opinion, Kurt was smart enough to know that the writing was brilliant—and that if those scenes weren't there, it made his character and the story less. Realistically, we got almost everything back in the script—and I give Kurt, and certainly Val, and Jim Jacks a lot of credit for fighting to keep this great script together and to shoot it. Our attitude was, 'Hell, yes! Let's do this movie.' We had really juicy roles and you could see everyone just chomping at the bit to get at them. All of the distraction just brought us closer together."[36]

Dana Delany agreed: "[Kurt] was our leader, the captain of our ship. Wyatt Earp had a really good sense of justice and right and wrong. Kurt's very much like that in real life. He was able to mediate between all the egos. It's very difficult when you have a lot of good actors. They have to all have their little moments and get the attention they deserve."[37]

Michael Biehn acknowledged that Jarre's dismissal was hard to take: "It was sad for me. I liked Kevin a lot. He really wanted that script to be the way he wanted it to be. He wanted to cast it the way he wanted to cast it. He wanted the saddles to look the way he wanted them to look. He wanted the spurs to be a certain way. He wanted the mustaches to be a certain way. He wanted the dialogue to be a certain way. He wanted it shot a certain way. He wanted everything exactly the way he wanted it. And, you know? The filmmaking business is a little more collaborative than that."[38]

While the actors may have been a bit upset, many in the crew took it as a positive change. "I think a lot of people said it was about time," confessed camera focus puller Michael Walker, "because they could tell things were running roughly. I think they were almost happy about having the change because it was a tough set. They were open to the idea of getting a new director—fresh blood to put some life back into the crew and the movie. Time is of the essence when making a movie. Producers want things to run smoothly and quickly. Otherwise they're spending a lot of [needless] money." Bill Fraker may have been pleased as well. A crew member suggests, "[The dismissal] probably relieved Bill from the frustrations that he had with that director. He was frustrated with the way things were happening and the obstacles that the director put up against him to try and make a movie. From a camera experience point, the way things should be done, and the way a traditional camera director at the time is used to doing. I think he was kind of happy about it."[39]

Yorgo Pan Cosmatos was born in 1941 to a Greek family in Florence, Italy. He studied film at the London Film School and, in 1960, was an assistant director to Otto Preminger on *Exodus*. After experiencing success in Europe with *Massacre in Rome* (1973), *The Cassandra Crossing* (1976) and *Escape to Athena* (1979), he migrated to North America where *Of Unknown Origin* (1983), *Rambo: First Blood Part II* (1985), *Cobra* (1986) and *Leviathan* (1989) quickly followed. Known for blockbuster and action films, Cosmatos "developed a reputation for his ability to handle complex action shoots, aerial photography, and for turning around troubled projects." According to director Richard Donner, "George was just a wonderful, bigger-than-life character. You never forgot his entrance and hoped there would never be an exit." The loud, profane, cigar-chomping, chain-smoking Greek was often blunt, gruff and politically incorrect. These traits would be soon experienced by one and all on the *Tombstone* set.[40]

Despite Russell's apparent support of the incoming director, all was not what it seemed. Cosmatos had never directed a Western. He had never even worked with horses. Actor Tomas Arana observes, "Cosmatos showed up knowing almost nothing, not even which actor was playing which role. He obviously hadn't done research or prep or any of that, due to being hired shortly before." Despite his credentials and experience, how could he possibly take on a project of this genre? The only answer was a "ghost director." In this scenario, one director gets credit for the film while another is silently calling all the shots and working with the actors and crew. Over the years there have been numerous relatively successful films where a more-experienced director or even an actor has stepped in to assist a struggling novice. In some instances, the ghost director didn't want the credit; in others, they were contractually blocked from "officially" directing for whatever reason. The following films may have been ghost-directed: *Black Magic* (1949) director Gregory Ratoff–ghost director Orson Welles; *The Thing from Another World* (1951) Christian Nyby–Howard Hawks; *Poltergeist* (1982) Tobe Hooper–Steven Spielberg; *Return of the Jedi* (1982) Richard Marquand–George Lucas; *Rambo: First Blood Part II* (1985) Cosmatos–Sylvester Stallone; *Cobra* (1986) Cosmatos–Stallone; *Tango and Cash* (1989) Andrei Konchalovsky–Albert Magnoli, Stuart Baird; *Dances with Wolves* (1990) Kevin Costner–Kevin Reynolds; and *Super Mario Bros.* (1993) Annabel Jankel, Rocky Morton–Dean Semler, Roland Joffe.

Kurt Russell ghost-directed *Tombstone*. Not only have several cast and crew members vouched for that statement, but Russell himself confirmed it. Explained Russell, "I said to George, 'I'm going to give you a shot list every night, and that's what it's going to be.'

I'd go to George's room, give him the shot list for the next day, that was the deal. 'George, I don't want any arguments. This is what it is. This is what the job is.' And I said to George, 'While you're alive, George, I won't say a goddamn thing.'

"The vision that Kevin had as a writer, he couldn't realize as a director. That's an unfortunate reality. Within three weeks he was replaced by a man who had no concept of the screenplay but a very good eye. At that point, George and I had to become bed buddies ... here's this poor guy coming in on one day's preparation, and what's he supposed to do? Because of my position in the film, the task fell to me to make sure the whole thing didn't just fall apart.... I believed in the material and in Kevin's vision."

Some of the issues were very basic. "Logistical decisions—the base camp was an hour-and-a half's drive from the location," explained Kurt. "From the beginning we needed to cut 25, 30 pages of the movie but Kevin never got around to doing that. And I was the only one left who knew the script." Extra Glen Gold agreed: "It was quite obvious that [Russell] had quite a bit to say about how things were set up and how they were going to do them.... Russell would [give instructions], or they'd be talking and you'd see him change the lighting or change the camera angle. It was quite obvious that Russell was [directing activity]. Russell had some input on what they [were] doing." Another extra observed, "Kurt was essentially, very much an ad-hoc director. He was always consulting with George and when they would film a scene, Kurt would say, 'Hey, let's do it this way.' George would acquiesce without argument. [Cosmatos] would say, 'Do another one?' Kurt would say, 'No, that's good.' Or George would say, 'Okay, I like that,' and Kurt would say, 'Let's do it one more time this way.'"[41]

As Russell had indicated, he, Kilmer, Fasano and Jim Jacks would convene each evening in Kurt's room where they would craft the next day's schedule. Conspicuous by his absence was Cosmatos. Seconded Kilmer, "[Kurt] and I worked so hard, I eventually moved in with him and slept on the sofa when Goldie wasn't in town, so we could use the extra 20 minutes writing or going over [the] schedule, etc. We had to do a lot of work—lobbying for ways of looking at the screenplay to allow for stuff that was missed. We had challenge after challenge. Kurt is solely responsible for *Tombstone*'s success, *no question.* I was there every minute and although Kurt's version differs slightly from mine, the one thing he's totally correct about is, how hard he worked the day before, for the next day's shot list, and [the] tremendous effort he and I both put into editing, as the studio wouldn't give us any extra time to make up for the whole month we lost with the first director. We lost our first director after a month of shooting and I watched Kurt sacrifice his own role and energy to devote himself as a storyteller, even going so far as to draw up shot lists to help our replacement director, George Cosmatos, who came in with only two days prep. I was very clear and outspoken about what I wanted to do with my role, and actors like Powers Boothe ... and Bill Paxton, were always 100 percent supportive, even in the blistering heat and sometimes as the day would fade, at the possible expense of their own screen time. Kurt did this for the film virtually every hour. I would even go up to him and whisper, 'Go for another...' meaning another take when I thought he could go further, but in the interest of the schedule, he would pound on. Very Wyatt-like, come to think of it. I have such admiration for Kurt as he basically sacrificed lots of energy that would have gone into his role, to save the film. Everyone cared, don't get me wrong, but Kurt put his money where his mouth was, and not a lot of stars extend themselves for the cast and crew. Not like he did."[42]

Fasano had a similar recollection regarding the process: "We shot all day (or night), checked out the dailies from the day before, then after dinner Kurt and Val Kilmer would convene in my hotel room and we would dissect the scene [that] was going to be shot the next day. We argued. We talked about research they'd done on their own. They read the scene out loud. We played with variations, combining scenes to make the original point. As they paced and talked, the whole time I was typing—putting these new ideas into Kevin's original scene, stopping the bull session to read the complete scene to them when I thought it was ready. It went that way for seven weeks." Admitted Russell, "I ended up working every night until I had to pass out. After we worked all day, I would work on the script and on the directing. Usually after shooting I get a beer with the boys every time. But, I didn't do it this time because I had to work on the script every night."[43]

Robert Burke speaks for almost everyone when he describes Russell's work ethic: "Say what you like about Kurt Russell, but he put his heart and soul into it. He was trying to pick up the pieces. He was the guy staying up late. He was the guy saying, 'No, the camera angle's wrong.' And, goddamn it, he was always right. He had a feel for this thing. George was terrific but [Kurt] was coming in with camera shots and shot lists the next day and passing them to George. 'Oh, we need to get this,' or 'Oh, I want another rain truck here.' Very rarely do you see somebody of his caliber just want to push that up the hill every day. Could he be abrasive? Yeah, sure. But he was under a lot of pressure and it was always, I believe, with the best intention. Kurt was up at four o'clock in the morning, get to the set at five, shoot four scenes from six o'clock to four in the afternoon and now he's done. Yet he's still in costume, standing behind George's chair for another five or six hours. This guy wasn't [just] punching the clock, he was definitely [its] heart and soul."[44]

Slowly, steadily, by shaping, rewriting and eliminating, the group created a newer, leaner script to accommodate the revised schedule. But even though there seemed to be a tentative agreement with the new regime, many disgruntled actors were still leery, mostly about their roles and how they might be modified. Russell even volunteered to have his own lines cut and scenes reduced. Some, such as Boothe, felt Russell's involvement was the most essential ingredient: "Kurt took on something that no actor should be asked to do and he held this movie together. He fought for scenes for everybody. It wasn't just saving himself."

Fasano challenged the actors on their roles. "On their days off," explained the writer, "the individual actors would come to my room and I'd say, 'Okay, Bill [Paxton], you have these four scenes. We can only have three. What is important in this third scene to you?' That way I reduced the length of the script to fit the rest of the shooting schedule." But, he was also sensitive to the actor's needs and desires. He sat down with each lead actor and asked, "Why are you doing this role? What is it about this role that is important to you?" Based on their replies, he tried to make sure their character's important lines were not lost. While some feared their best lines and scenes would be eliminated, Kilmer wasn't so discouraged. Fasano: "I remember one day where I was a little frightened to tell Val that some of his lines had to be cut out of a scene we were about to film. He smiled and said, 'I have this makeup on. I have this accent, and I have my cup. You could cut all of my lines and I'll just sit there and cough quietly and steal the scene.'" ("I went to a dinner and Kirk Douglas was there," says Kilmer, "and he started poking me in the chest, laughing about the Doc Holliday thing, and he said, 'I don't know if it was true for you, but the hardest thing was [deciding] when to cough, 'cause you never know how much or how little.'")

Michael Biehn believes the film was saved by tearing scenes out: "Powers Boothe would lose a scene. I would lose a scene. Bill Paxton would lose a scene, or two scenes, or three scenes. Everybody's ego had to be massaged at that point. We were watching our characters disappear. Without Kurt's leadership, that movie would have folded at that point."

Others weren't as positive about these developments. Says John Philbin, "Some actors were upset about their parts getting smaller. That's normal for actors of that caliber when they sign up to do a thing and it turns into something else. A lot of actors were really fucking pissed, because they [had] signed up to do Kevin Jarre's script. [Then] when they got the new draft that they were going to be shooting, obviously, most of their parts had been cut. And they were pissed. I just watched that drama and said, 'Wow. This is tense.' George was not a friendly, warm, fuzzy, understanding director, so he's yelling at all these people that are great actors who decided to do this thing, and George just doesn't know how to direct actors. So there was tension." Tomas Arana agreed: "When Jarre was fired, the studio chopped the script apart and then eliminated all the Clanton base scenes and the Old Man Clanton role. They also then blended together many of the Earp scenes, maintaining most of Kevin Jarre's wonderful dialogue using words of the 1800s, but combining different scenes. So Stilwell's part and various other Clanton gang scenes were gone along with their various backstories and it became just all about the Earps and we Cowboys would just interact with them. It was a pity, because I believe Jarre wanted to show that the Clantons and the Earps were not all that dissimilar and that they had many common family things, etc." Some cast members even felt the production had turned into the Kurt and Val Show. Said one unidentified actor, "A lot of guys, Buck Taylor, Peter, all the other guys, even Sam Elliott [originally] had a lot more lines and a lot more [to do] in it. Paxton and all of them, and they took all their lines away. Kevin's script was more into the town and the people, the individuals that were in the movie, they had lines and more into their life … it was completely different than just an action show. And that's what we called it, the Kurt and Val Show. [However], I don't know it would [have] sold with Kevin's way of doing things. I think it would have sold but it wouldn't have been such a power-packed sell." Another actor claimed that most of the story "was about the five guys in the Vendetta posse. So Kurt cut all that out. He said, 'No, it's about Doc and I. Give us all the lines. Give us all of that stuff.'" Even producer Jim Jacks supposedly was upset about the direction the script was taking, and asked, "What about [everybody else in the film]?' Russell reportedly responded, "Rooker pissed me off. Buck Taylor is a has-been and nobody knows Sherayko." (Of course, one must consider who said this, and the circumstances under which this statement was made, in order to determine the veracity of the claim.) According to Philbin, Sam Elliott said that had he read the script the way it was finally filmed, "I wouldn't have agreed to do this shit." When Elliott nursed a beer in a bar one evening, someone approached and said, "Sam, you should have been playing Wyatt Earp." Sam just looked up at him with that look that he gives, and he said, "Tell me about it," and went back to his beer. Others weren't even sure they wanted to continue with the production.[45]

Jarre had hired Forrie Smith and the actor was extremely loyal. "When I was going to quit, I went in to talk to Val Kilmer," recalls Smith. Val quickly reached the heart of the matter: "What we have here is a Shakespearean play and we lost our Shakespeare." Forrie protested, "Well, I didn't come here to talk to Doc Holliday. I came in here to talk to Val Kilmer," to which Val replied, "Val Kilmer does not exist. Only the characters he portrays." Smith then went to see Kurt and Sam, who immediately changed Forrie's mind.

"Are you crazy?" asked Sam. "You're going to quit this job. You're healing up from a broken leg and getting paid all this money while you're doing it. Don't be crazy." Forrie remained.[46]

Smith wasn't the only one who wanted to leave. Lisa Zane recalls, "While on set, I heard Kevin got fired. I seriously can't remember if I was stunned by the news or not at all." She confided to a Buckaroo, "I don't know what I'm going to do. Looks like I don't have a job." That night, she and Jarre (already back in L.A.) were on the phone, and he urged her to stay on the picture if possible.

Matt Marich spent an entire day with her and discussed the scene she was going to perform at the Bird Cage. "I took a lifecast of her that day," remembers Marich. "Started sculpting the face and then I was supposed to have dinner with her and Catherine [Hardwicke] that night. So I called her room. Catherine answered and said, 'Man, it's a really, really bad time, I'll talk to you later.' Well, the way things happen in Hollywood is, you go back to your hotel and they have your stuff packed up and they tell you to leave. It was very abrupt and very short and I'm sure heartbreaking for that young lady."[47]

Tuesday, June 12, 1993. Iron Springs set, Sabino Canyon, Tucson. The cast and crew finally got to meet their replacement director, whose inauspicious greeting—"Where's my god-damn director's chair with my god-damn name on it?!"—quickly disabused any who thought they'd be working for a lightweight.

Billy Lang: "[The] first day George was on the set, we all go down to the set [in our] badass-looking costumes. We've got our guns on and our red sashes. Here comes George walking down the road. He takes one look at us and he screams at the top of his lungs, 'Adam!' Here comes Adam [Taylor]. 'Yes, George?' 'Who are these men with the rags? I want them out of my movie! Get them off the set!' 'Well, George,' Adam replied, 'they're the red sash gang. They're the bad guys.' George kind of looks at us and strokes his chin a little bit. 'Ah, I like these guys.'"

Cosmatos' bluster would set the tone for the rest of the production. Loud, crass, abusive, creative and talented, George deliberately set everyone on edge with his outrageous behavior. But why did this surprise anyone? Cosmatos had viewed this technique first-hand from the "apoplectic Prussian bully" Otto Preminger while on the set of *Exodus*. Demanding, confrontational, manipulative, abrasive and spectacularly ruthless with an intimidating treatment of actors, Cosmatos seemed to emulate the aforementioned traits of the man known as "the greatest producer and worst director in Hollywood history."

"[Cosmatos] was a whole different animal," said Sam Elliott. "George came into an impossible situation, and he came in with great passion. You can never say the man does not have great passion. Treated everybody not too good. I always go to the set and stand around when I'm not working, just to watch. I remember George coming up to me with his dark glasses, looking up at me from the top of his glasses, sticking his nose right in my face. And he said, 'Am I going to have trouble with you?'" Sam paused a second, looked him right back in the eye and said, "I don't know. Am *I* going to have problems with *you*?" George just laughed and replied, "Ah, we're gonna get along fine." They did. Stephen Lang agreed: "George had very rough edges, he didn't communicate in the best way some of the times, but once you got to know him, you had tremendous affection for him." Cosmatos was an acquired taste; he wore a ridiculous, cheap, straw cowboy-type hat, black socks and white tennis shoes, smoked five packs of cigarettes and drank 40 cups of coffee a day. No wonder he was so wound up![48]

Property master Steven Melton remembers, "When I met George, he just kind of screamed out in front of all these people, 'What was the last thing you worked on?!' 'Well,' I said, 'I just finished *Hard Target*.' He goes, 'Okay, I like John Woo. He's good. You're okay. You're okay.' And that was it. I was very fortunate that he liked the movie I had just done because many times someone new would show up on the set and George would scream at them, 'What are you doing on my set? What do you do?' And they would reply whatever. 'That movie is a horrible movie, horrible. We don't want that on this film. I don't want you.' So, that was George's interviewing process. He was really, really mean. And I remember so clearly Catherine Hardwicke, who if you didn't know she was a production designer back in those days, you'd think she was just an art department girl. Because she always had shorts on and a fanny pack and she was just full of energy. She came in with an original drawing she had done and George tells her how terrible it is and literally just crumbles it up and throws it on the ground. You could see tears in her eyes, she's on her knees picking up this drawing and George is saying, 'You dress horrible. I'd never, ever hire you as my production designer. You have no style!' Just screaming at her and walks away."[49]

Catherine clearly recalls her first meeting with Cosmatos: "I put out my hand to shake hands with him, and I was not only left hanging, he stared at my hand like it was a dirty diaper. He looked at it with disgust and said, 'You are the production designer? Who hired you?' He did not want to work with a woman; he told me I should have been a man. He said I should have been tall, with an English accent and wearing safari clothes, and not a woman. He was disgusted that he had to work with me, sight unseen. He would berate me all the time. 'You dress like shit.' And I'd be wearing stylish cut-off jeans and work boots. I didn't look like shit, but he did. 'What on Earth do you want me to be wearing?' Hardwicke asked him. 'I'm working out in the desert with rattlesnakes. I have boots and a water bottle and a hat. What do you want me to be wearing?'" Cosmatos' reply, "I want you to be wearing a long black dress and carrying a cigarette holder," was surprisingly weird, and Catherine was nonplussed. "At least what he said was kind of funny. But it was outrageous on a daily basis."[50]

According to medic Chris Swinney, "I made it all the way through without getting yelled at because I had kids and Cosmatos liked [my] kids and was always asking about [them]. The last day of filming, one of the actors came up to me and said, 'I don't have any footage. Here's my little camera. I've gotta go and do this scene. Would you shoot some footage for me of people and cast and crew and stuff?' So I was walking around shooting here and there and they did the scene and George yells, '*Cut!*' And he looks straight at me and goes, 'You!' and he points right at me. 'Who gave you permission to shoot on my set. Get off of my set!' The actor came by, 'Oh, dude. I'm sorry.'"[51]

Even animals weren't safe around George. One day the crew was on the Babocomari and Cosmatos wanted a simple shot of a horse drinking water. But he didn't tell the wranglers beforehand, so the horses had already been watered. George commanded, "Set up the cameras here. This is what I want. I want the horse drinking water right here." The jittery horse was now scared because Cosmatos was hollering. Bo Gray, who played the part of Wes Fuller, recalls watching all this with Sam Elliott. According to Bo, "Sam's right next to me and I'll never forget his words. Cosmatos just went off on this poor wrangler. Cosmatos said, 'Goddammit. He's not drinking. What do horses eat? They eat meat.' And everyone started to snicker. And the wrangler replied, cool as hell, 'All the horses on this set are vegetarian.' Sam elbowed me in the side and went, 'Goddammit, Gray. They shouldn't allow a director on this set that doesn't know that about horses.'"

So, production was halted about 45 minutes while this poor wrangler "is hauling ass in his pick-up, dirt's flying, to go get some oats to put down. Meanwhile, Cosmatos went over to craft services and threw some meat in front of the horse. "Have the horse stay right there," he yelled at the wrangler. According to onlooker John Philbin, "Russell and Elliott looked at each other and went, 'This fucking guy has no clue.'"[52]

Too bad Cosmatos didn't ask Buckaroo Jeff Dolan for advice. "Directors generally don't know anything about horses," admits Jeff. "Show me where you want the horses in the scene, you block the scene. We'll put the horses where you want them and once you're satisfied with where the horses are standing, we'll take the horses away and then you can finish lighting the scene, getting ready. Then when it's time for the horses to come back and you're actually going to shoot, we'll bring the horses in and put pellets on the ground and they'll stand there for you. They won't have to have halters on them and lead ropes, they'll just stand there. I'll just give them a snack and that should work for the length of time that you need to get your scene shot. It's stuff like that that a lot of guys don't know. They just don't understand—that happens a lot … planning and not being aware of what horses will do and won't do."[53]

"One time Kurt Russell kind of screwed up and George was very upset," notes Lee McKechnie. "And [Cosmatos] can't get upset with the actor, so he looks for an extra or someone who is expendable. [Then] he took an empty water bottle, and he was so upset when he was looking at the monitor, he looked around. He wants to throw it at Kurt and, of course, he can't do that. So he took the bottle and hit an extra with it who had nothing to do with the scene."[54]

With the replacement director's debut thus featuring such a bombastic series of tactless behavior, members of the production doubtless were asking themselves just what they had gotten themselves into. And why was the new fellow so belligerent? Perhaps it was insecurity. He had never directed a Western or a cast of this caliber before. Also, in many cases, a lack of confidence and uncertainty often manifests itself in self-doubt, nervousness. In other cases, recognition, bragging and narcissism with lacerating attacks against those who oppose them. Some directors are notorious for doing anything they can to get the performance they want and need on film. It may mean firing multiple people, making enemies, raising their voices and terrifying people, as opposed to gently holding someone's hand and working with them. Said one crew member, "I remember George Cosmatos looking around on the first day of shooting and he said, 'You know what the problem is? There's too many actors in this movie.' 'Cause he had to deal with all these fucking actors, and good actors who have opinions, and he knew nothing about Westerns." Cosmatos said to an actor, "You know why this film is going to be wonderful? Because I'm cutting all the women out."[55]

Nevertheless, Cosmatos knew how to ramrod an action film, which is what *Tombstone* turned out to be. And he knew what his role would be. Cosmatos angrily admitted, "I know what's going on. I know what I'm doing. My reputation is to rescue movies. I rescue movies from defeat and that's why I'm here and we're going to make a great movie."[56]

The first scene Cosmatos scheduled was the Iron Springs ambush where Wyatt kills Curly Bill. It was filmed over a three-day period at the lower Sabino Canyon recreation area of the Coronado National Forest, about 200 yards upstream from the dam. A popular area for hiking, jogging, wildlife-viewing, photography and picnicking, the location offers mountains, canyons and plants and animals in great abundance as Sabino Creek winds its way through miles of canyons before reaching the Sonoran Desert.

Cosmatos' concept of Curly Bill's demise wasn't what Kevin Jarre had in mind. Explains makeup artist David Atherton, Curly Bill was going to be] killed with a shotgun "which almost split him in half ... it was [to happen] just somewhere out on the ground, it wasn't in the river. And so in pre-production I had built a whole apparatus for Powers to wear. It was a body and you buried Powers into the ground halfway and you've got a body that's just shredded by a shotgun. So in the meetings [Cosmatos] would be telling me the things he planned to do differently so we could be prepared. He changed that whole scene into a river scene and Powers was just going to get shot ... and that was that. There was nothing prosthetic-wise or anything fancy." However, according to Blumes Tracy, second unit SFX, "That might be giving George a little more credit than he is due. The reason the water shot was changed was because we had a flood. When we scouted it, it was different than when we actually went and shot there. That was because there was still water there when we shot it." Changing the film's direction by Cosmatos, or the focus of particular scene, was not unexpected as the director had previously reviewed Jarre's footage and rejected almost all of it.[57]

The production team was ensconced at Sabino Canyon for several days. According to the script, Wyatt and his posse attempt to ambush the Cowboys at the waterhole. They dismount and creep toward two cowboys sitting around the campsite, seemingly undetected. Doc Holliday has a coughing fit and suddenly the opposite side of the creek explodes in gunfire. It's an ambush! Vermillion takes a graze, Johnson is hit by a ricocheting rock, Holliday is dragged to a tree truck for cover. All hide behind whatever cover they can find. Soon they are almost surrounded. Curly Bill laughs and baits the posse. Unexpectedly, Wyatt, with an almost supernatural calm, takes his shotgun, rises to his feet and advances toward the Cowboys. His clothing jerks as bullets rip through it, yet he remains unharmed. Curly Bill waves away his men's fire and walks out to meet his nemesis. He empties his six-shooter at Wyatt to no avail. He then raises his shotgun to end this shootout. But before his is able to do so, Wyatt fires both barrels of his shotgun, shredding Curly Bill and ending the dispute.

The first segments they filmed were of Wyatt's posse riding into camp, Turkey Creek and Texas Jack getting pinned down in the crossfire, the posse cleaning its guns after the shootout, etc. They also filmed an interesting scene featuring several Apaches watching the gunfight from the canyon's rim, but it was not included in the film. As this was Cosmatos' first day on the set, he was naturally a bit nervous, which translated into tension on the set. Stuntman Dickie Stanley attempted to ease the strain: "While we were practicing ... everybody was saying *bang* for their intended shots. Another person [and I] starting joking about something less mundane than *bang*, so we designated a different sound effect to all the outlaws. Ping, pow, pop, zing, whiz, etc. Well, when we set up for the next practice, everybody had new sounds for their simulated shots and when 'Action' was given they followed suit. As the sounds were being made, the posse stood up and was bewildered at what was going on. Before long, Kurt and Val started shooting imaginary machine gun fire at us and throwing fake grenades. It was a very interesting exchange. Most of the crew started laughing and it really calmed the mood. George came over and asked who was responsible. Several of the guys pointed at me, and he said he was grateful. 'But we really need to get back to work.' The rest of the day was very calm and pleasant."

Almost. Explains Cosmatos, "This was the first scene I shot in the movie ... it was written on land but I put the river between them to give it more quality, make it ... walk

George Cosmatos gives instructions to Kurt Russell, Val Kilmer, Peter Sherayko and Buck Taylor on the Iron Springs set at Sabino Canyon north of Tucson. Powers Boothe can be seen through the branches on the far right (courtesy Larry Zeug).

in the water and splash, it helps, an added dimension. Another level. I was waiting for a crane for this, a small [python jib] crane. I waited one hour, it was late [and] really delayed me the first day."[58]

Film aficionados know that all the elements of a particular scene—dialogue, action, stunts, special effects and sound—are not usually filmed or recorded at the same time or even at the same location. Weather, actor availability and many other factors come into play. And so it was with the Sabino Canyon scenes. At times the creek that ran through the canyon was bone-dry. "So, what they had to do is take white buckets and fill them full of water and put squibs in them," explains Buckaroo Larry Zeug. "As they're fanning down the Cowboys, if you see water popping up it's because they had squibs in these water buckets [to give the effect of bullets hitting the river's surface]. As this was the only scene of the Cowboys shooting, they could lay the camera track right down in the bottom of the river." (Squibs were also used to kick up the sand in front of both the Cowboys and the posse.) At other times, the creek was a mere trickle so water trucks were brought in to fill the stream bed. Then, the cameras were turned to the opposite bank to show gang members shooting at the posse. Some of the gang members were Buckaroos while others were stuntmen. Continues Zeug, "At first we only shot from the angle of Wyatt's posse firing and you never saw the Cowboys [in the brush]. I was running around helping everybody load. Being a gunsmith, I was helping the armorer because he couldn't take care of all the various scenes. So I was loading the guys but you don't see anybody, you just see the gunfire and smoke coming through the trees."[59]

A special effects guy who was shooting dustball hits at Wyatt's posse accidentally shot a hole in Kurt's hat that was lying on the ground. Russell blew up, saying he wanted to keep the hat and the special effects guy ruined it. Pressures and tensions were high and Peter Sherayko, who was within five feet of the incident, said the dressing down Kurt delivered wasn't pleasant. After that segment was complete, Cosmatos began to film the next portion of the scene when Earp shouts, "No!," emerges from his cover, and starts to cross the stream toward Curly Bill. The Buckaroos were shooting their rifles from across the stream and production had previously informed them, "Okay, when Kurt gets to the water, stop shooting for dialogue." Prior to filming the scene, Powers Boothe gave the team a real pep talk and told them they were unstoppable bad asses, whereupon several members apparently got carried away and kept shooting their rifles. According to John Peel, after this happened a second time, "Kurt walks all the way across the creek, still in full Wyatt Earp mode, walks up the bank right in the middle of where we are, looks at us and gives us an ass-chewing. He says, 'Guys, this shit is costing us about $5000 a minute and every time you fuck up this setup, it costs money! And when I say stop firing when I get to the edge of the water, that mean stop fucking firing!' And, of course, we're all as small as we can be as we've already seen a lot of guys get fired. No one wants to get fired."[60]

Rick Terry was also present that day but has a slightly different memory of why they were told to cease firing: "The reason for that is safety. There's a little wadding in the blank that actually comes out the end of the barrel and it's not a very long distance but we didn't want to take a chance of hitting Kurt with one of those wads. [After Kurt got upset,] we got this big lecture about safety and the next day when we got our call sheets, there was a big notice on there about safety, safety, safety, and being retold to be careful."[61]

Based on Garrett Roberts' suggestion in an attempt to ease the tension, Boothe gathered all the Buckaroos together and told them, "One last photo before we're all killed," and posed with 12 Cowboys: Logan Clark, Garrett Roberts, Rick Terry, Jeff Dolan, Bill Luce, Chris Ramirez, Charley Ward, John (Bronc) Peel, Reggie (The Apache Kid) Byrum, Billy (Billy Concho) Lang, Chuck Milner and Tom Ward. Other Buckaroos were present but were not included in the scene. Jerry Tarantino was bluntly told by Cosmatos, "Hey, you! Wild Bill Guy. Outta here!" Apparently, Jerry's Hickok appearance was so unique and recognizable that the director didn't want him appearing in too many scenes. Jerry had been hired by Peter Sherayko, as had four other Norco Desperados: Curt Stokes, Marty Kottler, Len Ellonero and David Bireo. Jerry was the only one to appear in the film; his wife Kathy was Dana Delany's stand-in.[62]

The scene continues as Curly Bill and Wyatt meet in the middle of the stream. During rehearsal, Boothe is brought out into the water in a small boat, then steps off into the river. Once filming starts, Bill fires a shotgun, misses Earp, throws the weapon into the river and pulls out his six-shooters. "Well, that was my shotgun," said Zeug. "I didn't see the gun until we're shooting this scene and they brought it out and somebody was blowing it out with an air hose. I said, 'What the hell did you do to my shotgun?' All of a sudden I hear my name called over the speakers. Everyone's hollering, 'Where's Larry? Where's Larry?' So I go down there. 'What's the matter?' Right before lunch, they broke the mainspring in that Stevens shotgun. There are two mainsprings because it's

"One last photo before we're all killed." Powers Boothe and the Red Sash gang at Sabino Canyon. Front, left to right: Logan Clark, Garrett Roberts, Powers Boothe, Rick Terry (behind Boothe), Jeff Dolan, Reggie Byrum (kneeling next to Boothe), John Peel, Billy Lang, Chuck Milner, Tom Ward (photo's edge). Middle three, top to bottom: Charlie Ward, Chris Ramirez, and Bill Luce (courtesy John Peel).

double-barreled and there are two locks on each side. 'Larry, we need you to see if you can fix this gun. The production company doesn't know it's broken.' They'd shot one scene with Kurt Russell and now it's broke. We're out with our trucks and stuff. I said, 'Got my tools out here but there's no power to run an air compressor.' And I didn't have an air compressor with me. What we did, we went up to the special effects trailer, hooked an air hose to a nitrogen bottle and I made a mainspring during lunchtime. The production company never knew it broke and after lunch we went back to shooting that scene."

The shotgun that Kurt Russell used was a J. Stevens three-trigger shotgun: When you pull the front trigger, it allows the barrel to tilt forward to eject the empties. Explains Zeug, "Fred White loaned the real Wyatt Earp his shotgun, which was originally a Stevens shotgun. So, Peter had picked [one] up and we had it re-blued. Three stocks made by Bishop. But there was only one shotgun."[63]

They filmed that portion of the scene several times and, apparently, when the shotgun discharged, it didn't sound loud enough. So someone had the bright idea of adding additional powder to make a louder explosion. Rick Terry describes what happened next: "So when Kurt marches out to fire the gun off, there was a cameraman who was holding the Steadicam pretty close to [him]. When he fired that shotgun off, that powder set that guy's clothes on fire. Of course, everyone ran and put the fire out; it was kind of an embarrassing deal because after we had the big safety lecture, those guys on the other side of the creek went and did something like that."[64]

Interestingly, dialogue that embodies the essence of this film is included in the scene's aftermath, yet it wasn't even written for *Tombstone*. As Wyatt sits by the river's bank, Holliday, Sherm McMasters and Turkey Creek Johnson squat near a tree. After Holliday

Exhibition shooter, armorer, stuntman and consultant Thell Reed guards the weapons at Sabino Canyon (courtesy Christian Ramirez).

has yet another coughing fit, Johnson asks, "Doc. You ought to be in bed. What the hell are you doing this for, anyway?" Doc simply replies, "Wyatt Earp is my friend." "Hell, I got lots of friends," says Creek. Holliday's response ("I don't") says it all. According to historian Jeff Morey, this exchange came from a script Kevin Jarre had written for a proposed but unproduced new version of *The Magnificent Seven*. Apparently Jarre didn't care for John Sturges' version.[65]

Buckaroo Larry Zeug was also the production's gunsmith. One day there was an issue with the 1873 Winchesters. Peter Sherayko told Zeug, "Larry, I got a real serious problem. All the original '73 Winchesters … when you kick the level down and pull it forward, the firing pin sticks back and the bolt goes forward and the gun's jammed up. Well, there's a part that goes in this action that goes into the firing pin which drags the firing pin forward that stays in the bolt. Oh my God, What are we going to do? All these guns are missing this part—they're all not working." Zeug was able to solve the problem but when they were filming the scene at Sabino Canyon, a more serious issued raised its ugly head. Says Larry, "Buck Taylor was shooting an original Winchester '73 and [he told me,] 'I don't know what [second unit armorer Johnnie Mitchell's] done with this thing but I told him I wanted an empty casing to fly out of the gun when I lever it for this scene.' [The scene Taylor is referring to is the one where a bullet hits the tree in front of Texas Jack and scatters wood all over his face.] I looked at it and said, 'Buck, somebody's jammed a .45 in this thing.' These are all original rifles—they're .44–.40s. So I had to strip the gun down to get this [bullet] out. I told Buck, 'I've got .44–.40s dummies in my gun belt but I got to go back to the truck.' Buck said, 'Don't worry about it, Larry. The hell with it. I'll shoot the scene without it.' About that time, Mitch came out and said, 'What did you get out of it?' I said, 'Somebody put a goddamn .45…' He said, 'They're all .45s.' 'No, they're not. The originals were .44–.40s. They never made .45s.'" Problem solved.[66]

The company later convened near a small stream on the Babocomari to film Texas Jack and Turkey Creek discussing the battle's aftermath. As Wyatt "walks on water" in the background, Jack asks, "You ever seen anything like that before?" An incredulous Creek can only reply, "Hell. I ain't never even heard of anything like that." On Saturday, August 9, they finalized the Iron Springs shootout and returned to Sabino Canyon, but the stream was dry. So they went back to Mescal, built a small wooden platform and as Russell shouted, "No!" and fired his shotgun about two dozen times, they filmed him with the sky as a backdrop. That cut lasted less than two seconds but it showed Earp's determination.[67]

FIVE

Culture Shock

John Henry Holliday was born August 14, 1851, in Griffin, Spalding County, Georgia, the only son of Major Henry Burroughs Holliday and Alice Jane McKey. The latter died of tuberculosis when John Henry was 15. Just three months after Alice's demise, his father married 23-year-old Rachel Martin. Since his mother's bacterial infection was highly contagious, John Henry was later diagnosed with pulmonary tuberculosis as well. Holliday was also born with a cleft palate that was surgically repaired by his uncle, John Stiles Holliday. The youngster had speech therapy as well as piano lessons, both to help him overcome his shyness. A Southern aristocrat, Holliday earned a Doctor of Dental Surgery degree from the Pennsylvania College of Dental Surgery in 1872 when he was but 20, and shortly thereafter began his practice in the Atlanta office of Dr. Arthur C. Ford. After an alleged incident where Holliday may have shot and killed a Negro in a whites-only swimming hole, and in the hope that the Southwest's dry desert air might prove an effective remedy for his poor health, Holliday boarded a Western & Atlantic train in September 1873 and traveled west to Dallas. After a short stint there as a dentist, his continued poor health and subsequent lack of patients forced Holliday to find another source of income. Given his education, intelligence, dapper appearance and refined manners (he looked and sounded like a gentleman), he gravitated toward a profession where such assets could be put to good use: professional gambling. To protect himself from unhappy patrons, he carried a gun in his shoulder holster and another on his hip, and a knife as well. Professional gambling was a dangerous, unsavory trade, and over the next several years, Holliday built his reputation and was said to leave a trail of bodies in cow towns from Texas to the Kansas Territory, and from Wyoming to New Mexico. Virgil Earp once stated, "Tales were told that he had murdered men in different parts of the country; that he had robbed and committed all manner of crimes, and yet when persons were asked how they knew it, they could only admit that it was hearsay, and that nothing of the kind could really be traced up to Doc's account." A book written by distant relative Karen Holliday Tanner states that while Holliday had been arrested 17 times before the O.K. Corral shootout, only once was it for murder … and he was acquitted.

In Fort Griffin, Texas, Holliday met an attractive dance hall girl and prostitute who had a rather large proboscis—the Hungarian-born Mária Katalin Horony, better known as "Big Nose Kate." Fort Griffin also is where Holliday supposedly killed fellow gambler Ed Bailey. In a story attributed to Wyatt, Bailey and Holiday were playing cards and Bailey continually looked at the discard pile, which was against the rules. After warning Bailey several times to no avail, Holliday took the pot without showing his cards, which was also within the rules. A furious Bailey went for his pistol but Holliday was quicker and stabbed him with a knife. Bailey died and Holliday was detained in his hotel room. The resourceful Horony started a fire in a shed behind the hotel as a diversion, and while everyone ran to put out the flames, she walked into Doc's room, gave him a revolver and the duo calmly left for Dodge City. Great story, full of intrigue, death and romance, but unfortunately, it's not true. There is no evidence in any newspaper articles or court records of this incident, although Holliday was held under guard in his hotel room for "illegal gambling." Horony did set a fire, however, and the couple did escape to Dodge.

While Wyatt tried to maintain the peace in Dodge, older brother Virgil and wife Allie were living a prosperous life in the Arizona Territory. Virgil was busy—stagecoach driver, night watchman, owner of a sawmill, Prescott constable—and in November 1879 even became a deputy U.S. marshal for the area that included Tombstone. According to Wyatt, by 1879 Dodge City "was beginning to lose much of the snap which had given it charm to men of restless blood." So in September he resigned his position and, along with Mattie, his brother James and wife Bessie, left for New Mexico to take advantage of the area's silver-mining boom. Holliday and Elder joined the foursome in Las Vegas, New Mexico, and after a short stop in Prescott where they met Virgil, the Earps continued on to Tombstone. While James found employment there as a bartender, Wyatt staked several mining claims. He'd even brought along 15 horses and planned to start a stagecoach service, but when he got there, he found that there were two stage lines and sold his outfit to one of the other companies. Wyatt eventually found work as a Wells Fargo security guard. Brothers Warren and Morgan arrived in the summer of 1880 (as did Holliday). For the first time in a long time, all the Earp brothers, save Newton, were together again. Shortly thereafter, Wyatt joined Virgil as a deputy U.S. marshal only to resign three months later. But before he did, Wyatt was involved in the arrest of Curly Bill Brocius for the murder of Marshal Fred White.

Liked and well-respected by the Cowboys, White was considered far removed from the complex business, personal and political rivalries that involved so many Tombstone residents. On the night of October 28, 1880, White successfully disarmed numerous Cowboys who had entered Tombstone and began drinking and shooting into the air—"disrupting the peace." Confronting the drunken Curly Bill, White demanded his weapon. Brocius obliged, handing the half-cocked six-shooter to White barrel first. When White grabbed and pulled the gun, it discharged, the bullet striking White in the groin. Wyatt, coming upon the scene, didn't realize that Brocius had dropped his weapon, and so pistol-whipped the outlaw, knocking him unconscious. At this point, he and Morgan arrested him. Curly Bill was taken to Tucson and held in protective custody. Before he died, White testified that the shooting was an accident and Brocius was subsequently acquitted. However, hostility was brewing, and Earp's treatment of Brocius only increased the tension between the Cowboys and the lawmen.

This increasing animosity was at once both complex and elementary. The Earps represented law and order, and were sworn to uphold the peace in an increasingly violent town. The Cowboys, unaccustomed to being told what they could or could not do, resented any authority over affairs conducted outside city limits. On September 18, 1881, the Tombstone Epitaph bluntly told its readers, "It has come to pass in this county that life and personal property are unsafe; even in the town of Tombstone it seems as if one of the leading industries is to be destroyed. There is not a teamster today who is not in fear and dread of the cowboys, or so-styled "rustlers" depriving him of his hard earnings…. How must such men feel to be robbed by a hand of thieves and cutthroats, who take pride in announcing to the public that they are 'rustlers!' These chaps seem to have no difficulty in evading the law, *while others, not inclined to work, daily join the band and they are increasing fast in numbers." But this was more than just a matter of authority vs. free will. It was politics. The creation and settlement of Tombstone had brought along with it Northern (i.e., Republican) sympathizers, carpetbaggers and industrialists who sought to civilize the West. The result was a fundamental conflict over resources and land, and development vs. agrarianism. As these citizens increasingly dominated local law and politics, ranchers and those who supported them (i.e., Democrats) felt their tenuous control of the wide-open ranges slipping through their fingers. However, the latter found a friend in corrupt Cochise County sheriff Johnny Behan, who tended to side with the Cowboys and ranch owners in all matters—the sheriff allowed them free rein as long as they paid him a ten percent tax on their stolen cattle. As a result, Behan casually ignored horse thieves and cattle rustlers, which further intensified ill will with the law-and-order factions. As Georgetown University assistant history professor Katherine Benton-Cohen says, "Federal officials in the U.S. and Mexico ... wanted the Cowboy violence contained to avoid an international controversy with Mexico. Cowboys were going into Mexico, stealing cattle and murdering their Mexican owners. Officials were calling for a Border patrol—not to stop Mexican migrants coming north, but to apprehend American criminals going south." Monies and cattle "procured" from these nefarious enterprises naturally found their way into the hands of Tombstone's saloon owners and local businessmen, who of course supported the Cowboys' generous spending habits. In a May 27, 1882, interview with the* San Francisco Examiner, *Virgil Earp stated, "Concerning the fights between the Cowboys and myself and brothers, it has been stated over and over again that there was an old feud between us and some of our enemies, and that we were fighting only to revenge personal wrongs and gratify personal hatred. All such statements are false. We went into Tombstone to do our duty as officers. To do that we were put in conflict with a band of desperados, and it resolved itself into a question of which side could first drive the other out of the country, or kill them in it."*

Upon Wyatt Earp's resignation, Johnny Behan in November 1880 was appointed undersheriff of Pima County. Behan had held numerous governmental positions that included sheriff of Yavapai County, delegate to the Arizona Territorial Legislature, census marshal, sergeant-at-arms and Mohave County deputy sheriff. He'd also been a saloon keeper and livery stable owner. While in Prescott in 1875, Behan had divorced his wife Victoria Zaff when he'd begun a liaison with prostitute-courtesan Sadie Marcus-Sada Mansfield-Josephine Marcus. After a brief return to her family in San Francisco, Josephine may or may not have arrived in Tombstone on December 1, 1879, as a part of the Pauline Markham troupe, and performed in the stage production H.M.S. Pinafore. Eventually, she and Behan lived together as husband and wife although no marriage record has been found.

In February 1881, the eastern portion of Pima County, which included the area around Tombstone, was split off to form Cochise County, and Behan was appointed county sheriff. It seems Wyatt and Behan entered into some sort of deal—if Wyatt agreed not to oppose Behan's appointment, Johnny agreed to name Earp the new undersheriff. Once appointed, however, Behan reneged on his promise and instead named prominent Democrat Harry Woods to the post. Naturally, Earp was furious and vowed revenge. At some point that same year, Josephine found Behan in bed with the wife of a friend and kicked him out of their house. Shortly thereafter, she may have begun a relationship with Wyatt.

During the period between July 1880 and October 26, 1881, Earp held several positions, including U.S. deputy marshal, Pima County deputy sheriff and Tombstone deputy city marshal. During those same 15 months, he was also involved in a series of altercations with

Behan and Cowboys: the return of his race horse after Billy Clanton had stolen it … stolen government mules … the court's repeated failure to convict Cowboys … and constant death threats. Other events fueled the fire: That July, Behan arrested Holliday for alleged involvement in the murder of a stagecoach driver, and in September, Virgil arrested Frank Stillwell, one of Behan's deputies, and Pete Spence for another robbery. The tensions all came to a head at the O.K. Corral.

With that portion of the filming complete, Cosmatos moved back to the Hooker Ranch set on the Babocomari, where during the week of June 21, several additional scenes were filmed: scenes 118, 135 and a reshoot of scene 121 (all later eliminated from the script); scenes 122 (Wyatt bids farewell to Josephine), 133 (Earp, Johnson and Vermillion ride off from Hooker's Ranch), both reshoots of Jarre's footage; and scenes 124 (Fuller and Claiborne are killed by Breakenridge), 125 (Breakenridge brings their bodies to the Hooker Ranch), 128 (Cowboy gives message to McMasters from Ringo), and 130 (McMasters' body is dumped near the Hooker Ranch house). Interestingly, these last two scenes were filmed several different times. On Monday, May 24, Jarre filmed four takes of Buckaroo Bob Vincent riding down a rather long, steep hill. Once he reached its base, Vincent dropped McMasters' dead body from across his saddle. Each time they did a countdown to the drop zone so when Rooker was pulled off the saddle, he could land on his feet, then drop and roll. Cosmatos later replaced Vincent as he thought the Buckaroo looked too much like Sam Elliott and it might confuse the audience. Cosmatos then re-filmed this last scene; Buckaroo Frank Castanza originally delivered the message to Kurt Russell, but when it was later reshot by Terry Leonard in mid–August, Castanza had already departed the set to work on *Geronimo*, so Matt Feitshans was used instead. But by now the grass in the original scene had turned from green to brown, so a neutral background was used when Feitshans delivered his lines.[1]

On Saturday, June 26, the shooting schedule moved production to Old Tucson where the first few days were dedicated to soundstage filming. While the studio was closed to the general public when production filmed outside, tourists were allowed on the grounds when filming took place inside on the soundstage. Extras accessed the set through the use of special passes. A portion of its massive 12,800-square-foot interior had been configured to represent the opulent, gilt-edged Bird Cage Theater, complete with raised stage and the balcony's "entertainment" partitions. The set decorators took pains to assure that the stage curtain accurately advertised period-authentic stores: G.F. Spangenberg Gunsmith, J. Myer(s) & Bro. Clothiers and J.A. Hoff, Assayer. The curtain was decorated with a replica of the famous portrait of Fatima (Farida Mazar Spyropoulos), the belly dancer who performed at the Bird Cage in 1881. Bordering the bottom of the curtain was the town motto: "Pure Water. Wonderful Climate. Good Schools." Hand-painted murals lined the outer facings of the balcony while red velvet curtains bordered the partitions. Even though the soundstage contained adequate modern lighting, the scenes filmed there required period gas lamps, candles and stage footlights, all of which added to the overall ambiance but also created an almost unbearable heat. Buckaroo Kane Rubalcaba: "We're sitting there, it's like 110° outside, and 120° inside and we're dying. And Harry Carey, Jr., kept screwing his lines up. I swear I lost 30 pounds just sweating my ass off for this thing. Of course, we're sitting there smoking cigar after cigar after cigar, drinking whiskey [that] was apple juice, [and it started to get sour]. And we kept going, 'Back to one. Back to one.'" Eventually, they decided to continue filming the scene but shot Carey's segment

The interior of the Bird Cage Theater, constructed on the Old Tucson soundstage and ready for the *Faust* sequence (courtesy Larry Zeug).

separately. A small orchestra, complete with timpani drums and bass, provided musical entertainment while benches and chairs for the patrons were strategically arranged on the floor.[2]

The etymology of the name "Bird Cage" is both interesting and entertaining. One version explains that the balcony containing the private "entertainment" sections appeared like a bird cage suspended from the ceiling. Another version suggests that the "percentage girls" (prostitutes) who served drinks to the compartment patrons were always cheerful and sang like birds while they worked. Drinks were sold for a dollar each, the waitresses received 20¢. Still others said the name was given to the theater after entertainer Eddie Foy played the venue and had a conversation at the bar with songwriter Arthur Lamb. Lamb asked Foy, "What do you think of Tombstone, Eddie?" Foy replied, "They should have called it a coffin, long and narrow." Lamb laughed as he pointed to the cribs overhanging the casino and said, "This place reminds me of a bird cage, you can see those girls with the feathers in their hair, serving kisses and champagne and giving other favors. Those women are like birds in a gilded cage." Foy replied, "Sounds like a title to a song." Lamb began writing the words on a napkin and when Foy read the lyrics, he insisted, "That's a song that only a woman should sing." Lamb gave the lyrics of "She's Only a Bird in a Gilded Cage" to Harry Von Tilzer for musical arrangement. Von Tilzer insisted that he would not write the music unless Lamb made it clear that the girl in the song was a rich man's wife, not his mistress. Later, the famous singer Lillian Russell made "She's Only a Bird in a Gilded Cage" one of the most popular songs in 1900 when it was published; the theater then changed its name to the famous moniker. However, newspaper articles at the time clearly show that the theater was known as the Bird Cage Opera House on December 27, 1881, the day of its grand opening. Built on 30 × 120-foot Lot 9, Block 5, on the south side of Allen Street, the theater was first known as the Hutchinson Variety Combination, then the Hutchinson Variety Theater, and the Bird Cage Opera rooms before it finally became the Bird Cage Theater.[3]

Even though it is only seen on the screen for a second, a great deal of effort went into creating an eight-page prop program for the evening's show. Titled *Pinafore on Wheels Presents the Pauline Markham Pinnafore Troupe*, the presentation consisted of three performances: "Prof. Gillman and his Ballet of Gravity," "Selections from the Bard by Mr. Romulus Fabian Tragedian in Excelsis" and "Faust—Or the Devil's Bargain." The meticulously detailed program featured advertisements for such period-correct products as Robert Bacon cigars, Dr. Price's Cream baking powder and Magic starch, as well as a full-page ad for an "Improved High Arm Sewing Machine." Apparently, a three-act, six-scene play was also planned for the evening as a list of the stage show's "actors" and the characters they played was included in the program, which even contained a plan of theater exits in the event of a fire. In all, it was quite a brochure for something that no one would ever see.

As scene #20 in *Tombstone* begins, the houselights dim, the curtain lifts and a spotlight illuminates an easel announcing "Prof. Gillman." A slender man in top hat and tails appears, holding three objects, but before he can begin his act, it is disrupted by gunfire. Initially, actor Charles Schneider had been hired by Kevin Jarre but by the time the juggler arrived for his scene, Jarre had long since departed. Despite having practiced for weeks, Charles had neglected to ask Jarre one important question: "What will I juggle in this scene?" Imagine his surprise when he learned the answer. "The morning I arrive on the set, I'm in my costume, everything's beautiful, I look pretty cool," admits Schneider. "The prop department approached me and … handed me my juggling clubs. They are much smaller, authentic 19th century juggling pins, and worst of all, much heavier than I dreamed they would have been. One of them has an explosive charge in it.

"I'm no master of juggling clubs, much less balls. In fact, I've just acquired this skill and was barely able to get two or three revolutions of the plastic larger clubs you might find in any hobby shop. These wooden clubs were a whole new ballgame to me and I immediately tried to juggle the three no-gimmick props … and could not do it. I pulled an assistant director aside and said, 'I cannot believe this. I can't deal with these things. I don't think I can really pull off juggling these fully. Maybe just one spin.' The assistant said, 'Just wing it. Hopefully, it will work out, man. It's going to be a little bit brutal but we'll see what happens.' I remember kind of having a panic attack and freaking out. I ran up to Billy Zane. He was a true trooper and he took me aside and said, 'It's going to be okay, take some deep breaths.'"

Even though they wouldn't appear in the scene, several actors, including Boothe and Lang, were on the sidelines watching the filming. A special effects assistant walked up to Schneider with a harrowing warning: "Charles, I've got to give you specific advice that nobody else is telling you. We're going to blow up a fake pin with a charge of gunpowder.

You're not wearing any protective goggles, you're not wearing anything. This is going to be about a foot or two over your head. Try to aim it in this direction but those shards are going to be flying all over the place. Keep your eyes shut. Turn your head away at that moment, no matter what they say. We want you to be protected … no matter what they tell you, keep your eyes away. We don't want you to get hurt." Stunned, Schneider desperately replied, "No. I don't think I can juggle these pins." Suddenly, Cosmatos bellowed out of the darkness: "What?! The fucking juggler can't juggle? What the fuck… Who fucking hired you? Who cast you in this?" Without missing a beat, the terrified juggler replied, "Kevin Jarre." There was a collective gasp.[4]

Powers Boothe, holding a copy of the pink-paged script, stood up and interrupted the tirade. "Excuse me, George," he said. "There's really no reference directly here in this currently re-written scene of Prof. Gillman actually juggling." An earlier draft had suggested he toss a pin up in the air with a few revolutions. Added Boothe, "Looks like the current draft suggests he could come out, do a little something, toss that pin up and it's blown up out of the air right away." Boothe then winked at Schneider, who immediately took his lead and said, "Exactly, George. Check this out. I'll come out, do a really Victorian frilly bow and curtsy and how-do-you-do. And with a great flourish, I'll make a couple of revolutions and just lob that little pin up over my head and whammo! If I can, I'll give it a revolution. I'll try it the best I can. I deeply apologize. I'll just come out and do that." Schneider then glanced at Boothe with great appreciation and a look that said, "Thank you, man. You save an actor's ass." An exasperated George said, "Just fucking do it." Five takes later it was over.

After the scene was completed, a large, rather tall grip approached Schneider and said, "You're not alone, Charles. You did a good job. He's been screaming at all of us for days. He's a screamer. A lot of us aren't crazy about this guy and I know you need a hug." And she hugged him.[5]

The scene continues as Gillman races from the stage and yells, "They're shooting at us, they're shooting at us!" Shakespearean actor Romulus Fabian, played by Billy Zane, then mutters, "We won't have to wait for our notices," walks onstage and delivers the St. Crispin's speech from *Henry V*, Act IV, scene iii 18–67. Upon its completion, the audience erupts in cheers and wild applause, firing six-guns at the ceiling. (Portions of this sequence were completed at the Mescal location in early August.) Scene 21, where Fabian discusses the audience's reaction with an actress before he goes onstage, was eliminated.

The final portion of the film's evening entertainment sequence is a rendering of *Faust—Or the Devil's Bargain*. Set choreographer Lisa Zane explains the concept: "I said [to Kevin], 'Let's set it to Saint-Saëns' 'Danse Macabre' and let me choreograph it,' and he said, 'Great!' He often said, 'Great!' So I created this ballet to one of my favorite pieces; it was humorous, elegant and quirky, a little Ballet Russe in flavor." The orchestra whirls into the music as the rising curtain reveals a black and red, wild-painted backdrop, covered with images of death and damnation. An ancient white-bearded scholar sits alone with his books while Satan dances across the stage, tempting him with images of wealth and youth in the form of a shimmering blonde ballerina. As the curtain falls, Satan, exultant and triumphant, is ready to collect the debt. Cosmatos admitted, "This piece was very long and I had to cut it because it went on and on and all we had to do was establish different people and that [Wyatt] sees [Josephine] again and he's interested." Set dresser Matt Marich created the flame effect with silk cloth and fans. Cindy Wykes played the part of the first monkey holding a scroll and clearly remembers rehearsals with Zane, who informed the dancers that Jarre had been let go. Naturally, when Kevin was fired, Lisa was released, and her brother Billy was furious. "That night Kevin and I spoke on the phone," says Lisa. "He was already back in L.A. I said I wanted to walk, I was done. He said, 'Don't. Stay on, represent.' He was adamant. Everything felt so moribund that the word Tombstone had become like a joke. I was firmly in Kevin's camp, and they were cleaning house. Within a week, Bint [her dog] and I were out of there."[6]

"The [*Faust*] scene was shot during the day," says Cindy. "It was really, really hot. They wanted all the smoke in the theater to remain still, so no fans were blowing." Along with the Faust mask, Marich also created two monkey masks with fiberglass. There is a section in this scene where a Bird Cage employee (Buckaroo Art Craffords) tries to replicate a psychedelic effect by passing jars of colored liquid in front of a leather-wrapped, yellow spot projector. For filming purposes, the lens mount actually was a Home Depot plastic toilet flange. A brass trim piece was supposed to cover the lens. Marich: "When they came and got that piece, I wasn't in the shop, I was out dressing sets. We made [the trim piece] in brass like a lace doily with a hole in it that was supposed to sit over [the lens] so it looked very Victorian and fancy. [Unfortunately], it never got put on, [and you see the flange] in the film. My fault."

There were several other Buckaroos in the Bird Cage scene, including Red Sash members John Peel, Reggie Byrum, Rick Terry, Jerry Tarantino and Bill Weddle, the bartender who serves Curly Bill. And there was a hidden cameo as Mrs. Sam Elliott—actress Katharine Ross—was also in that scene. According to background player J. Nathan Simmons, "She kinda mingled in the back, she kind of snuck in the background like we did. Very cool. We didn't realize who we were talking to, of course, We thought she was one of us. She was in costume and we thought she was one of us."[7]

As filming of this scene began, Stephen Lang, still in costume, and maybe even still in character as Ike Clanton, stood in a corner of the soundstage, looking on. Recalls Schneider, "I looked over … and he was acting like he was a conductor. So there he was looking like he was red-faced, shit-faced, drunk out of his mind with his eyes all bleary-eyed, all crazy, and he was acting like he was a fancy man directing an orchestra, with his nose in the air and his hand [waving in movement to the music]. Like he was waving a baton, all aloof and funny … and no one saw it but me…. I don't know how his eyes got that bloodshot and yellowed at the edges, and his face so lazy and engorged unless he was truly in his cups. It was a magical moment—he may as well have been on screen. It's the way his character would have reacted if he had seen some fancy orchestra. Wow, I'm watching Stephen Lang being that guy totally in the moment having fun."[8]

Obviously, from the aforementioned recollections, Cosmatos was a great action-oriented director—talented, passionate, creative and enthusiastic. But he was also extremely vulgar, peppering his language with F-bombs as naturally as other people would breathe. Disney Studios had warned the production company, "Watch your language. Children are present on the set." Recalls Zeug, "There's a scene out in front of the hotel and George, unfortunately, his language was unreal. Everything was 'Fuck this, fuck that. Where's my fucking Cowboys?' We were upset about it because we don't use that kind of language. There were memos that came out from Disney, saying that we have children on the set and there will be no swearing. Well, we weren't swearing anyway but that didn't stop him. It never stopped [him]."

Sam Elliott was perhaps the most easygoing, professional, likable actor on the set, but sometimes even Elliott reached his limit with Cosmatos. On one occasion, the actor

The cover of the eight-page prop program used during filming of the Bird Cage sequences (courtesy Jerry Tarantino).

was outside a saloon going over his lines when George yelled, "Sam! Where the fuck's my Sam? Sam? Where the fuck are you?" Enough already! Sam threw the script down, opened the door, stuck his head in and hit George with, "George, I fucking hear you, George!" He then slammed the door and backed out. George was very quiet after that scene, Elliott then admitting, "In all the years that I shot, I never had to deal with this kind of shit." According to Zeug, Kilmer was not immune to George's nonsense, either. One day, out in the middle of the street in front of the Grand Hotel, Val was getting prepared to film a scene when suddenly, the first AD got into it with George. They were going back and forth, yelling at each other. As Zeug recalls, "Finally, Val gets fed up with this, takes the script, throws it on the ground and says, 'Fuck it. I'm out of here.' With that, everything stopped, they told us, 'Go on home. We'll be here tomorrow morning.'" The next day, the AD was gone.[9]

Donna Cline vividly recalls, "I heard a rumor that someone in the Pima County Sheriff's Department was stalking George because they had heard that he had a habit of peeing on the set in broad daylight. No bush, no hiding anything and he would just turn around and pee. One [night] we were filming at Mescal, and we were doing close-ups of Kurt. Half of the crew had already gone to lunch as it was one in the morning. George calls 'Action,' and the boom operator soon intervened, saying, 'Wait a minute. Hold on. What's that sound?' Apparently, [George] had turned around and was taking a whiz and yelled, 'Action' over his shoulder. [The boom mic picked up the sound.] Even Kurt said, 'George, come on, man.'"[10]

And it wasn't just that. The director had a penchant for soft-shelled nuts and subsequently ruined more than one shot by cracking the nuts and eating pistachios. He'd also go to craft services, get cans of Cheez Whiz, and squirt it into this mouth. Then he'd yell, "Action!" or "Cut!" and it would fly everywhere. One day he was eating a sandwich and yelling at script supervisor Faith Conroy, spitting food at her. Finally, she said, "I've had enough. I'm gone!"

Donna Cline: "One night I went out to show him some storyboards. I had been up since five in the morning working, almost 24 hours, and I was so tired. George was in a foul mood. They were filming and I saw unit production manager Terry Collis and asked, 'Do you think maybe I can [show this to] him? I really need this for the editors.' Collis said, 'Just stand here for a minute. Let me talk to him.' So Terry says to George, 'Hey, Donna really needs to show you these boards.' [George] went off on me ... he screamed and screamed at me. I don't take that so I just walked [away]. He saw me leaving and yells at me, 'Oh, that's a good job.' Yeah, right. I went to the shuttle and was told, 'Welcome to the club.'"[11]

After many hours of hard work, it became almost comical to hear one of George's invective-laced tirades. If you didn't already have a harsh vocabulary, you could certainly learn new ways of swearing just being around him. But not everyone believed the director was an uncouth lout. One evening, actor Pat Brady witnessed a typical outburst. When someone asked him, "Man, can you believe what you just heard?" Brady replied, "Well, I know George and he's a friend of mine. In private life, he's actually very charming." Cosmatos was an avid collector of classical English literature and had amassed quite a library of original signed works. Why he chose to act the way he did while on the set was anyone's guess.[12]

By now, everybody was aware of Cosmatos' presence, and actors weren't the only people frustrated with the new director. According to B-camera focus puller Michael

Walker, cinematographer William Fraker had warned the camera crew of Cosmatos' reputation: "The party's over. We got another director coming and he's a bit of a ball-buster. It's going to be different now. Get ready." No doubt the change of directors relieved him of all the frustrations and obstacles Jarre had caused. Fraker admitted, though, that the only reason he'd signed on in the first place was because Kevin was an inexperienced director and Bill thus felt he (Fraker) would have more control over the project. Fraker always felt that "the most exciting part of walking on the set in the morning is that it's really inspirational. It's completely black, and I strike my first light for what I'm going to do and that becomes my first brushstroke. Then I add other brushstrokes along the way, different lights and so forth, until I come up with a complete picture. Then I look at it and say, 'Okay, let's do it.' The look of a picture is inherent in the material. I read the script and say, 'This is what I feel this picture should look like.' Basically, I have an idea of what I want my picture to look like—I call it *mine* because I'm working on it—and I talk with the director. It's usually me and the director who find a bond and form a marriage." However, when Cosmatos was hired, that bond quickly vanished. Said Billy Getzwiller, "We were watching dailies one night and Cosmatos is yelling, 'What is this piece of shit? Out of focus! Out of focus!' Bill Fraker got up, threw his glass at the screen, and said, 'I'm outta here. I can't deal with this guy.'" Actor Sal Cardile recalled there was constant tension between Fraker and Cosmatos: "George wanted things done a certain way and Bill would tell him you can't do that, or it wouldn't look right, [but] George would press the issue." After one particularly loud exchange, Fraker said, "When you figure out what the hell you are doing, I'll be in my trailer. You let me know and when I'm ready to come out, I'll come back." He then stormed off the set. One day, they even came close to fisticuffs. The two men were driving around the set in individual golf carts when they came face to face on the same road. Neither would budge so they came up with a safe, sensible solution: They crashed into each other. Bragged Fraker, "George fell out of his cart. I didn't." According to some, a fistfight then ensued. Fraker threatened to quit so many times, they made him an associate producer and gave him additional points just to keep him on location.[13]

Fraker had been given a modified Panavision lens case that held a bottle of liquor and it was hot-head technician James Danicic's responsibility to assure it was always Chivas. "There were times when we were doing the night shoot that I would go to the camera truck," explains Danicic. "There were plenty of shelves that were cleared and I would put a [furniture] pad over the shelf above, down across the front of me, and I would just lie there with the radio next to me, waiting for my name to be called, trying to catch a couple of winks. I would hear a golf cart pull up outside, [someone would] run in the truck, click, click, case opens, pour a drink, and then be gone. 'Uh, oh. Bill's up to no good. He's getting stressed out.' One night I hear the guy stomp up, make another Chivas, the footsteps stomp off, then they come back and [my cover] drops. It's Fraker. He goes, 'You little shit. I knew you were hiding somewhere.' 'Bill, I didn't hear my name. I don't know what's going on. I've got the walkie-talkie right here. I missed it. I'm sorry.' 'No, no, no. I don't need your ass. Get up and make a drink. Let's sit down.' They were calling for Bill on the radio. 'Just tell them I'm in the can. Bill's 10–1, still 10–1.' So we sat there and had a couple of cocktails before we went back to the set."[14]

Language admonishments were not the only restrictions the studio attempted to put in place. "Tombstone is a CLOSED SET. Our caterers are NOT PREPARED to feed visitors." "No photographs allowed." Naturally, these warnings didn't stop those who were

Director of photography William Fraker (known also for *Bullitt, Rosemary's Baby, WarGames, Looking for Mr. Goodbar, Honeymoon in Vegas,* and more) (courtesy James "Spud" Danicic).

prepared to incur the wrath of location security. Back in the day, iPhones with numerous apps, features and built-in cameras weren't yet available, so many folks took photos with Pentax, Nikon, Kodak and Canon SLR cameras. And those who couldn't afford such luxuries used the Olympus 35mm point-and-shoot, or maybe a Polaroid One-Step or the old Kodak 110 standby. Because not every extra appeared in every scene, there was an active "bootleg" market where extras shared their photos. Sneaky extras would peek around a corner, make sure no one was looking, and take a shot or two. And although they were cautioned about not bothering stars for photos, many stars like Sam Elliott were more than happy to pose with anyone who asked. One day some of the ladies who were extras bravely brought their cameras to the set and asked Sam if they could get picture with him. He was very discreet and told them if they would go down to the far west side of Mescal that, well, maybe … he could wander off and meet with them in about 30 minutes or so. He did and when he got there about 20 women were waiting. Gracious as always, Elliott took a photo with each and every one. Stuntman Lee McKechnie remembers that while the "no photographs" policy wasn't all that unusual, the *Tombstone* set was locked down tight: "You could get kicked off the set if they saw you taking pictures. Even if you knew the actors well enough to get a picture, or [if] the actors said, 'Hey, let's get a picture.' You'd have to sneak down an alley with them and say, 'Come here a second but don't let George see ya.'"[15]

But, these surreptitious photo-op tactics didn't always work for extras seeking autographs, as extra Glen Gold relates. Smiling, Gold recalls chasing an autograph from a visiting actress who wasn't even in *Tombstone*. "Dobie [Carey] and Buck [Taylor] baited me," says Gold, "and I went along with it. [We were] standing around talking [and] Kurt Russell went down the street headed for the set; right behind him [walked] Goldie. I said to Buck, 'That's Goldie, ain't it?' He said, 'Yeah, that's Goldie.' I said, 'I wonder if she'll give me her autograph.' Dobie kinda grinned. He said, 'Why, sure. Go get it.'" So he did. The only thing Gold had for her to sign was a business card with his name on it. "I said, 'Goldie, can I have your autograph?' And I was putting a little ham on it; I was being a little overboard. And she started laughing, that crazy laugh of hers. She broke out laughing and she said, 'Why, you sure can.' And I handed her that card." After signing, Hawn, still laughing, handed it back and took off across the street. When Gold rejoined Buck and Dobie, another young extra said, "That was Goldie Hawn, wasn't it?" Yeah, he was told. He said, "I didn't know she was here. I'm going to get her autograph." Ever helpful, Gold said, "Well, there she goes. Go get it." The young extra took off out in the middle of the street and stopped Hawn to get her autograph. About five minutes later, there was an announcement over the PA system: "All extras assemble in the tent in the holding area.

Tourists with cameras in hand stand behind a security rope on Kansas Street in Old Tucson and watch a scene being filmed. No photographs were allowed, although one tourist is using a video camera (courtesy Larry Zeug).

Immediately!" When they arrived, they were instructed, "We already told you there won't be any pictures. And there won't be any more of this autograph-seeking, either."[16]

Of course, the opportunity to interact with a Hollywood celebrity sometimes was just too enticing. Several actors had brought to the set wives, girlfriends and children, many of whom were actors or aspiring actors in their own right. One day a hotel house-keeper saw one actor's wife racing along the hallway toward the elevator. Throwing caution to the wind, she stopped the actress and politely asked for an autograph. Irritated at being interrupted, the actress grabbed a piece of paper, scribbled her name on it and, adding a few choice words, shoved it back at the employee and rushed down the hallway. The housekeeper looked at the actress, looked at the autograph, tore it in two and threw it on the floor. In another instance, Kurt Russell decided to take matters into his own hands. While he was prepping for a scene, a still photographer kept taking shots of him while the crew was putting on Kurt's makeup and trimming his hair. Russell waved his gun at the photographer, telling him, "No, don't take pictures right now. No pictures." The guy wouldn't leave so Kurt literally shot his .45 in his direction. Scared the hell out of everybody, but the photographer stopped shooting. When a girl asked Kurt for an autograph when they weren't filming, she was promptly escorted off the set.[17]

And then there were those non-movie folks who just didn't care about celebrities. As Buckaroo Bobby Vincent recalls, "Down in Mescal, there's a local store owned by some people; we took a break and Bill Paxton wanted to go [there] with us. So we go in and order some stuff and Bill [started] joking with the gal behind the counter. 'You know who I am?' goes Bill. This girl looks at him and says, 'No.' He says, 'I'm the famous actor Bill Paxton.' She turns around and says, 'So?' I laughingly told him, 'I'd like you to know, Bill, you're getting an ego there, bud. She wasn't impressed at all.'"[18]

After Cosmatos wrapped up the Bird Cage scenes, he began to film Wyatt Earp's arrival at the Tucson train depot. Visual and weather-related continuity issues were a constant problem on the set: first- and second-unit shooting, geography, the level of ambient light, shadows, pick-up shots, and the effect of a four-month filming schedule all contributed to mismatched backgrounds and, just like Sabino Canyon, it was the same with the train depot sequence. A close examination of the ever-changing sky shows that parts of this sequence were filmed at several different times over the summer. In the film, as Wyatt's train arrives in Tucson, he steps off the passenger car, notices someone abusing one of his horses and confronts the man. U.S. Marshal Crawley Dake and his deputy observe this scene and even before they can offer a law enforcement position to Earp, he declines. Wyatt then passes the horse's reins to a young boy and hears a familiar voice in the distance: "Boy, I'd know that sour face anywhere." It's his brothers, Virgil and Morgan. Wyatt turns, grins and hugs them.

The train upon which Wyatt arrived was #11, the historic 1872 standard-gauge Virginia & Truckee Railroad line steam locomotive *Reno* (4–4–0), that had been purchased at auction from MGM in 1970, along with a tender and passenger car. (The designation 4–4–0 means the engine had four unpowered lead wheels, four powered driving wheels, and no trailing wheels.) At various times over the years the train appeared in such films as *The Cheyenne Social Club, Support Your Local Gunfighter, How the West Was Won* and *Joe Kidd,* and had had either a straight cap smokestack or, as seen in *Tombstone,* a diamond stack with a sheet metal extension. The engine was pulling V&T Baggage Car #1, V&T Coach #19 and a 40-foot flatcar first used in the 1975 film *Posse.* Its window-sided, boxcar-type prop body was later removed. The locomotive, baggage car, and coach were left

The Reno at Old Tucson Studios (courtesy Chris Swinney).

painted and lettered exactly as they had appeared in the 1993 Mario Van Peebles film *Posse*. Perhaps someone in the art department thought Western Pacific Rail Road (W.P.R.R.) looked appropriate on the rolling stock but that line never actually serviced Tucson; Southern Pacific did.

Since the *Reno* had first been a wood, then a coal, and then an oil-burner, its boiler had deteriorated, which is why a large air compressor was installed in the baggage car in the winter of 1988–1989 to provide movement for the locomotive. Compressed air was piped forward to the cylinders which in turn pushed side rods allowing the engine to move, and the fuel tank was removed to lighten the load. Steam and smoke effects completed the visual illusion with sounds effects added in post-production. As the Old Tucson Studio track was only 1000 feet long, it wasn't possible or practical to film the train's arrival in Tucson in a wide-angle shot. According to Old Tucson historian Paul Lawton, "Distance combined with a long-lens camera made the train appear farther away than it actually was. It was partially screened by brush, and a cut in the land made it appear as if was steaming under full throttle."[19]

Portions of this arrival scene were filmed at different times. The conversation between Dake and Earp, as well as the segment when Wyatt turns over the reins to a young boy, were both filmed during the last week of June, but Earp's arrival and his confrontation over the horses were filmed on August 23, hence the differing appearance of the sky. Thirteen-year-old Sam Dolan, son of Buckaroo Jeff Dolan, played the boy. Sam was eventually hired as a full-time Buckaroo in addition to being a member of the Red Sash gang. He and 15-year-old Charley Ward were the youngest Buckaroos on location. (Belonging to the Red Sash gang earned Sam the moniker of "the sweetest little outlaw," courtesy of Stephen Lang.) The fellow Earp hits with the quirt was wrangler Byron Wilkerson. Sam recalls, "[There were] not too many [takes of my scene]. It seems like we started shooting that dialogue before lunch and a lot of it was shot in the afternoon hours, right after lunch because the sun was real high and hot."[20]

Originally, the scene was to be much more intense than what appears on film. Wrangler Gary Gang, a member of the "House of Men" rides, says, "I was supposed to have a part in the train scene. I had trained this horse to rear, which ended up not being used in the final cut because the head wrangler didn't want me on set, and they wouldn't let me rehearse the horse on the flatbed train car. The horse goes up there cold [but] wouldn't rear at first because I wasn't rearing him. The horse looked great but they didn't use the gag the way it was written in the screenplay. I [had] taught this horse to fight—when he goes up in the air, his feet are striking out. You gotta know where to stand. They had Kurt working the horse when he was rearing [and] the horse was in his face. It wasn't the way the scene was supposed to go. That was all Kurt needed was that horse slashing his face. So he got pissed and said he wouldn't do it. 'I'm not doing this shit.'" At the conclusion of this scene, they filmed the remainder of the arrival sequence where Wyatt guides the family to a train station house window and gazes upon the group's reflection. As the three brothers walk along the station platform, Bill Paxton throws a half-eaten apple in the air. "Bill Paxton wanted to eat eggs, hard-boiled eggs," says Greg Poulos. "And we told him you'd get sicker than a dog if you start eating eggs. [But] he wanted eggs. After about the fifth egg, we had to switch to an apple so he could throw it. The eggs started getting to him. The heat was too much." For the Earps-and-wives-group-pose-reflected-in-the-window scene, Dana Loraine Goodge was one of the ladies' reflection stand-ins, and recalls that some of the actors were less than pleased by having to wait and wait. "The women were late to the set all the time," remembers Dana. "They were late getting to Mescal or Old Tucson; they were late getting to the set. That particular day, we stood out there so many times. We thought the women were supposed to be there and they kept me having to stand out there [and each time they had to] redo the lighting because the women hadn't shown up yet. I was sitting in the train at one point and I heard Sam Elliott talking to George: 'These fucking so-called actresses … these extras and stand-ins are more fucking professional than these so-called actresses. Get these girls out here.' There was anger at the women." No doubt it had to do with the heat and everyone getting tired and frustrated. As the week progressed, Cosmatos filmed scene #90, Doc's departure from Kate at the Grand Hotel. In this scene there is a reference to the Frankie Laine song "Gunfight at the O.K. Corral" from the 1957 film of the same name. Doc asks Kate, "Have you no kind word for me before I ride away"—a direct homage to Dimitri Tiomkin's song. This scene was not included in the film's original release but later was added to the Director's Cut.[21]

One reason fans are so enamored by *Tombstone* is its vibrant, authentic detail. Using archival photographs, the filmmakers recreated specific buildings of the actual western town, and although the gambling halls and theaters had a gilt-edged Victorian glamour, structures alone were not sufficient to create this effect. So each scene was also filled with a great deal of atmospheric richness and activity. If one disregards all foreground movement and dialogue, and instead concentrates on the background, it's amazing to discover what is happening in the town. For example, we see suffragettes actively advocating for women's rights: a woman carrying a placard asking for the vote for women marches through the frame at one point, and later, a wagonload of women crosses the screen, all carrying signs, "Equal Pay for Equal Work." What helps such scenes work even better is that everyone was in period-correct clothing.

Joseph Porro had discovered a cache of calicos and linen dresses that had been purchased in the U.S. during the film's actual time period. They had never been worn, and were sitting in a warehouse for 120 years. But the proper appearance wasn't only limited to the female gender. Although the Buckaroos wore period-correct Western clothing,

The Earp brothers and their wives await the beginning of a scene at the railway station on the Old Tucson set. In costume, left to right: Kurt Russell, Dana Wheeler-Nicholson, Lisa Collins, and Bill Paxton (courtesy P.J. Lawton, Old Tucson Studio).

there were also those who specialized in military apparel and Civil War apparel. Known as "stitch-counters," they had a responsibility to accurately portray history in everything they do, from the buttons on their coats to the buckles on their shoes. Re-enactors who sew almost always do so by hand, and try to replicate the sewing methods and techniques that were used in the time period they are portraying, not just the overall look of the finished piece of apparel. Two such individuals were Kane Rubalcaba and Curt Stokes. In the train station sequence, they wore sky-blue trousers, civilian shirts without their military jackets, either 1872 Andrew campaign or common slouch hats, and were getting their boots shined by a shoeshine boy.[22]

Usually, the first assistant director or key set production assistant organizes these background activities. In this case, it was James Alan Hensz, who came up with the vignettes that seem so innocuous but add so much realism to the film. As a result, you can almost feel the blazing heat, taste the grit in your teeth, smell the sweat of the cowboys and the stink of manure in the streets. Often, Hensz was just told, "I want to see some action over there," and he would create whatever came to mind. Sometimes it works, sometimes it doesn't. Explained Rubalcaba, "We were doing a night scene in town and Jim asked, 'Do you guys have any other looks?' We had brought our military uniforms so we switched out all our saddles and tack, put on our McClellans Saddles, all our military tack on. Polished up our saber belts, had our kepis. We're riding into town and over the radio we hear, 'Cut!' It was Cosmatos. 'Where [did] these fucking soldiers come from? I'm making a western, not a war movie.' It was hilarious. So we do a quick change [but said], 'Here's Tombstone. You got Cochise and all these guys raiding around southern Arizona. You got black folks, you got Chinese, you got Indians in town. Fort Huachuca ain't that far and there's no soldiers on leave in town? Come on.' But they wrote that right out and re-did it with something else."[23]

The street altercation between Holliday and a drunken Ringo was filmed over a two-day period at the end of the same week. Although it appears it was shot on the Mescal set, it was actually staged on Kansas Street in Old Tucson. This scene, with different characters, was based on an episode described in Walter Noble Burns' 1927 novel *Tombstone: The Iliad of the Southwest*. In Burns' book, Wyatt, Virgil, Morgan, Doc and Mayor Charles Thomas are chatting in front of the Campbell & Hatch Billiard Parlor while Ringo, the McLaurys and the three Clanton brothers lounge in front of the Grand Hotel. After Ringo confronts Wyatt and is rebuffed, he turns to Holliday, who utters the iconic line, "I'm your huckleberry. That's just my game." Sam Dolan also appeared in the background of this scene when he ran, grabbed two young boys and pulled them to safety as they sat watching the action. (What's a huckleberry? In answer to a challenge, it meant, "I'm your man." Then again, in Aurthurian lore, garlands made of huckleberry were given to Knights of the Roundtable for rescuing damsels in distress—a medal of gratitude, as it were. So the line could be translated into "I'm your hero." There are also those who believe that as the handle on a coffin used to be called a *huckle* and that the pallbearers were called *huckle bearers*, Holliday must have instead said, *"I'm your huckle bearer."* A huckle bearer was also known as one who sat near the gravesite in the event a bell rang. (A grave bell was used as a precaution to prevent someone from accidentally being buried alive. Thus it's possible the line is really a threat: "I'll put you in your grave." However, none of those explanations hold water as every draft of the script clearly reads *huckleberry*.)[24]

The first day was a long shot of the Earps walking up the street. As the scene ends, Ringo stumbles and falls into a stack of coffins in front of the undertaker's building. In later years, this structure was turned into a funeral-embalming museum at Old Tucson. For years, Mark Tovsen and his business partner had been accumulating mortuary-related items from numerous Tucson funeral homes and really didn't know what to do with them until they decided to donate the collection to Old Tucson where they could be displayed; in the meantime, they were used in the film. Although several of these items were peppered throughout the set, the only ones that appear in the film are the clothes Frank and Tom McLaury and Billy Clanton wear during the funeral procession and the glass-faced coffin they lie in. Made in Mexico in the 1980s, the coffin's style replicated those used in the United States in the 1800s. Tovsen had provided two such items but since the second one wasn't quite as elaborate, only one coffin was used, each actor taking turns lying in it for his close-up and each actor quickly regretting the lack of air inside. Tovsen also provided a fiberglass-and-wood replica of the famous Black Moriah curved-glass funeral hearse that transported the deceased to Boot Hill Cemetery. With sterling silver and gold leaf trim, the actual Black Moriah had been built by Cunningham Bros. of Rochester, New York, for $8000 in 1881, and was owned by the Watt and Tarbell Undertaking Parlor. Unfortunately, as the replica's front axle broke, wagons were instead used in the film.[25]

The next day, they shot Kilmer's huckleberry sequence and Jason Priestley's defiance of the Earps. Priestley, star of television's *90210*, was then at the height of his popularity and appeared in the prelude to the huckleberry scene. Throngs of 20-year-old female extras hovered around him, asking for autographs or photographs. Priestley appeared as

"I'm your huckleberry." Kansas Street, Old Tucson Studios. The Earps and Holliday (left to right: Kurt Russell, Sam Elliott, Val Kilmer and Bill Paxton) watch as Curly Bill Brocius (Powers Boothe) and the other Cowboys walk away from a confrontation (courtesy P.J. Lawton, Old Tucson Studio).

Deputy Billy "Sister Boy" Breakenridge; the diminished nature of the role must have rankled him. Jarre's earlier drafts had a much larger role for Breakenridge, but most of Priestley's efforts ended up on the cutting room floor. But overall, he considered it a worthwhile experience. "Working on *Tombstone* changed my life," admits Priestley. "It was one of the greatest times I ever had, sitting around listening to these actors tell stories. I had no stories of my own to tell. They reminded me of what it is to be an actor."[26]

As filming continued at Old Tucson, the production crew was putting the finishing touches on the Tombstone set in Mescal as the construction team, set decorators, greensmen and painters were still getting the town ready. An example of the emphasis on authenticity: One afternoon, two Buckaroos were asked to fire live ammo into the Tombstone sign for a rustic, weathered, violent look. Crew members constantly dressed and undressed the various buildings, and tents and unfinished frame structures were everywhere along with false-front buildings that filled in the gaps between other structures. As the historical Tombstone was still relatively new in the early 1880s, framed and unfinished structures would not be out of the ordinary for filming. The overall effect depicted a fresh, up-and-coming town in the process of being constructed. Through the use of numerous creative camera angles, the town appeared much larger than it actually was. And once Cosmatos came aboard, the size of the Mescal set increased substantially. According to set dresser Matt Marich, "They built more of the background behind the

Rear view of Fremont Street on the Mescal set. Note that many of the buildings are just false fronts or incomplete wooden structures. The O.K. Corral is located directly above the middle tent (arrow) (courtesy Larry Zeug).

O.K. Corral—they built an Oriental area back there. That whole area got huge. They built more of the entire background and part of [Allen Street]. Campbell & Hatch … was going to be a separate set; [it] was actually in the space next to [the Oriental] but there was a dividing wall. Well, when Cosmatos came on, they made them tear that wall down and build a second half of the bar, so it was now a giant U-shape and it was [as] if the Oriental spilled into Campbell & Hatch. Technically a flaw, not accurate at all. And that's why if you look carefully in the background, you can see all the taxidermy on the walls. That's supposed to be Campbell & Hatch. That was supposed to be a separate set but [Cosmatos] merged them together." In addition to the sets used at Old Tucson, more than 82 structures were either constructed or renovated at Mescal, including buildings, tents and unfinished, framed dwellings.

"I want the Chinatown, there was a Chinatown here! I want the Chinatown!" Cosmatos was screaming again. "I want you to build me a Chinatown today!" Hardwicke agreed to create a drawing and when she returned with it, she asked, "Do you want something like this?" The director's response was predictable, as Catherine relates: "He goes, 'What is this hen scratch? That is the worst drawing I've ever seen in my life.' I said, 'Okay, if you don't like it, I'm sorry. My art director drew it. If you don't like it, I'll draw you another drawing.' 'Oh, your art director drew it. Then you don't know how to draw, do you?' Then he started dancing around like Rumplestiltskin. 'She doesn't know how to draw.' He gets a megaphone, 'She doesn't know how to draw.' He's saying this to everybody on the set. So I didn't say anything. I went and got my drafting board and my pencil and I put it down on the desk, right next to him by the monitor, and started drawing. I drew this big elaborate drawing of Chinatown right in front of him. He looked at me, and steam was coming out of his ears. He was just so mad that I could [actually] draw. I said, 'Do you like this?' He said, 'Yes, I guess I like it. Now, let's see if you can build it.' I got some telephone poles … within two hours I had poles standing up, it was half-built. He drives by in a golf cart with a megaphone and I'm standing there and he yells into the megaphone, 'Hardwicke! Hardwicke! It looks like shit! You're doing a very bad job!' Then he steps on the gas and roared away."[27]

Apparently, there wasn't anything Hardwicke could do that satisfied the director, as two more stories illustrate: "One time, I'm building something on the set and I get called on the radio: 'Catherine, come down to the sheriff's office.' They were filming a scene in the sheriff's office, and I see all these actors just staring at him, and they're not filming. I walk in there [and say], 'What's going on?' George said, 'What … is … this … deer … head … doing … here?' He pointed to a wall-mounted deer head that was above the doorway. 'Well, it's decorating,' she said. 'There are photographs that show that there were those type things in the office.' 'What … is … this … deer … head … doing … here?' 'Like I said, it's set dressing. The set dresser just put it up there because he thought it looked very interesting.' And everybody is just staring at me, I'm staring at him, too. 'Bring me the set decorator, I'm going to fire him.' 'Oh, he's not here. He's in Tucson, so you can't fire him. You're just going to have to talk to me.'"

"'What … is … this … deer … head … doing … here?' I was trying to figure out what was going on. Has he turned into a robot, is he stupid? Nobody knew what to say. I finally looked at him and I saw him looking further toward the lens. I said, 'Oh, are you saying that maybe it's too high? It's not in your shot. Do you want me to move it down?' 'That's it. It's out of the shot. We're shooting with an anamorphic lens. You are an idiot. Why would you put it up there? It's out of my shot. You're a complete idiot.' He was yelling in front of Kurt and everybody. When he stopped his little tantrum, I said, 'George, you told me you liked to have low angles, cool wide-angle shots, all these different angles. So, I dressed every inch of the set so you could put your camera with whatever lens you want and shoot and there will be something interesting in your framework.' And he looks at me and goes, 'Oh … good idea. Okay. Let's roll.'

"Another time we're at the church, 'Why are these five crosses here?' I had five giant crosses. 'If you don't like them, I'll take a couple of them down. They're just in the deep background. They fill up the shot.' And then he started screaming, 'It's the fucking crucifixion. I only want three crosses!' He looked like he was going to kill me. A stuntman came up and jumped in between us because he thought he was going to punch me. He just couldn't articulate that he only wanted three crosses, instead of five. They wouldn't let him fire me because I was doing a good job … but, oh, he wanted to."[28]

While most of the town's buildings were historically correct, some were given the names of the crew's family members. Across the street from the Oriental Saloon is the Key West Cigar Shop. Although you don't see it in the film, set dresser Matt Marich's father's name "P. Marich" is painted on the front of the building as proprietor. This tongue-in-cheek approach even extended to the names on some of the Boot Hill tombstones, the most famous of which was Lester Moore. "Here lies Lester Moore, Four slugs from a .44, No Les No more." Had a Lester Moore actually existed? Supposedly, Moore worked as a Wells Fargo stage agent in the border town of Naco, Arizona. When Harry Dunstan arrived to claim a package, he found it badly damaged. After an argument, both men went for their guns and in a blaze of gunfire, Moore fell from four slugs from a .44. Dunstan also died from just one of Moore's shots. Moore, a harmless, inoffensive man, became world-famous with his epitaph, while no one knows what happened to Dunstan. In the film, Moore's name on the headstone is spelled "Moor."[29]

After Cosmatos completed filming Ringo's attempt at a street shootout with Holliday, the production broke for a well-deserved July 4 celebration weekend. Upon their return the following Tuesday, they moved on to scene #9, Doc's altercation with gambler Ed Bailey in the Prescott saloon. Frank Stallone, who played Bailey, arrived that day and immediately met Kilmer. "[Val] was terrific with me," says Stallone. "We sat down and he said, 'Let's go eat, man.' So we went over to a table by ourselves, I had a beer and we started running lines. It was just terrific. He was very, very helpful to me. [We] went over the lines and stuff like that and then we started shooting." Always in character, Val would sometimes listen to his Southern-accented dialogue on a tape recorder before filming a scene. He was worried he would lose the character and the accent if he dropped it even for a second. He was "Doc" the entire film. Explains Kilmer, "Southern aristocrats have a different dialect than even upper class and a real serious aristocrat has a very distinct style that you can tell if you're a Southerner. I called a friend of mine (Tim Monich) who was my speech teacher at Juilliard where I went to school. He now does movies and he's got an extensive library of sounds and voices. And I said, can you give me a Southern aristocrat, a contemporary guy but, you know, I want to have it seem like it doesn't exist anymore. So that was kind of what he did for me. Except the guy that he sent me (on tape) was so, you know, was *sooo* slow, it would have taken about five hours to say it. It just lulls on the voice, it went on for hours. I sort of adjusted it. I tortured just about everybody with this tape; he was a very entertaining character. The tape that the dialect coach gave me was too extreme. If I had done that, I wouldn't have felt comfortable even if it was more accurate. But he was from Georgia. But it's also strange in the Tombstone stories or O.K. Corral stories, [Doc is] very rarely done as a real Southerner, which is a real part of his character."[30]

Including master shots and POVs, they did ten takes, and in each take, Stallone would get stabbed. "One time when Val stabbed me, the knife didn't quite go back into the handle," explains Frank. "It was kind of like a dirk, dagger. Didn't quite go back into the handle so well. But that was okay." The curly-haired Stallone is a fairly good-sized fellow, and Kilmer thought it would be a good idea to grab Frank and flip him in the air, but he could never figure out how to manage it. The third gambler at the table was Bobby Joe McFadden, owner of Bobby Joe's Irish Pub in Mescal, where Buckaroos and PAs would hang out after a day's filming. Every day or so, Kilmer would send an assistant to the pub for a bottle of Scotch … no doubt so he could stay in character. (McFadden's wife Elly was the director of marketing at the Tucson Holiday Inn.) Later that day, they filmed scene #152 where Wyatt meets Josephine in her dressing room of the Denver Theater.[31]

Property assistant Greg Poulos was under the poker table and gave Kilmer a knife

Opposite, top: The Prescott Saloon at Old Tucson Studio where Doc Holliday (Val Kilmer) stabs and kills Ed Bailey (Frank Stallone). **Bottom:** Interior of Josephine Marcus' dressing room on the Denver Theater soundstage at Old Tucson (both photographs by Lee Gray/courtesy Catherine Hardwicke).

to stab Stallone's character. "You do so many takes," explained Poulos, "and [each take] you have to reset the table. It was 3 a.m., 4 a.m., and [first assistant director] Adam Taylor was kind of yelling; he wanted to get it done. 'Come on, Greg. Hurry up, hurry up and set the table.' Val took all the poker chips and threw them at him and said, 'If you can do it faster, go ahead.'" Taylor was under a tremendous amount of stress working for Cosmatos. After many scenes, Adam could be seen sitting dejectedly with his head lowered while his father Buck rubbed his shoulders, saying, "Take some breaths. You'll get through it." You could just see the migraine starting. Many were the times when Adam would say, "It's going to be a little rough. Would he just please stop yelling?" The way Cosmatos treated Taylor was absolutely brutal. "Adam! Adam! I want this done now, Adam!" Adam would just say, "Yes, sir," and do what he was told. One evening Taylor was sitting by the hotel pool, beer in hand, and he told Buckaroos John Peel and Billy Lang, "You know, George apologizes to me every night. He apologizes every night for being hard on me." Even so, Cosmatos fired poor Adam over and over again.

On June 14, Adam started his first day as an official first AD. By June 21, Brian Cook arrived on the set to take Taylor's place. Adam moved to the second unit with Terry Leonard. On Friday, July 16, while staging a scene, Cosmatos yelled at Cook, "Cookie! What are these shadows doing on my set? Get these shadows off my set." Replied Brian, "You moron, George. The sun is setting. It is creating shadows. I cannot change the sun." Of course, Cosmatos lost his temper. "Then you're fired! Fired! Understand? You're fired!" Brian Cook, who literally reeked of alcohol every single day, went right to the bar, ran up a huge tab, borrowed somebody's credit card and didn't pay it back. Production eventually had had enough of Cook's behavior and put him off on a plane as quickly as possible. By the time George got up the next morning, he had changed his mind. "I don't want to fire [Cook]. I need him back," he realized, as Cook was probably George's only ally. George wanted to un-fire him, but it was too late. Taylor was back on first unit and Cook was gone.[32]

"One night we're doing town stuff and they brought [in] 200 extras from Tucson and they costumed all these women," remembers John Peel. "And George was looking at some of the girls and said, 'I don't like those girls. Get rid of those girls. I want blonde with big tits! Lots of blondes with very big tits.'" Eventually, he must have been satisfied with the subsequent results as one female extra in particular seemed to be one he always chose to be in a scene. However, he never called her by name. Rather than just say, "Can I have that girl over there?" he would instead go to his first AD and say, "Hey, give me the girl with the big tits." And he'd say it loud enough so that everyone heard. Then he would command, "Okay, action. When camera roll, you, big tits, you come close and we shoot." The girl was humiliated. After numerous embarrassments, she had had enough and demanded that Cosmatos treat her with proper respect, telling him, "Look, this is my name. Would you please stop saying that? I take offense to that and it's very insulting." Despite her mortification, George refused. After filming was completed, the extra filed a sexual harassment lawsuit that was settled out of court.[33]

The shootout between Ringo and Holliday was filmed at the Oak Grove set on the Babocomari ranch in mid–July. Kevin Jarre had previously scheduled this scene to be completed the first week of June, but as with many other scenes, Cosmatos decided to re-film it. Due to inclement weather, the crew had to re-visit the site three times before the scene was completed. Michael Biehn remembers that he and Val spent a great deal of time preparing for their duel. "Val and I went out the day before we shot that scene, and we choreographed that scene together," recalls Biehn. "It was Val and I who decided that we weren't going to be walking ten paces, turning and shooting, like they've done in a million other movies. We thought, 'Well, wouldn't it be fun if we did it kind of close, where we're just, like, two or three feet apart from each other?' We went out and rehearsed that, and we spent six or eight hours rehearsing it, kind of doing that thing where we'd walk around each other, sizing each other up, and then how I got shot and how I still continued to pull the trigger even though I had a bullet through the brain. All of that stuff, Val and I rehearsed the day before we shot, and that's the kind of actor that I know Val Kilmer is. I mean, he is passionate and he wants to get it right, and he is like me ... and like a lot of people who are like, 'I'm making a movie here. I'm going to do the best I can, and if you're not with me, then get out of the way.'"

The scene is one of the climaxes in the film, and Biehn justifiably is extremely proud of his work in it: "Well, I always thought Johnny Ringo had a little bit of a 'suicide by police' mentality," the actor said in an interview. "There was nothing to live for, and he's smarter than everybody else and I think he was just jaded and wanted out.... There's a part in that movie, which I think is one of my greatest moments on film, and I don't sit around and look for it, but whenever I see it, I always think, 'Yeah, that's what I was trying to do, and that's what I got.' I have the line, 'All right, lunger. Let's do it.' And there's something that's like a twinkle in my eye, which is almost like because back then the only fun things to do were drink, whore, but [the prospect of the duel] was really exciting. That was really living on the edge, that was really life and death, and it was the only thing that really turned Johnny on. That was the height for him, like when guys skydive, or why people go to horror movies to get that scary feeling, that adrenalin rush." Kilmer's cigarette was about an inch and a half long and the scene had to be filmed several times from a variety of different angles. After each take, an assistant would cut a new cigarette to the correct length, light it and hand it to Val before they hollered "Action!" again. According to those present, they went through at least 20 cigarettes. And Greg Poulos found himself responsible for rolling Val's as he was the only one who could do it right. Says Steve Melton, "Val would literally roll it wrong—just tear it in two and throw it on the ground. Greg always did it better."[34]

"George really liked us because we worked hard and didn't give him any flak," explains Greg. "We would finish a scene on the set and George would call for me. He'd say, 'I want this, I want that.' He'd want all these props and set dressing [for his own personal use] and I kept putting them aside and I'd tell the producer, 'George wants this chair. Just put it aside and we'll figure it out at the end.' Every set, he'd want something from it and I became the guy that would just store it for him." Who knows where it all ended up; Cosmatos *was* given his personalized director chair.[35]

Cosmatos spent the remainder of that week filming the wedding massacre scene, one of the most complicated scenes in the film, in front of the Old Tucson mission. Shooting it took several days with both first and second unit involvement as well as 111 principal actors, stuntmen, Buckaroos, children and extras. Initially, the scene was much longer and more extensive than what appears in the film; it included numerous stunt gags, including several Cowboys being killed and a stuntman falling into the plaza's fountain. Many wedding guests also hurriedly departed the area when the Cowboys first arrived in town but it doesn't play that way on the screen. (The mission was originally constructed in 1939 for the film *Arizona* and, over the years, had appeared in numerous films with a variety of different facades. It underwent an extensive $750,000 facelift in 1986 for the film *¡Three Amigos!* and had kept that new appearance until it was destroyed in the 1995 fire.) Although the first unit moved to Mescal on Thursday, July 8, the second unit remained through Saturday to film the final stunt sequences. Written on July 1, the wedding massacre scene was not in any version of Jarre's script but was used by John Fasano as a substitute for the Old Man Clanton–Cowboy assault on the Mexican Rurales. However, much of Jarre's dialogue was included in this revised scene, including a portion of Revelation 6:7–8. "…behold, a pale horse: and his name that sat on him was Death, and hell followed with him." Wardrobe crew member Michelle Beauchamp played the part of the Mexican bride and Michael Garcia was the groom. Garcia also filled the role of a Rurale captain in several scenes that never made the final cut. In later interviews, Michael Biehn admitted he was particularly upset with that scene: "What they did, which I never liked, is that after Kevin left the show, they added the scene [where] Johnny Ringo shoots the priest at the beginning of the movie. Well, Johnny Ringo never shot any priest. That never happened. I always found it difficult to play and I fought against it hard, but I'm a nobody when it comes to that argument against Disney. It always hurt me that I had to play a character that was based on a true-life character and he was portrayed as somebody who would shoot a priest between the eyes. Disney wanted good guys and bad guys … with Kevin, it was a much grayer script." Biehn publicly apologized for his portrayal in that scene at a Texas panel discussion in 2012. Stephen Lang was none too pleased, either, admitting, "I hated the Mexican wedding massacre myself. The Skeleton Canyon ambush is a matter of record, and would have been a great opening scene. But it just wasn't going to happen."[36]

Prior to the addition of and subsequent filming of the wedding scene, the film originally was to begin with a confrontation between Old Man Clanton, Curly Bill, Johnny Ringo, several Cowboys and a squad of Mexican Rurales. (Several Buckaroos were dressed in Mexican uniforms and, made up with dark faces and mustaches, rode as a squad through the desert. Veteran actor Pedro Armendariz, Jr., filled the role of the Rurale captain. This scene was filmed, but it wasn't included in the final print. Armendariz then played the part of the priest in the wedding scene.) Wranglers and stuntman filling the roles of the Rurale soldiers included J.T. Hall, Kip Farnsworth, Jeff Ramsey, Hal Burton, Joe Getzweiler, Jerry Wills, Tommy Rosales and Richard Duran. Glenn Ford, Kirk Douglas and even Gregory Peck were contacted for the part of Clanton, but eventually Robert Mitchum filled the role. However, by the time they were ready to film the scene, Cinergi decided it couldn't afford it, so Mitchum neither appeared on location nor was ever fitted for his wardrobe. And rather than explain the financial issues, the studio's publicity machine instead announced that Mitchum had suffered a back injury after a few hours on horseback and thus had been written out of the film. In an interview he gave to *Trail Dust* magazine, Mitchum said, "I was to play Old Man Clanton, but I was having trouble with my back. I had it X-rayed and the doctor forbade me to do it because of the second scene. I'm lying there with a horse on top of me. So I had to beg off…. [T]hen they asked me to narrate it." And that was partially true. In August 1993, spurred on by genuine interest from George Cosmatos, Mitchum was approached to do the voiceover work for the prologue and epilogue "especially since [he] was unable to appear in the picture." This was literally months *after* Mitchum's scenes were to have been filmed. Interestingly, on the same day Cosmatos made this suggestion, Bob Misiorowski notified Andy Vajna that Hugh O'Brian was interested in doing the voiceover. Adam Taylor's wife Anne Lockhart Taylor explains how this offer was made to Mitchum: "As far as I recall, they said to

Old Tucson Studios. As a hat-wearing George Cosmatos gives Powers Boothe (Curly Bill Brocius) last-minute instructions for the wedding scene massacre and Michael Biehn (Johnny Ringo) balances himself on the plaza fountain, a goat watches the proceedings (courtesy Larry Zeug).

[Mitchum], 'Look. This part is basically not going to be there any more. But we'll pay you the same money if you come in and do an hour's worth of looping.'" And the late-addition wedding scene? Hot-head tech James Danicic says the wedding scene was written just a few days before it was filmed, revealing, "I was told, the scene was based on them seeing [wardrobe assistant] Michelle Beauchamp. 'Let's make it a wedding scene. She's got to be the bride.'" Other than the footage with Charlton Heston, the only other scene Jarre directed that remained in the film was an insert of the food-laden wedding table. A mariachi band is present in this scene. Terry Leonard even used the band as background music while he set up the next shot.[37]

Stuntman Jeff Ramsey has bittersweet memories of playing one of the Rurales in that scene. "There's a shootout in front of the church which involves the Red Sash crowd," says Ramsey, "and I was there to get killed. But I worked out all the time, and in the hotel where we were, there was a small gym setup, so I'd work out. I remember doing curls with a cable and a bar, a weighted machine, and I blew out L3 (a lumbar vertebra), because I had fused my back earlier in '89, 4 and 5. While doing these curls, typically too much heavy weight and I blew out L3, which is a painful situation. So the next day I'm praying that Leonard doesn't have me do another stunt in this sequence because I didn't have any Percodan with me, which I normally took on the job in case I got hurt. The fellas found

The Rurale wedding party and the mariachi band await the beginning of a scene on the Old Tucson wedding set (courtesy P.J. Lawton, Old Tucson Studio).

out. I said, 'Do you have any pain killers?' One fella says, 'Well, I have some Vicadin.' I never took that before. He said, 'You better take two.' So, I took two and it really knocked me down. We were inside one of those sets at Old Tucson, and I'm lying on a crash pad and I'm thinking to myself, 'Oh, my God. If Leonard calls me, I can't do anything. I'm almost paralyzed from these drugs.' I get up and drink coffee and I didn't know that coffee makes it even worse." Ramsey was there for just the one scene and then left the set for Los Angeles where he had surgery to take care of his issue.[38]

That weekend, the production moved its base camp to Mescal—the Buckaroos called it "Stalag 13"—and Sam Dolan remembers, "We were setting up our camp [at] the main ranch set for the old *Young Riders* TV show, about 200 yards from town. It was a little white ranch house with a barn and outbuildings, and we set up corrals down there and our tents around those buildings. There was a little bit of down time as filming wouldn't begin in Mescal until July 14. A typical day that July and August started out at sunrise. We would wake up, climb into our wardrobe—most of it pretty filthy unless we'd gone to the laundromat in Benson—and even then they wanted our clothes to look dirty and so they got pretty nasty. Then we'd feed and water the horses. While they ate, we walked over to the set and got breakfast with the crew. Then we'd go back and saddle our mounts for the day, get our guns, and ride back to set. Half the day was spent sitting around, waiting. Then, one of the ADs would place us in the street for a scene, but mainly we sat around under the shade of the awnings waiting or napping. At lunch we would water the horses, loosen their cinches and line up at the catering truck. The Buckaroos were allowed to have lunch most days with the crew and principal cast. There was a separate line for the regular extras."

Michael Garcia (Rurale captain and groom) and Michelle Beauchamp (bride) leave the church as Pedro Armendariz, Jr. (priest), follows with a group of stuntmen dressed as Rurale soldiers.

Jeff Dolan explains how the Buckaroos scammed the system: "At lunch, we'd always get a couple extra lunches. We'd say, 'Hey, we gotta get a lunch for Bill back in the camp.' And the cook would go, 'Sure, fine.' Of course, we ate like kings and they put together a nice lunch and that would be the basis for sort of Mulligan stew–kind of dinner. They would add beans and somebody else would pull out something and we had the basis of the two lunches and we'd make a small dinner for half a dozen of us. It was really fun."[39]

July in Cochise County that year was brutal. The horses all lost weight and the afternoons could be really unpleasant. The air around the set was filled with smoke from the bee gum smoke pots the FX crew burned all day. Flies were constantly all over everything, man and beast.

According to J. Nathan Simmons, "Sam [Elliott] was very cool about sitting with the background players. One time Kurt yelled towards Sam, 'You don't have to eat with those extras.' Sam said, 'Put my pants on the same way they do, one leg at a time.' Sam was a stand-up guy." Simmons recalls another Elliott incident that impressed him: "Kurt Russell was trying to fire a five-year-old kid for asking for an autograph. He didn't know any better. He's a five-year-old kid. If I remember correctly, Sam Elliott stood up for him. 'He's a five-year-old kid. If you fire him, I'm walking off the set. And the only stipulation is that you leave him and his family alone for the rest of the movie. And you don't speak

Red Sash gang members await their turns at the catering wagons (courtesy Larry Zeug).

to the background [players]. You don't need to speak to the background. That's not your job.' I remember that. That's one of the things I admired about him. He knew we were there to work just as hard as he did."[40]

Donna Cline was also impressed with Elliott's behavior. "All of the women, every one of them—we were in love with Sam Elliott," she gushed. "He was a cowboy and a gentlemen and he absolutely had his priorities right. One night we were shooting all night long and George was acting up. It was about five in the morning. Finally, Sam said, 'George, stop this right now. We have all been up all night. You are tired. So are we. We're trying our best, so stop yelling.' I was so happy and proud of him—he stood up to George. [Another time, Sam] was in the production office and apparently George made him angry. He was wearing that big old cowboy hat and he was mad as hell. He was cussing and we were all surprised by this unusual display of temper. Sam turned around as he was leaving the office. There was a small dog gate stretching across the door because we always had animals in the production office. He stepped over it, turned around, took off his big hat and said, 'Ladies, please forgive my language.' We did, of course."[41]

One day on the set, Cosmatos told property master Steve Melton, "I need flies. I want flies on these dead people." So they had to figure out how to catch some flies. There are ways, as Melton explains, "We found out if you put a fly into a freeze for 30 minutes, it sort of stuns it and numbs it and then you pour Gatorade on the actor's face and literally set these flies on the actor's face, roll camera and then the fly sort of comes to life and starts to move and buzz around and there you go. You've got your shot. George told us how to do that and the flies weren't moving and he's screaming, we're ruining his movie and why aren't the flies doing anything. He was just really bizarre; basically he just screamed and spit a lot."[42]

As the shooting schedule extended into mid–July, the days on the set became longer and both temperature and tempers began to rise. People were fired left and right for little or no reason and in some cases just because they could be. One night, for instance, Cosmatos told production assistant James Alan Hensz to pick up a granola bar wrapper lying in the street. Egos being what they were, he refused to do so and was fired. All the other ADs and PAs liked Hensz, so for several days people wore granola bar wrappers pinned to their jackets and shirts as a silent protest. It didn't last very long but they made their point. It was said that over 100 people were fired from the project. Of course, many were swept away when Cosmatos cleaned house after he arrived on the set. Property assistant Greg Poulos' experience sounds fairly typical: "I was asked by Michael Courville to go down there with him and Jim Falkenstein to do the movie. [John Sanders, the] first prop master, had been fired and Michael replaced him. [When the first property master left,] his whole crew went with him. If the prop master leaves, usually the crew will go with him. They're pretty dedicated to who they work with. They keep their crews, they know they can trust them. They know what their job is and they do it. So it's pretty normal." Later, Courville and Falkenstein left to do sitcoms, and Steve Melton took over as first property master. Other crew members left due to Cosmatos' abrasive personality and general lack of directorial skills. Some remaining crew members began wearing *Tombstone* T-shirts with the names of those fired listed on the backs with a line drawn through their names. When Cosmatos would offend or fire someone, Stephen Lang admits that he (Lang) would "just start to laugh and sing, 'And another one bites the dust....'"[43]

According to James Danicic, hot-head technician for the film, "Cosmatos decided he wanted a remote-head guy for cranes. When you're filming with horses and stuff like that, you like to have the camera [higher] up and get more dynamic shots. He wanted a crane for every set; a small one, a long one, medium in between. [Sometimes] I had a long 70-foot crane, high with a wide-angle lens. It was interesting that so many people were let go so quickly over a lot of little things. People cycled through so quickly. It got to the point with camera people that I just stopped introducing myself.... [F]ocus pullers would be there a day or two days and then [be] gone. It was a big movie with several cameras and people missed shots from time to time, but you could have one bad night and you were gone. I know at some point there were at least two crew members who put their names on the tombstones at Boot Hill. There was also a rumor ... that we had extra camera people at other hotels ... just standing by that if you pulled a bad shot, they'd take you off the set that night and have someone on the way to replace you."[44]

Animosity on the set wasn't confined to just Cosmatos and the cast and crew. Many of the wranglers and stuntmen hated the Buckaroos because, in their opinion, the re-enactors were taking their jobs. Some of the wranglers drove wagons in the background and cut off the Buckaroos just for spite. Chris Ramirez recalls, "We'd ride by the wranglers in their jeans and jacket and modern cowboy hat and they'd look at us and go, 'Scab. Why don't you fuckers go home?' And we'd just ride by. Really uncomfortable."

"I argued with those wranglers every day," says an exasperated Sherayko. "We almost had a fistfight a couple of times because they wanted to get their buddies in to ride instead of the Buckaroos. They hated the Buckaroos. They said, 'These guys, they haven't been on [a movie set,] they can't ride.' That's what (the wranglers) want to do. That's what 90 percent of them do. They're good cowboys, they're good horsemen, but they're rodeo ropers. The wranglers are a close group of people that bring their own friends in [as well as] their own saddles, which were modern roping saddles. We (Buckaroos) kept saying, 'No. We have to use Sam Stagg–rigged, half-seat slick forks. You can't use [a modern] saddle.' I remember one of the guys … was taking a *Boss of the Plains* hat and he was creasing it and crushing it and curling up the sides, and I kept saying, 'Don't do that. Don't make it look like a modern rodeo hat. It's not.' They said, 'Well, that's the way a cowboy's hat supposed to look.' They just got so mad at me. (*The Boss of the Plains* is a high-crown, stiff-brimmed cowboy hat designed by John Stetson in 1865.) One of the assistant wranglers challenged me. He said, 'Oh, the Buckaroos can't ride. Your guys are no good.' I said, 'Look, you guys are (the) roping cowboys.' Every wrangler I know is a rodeo cowboy. I had three or four guys that were real live rodeo cowboys. So I challenged [the wranglers]. I said, 'Okay, let's put $5000 down. We'll have a contest. You take the best three of your guys for roping, I'll take the best three of my guys for roping. You take the best three for shooting from horseback at targets, I'll take the best three of my guys, $5000 each and winner take all.' I knew that even though they were good ropers, they were lousy with a gun on a horse. So I knew we'd win three out of those and I knew at least one of my ropers would win out of the three. So, I'd be four to two ahead and we'd win. They wouldn't take me up on it. 'No, fuck you…' So we had arguments all the time."[45]

Frayed tempers and excessive heat made filming almost unbearable. On many days, the cast would leave the hotel at six a.m., with the first shot of the day scheduled for 9:00 a.m. They would have lunch at 1:30 p.m., and would be back filming again by 3:00 p.m. The day concluded around 7:00 p.m. If night shooting was planned, the schedule was even tougher: Leave at 5:00 p.m., first shot at 7:00 p.m., lunch at midnight, start filming again at 1:00 a.m., and wrap up the evening at 6:00 a.m. One Buckaroo spoke for everyone when he said, "During the last month or so, you learned to keep your head down. You talked to the cast members you developed friendly relationships with, but you stayed away from George and the first-team people unless spoken to. Our horses were tired. We were tired. Those last few weeks were tough. Our tempers were short and sadly, we were not always at our best…. [T]he truth is we were worn out and ready for it to be over." And Southern Arizona's summertime heat was unbelievable. Not only would the call sheets detail what scenes were to be filmed, who was present, leave and crew call times and special instructions, they also identified sunrise and sunset times and the temperature. And it was damn hot. Temperatures were always in the very low 100s and on June 28, it reached 114°. "I found it a little inconvenient that Jarre insisted on our wearing real wool," complained Kilmer. "'It has to be wool. You can tell the difference,' he said. Well, you can't, Kevin Jarre. You can't tell the difference between real wool and any blend, even in a macro close-up, okay? When it's 134° inside the studio … you didn't really have to think about diet much…. It really was that hot. Someone put a thermometer in the theater scene—it was 134. In a wool suit, being Doc was easy to do. That was my theory about why Doc killed so many people. It's just like he wore wool, in the summer, in the Arizona territory and that made him mad."

When they filmed in the evenings, it was usually in the mid–80s—tolerable but still warm when dressed in period costumes and acting under the hot lights. As a result, staying hydrated became mandatory because failure to do so resulted in dire circumstances.

When asked what the greatest challenges were from a production standpoint, producer Bob Misiorowski said, "Heat and horse manure. Moving the horses, shading the horses, watering the horses, cleaning up after the horses. Flies, water, ice and salt tablets. All the cast and crew were constantly reminded to drink plenty of water." The heat even cut down the director, according to at least three witnesses: Buckaroo Jeff Dolan: "[George] passed out one day from the heat. He fell over [while] overcome with heat exhaustion working hard out there in the sun, trying to get it done." Property master Steve Melton: "I remember him falling over one day from heat exhaustion and literally no one, the crew was just walking right by him. He fell over in a chair. Finally a medic came and they had to give him water." Bobby Vincent: "Cosmatos was a pretty hefty guy. It was so hot, they had a 15-passenger van that they ended up taking the seats out of it because he over-heated. They poured a bunch of water on that poor guy and ended up turning the air conditioning on and finally got him cooled off." (Extras and crew members would humorously call the director "George Comatose" or "The Screaming Greek" or "Zorba the Hut.") Adds Vincent, "I was sitting on my horse talking to a production assistant one day, and I said something and she didn't respond; she'd fallen over flat on her back. So I yelled out and somebody came over and took care of her. There was a lot of that. I drank Gatorade and water like it was going out of style. You'd never go to the bathroom—you drank water all day long and never have to pee because it just came out of your pores: 112, 113, 114°. It was really hot for a while there, really hot. I had a black horse but he lost a lot of weight, partially because he was dark. And it was so hot and having the saddle on him all day long. He literally got sunburned." Even the Buckaroos, who were sleeping in their tents and should have been fully acclimated to the temperature, found it difficult.

Cosmatos didn't make it any better. One day he looked around and said, "This is supposed to be October, why is nobody wearing coats?" And, of course, it's the middle of August outside of Benson. The next thing you know, everybody's wearing coats. They were told, "Wear a coat. Wear winter clothing." No wonder everyone couldn't wait until filming was over. Focus puller Michael Walker humorously remembers, "You can just see [the actors] start to wobble. 'Oh God. There goes another one.' Back then we were burning 18Ks to get the lights, the shadow underneath the hat and exteriors. We have five or six 18Ks burning just to get the exposure for underneath the hats with the sun beating down on them, the backlight. It was a very hot set, especially wearing wool, it was brutal. It was brutal for me lugging camera gear around. It was a tough location."[46]

The excessive temperatures not only affected the actors, the production equipment also began to broil under the heat's wrath. Trailers began to flex, shrink and expand, and "problems [occurred] with the electrical outlets—several meltdowns happened." But as usual, creative minds resolved the issues. Says James Danicic, "When they did the interior shots, they had these big trailers with AC units on them and they'd run these big pipes right by my truck into the set. They had all these sections they put together and I would open up a section and take a couple of space blankets and attach an offshoot tube and throw it into my truck so I had some air conditioning because they wouldn't let me idle the truck and run AC all day. But I'd sit there with a [walkie-talkie] and wait for my name to be called on the camera channel."[47]

Many actresses wore big, heavy petticoats and the wardrobe department warned the medics that "some of these dresses are five to ten thousand dollars so if something happens, don't cut them off." It was fortunate that medic Chris Swinney had a motor

Lounging on the porch of the Grand Hotel, Mescal. With temperatures in excess of 110°, any shade was a welcome relief. The porch roof collapsed from the excessive weight of camera and lighting equipment and crew when filming *Lightning Jack* (photograph by Lee Gray/courtesy Catherine Hardwicke).

home with two air-conditioning units parked on the set in case somebody needed attention. "I once went to check on [actress] Lisa Collins," says Chris, "who said she was fine. I told her, 'You're crawling on the ground. You're not fine.' So I got her in the motor home. Wardrobe ran over to help me with the petticoat."

Special effects coordinator Dale Martin wasn't as fortunate. According to Swinney, "He was having some problems. I don't know if it was just the hours or the weather or the stress. There was a day that I checked him out and his vitals were all over the place. The producers and I got together and they ended up sending him home; he later passed away."[48]

As would be expected, in addition to all the conflict and tension, the production seemed to have more than its share of incidents:

- Cows gave birth to calves while others died of natural causes.
- Meryle Sellinger's German shepherd bit prop master Michael Courville on the arm.
- Several cast and crew members, including Michael Biehn, transportation coordinator Jon Carpenter and wardrobe assistant Amber Dunn were involved in deer-related car accidents.
- A vehicle was deliberately scratched in the hotel parking lot.
- Carpenter John Ashley received an eight-inch laceration on his leg from a power saw.
- A mule died.

Of course, such misfortunes didn't affect just crew members. Stephen Lang joined first assistant director Conte Matal in battling a flu bug. PA Donald Murphy slipped and twisted a knee, as did George Cosmatos. Actor Michael Rooker received a cut on his cheek. Extra John Wayne Galloway suffered cuts on his hands and arms after he went through a plate-glass window. And on top of all that, some of the film actors felt that the television actors weren't taking the project seriously—joking around, having too good a time.[49]

Expecting something different was pointless, so for many, humor was the only solution. In addition to the aforementioned "termination" T-shirt, Catherine Hardwicke created another, more eloquent version that made the rounds. This one listed numerous memorable comments the director had made during filming:

That ain't bad. You're biting me! SPAK, NOT GAK. What exactly is it I'm supposed to be doing? *How do you expect me to do THAT?* Madga and Shannon Finch will be handling that. I'm on a higher moral ground than you are. I think that was the oil pan back there. Just hire a couple of Rons. Could I leave early today to see my parole officer? *He's a stripper, Gene. He's hired.* Anybody seen the Oriental foo-foo? *That job should take two minutes.* Anybody seen Eddie? Love on the rocks—ain't no big surprise. It's made of people! *I know 100 people in LA who would come out here and work on a moment's notice.* Rob, you can strike Hooker's today. I'm absolutely exhausted. I've been Partying all night with Jason Priestley. Rob, we're shooting Hooker's tomorrow. Hel-loo! *Put this in the I don't even want to see it on any planet file.* LET ME SHUT UP. The movie is over. Rob, you can strike Hooker's today. You better work. Why don't you lick it? Rob, we're shooting Hooker's tomorrow. YOU are the so-called Production Designer? *Carla, your lover Tino called.* Who hired these people? I don't know what a phone instrument is, but I'll find out and I'll have one there tomorrow. *Underwater bridge? Fine, I'll send 20 guys with a truckload of shit and they'll stand around and go Duh?* You want ME to be there? You want Me to go to the set? If you can see me on the set, you know something's wrong. *Would Stanley Kubrick have this in his movie?* This is the Crucifixion, don't you see it? I can't do that, I'm sun sensitive. Who do you think you are, Patrizia Van Brandenstein? Mara? She's absolutely worthless but compared to your other incompetents, maybe she's not so bad. KAAAATE!! YOU'RE DOING A VERY BAD JOB! THIS LOOKS LIKE SHIT. *Equal sex for equal pay regardless of work.* I can paint that whole fucking wagon in 20 minutes. Okay, I'm timing you. Brian, do something about these shadows. If I see anyone standing around watching filming, they're fired. If anyone parks in town, they're fired. If anyone buys anything at Payless without an approval, they're fired. If anyone walks into the shot, they're fired. You're fired. Do you know what that means? (Just put on a different t-shirt and go back in.) *Who is this Serdena? Is he Italian?* Maybe you'll get to know me better and know why I drive women crazy. I'm taking antibiotics. I'm just not healthy. There is no construction coordinator on this film. Day players don't get lunch. THIS SHOW IS OVER. *I could buy this chair at Wal-Mart for ten dollars. Sir, that chair is worth more than you'll make on this entire movie.* Where's Eddie? I made Bambi's list? I've never been so abused in my life. I can't even go out partying. Of course, you did see me having one drink last night. Rob, you can strike Hooker's today. How's YOUR movie going? Rob, we're shooting Hooker's again tomorrow. *I'm all over it. What was it that I was all over?* MR. THING. Who put this deer head up here? Bring the man here right now! You get an "F" today. Yeah… Right! *You look like you need a Corvette.* You get a spanking. Anybody got a screw for their old man? Is anybody on the radio? … This is Seth… I'm in the O.K. Corral… Does anybody need me? 10–4. I'm on it. Get the FUCK out of the shot! Everything's in the fucking shot! A-DAM! *I've been begging people to do this for weeks.* I asked you 100 times three weeks ago to fix that board. Where the fuck is David Solomon? Gene, could we just finish Virgil's? *I'm not an infant.* You dress terrible. You should wear a long black dress and carry a cigarette holder and call yourself "von Hardwicke." That is SWEET! KILL IT!

Laughing, Catherine confesses, "I made 25 T-shirts for my art department and it was all the most outrageous quotes that [Cosmatos] said. I was handing them out to people and [George] came up and said, 'What the hell is this?' 'These are all your crazy quotes, George. It's kind a tribute to all your poetry.' 'Oh, it's all about me? I want five of these in each size.' And he demanded that I send him five of the T-shirts." Later, when he heard that she had a professional photographer take photos of the set, he also demanded 8 × 10s of them, and insisted that Hardwicke pay for it![50]

For others, the classic rubber chicken was enough to break the tension. The origin of the gag is unknown but it never fails to get a laugh. Some of the Buckaroos would ride around with a rubber chicken on their saddle and they'd pass it back and forth. Many would stuff the chicken in a saddle bag with the feet sticking out, or in a rifle scabbard, or just hang it from a saddle horn. It was even hung from balconies and railings. The trick was to insert it into a scene unbeknownst to anyone and then hope no one would catch it. Although Reggie Byrum wasn't in the O.K. Corral gunfight scene, he still wanted his chicken included. "[I] wasn't involved in the [scene] but I was going to play a joke when they were filming it. I was going to throw the rubber chicken in the middle of the gunfight. But every place I was going to do it, there was somebody there filming so I [couldn't]. [On another occasion] we put the chicken inside the saloon where [Kurt] jumps through the window, but it disappeared. I had it in my saddle [and was] using it for a horse quirt. One guy had it sticking out of his bedroll. We'd take turns carrying it around [but, if it was ever filmed in a scene], they cut it out. Sometimes, they even used rubber snakes."[51]

There were several kids around, including Norman Ritter and Cassandra Swinney, and they had a great time being on the set. Josh Swinney recalls, "There was a bunch of abandoned buildings we would play around in. I just remember hanging out with all the kids; it was a big jungle-gym to us. Sometimes we'd go in a building and watch them film a scene from up on the second floor, looking through the curtains. I always wondered if we were going to get in the scene. They didn't keep track of us as much because we didn't listen to them very well from what they told us to do when we were out there. But, when we weren't on the set, we were running around…. [One day] they made a call over the radio looking for kids to be in a scene." Cosmatos had approached Chris Swinney and asked if Swinney's kids were on location that day. "We have no children in this scene," Cosmatos told him. "I want children in this scene. Will you go get the kids and take them to wardrobe and have them dressed and bring them to me?" Swinney recalls, "I went over and got Yanez, Tomas Arana's son, Wyatt (Russell), my son Christopher and my stepson Michael (Ritter), sent them to wardrobe, and he put them in the scene." Josh Swinney: "My dad came and found us, we were playing around in this old barn. Every day I would come in, we'd be playing and then they'd say, 'Okay, go get dressed.' We would get dressed and we would play in all the other barns and everything we would do normally, and then when they needed us, they'd come find us. We were already dressed up. It really didn't matter how dirty you got because it was kind of the thing. They didn't want us tearing the clothes, but at the same time it didn't really matter how filthy we got. I guess the filthier, the better. They even sprayed dirt on us for one scene. There was dirt in the little pump cans that they sprayed—it was kind of like mud. Just kind of mist it on you because you come in and I had blond hair, blue eyes and fair skin. I'd come in, I was kind of glowing. Knock you down with some dirt, put some makeup on your face."[52]

Goldie Hawn visited Kurt on the set a number of times, with their son Wyatt and her daughter Kate Hudson. Wyatt would pick up his father in a golf cart and drive hellbent for leather to wherever he was going. Val Kilmer's wife and children came to the set at least once, as did Michael Rooker's children. On one occasion, Rooker grabbed one

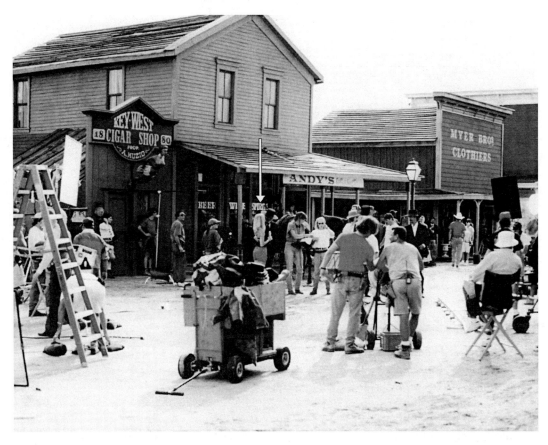

Cast and crew members patiently wait the setup for the scene in which Fred White (Harry Carey, Jr.) introduces the Earp brothers to the political aspects in the town of Tombstone. Kurt Russell stands with his arm around Goldie Hawn (see arrow) in front of the Key West Cigar Shop on the Mescal set (courtesy Larry Zeug).

of the sugar glass bottles from the prop table and smashed it over his head in front of the kids, who were horrified. "Don't worry," he said, "it's just a movie bottle." Rick Terry recalls another humorous incident: "There's a scene where Val plays the piano in the saloon. He was rehearsing, it was during the day and he was inside, practicing [on] the piano what he was going to play. We were outside sitting in the shade, listening to it, not thinking much of it. He had on this cape that he wears in the shootout, and the makeup that he had on kind of made him look pale—it was kind of white. And I remember one of these extras, a young kid, maybe 10 or 12, a couple of them [were] hanging around. So he gets done and Val comes walking out onto the boardwalk where we are sitting and this kid looks at him and says, 'Who are you supposed to be?' And staying in his Doc Holliday character, Val said, 'What's it to you?' It made the kid kind of embarrassed. So Val walks away and the kid says, 'I think we oughta start calling him Count Docula.' And then it got around. People started calling him Count Docula."

Kilmer wasn't happy with his piano-playing performance. "I'm musical," he admits, "but I'm no pianist. Learning a nocturne for *Tombstone* was a real bitch! It took four months and then they blew the edit. I can play one minute of Chopin and Chop-sticks. That's my entire piano repertoire."[53]

SIX

Back and Forth
and Back Again

Wednesday, October 26, 1881. Tombstone, Arizona Territory. Four men—three peace officers and a deputized gambler-cum-dentist—walked defiantly up Fourth Street toward Fremont and a date with destiny. Awaiting them in a small lot next to the Fry house behind the O.K. Corral were two sets of brothers and a fifth individual, collectively known as Cowboys. Little did any one of them realize that three of these outlaws would never see another sunrise.

Ike Clanton and Frank McLaury had arrived in Tombstone the previous day with a wagonload of beef for sale. They dropped their wares off at the West End Corral and Clanton headed over to the Alhambra Saloon where he soon ran into Doc Holliday. Due to previous altercations, an argument ensued when Holliday referred to Clanton as "a damned liar" and a "son-of-a-bitch cowboy." Holliday continued his taunts with a challenge: "You son of a bitch. If you ain't heeled, go heel yourself." Morgan Earp, who was in the Alhambra, broke up the argument but stoked the fire by telling Clanton, "Yes, you son of a bitch. You can have all the fight you want, now!" Earp then escorted Holliday out of the saloon, followed by Ike. Later, a still-furious Clanton encountered Wyatt Earp and challenged him to a gunfight, but Earp declined. ("I told him I would fight no one if I could get away from it, because there was no money in it.") Undaunted, Clanton replied, "I will be ready for you in the morning." Curiously, though, Clanton, Sheriff John Behan, Virgil Earp and Tom McLaury then retired to the Occidental Saloon for a five-hour poker game, which eventually wrapped up with yet additional threats from Clanton, this time aimed at Holliday. "That damn son of a bitch has got to fight," he told Virgil Earp. When Earp cautioned Clanton to watch his step, Ike replied, "You may have to fight before you know it." As a result, over the next 12 hours, Clanton continued to drink and several townspeople reported he endlessly threatened the Earps. The next morning, after searching for Holliday at Fly's boarding house, Ike retrieved his rifle and revolver from the West End Corral, where he had deposited them the previous day. Warned that Clanton was armed and had threatened them, Morgan and Virgil confronted Clanton outside the Capital Saloon, then buffaloed and disarmed him. Wyatt then escorted Ike before Judge Albert O. Wallace for violating a city ordinance. Clanton was fined $25 plus $2.50 in court costs and released; his weapons were deposited at the Grand Hotel and retrieved several days later. By now, Wyatt, tired of being threatened and believing he and his brothers would be assassinated at the earliest opportunity, challenged Clanton in the courthouse. "You damned dirty cow thief," he told the Cowboy. "You have been threatening our lives and I know it. I think I would be justified in shooting you down *any place I should meet you, but if you are anxious to make a fight, I will go anywhere on earth to make a fight with you, even over to the San Simon among your crowd!" Clanton bravely replied, "I will see you after I get through here. I only want four feet of ground to fight on." After more threats and provocations, Wyatt left the courthouse and almost bumped into Tom McLaury, who reportedly also challenged Earp. Face to face, they exchanged words when, suddenly, Earp demanded, "Are you heeled or not?" According to Wyatt, McLaury replied, "If you want to make a fight, I will make a fight with you anywhere," whereupon Earp slapped the Cowboy with his left hand and struck McLaury once on the side of his head with a pistol. McLaury was left lying bleeding in the street. After a sleepless evening of drinking and gambling, neither Clanton nor McLaury was in any mood for forgiveness, particularly after each had been pistol-whipped by an Earp.*

By 1:30 p.m. on the 26th, the outlaw duo now had been joined in town by Ike's brother Billy and Frank's brother Tom. All were armed and dangerous. By all rights, as per the town's requirement, they should have left their weapons at the Grand Hotel when they arrived ... but no one did. Eventually, the group was joined by Billy Claiborne. The McLaury brothers and Billy Clanton met Ike at Spangenberger's gun shop, purchased cartridges for their gun belts, and then split up. (Ike Clanton had attempted to buy a revolver in the shop but was refused.) While Ike went to the Occidental Saloon to continue fueling his courage, the others went to the Dexter Corral "to get something (Billy) left there." Eventually, all gathered at the O.K. Corral where, once again, witnesses heard them threaten the Earps. They then walked out the back of the corral and, along with two horses, turned west and stopped in a small vacant lot, a mere 20 feet wide, that sat between William Harwood's and C.S. Fly's boarding houses. The stage was now set: Tensions escalating and confrontation inevitable. All that was missing were the rest of the participants.

Several townspeople had notified Sheriff Behan and Marshal Earp that the Cowboys were armed, and many offered the marshal their help in apprehending the gang. While outside of Hafford's Saloon, Earp asked Behan for his assistance but was quickly rebuffed. Rather, the sheriff offered to go himself to see if he could disarm the gang. After waiting 20 minutes for Behan's return, Earp was informed by John L. Fonck of the Cowboys' actions. Virgil told the local businessman he wouldn't interfere "as long as they stayed in the corral," but if they remained armed and walked the streets, then he would "disarm and arrest them." Fonck responded, "Why, they are all down on Fremont Street now."

Behan had quickly located, approached and asked the five outlaws if they were, in fact, armed. According to his subsequent testimony, Behan said Ike Clanton told him he was unarmed, and Tom McLaury pulled open his coat to show the sheriff he wasn't carrying a weapon. (Behan said he put his arm around Ike's waist to see if he was armed; he didn't bother to search McLaury. This, despite the fact that there is no evidence that the Cowboys had ever deposited their weapons anywhere in town in accordance with the local ordinance.) Behan further testified that although Frank McLaury was armed, the Cowboy wouldn't relinquish possession of his weapon unless the Earps did so as well. The sheriff ignored Claiborne, who said he wasn't involved in the quarrel, and made no attempt to disarm Billy Clanton, who told Behan that he was on his way out of town. Behan then told the Cowboys he would "disarm the other party" and left to find the Earps and Holliday. When later asked if he had arrested the group before he departed, Behan was his usual ineffective self: "I considered the Clanton party under arrest, but I doubt whether they considered themselves under arrest or not."

Faced with no alternative but to neutralize the Cowboys himself, Marshal Earp, along with his brothers Wyatt and Morgan, and the deputized Holliday, marched north up Fourth Street. Virgil exchanged his shotgun that he had earlier retrieved from the Wells Fargo office with Holliday's walking stick and told Doc to conceal the weapon under his long coat. Wyatt and Morgan held their revolvers in their hands. As the four turned west onto Fremont Street's wooden sidewalk, they passed the Capital Saloon, the Tombstone Nugget *newspaper* office and the post office before they reached the rear entrance of the O.K. Corral. According to Tombstone housewife Martha J. King, who was shopping inside the butcher shop, the Earps walked four abreast as they passed the Union Market, but, because the sidewalk was too narrow, the two outside men were slightly in front of the two inside men in a bow-like formation. An anxious Behan attempted to detain the foursome in front of Bauer's and warned, "Gentlemen, I'm the sheriff of the county and am not going to allow any trouble if I can help it." As the Earps walked on toward the corral, Behan claimed he told them he was down there "for the purpose of arresting and disarming" the Cowboys. However, Wyatt said when he heard Behan say to Virgil, "For God's sake, don't go down there or you will be murdered," Virgil replied, "I am going to disarm them." Undeterred, the four quickly brushed past the sheriff, moved into the center of the street and continued their dramatic walk as Behan yelled, "I have disarmed them!" If so, then where were the Cowboys' guns? And why would he warn the Earps of their possible murders if he had already disarmed them?

Nonetheless, the Earps must have somewhat believed Behan as Wyatt put his revolver back in his overcoat pocket and Virgil later testified, "I had a walking stick in my left hand and my hand was on my six-shooter in my waist pants, and when [Behan] had said he had disarmed them, I shoved it clean around to my left hip and changed my walking stick to my right hand." Imagine the Earps' surprise when they reached the corral and observed that not only were Frank McLaury and Billy Clanton armed, but rifles also were visible in their horse scabbards. Behan had lied! Looking north toward Fremont Street, the four aligned thus: Wyatt stood on the far right, next to the sidewalk, Virgil was to his right, Morgan stood to Virgil's right, and Doc Holliday on the far left, still partially on Fremont. The Earps stared back, noting both the McLaurys and Billy Clanton leaning against the Harwood house, Tom holding the reins of a horse, and Ike Clanton, Billy Claiborne and Wes Fuller standing in the middle of the vacant lot. Only a scant six to ten feet separated the two groups as Virgil Earp raised his walking stick and, according to Ike Clanton, exclaimed, "You sons of bitches. You have been looking for a fight, and now you can have it. Throw up your hands." Wyatt's recollection of Virgil's demand was slightly different: "Throw up your hands. I have come to disarm you." Immediately, Frank McLaury and Billy Clanton both drew and cocked their revolvers. Trying to defuse the situation, Virgil shouted, "Hold on. I don't want that!" Nevertheless, shooting began within a matter of seconds.

Although who actually fired the first shot is still debated, most historians believe Billy Clanton and Wyatt fired virtually simultaneously—Billy at Wyatt, and Wyatt at Frank. Clanton missed, but Earp, knowing that Frank was the most skilled and dangerous of the Cowboys, shot him in the stomach, the first of two wounds Frank received. Wyatt then turned toward Tom McLaury, who was partially hidden behind the horse he was holding. As Earp fired at the horse's withers, it partially bolted. Tom, unsuccessful in his attempt to pull his rifle from its scabbard, twice fired his revolver over the horse's back, but Holliday stepped around the steed and shot McLaury with a double-barrel shotgun at close range. Contrary to popular belief, there is no evidence to suggest that Holliday first fired one barrel of his shotgun into the air to scare the horse before shooting Tom. A witness said he saw

Tom stagger down the street and collapse at the foot of a telegraph pole at the corner of Fremont and Third. Holliday then tossed his shotgun aside and pulled out his nickel-plated revolver to continue the fight.

Ike Clanton rushed toward Wyatt, shouted that he was unarmed and didn't want to fight. Wyatt pushed him away, yelling, "The fight has commenced! Go to fighting, or get away!" Behan, who had followed behind the Earps down Fremont, pulled Claiborne to safety as the cowardly Clanton rushed away through the O.K. Corral, across Allen Street into Kellogg's saloon, and then onto Toughnut Street where he was arrested. Some witnesses claimed Clanton drew a hidden revolver and fired at the Earps before he disappeared. Morgan Earp then shot Billy Clanton in the right wrist, but the Cowboy shifted his six-shooter to his left hand and continued to fire until he was out of bullets. The gunfight quickly escalated into a wild mêlée. Morgan tripped and fired from the ground. Wyatt shot Frank McLaury a second time; Frank struggled with his horse's reins as he, too, lurched across Fremont Street, firing his revolver as he went. Morgan, standing once again, and Holliday fired again at Frank McLaury. Frank's return fire grazed Holliday in his pistol pocket. Though both Frank and Billy had been wounded, they continued to return fire as Clanton hit Virgil in the calf and may have also hit Morgan, who yelled, "I am hit." The bullet struck both shoulder blades as well as a vertebra. Morgan fell to the ground a second time, then stood once again. Frank fired twice more, then challenged Holliday, "I've got you now." Doc replied, "Blaze away! You're a daisy if you have." Both Morgan and Holliday then fired, hitting McLaury in the left breast and in the head below his right ear. The Cowboy finally fell to the ground, mortally wounded.

Billy Clanton, who had been shot in the wrist, chest and abdomen, slumped to the ground. After he ran out of cartridges, he asked for more to no avail. C.S. Fly eventually relieved him of his empty revolver. The shootout lasted between 25 and 30 seconds with 30 total shots being fired. Virgil and Morgan were wounded, Holliday nicked, and both McLaurys and Billy Clanton lie dead or dying. Only Wyatt was unscathed. Morgan and Virgil were carried in hacks to Virgil's home where they were attended to by their wives. Doc retired to his room in Fly's boarding house where, according to Kate Elder, he sat on his bed and wept: "Oh, this is awful—just awful." As Wyatt left the scene, Behan approached the lawman and said, "I will have to arrest you." Still laced with adrenaline, Earp roared, "I won't be arrested. You deceived me, Johnny. You told me they were not armed. I won't be arrested, but I am here to answer [for] what I have done. I am not going to leave town."

The gunfight was over but the legend had just begun.

Before they began filming in Mescal, Cosmatos had a few scenes to wrap up: Doc's final confrontation with Ringo, Wyatt and Doc's conversation about Ringo at Hooker's ranch, and Wyatt and Josephine's horseback encounter at Mt. Lemon. Emily Blanton, who stood in for Delany during the horseback-riding sequence, recalls, "I would stand-in in some pretty precarious places. When she was on horseback, right next to the end of the cliff—that was a scary spot.... It's not always the glamour it's portrayed [to be]. The hours are ridiculous, but I really love the business, so I was willing to put up with a lot of stuff like that." Cliff McLaughlin is Russell's double in both the race through the woods and the downhill ride. Billy Lang says, "That horse popped [Cliff's] ass right out of the saddle [as they went downhill]. Cliff said, 'I was gone,' but his momentum was just right and he sat right back down."[1]

At the end of this sequence, Wyatt and Josephine express their love for each other as Wyatt falls to his knees, clutching her in his arms. But the area where the scene was filmed in had to be created as, in the words of Cosmatos, "We came here [to a valley] and it was full of bullshit. So we had to put ... those flowers all around to create a more beautiful atmosphere. We arrived there [and] the trees had shed [so] we tried to jazz up the scene by putting flowers in the background. Planting them and then we used pollen, we shot it through the scene and suddenly this cow field became a place where they could meet. The scene went longer and they kiss in the original scene and we thought that it was not a good idea that they kiss. Leave it open. Something happens but don't show it on the screen, it's much more powerful. Also, it was too obvious. So it's just the looks. I cut it because I didn't want the love story to be consumed so fast."[2]

Perhaps they didn't get adequate coverage or didn't like what they saw in the dailies, but these scenes were reshot in the final days of filming: McMasters' meeting and scenes #26 (Holliday and Wyatt inside the Oriental Saloon), #39 (Wyatt's attempt to retrieve his horse), #81 (Florentino ducks in a shadow as Virgil walks by), #129 (McMasters' confrontation with Ringo/Ike) and #143 (the aftermath of the Holliday and Ringo gunfight). While Cosmatos was ensconced in Mescal, Terry Leonard was busy on second unit, filming a variety of atmosphere shots that included horse falls and numerous "Vendetta Ride" stunt gags. On some days, they would combine with the first unit as in early July when they filmed the Wedding Massacre scene, or Wyatt and Josie's wild horse ride at Mt.

Kurt Russell (Wyatt Earp) adjusts his hat as he and Dana Delany (right; Josephine Marcus) prepare for their scene on Mt. Lemon (courtesy James "Spud" Danicic).

In a sequence that can only be seen in the extended version of the film, Sherm McMasters meets Johnny Ringo and the rest of the Cowboys at Rustler's Park on the Babocomari. McMasters is subsequently killed and his body is dragged by horseback to Hooker's ranch house (courtesy Larry Zeug).

Lemon. Later that month, Terry filmed the deaths of several Cowboys during the Iron Springs ambush as well as the escape of its two lone survivors. On July 23, he filmed the Earp posse as it rode of out the sunset. Five stunt doubles stood in for the quintet: J.T. Hall, John Hock, Bob Lester, Russell Solberg and Tony Boggs.

On July 30, Leonard filmed a gag where Wyatt rides his horse through the plate-glass window of the Galeyville Saloon. Located on the set around the corner from the Oriental Saloon, the exterior of the building was decorated as Spangenberg's Gun Shop, while the interior was the saloon. It was a very complex stunt, so preparations had begun immediately after pre-production. Veteran stuntman Leonard explains the process: "What wood are you going to use? What surface are you going to have the horse on so it doesn't lose its footing jumping in and lose its footing going into the building? What kind of glass were you going to use? How thick is it? What kind of shatter do you want to see? Can we use a three-sixteenth, an eighth- or quarter-inch of candy glass? It's a polymer material. How do you want to see it break, how do you build it, how much tension is there? There's all kinds of things you've got to think about ... but you gotta make sure all your ducks are in [a row]. We're working those horses for weeks in advance. We're in charge of construction and how [the building is] built, how it's put together. We're the ones that shoot it but I also go to the director and say these are the angles I have in mind. You don't do anything at the last minute with a horse; it's all prepped." In this scene, Cliff McLaughlin doubled for Kurt Russell as the horse jumped through the window. Once inside, Russell took over and finished the scene. Nine stuntmen were involved in that scene including Ben Scott, who was sitting in the barber's chair when his character was shot.[3]

Originally, two long-haired Buckaroos, Reggie Byrum and Jerry Tarantino, were supposed to be inside the barber shop. "They asked me to cut my hair," says Reggie, "and I said, 'I'm Native American and I really don't want to cut my hair.' So when I was a Cowboy [my hair was] up in a little Navaho bun and covered inside my hat. Then, when I wasn't a Cowboy, I had my hair down to my shoulders. Terry Leonard was directing those scenes and George came in there and said, 'I see [Jerry] too much.' He pointed at Jerry and the next thing I know, I'm out, too. The next day when they're filming that scene, I'm outside [the barber shop wearing] a top hat. They stop [filming] and George is talking to somebody and the guy comes over and asks, 'Reg, can we see your hat a minute?' I had a top hat with feathers and an Indian choker around it and they took it and they borrowed it for somebody else and I never saw my hat again."[4]

Leonard also shot the 13-second opening scene where 18 Cowboys gallop across Douglas Dry Lake, located just south of Wilcox. The Buckaroos trailered their horses over to the lake from the Babocomari Ranch. The Buckaroos and stuntmen, including Teri Garland dressed as a Cowboy complete with red sash, were located about a mile away from the camera setup. As Reggie Byrum recalls, "When we did the beginning and we're riding on Douglas Dry Lake, they had us ride way out. One guys said, 'Hey, we've got this big lens, we could count the hairs on your butt.' So a couple of us mooned him. What was really cool and I thought they should have used it in the scene, we were riding and all of a sudden there was a whirlwind, a devil's dust bowl come flying up and we came riding out of the middle of that." Larry Zeug notes, "We started that gallop from a mile out … and they would focus in as we got closer. We could see lightning strike the ground while we were out there and it was pretty scary." Chris Ramirez hasn't forgotten that it was hotter than hell out there: "We get out to the dry lake bed and it was probably 116° that day. Obscenely hot and the reflection coming off the dry lake bed was intense. It was burning us, it was so hot. We did that shot over and over and over and over. And the production crew … didn't bring any water for anybody. We just happened to have water … that we burned through pretty quickly. By the time we finished shooting that scene, there was no shade, so we crawled underneath the horse trailers, which was about 12 feet of clearance. We were just dying." As the scene was finished, several Buckaroos, including Larry Zeug, Curt Stokes and Kane Rubalcaba, noticed that an Amtrak train had stopped nearby. Someone said, "Let's go rob the train!" So, in full Cowboy mode, they raced toward the train and rode back and forth for a while. One can only imagine what the train's passengers were thinking.[5]

The days were pretty hectic and it seemed the Buckaroos didn't know from day to day where they would be or what scenes they'd appear in. "Some days our call time was 5:30 in the morning," recalls Billy Lang. "And we'd get up and shoot a scene and then in the afternoon one of the PAs would come up and say, 'I need a couple of riders up here to do this today. Do you guys want to go?' Yeah, okay. So we'd go out to shoot a night scene, work all night. And they'd need someone at five or six or seven o'clock in the morning. A lot of us were doing that. It's like, 'Where are you guys going today?' 'Oh, we're going to Dry Lake. Where are you going?' 'Oh, we're going to Old Tucson.' Depending on what it was, we need four riders for this set. We need five riders for this set. We need five guys for this set and a wagon. The PAs set the things out and made it so they had an adequate amount of people there." Thus, each Buckaroo had to be available every day, whether used or not. "We'd been in the set a few weeks," adds John Peel. "The call sheet would say for the next day, 10 Buckaroos or 20 Buckaroos. Any time it said Buckaroos, that meant we had to be at the spot with horses, gear, guns and outfit. One day the call sheet said 30 Buckaroos. Well, what happened was that the call sheet said 20 Buckaroos and we'd all show up and like most movie work, you stand around all day and do nothing. And they wouldn't use us. Some of the guys started anticipating this and one day they had a call for 20 Buckaroos."

Reggie Byrum continues: "Well, will 12 do?" "No, we need 20." "You sure 12 won't do?" "Why, what do you mean?" "There's only 12 of us here." From that day on, everyone had to be there from six to six, regardless. "Whether they used us or not, we were there and ready every day."[6]

Everyone had to find ways to blow off a little steam. On some weekends, they took the crews out to one of the Tucson parks to play baseball. Stephen Lang's team, the Clantonistas, wore black T-shirts with a tombstone on them. Lang once dislocated a finger but medic Chris Swinney reset it. "I got a hold of [the finger]," says Swinney, "and he looked at me and smiled and said, 'This is going to hurt, isn't it?' I reset it with a loud pop!"

"We'd play on Sundays," says Lang, "and get kinda bombed. We laughed a lot." "There were people just watching them playing," added Chris' son Josh, "and [Kurt] had this giant mustache and sideburns and a baseball cap and you'd never know that it was him. The people in the [stands] would say, 'He looks like somebody.' They would say a couple

Riders and horses are staged in line on Douglas Dry Lake for the opening sequence, where the narrator says, "Attracted to this atmosphere of greed, exiled outlaws band together to form the ruthless gang recognized by the red sashes they wear. They emerge as the earliest example of organized crime in America. They call themselves 'The Cowboys'" (courtesy Larry Zeug).

of people looked like somebody they knew, but they had no idea who it was. None of us was supposed to say anything." The Buckaroos would play poker in the numerous tents that were pitched all over the set, or go out for long trail rides just to keep the horses exercised. For those interested, there was a large screening room at the Holiday Inn where the dailies were shown nightly; pizza and refreshments were available each evening. The crew hung out, hit the bars and on days off, some even visited the real Tombstone. Recalls Michael Walker, "I remember going to Tombstone with my A camera first and film photographer where we met up with [Wyatt Glen Earp]. We hung out with him quite a bit, walked around the O.K. Corral, checked out the city." Lang, Mitchum, Billy Zane and Stallone hung out at the cowboy camp. Stallone brought along his harmonica, and Terry O'Quinn (John Clum) his guitar for a little entertainment. One Sunday, Lisa Collins visited the camp and wanted to go horseback riding. She said, "There's no wranglers around. They told me to come out." Buckaroo Zeug replied, "You want to ride a horse? Just remember, he rears on command and he'll run the socks off of you." So she took off and rode him for a couple hours. "Oh, I love this horse," she exclaimed upon her return. Whereupon she was told, "If you'd been dressing right, you'd have to ride him sidesaddle." Charles Schneider and several others spent their spare time doing water colors and sketches. Buck Taylor did a numbered self-portrait—one through 400 for the cast and crew. Russell received #1, Sam Elliott #2. And there always were liquid refreshments to lighten the mood including homemade apple pie moonshine.

One evening an actor was feeling extremely depressed, so upon his arrival on the set, he immediately headed to his dressing room. A crew member, sensing his mood, asked what was wrong. Informed of the reason, he then talked with the first AD. He then told the actor, "Adam said there's about 13 set-ups before your scene tonight and they're damn sure probably not going to get to it. I'm going to run down to the store and get you some beer." So the crew member went to Mescal, got some beer and a bottle of whiskey, and came back. But by that time, three actresses were in the actor's dressing room. Says the depressed actor, "We smoked pot and drank whiskey and beer. When they finally realized they weren't going to use me, I was so intoxicated I could hardly sign out."[7]

Meanwhile, back in Mescal, Cosmatos started to pick up the pace. On July 14, he filmed the Earp caravan's arrival in Tombstone. As the families pass Boot Hill, they continue on to the edge of town where they see Frank Stillwell and Pony Deal throw a family and its belongings out of a small cottage. John Philbin ruefully recalls, "There's one scene where the [covered wagon] rides into town and [the Earps are] looking at Tombstone and all the crime on the streets. On the corner, just as [the wagon] goes by, there's a bunch of cowboys just pillaging and terrorizing these homesteaders' house. We were working so hard in the background, thinking all that was going to get covered (by the cameras)—my best work ever. [But] you can't even see me when the camera goes by because you've got Sam Elliott and Kurt Russell." As with many other filmed scenes that explain the antagonism between the Earps and the Cowboys, this scene was not included in the final print.[8]

Earlier in that scene, two horsemen ride past the Earps' wagon just before it passes Boot Hill. "We were told to ride by them real fast," explains Rick Terry. "Well, in the street, there's all these people walking around, so you're riding your horse trying to avoid hitting everybody. We did that shot a couple of times. There's some guys off to the right carrying this coffin [into Boot Hill] and as we ride down the street we're supposed to ride around them. One of the times I did that, they came right out into the middle of the street and I almost ran into them. So, to avoid them, I cut inside between them and the side of the road to get around and to make sure I didn't run them over. When I came back, the continuity girl just chewed me out. 'You're supposed to do the same thing every time. You screwed up that shot!' Okay, whatever. Well, the next day she was gone, she was fired. She must have been yelled at about something and was taking it out on me but the next day she was gone." In one of the film's continuity errors, as the Earp wagon passes the cemetery, viewers can see four individuals carrying a coffin into the cemetery's entrance, followed by a woman. A second later, in an over-the-shoulder shot from inside the wagon, the coffin procession is still about 30 feet from the entrance. They then cut to a view from inside the cemetery and one can see the aforementioned woman on the far right-hand side of the shot. Two other Buckaroos, Jerry Brown and Reggie Byrum, are seen riding behind the Earps' wagon.[9]

Hot-head tech James Danicic recalls there was a great deal of external pressure the day they filmed that scene: "The production manager came to the set and he said, 'The suits are on the set today. … If anything goes wrong…' I was fighting, everybody was fighting with their equipment because of the heat. [The production manager] went around to every department, 'Everything has to go smooth, the suits are here.' Sure enough, we do the ride into town and reset the crane to pull them into town, and the head goes down. Back then, the old-style head ran on fuses instead of circuit-breakers and there were no backup fuses. So the head goes down just before the big shot and the production manager goes 'What do we do? Can you fix this?' 'I don't know, I need five minutes.' So I quickly walked over to craft services and grabbed a pack of gum…. I took the foil and wrapped it around the fuse and set it back in there and said, 'We've got 15 minutes before this goes dead.' Boom, we got the shot. A cheap fix but it's a risk of blowing other things up. But [the PM was] freaking out, 'How much longer, how much longer?'"[10]

During the next two days, they filmed Behan's greeting to the Earps, Fred White's explanation of the town's criminal dynamics, Holliday's street conversation with the Earps and Johnny Tyler, Doc's sickbed conversation with Earp regarding Ringo, and the confrontation Turkey Creek and Texas Jack have with the two drunks outside the Crystal Palace.

Once the Earps arrive in Tombstone, their wagon stops in front of the Grand Hotel where County Sheriff Johnny Behan greets Wyatt. If ever one wondered if Russell truly was a professional, the following story puts that question to rest. Says stuntman Lee McKechnie, who witnessed the scene, "I do remember a little scene with Kurt. He was standing next to a [wagon]. [Sheriff Behan] was talking to him about finding a place to stay. The horse [in the scene] had to go to the bathroom, on camera, and Kurt is standing there trying to be serious. He must have been a farm boy because as the scene was [being filmed], he reached over and took his hand and put it on the horse's butt. [The horse's discharge] was going through his fingers and his hand while he was talking. Okay, that was pretty brave. Of course, they didn't use that take." And, if you've ever ridden a horse for any extended period of time, what's the first thing you do once you dismount? Stretch your legs, which is exactly what Kurt Russell did once he got off his horse. Tired from a long journey, with cramps in his legs, he twisted his back to loosen his muscles and squatted down to lend a touch of authenticity to the scene.[11]

As usual, at least according to some, the actresses were nowhere to be found, and Dana Loraine was called on to fill the time: "There was a day in Mescal when we had the huge street scene when the Earps come into town and pass the graveyard. I was sitting at the corner in front of the Birdcage. That day we had 200 extras on the set and we're just the street scene. All of a sudden I heard a golf cart slam on the brakes. Dust flying. I was just sitting there talking to somebody and I heard, 'Dana. Get the fuck in this cart now!' As I get in the cart, I can hear on their walkie-talkies, 'Where is she? Where is she?' They were just screaming and yelling. And I got there to the top of the street where they were filming where the Earps got off the wagon. The women weren't there so they had to have me get in the wagon and practicing getting in and out of the wagon for lighting because the women weren't there yet."[12]

Glen Gold recalls playing the part of a drunk miner in the same scene: "They pull up to the hotel and Sam Elliott gets off the wagon, Russell gets off of that old stud horse and pulls up to the hitching post. Well, I'm the old miner that's coming down the steps of the hotel and was supposed to be a drunk miner and I walk right in between them and turn to the left and walk down the street. They said, 'You just struck it rich and everything and you're celebrating. Stagger a little bit. You're celebrating.' Well, [after] about eight or ten takes of that, George said, 'On this next cut, we're going to do it one more time. And when I say 'Cut,' I want everybody to freeze exactly where they're at and remember exactly where you're at and what you're doing. Because we've got the scene but we've got to move the cameras for the rest of the scene. We've got to reset. So, I want everybody to freeze when I say, 'Cut,' because that will be your starting [point] when we get the cameras reset for the rest of the scene.' So when he hollered, I was standing at the top of those stairs…. I hadn't started down the stairs yet. I was staggering some, trying to be a nonchalant drunk. When he put us in action on the pick-up, here I come down those stairs and I done it that way I'd been doing it for eight or ten other takes. He said, 'All right, cut. Back to one.' When I went back up to the top of the steps, Sam Elliott had gotten off the wagon and was standing there and cocks his head to the side like he does. Then he looked over at George and he walked over there. And the next thing I know, him and George are looking at me. I'm kind of getting antsy. Well, George says something to Adam and they look at me, then Adam comes over [and says], 'When we start the action on the next take, do not stagger.' I mean, it hit me right then what was going on. Sam Elliott didn't want me stealing the scene from him and Kurt Russell because here was this drunk staggering down the steps right between the two of them. Three different ADs run over after Adam told me that. 'Don't act, don't act!' I just stood there laughing [and telling them], 'Don't worry, I won't.' I got Sam Elliott to laughing about it. He knew that I knew what he was doing and why, and he got a big kick out of it."[13] In the next scene, Fred White points out several Cowboys to the Earps and calls the Oriental a "slaughterhouse."

Harry Carey, Jr., had been a key member of director John Ford's stock company and was well-versed in both Western and cinematic history. Although he wasn't the first choice to play the part of Marshal Fred White, Carey bridged the Western genre between John Ford's *My Darling Clementine* and *Tombstone*. According to Carey, it wasn't a very pleasant experience, and he noted one big difference in particular. "I worked on *Tombstone* and I didn't find any laughter any more. There always used to be laughter on a movie set. None [now]. None. It was like everybody was going to a lynching or something." But Carey's mere presence reminds the audience of Western films of the past, a fact not lost on Sam Elliott. Reflecting on what the veteran character actor Carey meant to him, Elliott simply says, "It's 'Dobe' [Harry's nickname]. It's everything he represents, that morality and that character he represents. It was like the antithesis of what Dobe was all about. It's kind of like the end of an era somehow, even within that little piece. There's a certain element in making a western film that the filmmakers need to be true to. It's not about body count. It's not about whores and cowboys in bed. It's not about gratuitous anything, whether it's murder, sex or whatever. You've got to be true to those elements that we all know from our childhood. You've got to be true that a man's word is his bond. You got to be true to solid morality. There shouldn't be too much of a gray area between the good guy and the bad guy." As the character Fred White, that's what Carey represented.[14]

Tucson casting director Holly Hire had used extra Terry McGahey in the past so it was only logical that she would find a role for him in this film. "Originally, they were supposed to hire me to ride for them," says McGahey, "but it just didn't work out [because] me and one or two of the wranglers kinda got into an argument. They were laming up horses pretty bad. For every horse you see, they had two or three lamed up. I was standing outside on the street, lying against a post, and these two guys were talking. They couldn't figure out why so many horses were lamed up. Well, I'm a cowboy. I looked at them and said, 'Well, I can tell you why.' They [replied] with kind of a smartass answer, 'Well, why is that?' like they knew everything. I said, 'Well, your hoofs are cut too low in the heel and too long in the toe and you're bowing their damn tendons [when you shoe the horses].' They didn't want to hear that. In fact, that's one of the reasons I just walked off the set."

But when McGahey was there, they put him to use. "I was sitting on a pickle barrel across the street from [the Oriental] and [Cosmatos] was looking around. I saw him looking over my way. He said, 'Hey, you.' I acted like I didn't hear him. He hollered, 'Hey, you' again. I still acted like I didn't hear him. The third time he hollered and pointed at me. I pointed at myself and he said, 'Yeah, you.' So I walked over there. He said, 'I'm paying you to sit on a pickle barrel. I don't think so. You're going to be in this scene.'"[15]

The scene referred to was Wyatt's confrontation with obnoxious faro dealer Johnny Tyler, played by Billy Bob Thornton. McGahey is the cowboy at the table who constantly plays the same card, which upsets Thornton's character: "You back that queen again, you son of a bitch, I'll blow you right off that wildcat's ass. You hear me?" Dickie Stanley is the drunk miner at the bar. Before the scene was shot, Thornton told McGahey, "Now, Terry. Please listen to me. I'm really going to act mad at you. I hope you don't get angry. I did that to some girl one time and she started to cry." Terry replied, "Well, I don't believe I'm going to cry." It has been rumored that Billy Bob ad-libbed all his dialogue in this scene but that's not correct. Well, not entirely. All of Thornton's dialogue up to Russell's "Just want to let you know you're sitting in my chair" line was, in fact, ad-libbed except for the "back that queen" line. Everything after that was scripted. According to Cosmatos, "Billy Bob Thornton came as a favor. He didn't have to say much so I told him to invent, go on, just be a bully. Of course, [Kurt] wasn't smacking him—an old Hollywood trick. But his face is red for some reason."[16]

Russell was to go over to the dealer, slap him a few times, take away his gun and throw it to Pat Brady, who played bartender Milt Joyce. When they were blocking out the scene, Russell asked Cosmatos, "What do I do with the gun? Do you want me to put in into my belt?" They thought about it a few minutes and Cosmatos then said, "Just throw it over to the bartender." Kurt said, "I want to look cool. I don't even want to look at the bartender. I just want to throw the gun." Stanley was standing with his elbows on the bar and noticed it was a real gun. Dickie continues: "I ran out, 'Hey, hey, hey! What are you doing?' George said, 'Why are you leaving the bar?' I said, 'That's a real gun. I'm not going to stand there while he throws a real gun.' I had my back to him. [Cosmatos] said, 'No, no. That's not a real gun. That's rubber gun.' He turns to Kurt, 'Is that a rubber gun?' 'No, it's a real gun.' Somehow the rubber gun didn't get shipped, so they [were using an actual] 9½-inch Smith and Wesson. They swapped that out and gave [Kurt] a rubber gun. It was like a Nerf gun, very soft." They did about 14 takes and Stanley got hit three times. The first two times were good solid hits, right in the back of the head. The third time, it skipped across the top of his head and fell behind the bar. Finally, they moved Stanley a few feet and filmed the scene as planned. At the end of the scene, Russell threw in another ad-lib. "Oh, what do you say, Milt? Twenty-five percent of the house-take sound about right?"[17]

Historian Jim Dunham was initially asked by Kevin Jarre if he wanted an acting role in the film and Jim agreed. After a successful Tucson audition, Dunham signed a SAG contract to play a high roller in three scenes. His only concern was a two-week, mid-summer appearance at Utah State University's Annual Festival of the American West that he was committed to doing. "No problem," said Casting. However, upon Jarre's release, Jim naturally wondered if he was still in the film. "Rest assured," he was told. "You're still in but your character has been changed to a miner." Upon his return from Utah, Dunham's wife told him, "The movie people have been calling all day." Jim returned the call to learn that he was no longer in the film. "The director wanted to shoot my scenes [the next day]," says Jim. "They agreed that it was not my fault, but they shot [the scene] with someone else. They paid me per contract and therefore, I am listed in the credits but do not appear in the film."[18]

As a general rule, once the *Tombstone* production set up in a particular location, most sequences were filmed in script or chronological order, especially once they reached the night shoots in August. With some exceptions, many of the night scenes in and around the Oriental and the town's main intersection were generally shot in the order they appear in the finished film. After the Russell-Thornton street altercation was finished, Cosmatos filmed the confrontation between Texas Jack, Turkey Creek and two drunks outside the Crystal Palace. As the scene ends, Peter Sherayko's character spins his revolver several times before he holsters it. When Cosmatos asked him why he did so, Peter simply answered, "Because I can." This trick remains in the film. Sherayko tells an amusing story involving that particular scene: "Val Kilmer and I were good friends on the set. The first day I rode my horse, I saw the prop guy say something to Val. That's when I said, 'Your gun's half cocked.' Val said, 'So what?' I said, 'In the movie, someone is gonna say you don't know what you're doing.' Val ended the conversation by saying, 'I find that those who break the rules get ahead.' I rode away, but within five minutes he had a different gun in his holster. I looked at it in his holster and said, 'You got a different gun there.' Val put his head down and said, 'I broke it.' I knew then he realized I knew what I was talking about. The scene where we came out of the saloon after drinking all night and playing poker, we actually did that for real, too. We did that scene—where we meet with Doc and Virgil takes our guns. Later, Val kept looking at me when I walked down the boardwalk and he finally said, 'Hey, Pete, you were drunk in that scene.' I said, 'I find those who break the rules get ahead.' Val laughed."[19]

Cosmatos then filmed the arrival of a stagecoach carrying members of a traveling theatrical group. Red Wolverton provided the stagecoach so it was only natural he would drive the team. As simple as it appears, the stagecoach's arrival was not without its mishaps. Says Red, "They wanted me to come in at a gallop, come right up there hard, and stop right on the money. That's pretty damn technical. To do that … markers [are placed] so you know where to stop. So I come around the block and they [had] moved several cameras and lights from [where] they said [they] would be. So here it was, all my goddamn markers, I missed the mark by about two feet [and] overshot the cameras. So they said come around again. [This] time the water had run down [the street] and I didn't have my foot on the brake; I didn't realize it and picked up a bunch of water on the rear wheels. I had my spot picked out and I hit the brake but because of the mud it didn't slow the coach down. The horses don't stop the coach, you have to stop them with the brake on the rear wheels. So I overshot it again. [Cosmatos] got madder than hell: 'I spent all this goddamn money and here they got some bastard who can't even drive a goddamn stagecoach.' Somebody said, 'Let's try it one more goddamn time,' and one of my co-workers bet $20 I wouldn't miss the mark by two inches. So that time, I come around and kept my foot on the brake to keep the wheels dry, and I stopped right on the goddamn mark. A guy said, 'He can't do it again,' so my partner said, 'You want to double the bet?'" He didn't.

Wolverton had to dress in character just like everyone else, which led to an engaging conversation with the wardrobe mistress. Reporting to wardrobe, Wolverton was told to pay a $100 deposit for a hat an old-time actor had worn. As Red was flush, he happened to have a hundred dollar bill in his pocket, so it wasn't an issue. For whatever reason, though, the scene wasn't filmed that day, so Red returned the hat. When they were ready to film it several days later, Wolverton was told, "You know, you have to put up $100 to wear this hat again." "Aw, to hell with it," Red replied. "I ain't going to do it." Thinking that she held the better hand, the wardrobe mistress then challenged Red: "Well, then you won't have any job." Of course, she didn't know who she as talking to as Wolverton had the perfect comeback: "Well, then you won't have any horses, either, because they belong to me." (Wolverton had rented 17 wagons and 20 head of harness and saddle horses, not including the six-up.) Not knowing what to do, the girl ran off to get an answer. Five minutes later she came back, literally with hat in hand, and sheepishly asked, "Mr. Wolverton, will you please wear this hat today?" Red had some dialogue: "I did have a speaking role in *Tombstone*," laughs Red. "I get to say 'Whoa' when I drive the stage into town."[20]

During the next several weeks, filming alternated between interior vs. exterior scenes, and day vs. nighttime shooting. Wyatt Earp's legendary walk to the O.K. Corral was filmed over several days during the week of July 19. As the quartet begins the march into history, a framed structure in the background is seen engulfed in flames. "That was George," explains Sam Elliott. "We were all looking at it, thinking, 'Who in the hell lit the fire?' At the time it didn't make any sense. And then you see it on film, and it's evident that the Cowboys lit the fire, as kind of a diversion or whatever it was. Cinematically it was a brilliant decision." Well, maybe. On June 22, 1881, the first of two fires in Tombstone destroyed 66 buildings in the downtown area that made up the eastern half of the business district. It was reportedly started when a cigar ignited a barrel of whiskey in the Arcade Saloon. Perhaps the film's flaming building symbolized this historical event. Or it could also be an allegorical combination of the Biblical theme of Death coming and Hell following—an emblematic link between the wedding massacre and the shootout. Four instruments of justice emerging from the fires of redemption to extract vengeance on the unfaithful. During the director's commentary on the Vista DVD release of *Tombstone*, Cosmatos claimed, "I wanted them to walk by and everybody's putting out this fire but they don't care. They don't have time for that. People are running. They are disturbed by it but they have no time."[21]

Still, movie fires are carefully handled, and this one for *Tombstone* was no exception. A framed structure built on a skid was relocated from the opposite end of the Mescal set and fitted with flame bars and propane gas to create the blaze. Chris Swinney, set medic and Three Points volunteer firefighter, was on hand to assure its safety, along with Tom Mathews, Alex Dunn, Todd Pierson and George and Andy Swinney. In addition to Three Points, the Derxelle and Mescal fire departments were also represented. After the first day of filming this scene, Cosmatos was upset at the size of the fire and proclaimed, "No, bigger. I want *Rambo* fire," which caused laughter all around the set. Second-unit SFX leadman Joe Quinlivan looked back at the firefighters and said, "He didn't just say that, did he?" Special effects worked to reset the fire and the scene was shot again the next day. While the firefighters wore Nomex protective clothing under their costumes for safety, Chris Swinney is the townsman who bravely throws a bucket of water on the flames.[22]

After the retake, Cosmatos concentrated on filming various portions of the walk itself: passerby reactions, children playfully "shooting" at the Earps and Morgan's response, Holliday whistling. The child who goes "Bang! Bang! Bang!" is Chas. Wheeler.

"The flames of Hell!" As the Earps and Holliday begin their walk toward the O.K. Corral, a building burned in the background. Note that the structure is incomplete and gas canisters stored the propane which fueled the fire. Behind the large building is a white tent and single-wide trailer where lunch and dinner were served to cast and crew (courtesy David Russell).

The Earps and Holliday begin their long walk down Allen Street. A crew member stands on the left watching the scene while wearing a T-shirt that reads "Time to get Wooly" (courtesy Larry Zeug).

That portion of the walk wasn't in the script but was added to create additional tension. The shootout was to end with the same young boy who, upon seeing the carnage, drops his gun when overcome with emotion. The lawmen start out in front of the sheriff's office and continue only a short distance down Allen Street before they reach the front of the Oriental Saloon where they turn right onto Fourth Street. In reality, the Oriental and Crystal Palace sit opposite each other at the corner of Fifth and Allen. In 1881, the walk really began in front of Hafford's Saloon (also known as Hafford's Corner) at the corner of Fourth and Allen. However, camera placement on the Mescal set makes the walk down Allen seem much longer than it really was. A frustrated Rick Terry stood in the street as the four walked by. "You had to be standing in a certain place and they told me [where to stand]. I'm in the middle of the street, the fire is going on in the background, a couple of guys ride by on horses. The Earps and Holliday are walking down the street and some little kid comes out with a [toy] gun. When they turn and go down the street, I'm standing behind them in the background in the distance. They shot that a couple of times. Cosmatos comes up to me … every time he gives me a different direction. 'Stand this way.' Or, 'Don't do this. Don't do that.' For crying out loud, I don't think you can even see me in the shot. You got the feeling like whatever you did was wrong." The original walk was much longer than it appears in the film—people walking, shadows on the ground, numerous angles. But Cosmatos thought it was too long and felt "it was like the end of the movie." So he took much of the footage he shot and used it in the closing credits.[23]

Filming of the iconic O.K. Corral gunfight took place between July 26 and 28. However, preparations for this climactic scene had begun well before then. Jeff Morey and Jarre had discussed taking all the actors who were to take part in the gunfight to Tombstone to go through how it actually transpired, but when Jarre was dismissed, that plan evaporated. Nevertheless, rehearsals were required the weekend before the scene was filmed. According to John Philbin, "We did [it] over and over again, tirelessly. Over and over and over." Naturally, they tried to replicate the actions of each character, not only in movement but in the proper historical sequence as well. Philbin continues, "[During] the first master shot, we didn't know what in the hell was going on. [But the process] eventually got cultivated down into tight and dramatic timing. We rehearsed it a bunch of times and by our last rehearsal, we [timed] it to the second [of the actual gunfight] and to the [correct number of] shots fired and we all felt something very special. Everybody felt something at that point; everybody involved in that scene in that corral, felt something very powerful that day." Buckaroo Sam Dolan had a similar impression as the rehearsals narrowed down the action to match the intricacies of the actual gunfight: "All of the actors [were] in their regular clothes, shorts, T-shirts, flip-flops, all the six-guns firing blanks. They were working out the beats and kind of timing it out. The way it played out live was very quick like the actual O.K. Corral would have been."[24]

Once the rehearsals were finished, the actors adjourned to the Buckaroo camp where targets had been set up. After spending all day firing blanks, the actors predictably felt somewhat complacent. Thell Reed had the answer: The armorer-consultant-stuntman-extra-exhibition shooter extraordinaire wanted the actors to feel the recoil of real revolvers, so he arranged for them to fire live ammo. Everyone fired at cardboard targets with faces drawn upon them, Val Kilmer wisecracking, "One of those guys looks an awful lot like Doc." Some were better marksmen than others. According to Robert Burke, "I remember hitting everything. Once I hit this beer can and once it was up in the air, I drilled it again. Everybody went nuts because I had played RoboCop prior [to that] and they started screaming, 'Robo! Robo!'" Russell admits he wasn't the best shot. "Val Kilmer and Michael Biehn were the standouts. It was amazing how each actor could shoot just like his character. Val was very fast and accurate and so was Michael. I was very deliberate—very accurate, but slow."[25]

More fun followed as John Peel describes: "I had a gallon jug of milk I had brought out to blow up with a shotgun, and Kurt wanted to shoot the shotgun. I threw the gallon jug of milk in the air for Kurt to shoot, and he blew that up. Then Val and all the other guys started going, 'Thell, Thell, Thell.' So, Thell goes, 'Okay, fine.' He puts on his speed rig, loads a pair of guns and at about seven yards he draws, does six rounds, flips a gun into the air, swaps a gun to the main hand and then thumbs six more so quickly that literally everyone stood there with their mouths open. Live ammo, .45 Colt, full loads. He holsters his guns, takes them off and hands them to me, and he was done shooting; very much the professional." The actors then left for the hotel, amazed at the exhibition they had just witnessed.[26]

Before filming of the O.K. Corral shootout began, Cosmatos ran one last blocking rehearsal. According to actor Grant James, "If George wanted something different, he would tell the actors. Then they would pull in the stand-ins so they could set the lights, place the cameras, etc." George numbered each cut in the shootout sequence and gave every actor a detailed list of his specific actions. "I took every actor's what he had to do," explained Cosmatos, "and I put it in one column and I gave him the paper. And I gave the other actors [their list] so each actor knew exactly what he had to do at the certain time of the scene. Who came first, who came second, that one came third, so I can put the whole thing together to give it the speed and movement we needed to show everything but to show it fast."

Local Jay Gammons helped the set dressers prepare the blacksmith shop with 1880s touches: "I showed them how to put up that black hood ... and things like that [anvils, tongs, hammers, forge, etc.]. Where to put the lamps, etc. What I try to do, I try to keep it as authentic as possible. 'Cause some of your Hollywood people are not very authentic. They ... put in [items] they like from the 1950s and they think it's from the 1880s and it isn't, so you have to be careful with them. I had to go tell them." Catherine Hardwicke had done a marvelous job of compressing the six square blocks of stores, saloons, dwellings and livery stables that surrounded the O.K. Corral into a more compact "downtown" district. According to *Washington Times* reporter Gary Arnold, "This arrangement helped create a sense of intimate, right-around-the-corner violence missing in some of the earlier films about the subject...." Bill Fraker noted how it previously had been customary to place the O.K. Corral at the edge of town, permitting sky composition while expanding the field of fire for the actors. But now, with the corral placed authentically in the middle of town, in a 10 × 20 yard lot hemmed in by buildings on three sides, one realizes how the gunfight actually had featured a "point-blank decisiveness," which intensified and concentrated the minds and anxieties of each participant.

The attention to detail in the costumes, weapons, saddles and set-dressing is what made *Tombstone* so authentic. John Peel, Billy Lang and Jake Johnson assisted Thell Reed with all the guns while the gunfight sequence was filmed. "We cleaned all the guns between each take," remembers Peel. "Thell assigned us each an actor. He'd say, 'I've got Kurt and Sam, you do Bill and Stephen Lang. You're in charge of this guy's gun. As soon as they yell, 'Cut,' run in there, grab the guns, run out here and clean them up real quick, load them up and stand by until they're ready to go.' Reed didn't want us to give the actors loaded guns until the last possible second, especially at close quarters where the actors were essentially shooting blanks at each other. So we had a little wooden dowel and before we'd load a gun we checked the bore of the gun to make sure there were no obstructions in the bore that might turn into a projectile." Jake Johnson also helped modify Val's shoulder holster and replaced Kurt's holster, which fell apart early in shooting.[27]

As a part of his responsibilities, Adam Taylor conducted a safety session before the scene began. He discussed the weapons, how they operated, who was going to be using what, and confirmed that everyone knew how to use them. Every gun was going to be loaded with quarter-load blanks provided by Stembridge Gun Rentals. Full-loads are 28 grains of FFF black powder; 15 grains are used for a three-quarter load, ten for a half-load, and five for a quarter-load. There also are a variety of types of loads for blanks—some for more flash, some for less, some for redder flash, whiter flash, more smoke, less smoke, etc. Noise isn't really an issue as the sounds of gunshots are later added in during the Foley process. After the safety meeting, Kurt Russell walked up to Taylor, got in his face and said, "Wyatt Earp only uses full loads." Supposedly, according to some of those present, Buck Taylor went after Russell and said something on the order of, "Don't you ever speak to my son again like that because he's in charge of your safety." A compromise was reached. They would use half-loads.

The Earps and Holliday (left to right: Val Kilmer, Bill Paxton, Sam Elliott, Kurt Russell) continue down Allen Street past an opium tent and the Key West Cigar Shop. In the foreground, a crew member holds a boom microphone (courtesy David Russell).

Given the recent death of Brandon Lee in *The Crow*, it was critical that all the blanks and loads in the guns were properly checked, but Eddie Perez remembers finding actual bullets on some of the gun belts used in *Tombstone*. "I mentioned it to Thell Reed," recalls Perez, "and the next thing you know, I was looking at gun belts for him. He said, 'Oh, man. You're really on top of that. Why don't you look to see if they're any more of them?' I think I found five or six more bullets like that left in the gun belts." And it was a good thing he did. One scene in *The Crow* called for a close-up of bullets loaded in a revolver. To accomplish this effect, dummy cartridges fitted with bullets but no powder or primer were used to provide a realistic appearance. Rather than purchasing dummy cartridges, though, that film's prop crew created its own. After pulling the bullet from a live round, the powder charge was removed and the bullet reinserted into the cartridge. Unfortunately, a live primer was left in the rear of one cartridge and, at some point during filming, this bullet was discharged with sufficient force to jam the projectile halfway down the gun's barrel. Then for a subsequent scene, the dummy cartridges were exchanged for blank rounds—which feature a live powder charge and primer but no bullet—thus allowing the gun to be fired without the risk of an actual projectile. But since the bullet from the dummy round was already jammed in the barrel, pulling the trigger caused the bullet to exit the barrel with virtually the same force as if the gun had been loaded with a live round, resulting in Lee's death.[28]

As the party prepares to make a turn down the historical Fourth Street, George Cosmatos instructs the stand-ins. Chas. Wheeler holds a pair of wooden guns in mid-street (courtesy David Russell).

Concept and storyboard artist David Russell illustrated the wedding massacre scene and developed the O.K. Corral sequence, albeit under considerable pressure and time constraints. He consulted with Cosmatos on additional shots and alternate shots and concepts for both scenes. According to the artist, "George really had no vision for the respective sequences. I essentially 'directed on paper,' which is quite common in my profession," so most of those scenes were largely shot as storyboarded. In general, a storyboard artist is drafted during an early stage of pre-production but David wasn't brought on board until after Cosmatos had arrived. David explains, "The job entails working in collaboration with the director to create a comprehensive visual narrative of the film. The storyboards serve numerous functions: as a budgeting device, shooting guide, stunt and visual effects template, and more. The storyboarding process is usually completed by the time shooting commences, but in the case of *Tombstone*, Cosmatos urgently required assistance in planning several key sequences." Obviously, it was a successful collaboration. Others also assisted in the effort. The Buckaroos, for example, observed, "You know, there was a ditch, they were digging a ditch across the vacant lot at the time [of the actual gunfight]." So, production added a ditch.[29]

Prior to the start of the shootout, Behan enters Fly's Gallery after telling the Earps that he had disarmed the Cowboys. Inside, Josephine Marcus is seen having her photograph

The O.K. Corral set (photograph by Lee Gray/courtesy Catherine Hardwicke).

taken by Fly. This portion of the scene is intended to recreate the famous Kaloma photograph. Supposedly taken by Fly, it represented a 1914 photo of Josephine Marcus. She is naked but covered with a sheer gauze peignoir. When informed that Josie would have been 53 years old in 1914 and this woman looked more like 19, the author of the claim said the photograph was taken back in 1883 but only released in 1914. However, most reputable historians refute this. When the storyboards for this section are reviewed, it is clear that a much-expanded version of this scene was originally planned: Josie disrobes behind a screen, steps from behind it, and to the amazement of the photographer, stands in full-frontal pose, covered only by a transparent veil. She then admires herself in the mirror before the photo is taken. But only the latter portion of this sequence appears in the film.

After the above portions were shot, they finally were ready to begin filming the gunfight. Taylor shouted, "All right, people. Settle down, please! Quiet all around! Stand by! Kill those radios! There will be fire in the hole! We're using half-rounds!" And finally, filming of this version of the Old West's most famous gunfight began. Russell recalled, "Just as George said 'Action!' there was a large crack of rolling thunder. We began the master and ran through it like clockwork … it worked just right. When it was over, everything went quiet, almost as though a train wreck had just happened, and once again, a long crack of ominous, rolling thunder punctuated the end."

According to Cosmatos, the Earp-Holliday quartet was intentionally dressed in black

Fly's Photography Gallery in Mescal (photograph by Lee Gray/courtesy Catherine Hardwicke).

hats, coats and vests that conveyed grim intent. "If you look at the dark clothes, they look like undertakers," observed the director. Even with half-loads, though, the noise was ear-splitting. As no one knows who actually fired the first shot, Cosmatos had to find a way to start the gunfight. According to George, he suggested that Kilmer wink and Thomas Haden Church react. Jake Johnson recalls, "[T]hey shot the gunfight, like it was done, to as many of the [historical] records as they could. This guy shot first, this guy shot second. This guy did this, this guy did that. A lot of their actions are based on what really happened in the gunfight. So we would shoot from the beginning to all the way to the end of the gunfight from all these different angles, depending on the light, who was in the close-up and different things that were documented. So it's very accurate. [But] it did not get edited that way." After each take, crew members would run out to collect all the props, pick up the blanks and rearrange the set dressing to go "back to one" if required." ("Back to one" is a term that means all cast and crew should go back to their initial positions to prepare for another take.) Once Cosmatos was satisfied with the master coverage, different close-ups, over-the-shoulder, POV and atmosphere shots were filmed. All told, it took four days to film the sequence. In take after take, Stephen Lang refreshed himself by ducking his head in a barrel of water and then dramatically flinging his head back.[30]

Naturally, the heat caused problems. Remembers Perez, "When they were shooting the candy glass [window panes in Fly's studio], they'd shoot one [of the panes] and all of them would start [breaking] because of the heat. In fact, you can see broken glass in front of the building, because they had to put the [panes] back together." This sequence is yet another example of the film's continuity issues. A careful examination of Ike Clanton's actions inside Fly's studio shows that the broken window frames and wooden stiles appear and disappear from shot to shot. After Clanton bursts into the studio, grabs Behan's gun and breaks out the window, the viewer can clearly see the missing wooden stile on the left side of the center bank of windows. Both upper and lower window panes are shattered. In the portion of the shootout when Wyatt asks Doc to return Clanton's fire, the entire center window, including glass, minions and stiles, is now gone. However, as Doc starts to advance toward Ike, the window is back and unbroken. After the shootout ends and Wyatt assists a wounded Morgan, the left half of the window, including the stile, is missing. One can clearly see how pieces from the various takes were cleverly, though carelessly, spliced together. Cosmatos says that it wasn't carelessness, just a lack of material. "We had problems because we blew up some windows in the photographer's shop,

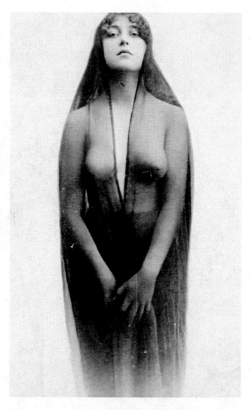

This image of "Kaloma" is believed by some to be Josephine Marcus. The image appeared as an art print and also on the cover of composer Gire Goulineaux's "Kaloma, Valse Hesitante (Hesitation Waltz)."

and we didn't have any more extras. In the film, now when you see it at the end, it has no glass in the frame any more. We took away everything and we just used it without glass. I ran out of glass because they were stupid and they brought me three panes of glass only. With all that shooting, three panes of glass is like nothing."[31]

Lee McKechnie stood in for both Val Kilmer and Bill Paxton when the shootout was filmed and vividly remembers how long it took to set up each sequence: "Sometimes it takes two hours to set up for that. Lights, camera, sound. Measuring the distance, changing lens. I'm [lying] down [in the street] there for a good 20 minutes or so, and it's hot and I'm wearing the same type outfit Paxton's got. Bill walks by, looks at me and pleads, 'Lee, please get up. You're making me hot. Can I do that?'" Declining the offer, Lee told him, "'Actually, I get paid to do this. It's cool. Don't worry about it.' [But] Paxton got down there [anyway] and he was down there another half hour by himself. That's the kind of guy he is." Quite the comedian, Paxton had a great time on location. He would imitate Cosmatos by walking with his chest out, talking with a Greek accent. Everyone thought it was hilarious but you didn't want to joke too much about George when he was on the set. During the O.K. Corral shootout, Paxton's character Morgan Earp is shot and falls to the ground. After the take was completed, Bill just laid there and exclaimed, "Game over, man," a line his character Pvt. Hudson made famous in *Aliens* (1986).[32]

A view from the front of the O.K. Corral looking toward Fremont Street. The two-story Tombstone Epitaph building is on the far right (courtesy Larry Zeug).

Several observers noted that actor Thomas Haden Church added a reflexive kick as his character, Billy Clanton, dies. This surprised Donna Cline: "I was there and I was watching that as he was shot and 'died,' falling against the wall and half reclining. He made a jerking motion with his leg…. I was so amazed because it was fairly realistic. I have a medical background—medical illustration. This reflexive kicking represented the waning of the blood pressure, the last semblance of consciousness; it was almost like the last hold on life. It was brilliantly done. (A scrabbling motion with the heel of his right boot, as if struggling to get back up.) I talked with him afterward, saying, 'Tommy, that was awesome. Very realistic. Where did you [come up with that?]'"

"'I just made it up. I don't know,' said Church, who told someone else, "[It was] one of those instinctive things that comes to you—everything's going for Billy and I try to get a little traction as I'm spiraling out of the old mortal coil." Church also repeatedly cocked and fired his empty revolver while speaking Clanton's last lines, "I need more cartridges, somebody load my gun." Neither action is seen in the film.[33]

Josh Swinney was one of the lucky ones who watched the shootout being filmed. "All the kids went and watched that. I remember the clean-up of the blood so they could re-do the scene. They would even take a blower and blow the dust around [to cover prints]. Re-setting the scene took a long time. Reloading guns, checking all the guns…. The actors would go back to their trailers, and then they'd come back and film it again.

Bill Paxton (Morgan Earp) draws a bead on Robert Burke (Frank McLaury) during rehearsal while other members of the Red Sash Gang contemplate their futures. Burke is on the far right, wearing a dark shirt and hat (courtesy James "Spud" Danicic).

[They would] have to go back and look at the camera to make sure that they got everything put back where it was supposed to be. [Filming of the shootout] didn't happen in little segments; they'd have multiple cameras set up. It took a really long time [to film that scene]. I remember they had [camera dolly tracks] they kept putting down. And then they had to move the tracks, put them down, lock them in place, and that took a really long time."[34]

Terry Leonard made an acute observation: Several horses are visible in the gunfight and one rears, turns and accidentally falls after Kilmer fires his shotgun. With cotton in its ears, the horse was protected from the shotgun blast, and the ground had previously been dug up and softened for just such an occurrence. Unfortunately, during that particular take, there wasn't a camera there to catch the animal's dramatic action. A frustrated Leonard cried, "What the heck! You guys need more cameras at different angles so you can catch that action!"[35]

Robert Burke, who played Frank McLaury, recalls a pair of mishaps: "I had a double-loaded squib that's supposed to be packed on my left shoulder. I'm tucking my head into my right shoulder because I know that thing is just going to let go. You have to agree to have a double load placed above your heart area because it's so devastating. I had worked with squibs and effects so I knew if I turn my left shoulder way out and hold my head back, it will be fine. Well, the fellow packed it on the wrong shoulder and I took every bit of the blast on the right side of my face and my ear and, rather than doing the scene over, I just kept going. Kurt came out to me; you would have thought his own kid had hurt himself. 'You all right? You all right? You all right?' My hearing was just gone on that ear and I had some burn marks under my neck. The joke was, before I hit the ground, the fellow who packed that charge was on a flight home. They took me to the hospital, I had some burns. No big deal. The next day we're back at the O.K. Corral and I take a bullet and go down but the tip on my shoes gets caught in this hole and I snapped my left ankle like you couldn't believe. Honest to God, I thought I broke it. [I'm] trying to get my boot off and I can't because it's swelling up so bad. Sam Elliott is standing with his back to the set above me and he said, 'What's the matter, Bobby?' 'My foot's swollen up,' and he pulled a Bowie knife out and he cut the boot off of me and I took the sock off. He said, 'You done just as well to break that thing.' I had this white patch on my neck, I had this balloon cast on my left foot and I go to the airport to pick up my pregnant wife and she's like, 'Are you kidding me?' 'No, honey. I'm fucked up.' Sam says, 'Oh, hell, Bobby. We'll [just] put a big boot on ya.'"[36]

During the last two days of filming the O.K. Corral sequence, the background extras were brought in and placed in the roadway facing the corral. Chickens, dogs, goats and sheep were running wild and the heat was getting to everyone. Dickie Stanley remembers, "One guy was making these goat sounds [while] they were filming. Everybody was laughing but nobody wanted to say who was doing it. Every time they'd go 'Action,' he'd go, 'Baaaahhh.' George was like, 'Where is that goat? Somebody find that fucking goat!' I don't know how many takes we did, [maybe] six or seven. Finally there were hardly any animals [left] any more, a couple of dogs, maybe a couple of chickens. All the other animals had been removed. [But] nobody pointed at [the culprit]. Everybody was laughing but it also wasted a lot of time." After the scene was finished, production decided to have a contest: How many shots were fired during the actual filming of that scene, including all the takes? The answer: 1137.[37]

Although Jarre had taken several historic liberties with the shootout, generally, his script followed actual events. The film's attention to detail in this scene is extraordinary. For instance, the real Tom McLaury wore a silver hatband and the actual Billy Clanton wore his gun cross-draw–style on his left hip—both examples specifically noted in actual testimony at the Spicer hearing conducted after the gunfight. Robert Burke and Thomas Haden Church did likewise. Val Kilmer whistled a tune as Holliday and the Earps marched toward the shootout, exactly as Stuart Lake wrote in his highly fictionalized, extremely controversial 1931 biography *Wyatt Earp: Frontier Marshal*. In fact, Jarre always took the opportunity to include several historical-literary-cinematic references in both the script and dialogue, and when faced with conflicting or contentious information, he didn't hesitate to incorporate it into his screenplay. A case in point is the Buntline Special.

Western mythology has it that Ned Buntline, aka dime novelist Edward Zane Carroll Judson, Sr., commissioned five .45-caliber, single-action Colt revolvers with 12-inch barrels as compensation to renowned lawmen Wyatt Earp, Bat Masterson, Bill Tilghman, Charley Bassett and Neal Brown, for "material for hundreds of yarns." Supposedly, each revolver came with a hand-tooled holster, a removable rifle stock and the word "NED" carved into the walnut butt of each gun. However, prior to Lake's inclusion of this event in his book, there was no known historical reference to any such special-commission activity. Colt did manufacture several long-barreled pistols between 1873 and 1876, but all those guns had 16-inch barrels that were left unattached. When someone ordered a shorter-barrel weapon, Colt merely cut off the barrel to the requested length. There are no records to indicate that Colt ever produced a 12-inch-long barrel revolver. Nevertheless, "This is the West, sir. When the legend becomes fact, print the legend." So Jarre decided to honor the myth and include the Buntline Special. Three specially manufactured EMF Hartford models with 12-inch gun barrels were acquired from Colt Firearms and shortened to ten inches. And because Tombstone bartender and Earp admirer "Buckskin" Frank Leslie once had ordered a ten-inch barreled Colt, Peter Sherayko made the case that Leslie likely would have wanted to carry a gun exactly like Earp did, hence the ten-inch barrel. "Buntline Special" was stamped into the top of each barrel and brass plates were created by John Innes and attached to the guns' grips. It read, "To Wyatt Earp

Peacemaker. From the grateful people of Dodge City. Apr, 1878." The saga of the Buntline Special may not be true, but if it isn't, it should be. After filming ended, both Russell and Cosmatos were each given one of the guns.[38]

It should be noted that in a *Guns & Ammo* magazine article (December 1997), historian Jeff Morey describes Stuart Lake's search for the five presentation guns via letters Lake wrote to Josephine Earp, Colt Firearms, Thomas Masterson (Bat's brother) and the editors of the *Wichita Eagle*, *The Empire* (Juneau, Alaska) and *The Nugget* (Nome, Alaska). Clearly, Lake believed the guns existed.

Some viewers relish the opportunity to point out historical errors in films such as this, and *Tombstone* is no exception. One inconsistency that is always identified is that there are *three* discharges from Kilmer's *double*-barreled shotgun—an impossibility. One observer noted, "The reason Doc shoots his shotgun three times is because there's two historical quotes where Doc shoots his shotgun into the O.K. Corral twice. But then there's another account that says Doc shoots his shotgun up into the air towards them and to scare them. So they covered both versions of that to see what would happen in the editing room and all three of Doc's shotgun shots end up in the movie. Stretched everyone's point of view, basically is what they did." Others have a different explanation. "I tell them [Doc] had a Drilling," says Reggie Byrum. "Most people don't know what a Drilling is. It's a European double-barrel [shotgun] with a rifle barrel in the middle." Drillings normally consist of two matching smoothbore barrels and a rifled barrel; the triple-barrel shotgun is generally laid out like a side-by-side shotgun, with the third barrel centered and below the other two. The barrels are all the same gauge. Most are break-action guns and use rimmed cartridges. But the film clearly shows that Doc's shotgun only has *two* barrels.[39]

In reality, though, this was simply an editing issue. An undated, handwritten document from the Old Tucson *Tombstone* files identifies 83 specific cuts in the shootout sequence. Not only does this *preliminary* document indicate that Wyatt takes the first shot, it clearly states that Holliday only fires his shotgun *twice*, before he pulls his handgun. Tom McLaury fires over his horse's neck, Holliday fires *once* into the air, cut to rearing horse as McLaury lets go of the reins, cut to Holliday who fires a *second* time, cut to McLaury whose side explodes in a red mist as he falls to the ground, cut back to a shot of Holliday just before he pulls the trigger for the *third* time and McLaury is *still* standing but his horse is now falling. The editor wanted to show as much action as possible from as many camera angles as possible and ended up showing the same scene more than once. In fact, Billy Clanton is seen falling to the ground *three* times!

Bo Gray was supposed to be in the shootout but was replaced by John Corbett. Says a still-fuming Gray, "I went up to Bob Misiorowski and said, 'Bob, am I cut out of the O.K. Corral?' 'Yeah,' he replied. 'They wanted John Corbett in there and he's more of a name and all that.' I said, 'Okay, you get me a van to leave. Get me the fuck outta here. I'm off this set. This is bullshit.'" Misiorowski tried to settle him down: "No, you can't do that. You gotta stick around for the funeral scene. You're already established." Gray shot back, "This is such bullshit, Bob." A sympathetic Misiorowski agreed: "Well, I'm with you but I can't do anything about it. I really can't." In the words of Gray, "I was so pissed off, I couldn't see."[40]

Given the constant action, the number of actors, takes and cameras, it was inevitable that there would be continuity errors embedded within the scene. In addition to the aforementioned windows panes, and the number of times Holliday fires his shotgun, an obvious example of this is Frank McLaury's hat. When the Earps and Holliday first approach, McLaury strikes a dramatic pose … wearing his hat. There is then a subsequent close-up where he is hatless, and then, when the gunfight starts, he's wearing his hat once again. No doubt, the hatless edit was shot just before his fatal head wound, by which time his hat was gone. Perhaps they were looking for a nervous close-up before the shooting began, grabbed it and inserted it out of order. Edit issues like this happen all the time.

On July 31, they filmed the death of Doc Holliday. Although the exterior of the building in which this was shot was the Alhambra Saloon, the practical interior set represented the Glenwood Sanitorium. "One of the areas I'm proud of is the last scene with Doc," Kilmer says. "We had to restructure the ending, because we'd run out of time and money, and I had this beautiful [five-page] monologue that Kevin Jarre had written. But dying of tuberculosis—I can't talk for five pages! And every time I rehearsed it, I just would start laughing… I mean, they were beautiful words, just not realistic. So I came up with a visual sequence instead, the card game. You know, Doc used to play cards a lot, and it's one thing he could enjoy that would take his mind off the pain. And it allowed Doc to move along the story points—to urge Wyatt to live life and go find that girl…. They were all ideas that Kevin Jarre had written but at that point we were on our own. And I knew the character well. I never talked to Kevin about it, but I hope he liked what I wrote."[41]

The Earps-leaving-Tombstone scene where Curly Bill smugly tells Wyatt, "Well … 'bye," was filmed next door at the Can Can Restaurant. In another scene filmed outside the same building, Wyatt tied a red sash around the boots of two Cowboys hanging from the Dragoon Saloon sign. One of the stuntmen stated they had to re-shoot the scene as he began to feel pressure around his neck from the hanging rigging. Prior to filming it, wranglers had shoved Kurt Russell's shotgun into his pommel sling without tying it down and, as a result, the sling flopped around a bit as he rode. Peter Sherayko was also in the scene and remembers it was pretty tight quarters. "When Kurt finished tying the sash, he turned to ride out and we all had to follow him, but he was always first. He got close to me and his shotgun [stock] caught my leg and broke." Take two![42]

Once Cosmatos wrapped up the aforementioned sequence, he began filming several interior and exterior night scenes. One of the first interiors filmed was the Latin-speaking, gun-cup twirling duel between Doc Holliday and Johnny Ringo at Wyatt's faro table. (Faro was a late 17th-century French gambling card game. Winning or losing occurred when cards turned up by the banker matched those already exposed. The equipment used was a layout table of oil cloth, canvas or felt with one of the suit cards passed or painted on top. An abacus-like casekeeper was used to keep track of the cards that had been pulled by the dealer. A dealer's box was spring-loaded to hold a deck of cards minus the joker face up.)

When Jarre first spoke to Kilmer about the scene, the actor was a bit apprehensive. Kilmer: "I was very concerned that the whole movie would be in trouble if I didn't beat [Ringo] in that moment. And so I said to Kevin, 'You know, what if this isn't funny—who knows what it will look like, a little tin cup kind of swirling around in these fancy gun moves. What if it's not funny?' And he looked at me and said, 'Yeah, I guess that's a problem.' So what I did was, for a couple of months, work the gun routine with both hands.

"I basically taught myself to do all that stuff with the .45 with the right hand, and also with the left hand—I was doing it with the .38 … and it's really tough to do that stuff. Guns are heavy. And it's also weird when you mess up—it's like hitting yourself with a hammer." So Val often was seen strolling around the Tombstone set with two guns, twirling them every chance he got, determined to make the scene believable—and funny. "I've got two guns, one for each of ya," drawls Holliday. The first was a 4¾ inch nickel-plated, ivory-gripped .38 Colt, 1877 Lightning. The second was a 4¾ inch nickel-plated, one-piece, ivory-gripped .45 Colt of EMF manufacture. Kilmer became extremely proficient in the handling of these weapons; he could twirl one forward and one backward at the same time. As for his lightweight tin cup, a weight was installed in the cup's bottom to offset the balance and thus help in the twirling motion.

Prior to filming this scene, Kilmer came up with an unusual technique to get into character. "I'm sitting in my cast chair outside the bar," says Forrie Smith, "and Val comes out and tackles me. We're wrestling around, we're in the dirt, and I finally get him in a compromising position. He goes, 'Okay, okay, okay.' I said, 'What the hell was that all about?' 'Well, I had to blow some steam off before I do the scene with the damn cup.' The wardrobe gal was all upset because he had dirt all over [him] and they had to brush him off." Before they filmed scenes inside the saloon, they would play the opening bars of Warren Zevon's "Werewolves of London" over and over to get the crowd in the mood, so to speak. "I'm pretty sure that's the only take we did," Kilmer recalls, describing his tin cup rebuttal. "And you always know when you're doing something right, because the crew laughs. They're usually just waiting for lunch, while the camera's rolling. But you know it's funny when you get applause from the extras and the crew and the camera guys and the other actors."

Michael Biehn worked equally hard at his gun-twirling skills. "The best thing is that I did the gun work myself for the barroom scene," says Biehn. "[Thell Reed and I] worked together to create a unique gun-twirling routine. I made up a trick here, and Thell made up a trick there, and we put that routine together in a matter of two or three months. I practiced the whole time to get the Colt .45 to do that. It took about two months to get it to that point. I just wanted to get it right. I even put in things that gun wranglers had never seen before! There was so much gun twirling and it all happened so fast, and of course film makes it look faster as well." Adds Michael, "I get asked to do the gun-spinning from time to time, but it took a lot of practice; you really have to do it over and over to get it right. It was certainly a difficult scene and took months and months of rehearsal and practice. When we did it, my hands started sweating. Those .45s are heavy. Dana Delany and Bill Paxton were sitting right below me. I didn't want to hurt them with a gun, and that was kind of nerve-wracking, but we did it." After filming was completed, Kilmer sent one of the cups to Cosmatos, inscribed "To George, from Doc."[43]

Jake Johnson recalls that Biehn practiced so much he broke the gun. "I know Michael Biehn worked with the guns a lot," explains Jake. "So much so that he broke the grips many times on the gun and I was always taking one of his guns to the gunsmith to have him replace the grips. Now, he got really good at it but in the process of getting good at it he dropped the gun quite a bit. He worked really hard to perfect those moves while he was out there. It's hard to say exactly what moves [Thell] taught him vs. what he wanted to do because I don't remember the specifics of what coaching took place. Thell wanted Ringo to look more like a showoff outlaw than a Johnny Mack Brown vaudevillian burlesque performance of gun-spinning and I think that's the difference you see when he's doing that. [Biehn] looks like he's serious, knows how to handle a gun. You can see from some of the angles that there were multiple takes but he was capable of doing the entire routine in one take. It was done more than once. I know I saw Michael practice repeatedly."[44]

Michael Biehn (Johnny Ringo) and Powers Boothe (Curly Bill Brocius) during one of the takes in the "Latin duel" sequence (courtesy www.moviestillsdb.com).

Dana Loraine Goodge usually was dressed as a townsperson, but in this scene she was attired as a lady of the evening. She preferred to call herself "a theatergoer" who had just arrived from the Bird Cage. According to Dana, "I thought [Val] was joking around. I swear to God I didn't think it was a part of the movie. So, all that laughter, it was just us thinking he was just goofing around." She also has a vivid memory of a somewhat notorious extra known as the Scene Stealer. "He was one of those extras who wasn't invited to be in a scene," says Dana, "but [somehow] he snuck in [anyway]. You see him in the faro table scene. All of a sudden he's standing against the wall [next to me]. He walks by and tips his hat. I yelled at him when we got out. 'How did you get in there and why would you do that in the movie?'"[45]

Both Biehn and Kilmer had become very proficient in handling their revolvers. It was said that one night they challenged Thell Reed to a quick-draw competition because, in the words of Frank Stallone, "I guess they thought once they're in their character, they're some kind of pistoleros. Thell said, 'No, I don't want to do this stuff,' but Val persisted. 'Ah, come on, come on.' Thell had a stocked-up, single-action, 4¾", off-the-rack Mexican loop holster. And he said, 'Okay, guys. You ready?' They never even cleared their holsters and he was out." That was the end of who was the fastest.[46]

Filming then moved outside to Allen Street. On the evening of Saturday, August 7, and continuing on to Monday, August 9, they filmed the scene where, after leaving an opium den, a hopped-up Curly Bill howls at the moon and shoots at passersby. Faced with no alternative but to arrest him, Fred White asks for Bill's revolvers but is killed in the process. Wyatt quickly rushes out, cold-cocks Bill and takes him into custody. Ike

Clanton and several other Cowboys then demand Bill's release. Unfortunately, someone forgot to fully load one of Curly Bill's guns, so when he fired at the moon, the gun would go, "Bang! Click. Bang! Click." Naturally, they had to film the scene again. In Cosmatos' commentary in the *Tombstone* director's cut, he explained, "I had to go up and up and up … and then the camera, I had it going back down towards him again until it came close to the guns but that was cut, so you don't get it here. It was like a double-crane shot. This was all one shot before and then it was intercut with the interior."

A gray-bearded extra is seen as a crowd gathers around the fallen marshal. He kept walking up pretty close to Carey, who played Fred White, and Cosmatos thought the extra was being a camera hog. It wasn't that, the man just didn't hear the instructions. They had tried to put him in deep background because the hearing aid he usually wore wasn't period-correct. But when he removed the device, he couldn't hear.[47]

Stephen Lang describes his characterization of Clanton: "[Ike] is as hard-bitten and bitter as Ringo, Doc or Wyatt, but he lacks their confidence and self-esteem. I think that Ike was whipped plenty by Old Man Clanton; [he] has something of the whipped cur in him. Vicious, somewhat dangerous, but also kind of sad and pathetic. That's good, playable stuff, and struck me as both unique within the story and historically plausible, and possibly very accurate. Everything I did as Ike represents a deliberate choice on my part." As the scene continues, Wyatt faces down Ike, and Virgil and Morgan rush from around the corner of a building, shotguns in hand. Billy Lang and John Peel were behind the building, loading and unloading the weapons, and Thell Reed had given them specific instructions: "Do not hand an actor a loaded gun until the very last possible second. They're actors, they're not gunmen. They could blow a blank off in somebody's face." After several takes (witnesses estimated as many as 14), Cosmatos called for one more. By now, it was after midnight. Morgan and Virgil had been filmed coming to Wyatt's aid at least a dozen times. But Sam returned to the side of the building once more and waited for his cue. As the scene played out, Sam dutifully ran around the corner, and … there was dead silence. Then, everyone broke out into a rousing "Happy birthday!" It was Sam's 49th birthday. Nancy Sykes from craft services had baked a cake and members of the cast and crew signed a huge birthday card for him. Katharine Ross also made an appearance that evening.[48]

Johnny Ringo wasn't present in that scene and there's a good reason why. Although Curly Bill is shown *leaving* the opium den, he is never seen *entering* it. Apparently, Ringo also entered the establishment and upon his departure, was supposed to grab a passerby, lift him a foot off the ground, and bodily throw him into a crowd of pedestrians. The scene was rehearsed several times but by the time it came to shoot it, Biehn was too tired, so he merely shoved the person. Though filmed, it wasn't included in the film.[49]

On Thursday, August 12, Cosmatos filmed the death of Morgan Earp. Grant James, who played the part of the historical Dr. Goodfellow, clearly remembers that particular scene: "The bloody pool table scene was on the schedule day after day after day in case of bad weather, which is one of the reasons that I was there as long as I was. They kept praying for good weather." But by the time they were actually ready to shoot, Cosmatos started fuming and yelling about what was wrong. Kurt calmed him down and said, "I'll lean back, you lean over, we'll shoot it again." James adds, "They made a prosthetic back for Billy Paxton with a hole where the bullet had gone in. It was attached to a tube that ran under the pool table where there was a guy with a bag full of blood. So I would jab those long tweezers in and out and squirt the blood. Billy would go, 'Oh, oh,' and the guy

The interior of the Campbell & Hatch Billiard Parlor where Morgan Earp (Bill Paxton) was murdered. The table in the foreground was removed for better camera placement (photograph by Lee Gray/courtesy Catherine Hardwicke).

would squeeze the bag and out would squirt the blood. It [looked realistic] to me and I was there." Originally, the scene was much longer, to show the bond between the brothers, but it was cut.[50]

That weekend, they filmed scene #49, the "Let's have a spelling contest" altercation between Holliday and Ike Clanton. (In the television movie script *The Tracker*, released in 1988 as *Dead or Alive*, starring Kris Kristofferson, Jarre first used the line, "How about a spelling contest?") John Philbin recalls that was a difficult scene to film: "There's this horrible poker game where Stephen Lang gets in a fight and bottles are flying all over. We can't match continuity, he's just losing it. Val's at the table, it's late, it's smoky. There were some tense moments. That was difficult when there's a lot of actors and a lot of props, a lot of action. It's hard to get the same thing to happen twice in an environment like that. And we were shooting in a practical environment, it's not a studio, it's a set. Catherine Hardwicke [had] built a bar. It's not a studio, and we had to match a lot of things over and over and a lot of actors that demanded coverage."

Stephen Lang admits that he really tried to get into character in that scene. "I don't know how many takes we did on the poker scene round table, lots of coverage," he says. "I think I may have knocked back a shot or six during the course of the evening. Not the way I usually work, but sometimes you just got to go with the flow. I won't speak for Val." Cosmatos confessed, "[Lang] told me he was most of the time drunk playing that part. I didn't realize it until after he told me." There are usually consequences for such behavior, as Lang ruefully recalls: "Immediately after wrapping, I flew to Colorado to work on *Tall Tale*, but I also played out my own private sequel or epilogue to *Tombstone*. It's called *Kidney Stone*, because I did four rugged days in the hospital in Glenwood Springs, struck down by a galaxy of kidney stones. That's what happens when you drink tequila instead of water for four months. Of course the great irony is that Doc died and is buried in Glenwood Springs, just a block or so from the hospital. And I don't think I've had tequila since."

According to Catherine Hardwicke, "One thing that stands out the most is the scene where Val passes out in the saloon and the boys [Kurt and Bill Paxton] carry him out. On the way out of the set, there is a step down [from the saloon doorway to the board-walk]. They were supposed to carry [Val] onto the dirt street, then let him down—but apparently forgetting the step down, all three of them went tumbling onto the street.... If you look hard, you'll see Val's body tip suddenly as he exits. It was funny seeing them all piled up in the middle of the street."[51]

Val also imbibed in alcoholic refreshment while in character, perhaps a bit more frequently than others. Property assistant Greg Poulos was his bartender of choice. "I was in charge of that. [Val] would always say, 'My flask is broken.' Some of the prop guys would go up and [try to] fix it. He would go, 'No. the only guy to fix it is Greg.' That meant he needed his $50 bottle of Scotch in it (which he purchased from Bobby Joe's Irish Pub in Mescal). He was Doc Holliday, every day. I enjoyed being with him because he was funny at times, hilarious. I'd see him in the hotel and kind of hide because I know he'd be Doc Holliday. He'd call out my name and I'd go like, 'Oh, no. I work with you for six days and I've got to see you on Sunday, too?' He was always in character, always. [Sam Elliott knew Val could be difficult] and he would give me a kiss on the cheek and then every night he'd say, 'Well, you made it through another day with Val.' When they moved to the Holiday Inn, they put [Val] in the room right next to me and he'd beat on my wall. 'Val, I got get up in three hours and you've got the day off.'"[52]

Eddie Perez recalls, "I remember one night in the saloon … they handed us prop beer. Being a young kid, I remember saying, 'They're going to have us working all night and here they are giving us prop beer.' That's when Val came over and showed me his flask and said, 'Well, here. Have some of this.' So I poured it into the prop beer, I figured, 'What the heck, if it's rum or something.' No, it was peach brandy. Val was drinking on set to get the character of Doc Holliday and he did an awesome job of doing it. That was the night I woke up at the Bell Gas Station because we got off at six in the morning. And we had to take the bus out there; I didn't want to drive because I was drunk. I woke up at 11 o'clock in the morning, out in my car, sweating my tail off. Knowing I had to be on the set at three o'clock. I had to drive to Tucson, take a shower and drive back. I tell you, that was the worst time of my life. And when Val saw me the next morning, we were still doing the saloon scene; he sat there and laughed at me because he could tell I was hung over. I was a beer drinker; I wasn't a whiskey drinker at the time."[53]

In some cases, liquor was deliberately used to achieve a certain effect. "I was in the opium den scene," remembers Poulos, "and Kurt's gun is on the table and I pick it up thinking it's the opium pipe and put it in my mouth and he shoots me. Val said, 'Go drink my Scotch so you look drunk.' Kurt had me drinking a couple of Miller Lights, it was 4 a.m. in the morning. Then they put this stuff on my eyes to make them red like I was wasted and stoned."[54]

On August 14, they filmed the scene in which the Earp brothers and their wives leave the Bird Cage after the theatrical performances and discuss spiritualism in the middle of Allen Street. In the June 24, 1993, revised fifth draft of the script, the characters suddenly stop in the midst of their conversation and gaze at the hills surrounding Tombstone, where they spot 15 Apache horsemen watching in silent contemplation. As the wives move closer to their husbands, the Apaches move off into the darkness. Originally, there was more of a pre-roll of this scene, with other characters leaving the theater before Morgan and Wyatt begin their existential talk. The portion with the silent observers was never filmed.[55]

Next, they filmed scene #23 in which the Earps and their wives gather outside the Birdcage Theater after the evening's performance. Virgil and Allie bid the group good night and head home. In an unused continuation of that scene, the couple walks past a person cooking dinner in front of a tent. The actor who played the townsman, J. Nathan Simmons, recalls, "It's cold that evening and I'm making this really nasty stuff in the pot 'cause they said, 'Well, bring it up. Let it percolate.' We had boiling water so I started adding all sorts of things to it. Sam walks by and said, 'What ya got cooking?' I said, 'Well, a little bit of this, a little bit of that.' Replies Sam, 'It doesn't smell very good so I think I'll pass on that one.'"[56]

On August 10, they filmed scene #47A, where Virgil posts an ordinance forbidding the carrying of weapons within town limits. Although it appears that the decree was posted outside the sheriff's office, due to the lack of space between the buildings, it actually was nailed up across the street when the scene was filmed. Wyatt then rides into town, dismounts and realizes that Virgil is now wearing a badge. Simmons was also part of this scene: "Actually, we were pretty darn quick on that. I think we might have done it maybe three times. It was a pretty fast scene, very easy done. They made sure we were aware of the horses; some of us hadn't been around horses before." Apparently, three extras also were supposed to say lines in that scene but it was not to be. "One guy ended up doing the lines from all three of us," grumbles Simmons. "I would say that was kind of a bummer for all of us; we wanted to kick his butt afterwards. It's like, 'Dude, we're all assigned a line in this movie and you end up saying them all?' We didn't see him much after that. He had basically done his part in the movie and he was done. But he stole our thunder as well."[57]

Two days later, Cosmatos filmed the aftermath of Morgan's death when Wyatt, with blood on his hands both literally and figuratively, staggers outside in the pouring rain. For whatever reason, Russell was in an extremely bad mood that evening and yelled a great deal. In this scene, Wyatt calls Josephine a "Jew whore!"—something later changed to simply "Get away from me!" The lightning was real, the rain wasn't. Tom Ford coordinated the effect. Three rain-making machines had been rented for the film, but due to budget constraints, one was returned. As a result, they could only simulate rain on a portion of the street. Viewers can clearly see a dry street behind Russell as he stumbles around. A large 8 × 15-foot lighting array made of aluminum pipes in the shape of a cube, and covered with bleached muslin, simulated the moon. It housed four 2500-watt HMIs (hydrogyrum medium arc iodide) and was hoisted 80 to 120 feet in the air by a condor crane to create artificial moonlight. Amusingly, some locals thought they were seeing UFOs and called the police department. It even made the news: "There were UFOs sighted off of I-10. Film at 11."

While a horse stands in the middle of the street, rain is pouring in Mescal and bystanders take shelter in the Grand Hotel (courtesy P.J. Lawton, Old Tucson Studio).

The lightning was both dangerous and terrifying. "One night, in the desert, a lightning storm came in around us," recalls Donna Cline. "We had three 60-foot cranes in the air. Honestly, if it hit one of those cranes, it might have killed us all. It seemed like they waited too long but they finally said, 'Okay, we're going to take the cranes down,' and everybody ran into the saloons and ran into places where we could get away from the cranes. It was frightening, because the storm was on us. I've never seen lightning like that before."[58]

During the night shoots at Mescal, the construction and set design team for *The Quick and the Dead* moved in and started to give the town a complete makeover, something that Sam Dolan woefully recalls: "Honestly, it was a little depressing. The transition signaled to us that our time at Mescal and on the movie itself would be drawing to a close. But there was also the sense that the brightly colored Tombstone that we'd called home for several weeks was being turned into something darker and dirtier. Nothing is really sacred in the business. They built the large fake brick building down the end of the street that served as the main saloon in *The Quick and the Dead* and very rapidly made a number of other cosmetic changes."[59]

During the Vendetta ride sequence, Kilmer and Buck Taylor's characters burst into a hotel room and kill a Cowboy (stuntman Cody Lee) who's in bed with two prostitutes. It was filmed inside the Grand Hotel, and Emily Blanton, who played one of the prostitutes, vividly remembers that night. Blanton was told, "Hurry up and go to the wardrobe trailer and grab your wardrobe because they're going to be blocking for this scene right now." Blanton says, "So I run over to the wardrobe trailer and they hand me a G-string and a bathrobe and they said, 'You need to put this on right now.' [Covered with the robe,] I run out to the set and both Buck and Val are out there. I told them how shocked I was that all I had on was a G-string. I think it kind of perked both of their interests. When they actually did the scene and busted into the room, I had managed to get my hand on a handkerchief—like a little scarf-y thing. So as soon as they busted into the room, I covered up my boobs because I wasn't prepared to share myself with everybody. George kept saying, 'We need to react slower.' I'm like, 'Okay, sure,' but I didn't follow his directions. We did it again. He goes, 'Emily, we need you to react slower.' 'Okay.' And again I didn't. I covered up my boobs and that's probably why that scene stayed in there. I didn't end up on the cutting room floor because I hid my nipples, pretty much. [As for the other girl in the scene, the first time] she bumped her head because she wasn't that experienced and she wasn't used to the squibs and how loud they were. We did three [takes]. Just three, and that's pretty good."[60]

Several other scenes were filmed inside the Grand Hotel, including the night Sheriff Behan confronts Josephine Marcus right before Virgil is ambushed. The interior was fully decorated thanks to Nell Peel, an antique dealer specializing in Victorian furniture (and mother of Buckaroo John Peel). Most of the pieces in the hotel, as well as the Earps' houses and Holliday's bedroom at the Hooker ranch, came from her. She also supplied linen and dishware to decorate the sets.[61]

Wyatt and Mattie's bedroom (photograph by Lee Gray/courtesy Catherine Hardwicke).

By now, everyone was virtually exhausted and it seemed that the closer it got to the end of filming, the faster the scenes were being filmed. "I did notice that there was an urgency in the last few weeks," admits Mark Rainsford. "We were trying to find out when we were going to finish. I left my home April 27 and got home September 3. The last few weeks, there really wasn't a hard finish date. Then they finally figured it out and … the scenes wore down." Even so, and perhaps for that very reason, a great many scenes ended up on the cutting room floor. A case in point are the deaths of two Cowboys. In scene #112, Ringo is notified of Curly Bill's death by Buckaroos Tom and Charley Ward, who played the two lone Iron Springs attack survivors who bring the news. Says Tom, "There was a night shot—filmed around two or three in the morning— and this was supposed to be after Sabino Canyon. Charley and I were part of the group shooting at Kurt's character. There was a shot … it was supposed to be after Iron Springs [and] we were reporting to Johnny Ringo. We were the only two survivors. They had a camp, there was an old railroad passenger car, it was a night shot. That was kind of the headquarters of the [Cowboys]. We're standing before the fire, it was about three o'clock in the morning. Biehn's there, he's squatting down with his silver pistol. He said, 'What happened?' So we went through all that stuff. Then he said, 'What I want to know is, why are you two back here?' He pulls his pistol and shoots Charley in the forehead and shoots me in the chest. Well, we really never did any stunts before that, so Terry [Leonard] is right there. He said, 'Let me give you some kidney pads,' and he did. He told us how to fall, and makeup put the makeup on Charley's forehead with the squib there. A squib was set up in my shirt. [Biehn] pulls the gun and shoots us and we fall over dead and they cut the scene. Terry came over [and asked], 'Are you all right?' 'Yeah, was it all right?' 'If it wasn't all right, they'd be doing it again,' replied Terry."[62]

Charley has a slightly different memory of that scene. "I was in hair and makeup two or three hours to get that squib on my forehead," he recalls. "I was really nervous about that. Terry Leonard was instructing us what to do. I said, 'Terry, I don't know what to do. I've never had a squib on before. I don't want to screw up the timing on this.' He said, 'Don't worry about it. You'll know when to fall. You'll feel a little thump on your forehead. Just fall and look down at your toes as you're falling. Just let your head whip back and come back up and look at your toes as you're falling. It'll be great.'" Not really, as Charley recalls how he felt after the squib went off: "I had an instant headache. I mean right then. I got up, I said, 'Man, Terry. That was a little bit more than a *thump.*' He said, 'I didn't want to scare you by telling you actually what it was going to feel like. I thought you were nervous enough. We've had guys go unconscious. Stunt guy have a squib on his head, it would knock him flat smooth out. It's a serious situation but I didn't want to scare you more than I had to.'"[63]

Later that month, Leonard filmed a scene on the Babocomari that, again, was omitted from the film's final version. However, it did serve to set up the death of the actor, Mr. Fabian. In scene #113, cowards Zwing Hunt and Billy Grounds sneak out of the Cowboys' camp rather than be held accountable for the terror they've caused. On their way out of the territory (Scene #120), they spy a stagecoach and attempt a holdup. Extra Kathy Tarantino, Buckaroo Jerry Tarantino's wife, describes what happened next: "There was a four-up hitch stagecoach and we were running full-blast through the desert and Cowboys, one on each side, were chasing us and shooting into the stagecoach. Of course, they didn't want to risk Dana [Delany]. So they risked my life. They paid me a whopping … $400 for that day. I just dressed like I normally do because it was far enough away so that nobody would know that it wasn't [Dana]. They could just see that there was a woman in there with a hat. It was fun and exciting but the stagecoach kept fishtailing. There was myself and two other guys in there, I had on a big satin gown and the seat covers were all velvet. The stagecoach was swerving back and forth and it was slippery and I was having a hard time just staying up. I was just laughing and I was hoping nobody could see that I was laughing. We only did it once. That was quite a thrill."[64]

Even though filming was almost complete, several crew members had had enough with the tension and confusion and decided to leave the production. Recalls B camera focus puller Michael Walker, "I left with about ten days left in shooting. There's a lot of pressure on the A camera first. George [Cosmatos] and Mike Latino were having a lot of problems; the director was crass and didn't like [Mike], who didn't put up with a lot of that shit from George. I think they had a lot of issues, personality issues against each other. So [Mike] decided to quit and I had a discussion with Billy [Fraker]. I said,

Kathy Tarantino stands in for Dana Delany in the Wolverton Mountain stagecoach (courtesy Jerry Tarantino).

'Look, if Mike leaves, I think I should probably leave, too, because [George will] just end up being even worse with me as well. It's a very stressful job to keep things in focus. It was a very tough show and I think Mike just had enough…. So I'll probably go with him.' Bill said, 'I don't blame you. I'll see you guys soon.' I left about ten days before the end of the shooting. [Later] I heard from a friend of mine that Kurt said, 'Keep Mike in the credits because he did so much of the movie.'" (Walker: "A camera would normally film wider angles while B camera focuses on tighter close-ups. The cameras may be positioned right next to each other so as to keep the same eye line. Sometime I'm off to the side getting some a different angle or reaction of an actor while the A camera focuses on the primary actor.")[65]

After 82 days of filming, the production could finally see light at the end of the tunnel. And everyone was dead tired. Tempers were frayed, actors were sunburned to a crisp, and even the horses were exhausted. If they could only get through the final six days, life again would be good. So, ironically, what scene did they decide to film that last Monday? What else but Wyatt and Josie dancing in the snow. Snow? What snow?

Kathy Tarantino was one of an unusually large numbers of extras used when the scene was filmed that evening. Extras were planted all around the set—inside the theater, in the street on horseback, even building a snowman. However, given the length of the scene and its focus on Russell and Delany, viewers don't actually get that impression.

Most background players were used for general, nondescript activity and even though it was way over 90°, many females were dressed in capes and gowns as if it were cold. Adds her husband Jerry, who was also in the scene, "They had guys on the rooftop of the buildings pouring huge plastic bags full of these tiny plastic flakes. It was very light, very small. We did so many takes on that, the plastic stuff was in our underwear. Every take they had to do, Dana [Delany] had to go inside and they had to take every flake of snow out of her hair so when she came out of the doorway it didn't look like she had [just] come in from outside. [They were] very meticulous." And the horses hated the plastic; every time they inhaled, shreds would go up their nostrils. Even a short scene like this (90 seconds) was very costly to create: $26,978, including $3500 to prep, shoot, wrap and strike the set; $2800 for the rental of statue, pedestal, trees, shrubs, park benches and fencing; $12,414 for snow blankets, blown snow, wind machine, tanks and guns, and even $200 for a snowman! If one looks carefully, after Wyatt throws his hat into the air, you can see it catching the wind and flying off into the distance. No doubt that was prearranged. After 10 to 15 takes, and set-up after set-up, everyone was exhausted. Too bad Cosmatos didn't listen to other suggestions: "I had an argument with some people that wanted to show them at sunset on the beach. I said, 'Let's do it in the snow because the snow is a contrast to all the desert we've seen.'"[66]

Over the next five days, another 12 complete or partial scenes were filmed, consisting of 188 set-ups that ultimately produced just 5:40 minutes of footage. Both the first and second units revisited numerous sites, including Old Tucson, Mescal and the Babocomari

Placement of "snow" in front of and on the Denver Theater in Old Tucson. Shredded plastic, snow blankets and wind machines created the wintry conditions (courtesy P.J. Lawton, Old Tucson Studio).

Ranch, where they filmed additional pick-up shots and did some re-shoots. On some days, they also ran split shifts—filming both night and day—to go easy on the crew and to also avoid various contract penalties. Several set-ups were of scenes Kevin Jarre originally had filmed in the first four weeks. Ironically, much of this new footage was eventually left on the cutting room floor. In one scene, Johnny Ringo was having an evening Cowboy meeting after the death of Curly Bill. It was staged at the end of the railroad tracks at Old Tucson Studios. Buckaroo Jerry Tarantino stood guard in the rain while the outlaws gathered next to a rail car. (This location was also used for Curly Bill's post–O.K. Corral eulogy.) Cosmatos noticed Jerry's wedding ring and told him to take it off. "Cowboys. They were never married," Cosmatos explained. Tarantino's hand was so tan from the sun that they had to paint the very obvious white, untanned band on his finger. Jerry's wife Kathy stood behind Cosmatos as they filmed the scene. "They had the camera right on Jerry," she remembers, "and I'm motioning [Jerry] to go to the left a little bit. No, go right. I was directing Jerry over Cosmatos' head."[67]

Known for staging complex aerial shots, Cosmatos wrapped up production with one that was both climactic and stunning. Usually, this type of shot is accomplished through the use of airborne devices like airplanes, cranes, drones or, as in this case, a helicopter. By definition, an aerial shot is an exterior shot taken high in the air and used to establish a sense of geography or scale. In *Tombstone*, it was used at the conclusion of the dramatic and violent Vendetta ride. Unfortunately, money was tight and as the production already was over-budget, several actors gave up their overages (an additional portion of their salary for every day the production ran over). In addition, one actor went so far as to ask his pilot friend to fly the helicopter needed for the aerial shots … and the actor paid for the pilot to come to the location out of his own pocket. Inclement weather caused the helicopter to be grounded that morning, but the weather broke shortly before lunch and the shots were completed. Cosmatos clarified, "I had them only for a few hours so I tried to [film] as many shots as possible with the helicopters." Russell, Kilmer, Buck Taylor and Sherayko are seen in this striking shot, riding their magnificent steeds as the camera dramatically rises away. Sherayko explains an amusing aspect of the scene: "There's a scene where we're riding the horses at the end of the movie with the helicopter shot watching us ride. Buck and I are always on the outside. We're on the outside because Kurt and Val weren't as good riders as Buck or I, so we had to keep them in to make sure they wouldn't run away. But Kurt also wanted to lead, he had to lead. Buck and I were on very fast horses, and Kurt and Val were on slower horses. And as much as they were getting them to go, we had to be pulling back. So if you look at that scene, you'll see they are trying to go fast and Buck and I are holding the horses back. 'Cause we can't have them in front of us. Buck kind of looks over at me and he says something, but it's all M.O.S. [without sound]. What he's doing is he's yelling to me, 'Slow down, Peter. We'll get fired.'"[68]

There is yet a continuity error within this Vendetta ride sequence. As the Earp posse chases Ike Clanton just before he discards his red sash, one clearly sees four posse members. Yet, three seconds earlier, *five* posse members, including Sherm McMasters, are seen silhouetted against the overcast sky. The McMasters character had been killed off earlier in the film. Sam Dolan details how that scene was filmed: "They lined up the doubles for Earp, Holliday, Johnson, Texas Jack, etc., and then sent me, my dad and some other crew people out every 50 yards or so with walkie-talkies and gave us each a number. As the posse rode right at camera, we were supposed to radio the camera team our number, so that they could pull focus. 'Approaching four … four…'—that kinda thing. It made for a long day, but when I saw the film on Christmas Day, 1993, I was proud of myself for having helped with that shot."

In the same Clanton-sash sequence, we also see Sheriff Behan, along with several Cowboys, scattering to the four winds. Jarre's original script had better-defined this relationship yet virtually all the scenes that addressed the Behan-Cowboy association were missing from the final release. To let them know when the shot began and ended, they also used a walkie-talkie in the wide establishing shot of several duster-wearing Cowboys riding into Tombstone. In the words of Larry Zeug, "It was lightning all around us and we were the tallest thing out there and wet." Although it wasn't raining at that exact moment, "we were in a rush for them to get the shot done." Buckaroo Bill Weddle was able to get a deal on yellow reproduction period rain slickers and many still have them. This second-unit shot was edited into the sequence just before the Clantons ride into town for the gunfight. A casual observer may think that these are the Clantons and McLaurys riding into town, as that was the way the scene was inserted, but it was really just a transition shot.[69]

SEVEN

"That's a Wrap!"

Initially, it seemed that the local citizens supported the Earps' actions. The response of the San Francisco Exchange *was typical: "The people of Tombstone have reason to congratulate themselves that they have marshals who are dead shots, and we hope the Tombstoners appreciate the fact." Still, the day after the gunfight, the bodies of Billy Clanton and Frank and Tom McLaury were displayed at the undertaker's beneath a sign that read "Murdered in the Streets of Tombstone." Slowly, inexplicably, public opinion began to turn against the peace officers. Within a matter of days, Ike Clanton filed murder charges against Wyatt, Morgan, Virgil and Doc; all were subsequently arrested. Wyatt and Holliday were jailed for two weeks during the hearing, while Virgil and Morgan were exempted because of their wounds. On November 30, after a lengthy hearing where Behan testified in support of the Cowboys and Clanton accused Earp of everything except the murder of Cock Robin, Judge Wells Spicer ruled there was insufficient evidence to indict the men: "I am of the opinion that the defendant, Virgil Earp, as chief of police, subsequently calling upon Wyatt Earp and J.H. Holliday to assist him in arresting and disarming the Clantons and McLaurys, committed an injudicious and censurable act, and although in this he acted incautiously and without due circumspection; yet when we consider the conditions of affairs incident to a frontier country; the lawlessness and disregard for human life; the existence of a law-defying element in [our] midst; the fear and feeling of insecurity that has existed; the supposed prevalence of bad, desperate and reckless men who have been a terror to the country and kept away capital and enterprise; and consider the many threats that have been made against the Earps, I can attach no criminality to his unwise act. In fact, as the result plainly proves, he needed the assistance and support of staunch and true friends, upon whose courage, coolness and fidelity he could depend, in case of an emergency."*

But Spicer's decision didn't end the matter. Less than a month later, on the night of December 28, Virgil Earp was ambushed by an unknown assailant or assailants while walking his rounds at the intersection of Allen and Fifth. The shotgun blast he absorbed was vicious—Virgil's left arm was sufficiently shattered such that Dr. Goodfellow had to remove five and a half inches from the humerus bone. Wyatt quickly wired for authorization to become a deputy U.S. marshal, and he and his posse searched for Pony Diehl and Ike and Phin Clanton—the three Cowboys they believed were behind the attack on Virgil. Fearing reprisal, Clanton turned himself in to Behan and even stood trial for attempted murder, but after a parade of convenient alibi "witnesses," the judge was reluctantly forced to release Ike. But Spicer also gave Wyatt some sage advice: "You'll never clean up this town this way. Next time you'd better leave your prisoners out in the brush where alibis don't count."

Morgan was next. On March 18, he was shooting pool in Campbell and Hatch's Billiard

Parlor and had his back to the door when several shots rang out. One bullet narrowly missed Wyatt, who was watching the game, but another struck Morgan, who pitched forward onto the table and then collapsed to the floor. Fearing another attack, Wyatt, Sherm McMaster and Dan Tipton dragged Morgan ten feet away from the rear door and close to a door to the card room. Drs. Mathews, Goodfellow and Millar were summoned to no avail; Morgan died within an hour. Pete Spence, Frederick Bode, Frank Stillwell, "Indian Charlie" Florentino Cruz and one other individual eventually were charged as suspects. Wyatt felt that Spence had nothing to do with Morgan's shooting, but believed that Stillwell, Cruz, Ringo, Brocius and Hank Swilling were involved. These two blows, just months apart, were too much for even Wyatt to bear. Virgil's maiming and Morgan's death changed Wyatt from peace officer to vigilante, vowing revenge on all Cowboys.

Arrangements were made to send Morgan's casket to his father in California, with James Earp accompanying it. Bessie and Mattie Earp followed five days later. Wyatt and his posse then escorted Virgil and Allie first to Contention and then on to Tucson. But as they waited for Virgil's train to leave the Tucson station, Wyatt noticed two armed men in the shadows near the train. Discovered by the vindictive lawman, Ike Clanton and Frank Stillwell made a break for it. Ike escaped. Frank didn't, as Wyatt shot him with a double-barrel shotgun. Other Earp posse members, including Holliday, Warren Earp, "Turkey Creek" Jack Johnson and Sherm McMaster, may have also fired shots into Stillwell as bystander George Hand described Stillwell as "the most shot-up man I ever saw." While it's highly unlikely, Virgil Earp still claimed, "Before Stillwell died he confessed that he killed Morg and gave the names of those who were implicated with him." When the angry Earp left to track down the rest of his brother's killers, he became a wanted man, supported by local businessmen and Wells Fargo, but now also hunted by Behan's posse, which included Johnny Ringo, Pete Spence, Johnny Barnes and 17 other Cowboys. Over the next two days, Earp killed Florentino Cruz at Pete Spence's logging camp, located off the Chiricahua Road, below the South Pass of the Dragoon Mountains, and Curly Bill Brocius at the Iron (Cottonwood) Springs waterhole in the Whetstone Mountains. Curly Bill and his men had ambushed Earp, who, unaware that his posse had abandoned him, advanced alone toward the outlaw, shotgun in hand. Curly Bill fired his own shotgun at Earp but missed; Wyatt fired a shotgun blast into Bill's chest, killing the outlaw. As the remaining Cowboys opened up, their shots shattered Earp's boot heel and saddle pommel, and pierced the coattails of his duster. Wyatt fired his revolver and hit Johnny Barnes, who later died from the wound. Earp then struggled to mount his saddle as his cartridge belt had slipped from his waist, but eventually he did and rode away. As daily local and national newspapers reported Earp's Vendetta activities, his support from those who had previously endorsed him continued to dwindle—the law and order populace could no longer abide by his actions. Earp and his men eventually made their way to Hooker's Sierra Bonita ranch, but faced with no viable alternative, they left the Arizona Territory for New Mexico in April 1882. Even the best of friends sometimes quarrel: Wyatt and Holliday had a falling out in Albuquerque, allegedly after Doc called Earp a "Jew boy" because of Wyatt's romance with Josephine Marcus. The Earps and Vermillion moved on to Gunnison, Colorado, while Holliday headed for Denver. It was over. The Vendetta ride had lasted a mere 17 days, but Wyatt's reputation had suffered irreparable damage because he now was viewed not as an avenging brother, but rather as a murderous retaliator.

On July 14, Johnny Ringo was found dead, a bullet hole in his right temple, at the base of a large tree in West Turkey Creek Valley, not far from Rustler Park. It was an odd scene, because his boots were tied to the saddle of his horse (which was captured two miles away), and a torn undershirt protected his feet. Ringo was armed to the teeth as a coroner's report stated: "His revolver he grasped in his right hand, his rifle resting against the tree close to him. He had two cartridge belts, the belt for revolver cartridges being buckled upside down. The undernoted property was found with him and on his person: one Colt's revolver, calibre 45, No. 222, containing five cartridges; one Winchester rifle octagon barrel, calibre 45, model 1876, No. 21, 986, containing a cartridge in the breech and ten in the magazine; 1 cartridge belt, containing 9 rifle cartridges; 1 cartridge belt containing 2 revolver cartridges." Over the years, although Wyatt, Holliday, Buckskin Frank Leslie and/or Johnny-Behind-the-Deuce (Michael O'Rourke) were either blamed or took credit for Ringo's death, the coroner's inquest ruled his death a suicide. Historians debate the truth of Ringo's demise to this day.

Four months later, Wyatt left for California. His life as a lawman was over.[1]

Babocomari Ranch, Saturday, August 28, 1993. After 15 weeks filming, the last day of shooting had finally arrived. Production began on May 17 on the Babocomari Ranch, and then moved to Old Tucson Studios, on to Mescal and then back to Old Tucson. Now it ended up here where it all started. Scene #41 depicts the meeting between Wyatt and McMasters as Earp attempts to retrieve his stolen horses. According to Larry Zeug: "We're set up in this bowl canyon that had one way in and one way out unless you went up over the hill. We're all stationed with tents around the hill, we're either supposed to either get on our horse or walk down when Wyatt comes to the camp." John Philbin recalls, "When Kurt showed up in character ... and got off his horse and shot that scene, he had Wyatt Earp down. He was different that day. He had acquired, briefly, the rage and power of that character. It came out in his eyes and his mannerisms and his voice. He actually changed. I remember him saying the last day, 'Fuck, I wish ... that's the character. I found him.' I was like, 'Better late than never. I think you had him all along but that was fucking insane, great work you just did.' It was powerful how he did that scene but it didn't end up in the movie. You're so busy doing so many things and the character comes to you at night or the next month."

Russell even apologized to Philbin for his perceived aloofness. "John, I ended up working every night until I had to pass out," explained Kurt. "After we worked all day, I would work with George on the script and on the directing. Usually after shooting I get a beer with the boys every time. But, I didn't do it this time because I had to work on the script every night. I've never worked on a movie where I couldn't just hang out with actors and have a beer afterwards."[2]

Interesting comments from one who never really wanted to act. "To go on about acting as art is ridiculous," claims Russell. "If it is an art, then it's a very low form. You don't have to be gifted just to hit a mark and say a line. And as far as I am concerned, hitting my marks and knowing my lines is 90 percent of the job. I'm always criticized for talking like that. Maybe the reason I do it is that I never got the chance to develop a real desire to act. I was acting by the time I was nine so it seemed like a natural thing to do. Anyone who finds acting difficult just shouldn't be doing it."[3]

Sam Elliott wasn't really satisfied with his performance, either. "Kurt and I had never worked together, and I'd been a huge fan of Kurt's since I was a kid," Elliott says. "And then we got together, and we're both pretty strong guys. And we had that rub kinda goin' between us, I think, during production, and it's evident on screen.... It made it tough at times, but it worked on the film. I don't know, I just felt like I went a little too far overboard with it. I think that's what makes it tough at the end—when you're not happy with what you did."[4]

As first AD, Adam Taylor had endured an ungodly amount of grief from Cosmatos. "He put up with more shit," admits Larry Zeug. "Nobody would have put up with as much as he did. They would have quit and walked away." The Buckaroos therefore wanted to give Adam a token of appreciation for all his efforts: a symbol for having survived that ordeal and representing the respect that the crew and actors had for him. "The last day of the movie, one of the guys … made a plaque," says Reggie Byrum. "[Mounted on it] was a pressure valve gauge that had the needle [bent] all the way over past the red mark." Reggie instructed the rest of the Buckaroos, "When I yell 'Buckaroos,' we'll all ride down and give Adam this [plaque]." One uneasy Buckaroo asked, "Oh, shit … what if…?" Byrum replied, "Hey, it's the last day. What are they going to do, fire us?" All the Buckaroos rode down en masse and presented the gift to Taylor. An extremely grateful Adam asked, "What does this mean?" His father Buck put it into the proper perspective: "That means you'll work for any asshole."[5]

Zeug continues, "Right before noon, we get hit with a rainstorm so they break for lunch. We had a flash flood come down through there. They had people walking through this water five-foot deep carrying a camera to keep it from going down the hill. And it virtually wiped out the Cowboy camp. The lunch wagon was there and they had steak and lobster for us. (A typical lunch menu could include BBQ prime rib, BBQ split breast, Alaskan crab legs, steamed green beans, steamed asparagus, baked potato, salad bar and sushi bar. Cosmatos had buttered white-bread roast beef sandwiches and caramel-crème brulle every day. Tux Wagon, the caterer, also handed out T-shirts to everyone present to commemorate the film's end.) And when this water came down the canyon, it physically washed out the whole set. They were lucky to save the cameras and some of the equipment that was out there. Everybody was rushing all over trying to save stuff. And, of course, we've got our horses out there. All this water went down and where we had parked our horse trailer, it was two foot of water. Instant mud. So we tried to drive out; some of us hooked up and pulled each other out to get our vehicles out. We loaded up our horses, but [when] the water was gone, Cosmatos is hollering, 'I want to set up.' We said, 'Wait a minute. We're wrapped. We're out of here.' He tried to call us all back but we said, 'No, we're not coming back. The movie's over.'" That's how the movie ended. Around three or four o'clock, production said, "Okay, it's a wrap." And after a few more close-ups of Russell on his horse, it was over. No speeches, no ceremony. Sherayko and a few of the Buckaroos were running up and down the ravine trying to collect the weapons that had washed away. One of the extras remembers Stephen Lang saying, "This is the perfect way to end this motherfucker!" The director, wearing his by now filthy white tennis shoes, slowly trudged through the muck to his car and driver. Once he arrived there, he stepped out of his shoes, got in the car, and was driven away. His tennis shoes were left stuck in the mud. Many extras drove home in their soaked wardrobe, and that was the end of *Tombstone*.[6]

The next day, Philbin met Russell, *sans* mustache, in the hotel lobby. Kurt had immediately shaved it off, as did almost all of the mustached actors. Kurt confessed that Goldie said of his mustache, "You may look great but I can't stand kissing you with that thing." According to Michael Biehn, "Everyone just grew a mustache. When it comes down to it, this goes back to Kevin Jarre…. He was very specific about how he wanted the mustaches. He wanted them to curl up on the end, which means, if you grow a mustache, and it grows long enough, you have to use wax on the end of it. Everyone was pretty proud that they grew their own mustache. There was one guy, Jon Tenney. He didn't get to grow his own mustache because he had a job right before that. They had to put a fake mustache on him. I think he always felt a little bit like the small dog of the group, because it wasn't his real mustache. He had to take his mustache off every day. I don't think anyone paid much attention to his mustache. Unless Kevin said, 'Someone work on Michael Biehn's mustache!'"

"I remember that last night of shooting," recalls Burke. "We were 100 percent sure the gate was clean, film's good, we were told we could shave off our mustaches. Everybody who had a mustache got into a trailer, and we all started to whack away. 'Jesus Christ. You're a good-looking son of a bitch, aren't you?' And we had a competition. Kurt won, Sam came in second. I think I came in third, or maybe Stephen Lang."[7]

To celebrate their bonding experience on the film, Russell and Kilmer gave each other gifts to remember the occasion. "I wanted to give him something that was special," said Val. "It was really fun and we became good friends working on it. So I bought him a piece of land in Tombstone. And because I knew he'd probably never go and see it and definitely not build on it unless he really hit hard times, I got a photograph taken with his chair on it with his name and framed it because I figured it'll be a nice-looking gift but legitimate sales slip for the land. He did the exact same thing except he gave me a gravesite inside of Tombstone. All the bodies are not actually in Boot Hill, they were moved to the Tombstone cemetery and he got me a tomb in Tombstone. Not a tomb, a plot. Framed with a picture of me with my chair there. Same exact gift we got each other. I got him a place to live and he got me a place to die. It's a 6 × 4 but it's mine and plot number 666, too, which is eerie. We laughed."[8]

After filming was complete, the cast and crew made their way back to Hollywood or wherever their next projects would take them. Paxton had left the production on August 25 to begin work on *True Lies*; Delany's next project, *Exit to Eden*, began on September 15, and Elliott started *The Desperate Trail* on November 17.

While many of the others took well-deserved breaks, Russell had already signed a deal with Canel+ to appear in *Stargate*, which began filming on September 13. As a result, he wasn't involved in any of the post-production activities. According to some, Cosmatos' first cut of *Tombstone* was in excess of 210 minutes, way too long for what Disney had in mind. Far from impressed with the script, cinematography or the acting, the studio just wanted to get the film released and out into local theaters a.s.a.p. to generate some sort of revenue to offset the costs. In order to get a jump-start on post-production, the editors had left the set and moved to Los Angles even before filming was completed. The initial post-production schedule was as follows:

> September 13 to September 18: Complete assembly of film
> September 20 to November 13: Fine-cut film
> November 1: begin Sound editing
> November 19: preview screening
> November 27: lock in Picture
> December 6 to December 18: ADR/Foley recording
> December 20 to December 23: music recording
> January 3 to January 29: pre-dubbing and final mixing
> February 1 to February 4: delivery to Disney

However, it quickly became apparent that a February 1994 release would be unacceptable as it was just too late, given that Costner was working on his own Earp project. And since his start of filming date had been July 19, 1993, who knew how long Costner would film or when his film would be ready for release? Disney needed to be the first one out, and a February release was just too risky. Russell acknowledged that there was "tremendous pressure" to reach theaters first. "Nobody ever said, 'You got to do it now and beat this other film,' but it was on everybody's minds," he says. "We'll never have enough time to make *Tombstone* the way we want. There is no point at which you go back to it and say, 'If I just had that…' I just say, go with the schedule that you have, go with the people that you can get, go with the screenplay that you have, make the movie as good as you can do it, do the day's work, move on, keep moving." So the studio accelerated the process by splitting the post-production activities into two parts: the first half of the film and the second half of the film, and called it the "Pressure Schedule." The fine cut was to be completed by November 6, music, November 18, ADR/Foley sound effects, November 22, and Dub & Mix by November 29. The editors then could begin printing masters and deliver their product to Disney. Including editing, music, Foley & ADR, dubs, 35mm interpositive and internegative prints, production dupes and answer prints, total post-production costs totaled $2,588,330.[9]

At 210 minutes (a three-and-a-half–hour movie) the number of daily showings was severely restricted. Alfred Hitchcock once said, "The length of a film should be directly related to the endurance of the human bladder." At a running time of two hours or less, it was felt that "audiences don't have a pre-built set of expectations about pacing and structure. You can keep people surprised and guessing the whole time without exhausting their excitement." Hence, the shorter the film, the greater the opportunity. So, in an effort to pare *Tombstone*'s length down to a more manageable two hours, numerous scenes were cut, including some that further explained the complex relationship between Curly Bill and Ringo. After Jarre was fired and Cosmatos was brought on board, the dynamic and balance of power between these two particular Cowboys changed significantly. According to Biehn, "Powers could have said, 'I'm the antagonist in the movie. I'm not going to support Michael Biehn—he was signed to support me!' But he was very, very gracious. Powers' reactions *made* Johnny Ringo—he had a comedic way of complementing my character as being someone he really enjoyed, that impressed him. If everybody around you is walking on eggshells, you don't have to do very much." Adds Michael, "We were all disappointed with the way our interpretations of the Cowboys came out. We had developed a very close fraternity, especially Powers and I. We rode horses together and read together and really Ringo only spoke to Curly Bill. None of that was shown in the movie."[10]

In an attempt at brevity, in addition to the aforementioned scenes, several others were also left on the cutting room floor: slow-motion dying at the O.K. Corral *à la The Wild Bunch*; Curly Bill's eulogy following the deaths of Billy Clanton and Tom and Frank McLaury; Curly Bill's attempt to convince Wyatt that Fred White's death was an accident; Wyatt's vulgar exclamation to Josephine Marcus after Morgan's death ("Whore! Jew whore! Get away from me!"); and Doc's farewell scene with Kate. On November 11, in addition to numerous looping changes and dialogue corrections and eliminations, producer Sean Daniel suggested to Andy Vajna that perhaps it would be best to include a lovemaking or kissing scene between Wyatt and Josephine: "If they don't, then many of the following scenes don't make any sense," Daniel pointed out. "Why is Wyatt so guilty when his wife accuses him? Why does he call Josephine 'whore' in the street? Why does Josephine forgive him? Kurt and Dana play the parts as if they had made love, and it shows. I also think women (who buy romance novels by the millions) will like the idea of Wyatt torn between two women." Daniel also suggested ten specific cuts to reduce the film's length: Claiborne and Barnes (John Corbett) meeting with Ike Clanton; the opium scene; the post–O.K. Corral scene between Wyatt and Mattie; the stagecoach heist; Breakenridge's pursuit of Fabian's killers; Behan's warning to Josephine; the attack on the Earp wives; the snow dance; and a trim of Holliday's death scene, including his comments about his lost love and Wyatt's book. Some suggestions were implemented, others rejected.[11]

The cuts also include an extended sequence where Billy Claiborne and Wes Fuller defect from the outlaw gang after Curly Bill's death and subsequently kill Romulus Fabian in a stagecoach holdup. Explains Bo Gray, "Someone says, 'Fuller and Claiborne did it.' But the footage was cut out where we actually kill him. [In this sequence,] Breakenridge tripped over a saddle and accidentally shot us dead with a big old buffalo gun. After Breakenridge kills [us], we're draped over our saddles for the ride to Hooker's [ranch]. Doc and Wyatt ask, 'Who's that?' and Breakenridge answers, 'It's Claiborne and Fuller. I killed them!'"

Gray also was extremely upset with the way the duo's death scene was filmed: "I talked to Jason about it, I said, 'Jason, take those damn spurs off, those big Spanish rowels. You can hear them coming and the sound is going to pick them up.' Priestley agreed, 'Well, that's a good idea.' But he didn't do it 'cause George said, 'I want the noise.' So Jason [now] sneaks up on us and scares us. Well, when a man is scared and embarrassed, what's his first reaction? He's mad? 'Sister-boy! What are you doing here??' We played out the scene and George said, 'Cut.' He never called me by my name until the [end of shooting]. He said, 'Hey, you. Come here. That is much too big.' I said, 'George, it's what I felt. I'm embarrassed; I'm pissed off at this little effeminate deputy sheriff. He scared me and he's got a buffalo gun in my chest. It's an honest reaction.' George [just] said, 'Look at the video-assist. Goddammit, you're too big.' I looked at him and I said, 'Shit, I oughta get an Academy Award.' Cosmatos replied, 'You get your ass back there and you're just playing really low-key.'" And the scene was cut.[12]

Bo, still furious, searched out Kilmer for advice: "I described that scene to him, and he said, 'Wait just a minute.' He went and got Kurt. So I did the scene for both of them [and told them], 'Guys, you know. I'm getting all this bullshit from the director about this. What's wrong with this scene?' Kurt looked at my face, put his hand on my chin and said, 'Look in the mirror. You've got a great-looking face. All you gotta do is what the director said.' Val told me later, 'Well, Bo. If it makes you feel any better, they had a giant fight over that scene between the producers and the director. Some wanted to keep it in, some wanted to keep it out.'"[13]

During production, several media outlets visited the set for publicity and specialty pieces, including *People*, CNN, the *Los Angeles Times*, Italian journalist Sylvia Bizio (*La Repubblica* and *L'Espresso*), *Premiere* magazine, etc. By June 18, just four weeks into production, Andy Vajna had already been contacted by the Buena Vista home video division of Disney regarding the anticipated video release of the film, which would include "special additional footage, director's cuts and talent and director's messages." It was felt such a product would not only generate extra public relations out of the video market, but the added content would enhance sales. Since video renters tended to be people who had not previously seen the film and had missed the theatrical promotions, Disney felt that "by having these extra pieces of film or extra bits, the video market has something to latch onto to generate hype and sales." Naturally, the studio would be careful not to cause additional expense or "incur ... the wrath of the set." Vajna approved the concept and asked that Patti Hawn coordinate the activity. As production was starting to wrap up, cast and crew publicity was required, so the official photograph was taken on August 8 in Mescal. The following day, portrait photographers Fred Tio and Greg Gorman arrived on location to shoot ad art with Russell, Paxton, Elliott, Kilmer, Delany, Boothe and Biehn. Delany was also asked to "write" a diary of her experiences by _Premiere_, but declined. To increase the film's "wow" factor, the production loaned numerous wardrobe items to Planet Hollywood, including Kurt Russell's black long coat, black jacket, vest, pants, white shirt and boots with lifts; Sam Elliott and Bill Paxton's gray pinstriped suits with white shirts and boots; and Val Kilmer's gray cape, black short jacket, pants, vest and gray shirt and boots.[14]

Composer Jerry Goldsmith, an Academy Award winner (_The Omen_, 1976), was contracted to write the musical score. Along with music editor Ken Hall, Goldsmith was scheduled to travel to London on October 24 where, along with scoring mixer Bruce Botnik, he would record and mix the score. The music would then be delivered by November 10. In fact, as late as October 10 in the post-production schedule, Goldsmith's name still appeared on one of the ending credit cards. Jerry, like Cosmatos, had had a long-standing, very close professional relationship with Andy Vajna. Goldsmith had also done a few movies with George so it would have been natural that Jerry was asked to work on _Tombstone_. However, by October 12, Goldsmith was forced to back out due to a scheduling conflict, and Cinergi approached Russian composer Vladimir Horunzhy, who expressed interest in using the Hungarian National Philharmonic to perform his score. Unfortunately, Horunzhy's delivery date wouldn't be until late November, which was deemed unacceptable. Goldsmith then recommended Bruce Broughton, who composed and produced the final score. Broughton recalls that he didn't have a great deal of time to compose: "Perhaps four weeks or less." The score was recorded by the Sinfonia of London orchestra and conducted by David Snell rather than Broughton as the latter wanted to produce from the recording booth. Patricia Carlin then edited the music. Broughton, given little guidance regarding what the producers wanted other than "Don't make it sound like a Western," was up to the task despite being puzzled by that directive. "This confused me," admits Bruce, "especially with the guns, horses and cowboys and classic O.K. Corral theme. I asked Jerry [Goldsmith] about it. He said simply, 'Bruce, do what you're going to do.' And I did." The composer succeeded admirably. Wrote Broughton in the liner notes for the _Tombstone_ 1993/2006 CD release, "The music to _Tombstone_ is not particularly 'Western' in that the orchestration depends not at all on the typical Western instruments such as the guitar and harmonica. It relies, in fact, on (a dark combination of) instruments of ethnic color like the Hungarian cimbalom, the Irish tin whistle and bhodran, and the French contrabass sarrusophone. The brass section includes, along with tenor and bass trombones, the more massive contratrombone."[15]

Before Broughton began writing the music, he saw a rough cut of _Tombstone_ with the temp track from _Silverado_. Also known as "scratch music, or temp-dub," a temp track is an existing piece of music used in the editing process to create mood and atmosphere, style and emotion, and can help the producer and director get a feel for the movie before the actual score is created. "Constructed by a music editor, in most cases, it is a blueprint of a film's soundtrack—a musical topography of score, songs, culture and codes in which a balance must be obtained between the director's vision, the music's function, underlying requirements of genre, and the spectator's perception." Broughton explains, "George asked me what I thought about 'his music' he had placed in the film. 'I love your music,' I said, 'but I hate it in this movie.' Actually, that music made the movie look stupid. *Tombstone* was nothing like *Silverado*. *Silverado* is very carefully crafted with classic good guys vs. bad guys and classic farmers vs. settlers themes. It's about friendship and family. *Tombstone* is much darker; even the heroes are dark. Wyatt Earp is a card dealer who two-times his wife, an opium addict, and eventually runs off with an actress. His best friend is a tubercular gambler and deadly gunslinger, Doc Holliday, who is also a terrific alcoholic and morally depraved, but who also happens to have the best wit in the film. The emotions are over-the-top; so is the music. Everything is on a big scale and is very dark, emotionally. It's often melodramatic, but practically always entertaining. To my mind, the music simply plays the scenes."[16]

Broughton continues, "George wasn't particularly enamored with the temp track. He just wanted to see what I thought about using the *Silverado* score. Although he could be a charming guy, he could be very difficult and quite mercurial. I played him a little bit of the theme that I was working on; he wasn't exactly complimentary. When I finished the theme, I played it later for Andy Vajna and Buzz Feitshans and they liked it." The music was recorded at the Sony Whitfield Studio in London. While Mike Trevor-Ross mixed the score. Andy Vajna attended the sessions; Cosmatos didn't. Perhaps George didn't appreciate Broughton's comment about *Silverado*. Nevertheless, due to a particularly tight schedule, the studio never had the time to temp-track the second half of the film, so when the film was screened for the media, it included Broughton's score.[17]

A pre-screening was held on November 18, 1993, with less than favorable results. All the media outlets were represented, including *Good Morning America*, CNN, HBO, *Entertainment Tonight*, *Turner Entertainment*, the *Associated Press*, MTV, *Knight Rider/New York Times*, and the *Los Angeles Times*, among others. The American Humane Association (AHA) sent a representative the following week and deemed the film "Acceptable." The AHA wrote that trained horses had been brought in on the set, and the ground was properly prepared for all falls and stunts. Quarter loads were used for the gunfire and cotton was placed in the animals' ears. Word on the street was that Cinergi hadn't delivered the completed film yet and that the December 17 release might not be met, but Disney countered that the film *had* been delivered and tested at the El Monte theater to 83 percent favorable results. Said one production source, "Frankly, I don't see any way to trim that much this close to opening and not seriously hurt the film's integrity." *Entertainment Weekly* wrote that Kurt Russell was livid after seeing the film—supposedly saying it was the "worst shit he's ever acted in"—but later published a statement from Russell that he only "disliked the soundtrack." The actor apparently must have only heard the temp track, because Broughton's score was both engaging and memorable. According to Broughton, the only change in the score was to expand the music over the end credits to make the score about a minute longer. This happened during dubbing because they lengthened the credits. Producer Jim Jacks was another one who felt the film could have been better. Shut out of the editing process, he confessed, "There was a great movie to be cut from the footage, and everybody did their best in a short post-production period. The result is a good movie, but it isn't the movie Kevin set out to make. That's the problem. We don't feel we quite delivered on the script.... It should have been a great movie. After one of the previews, George Cosmatos came up to me and said, 'You see, we were right! They loved the movie.' I said, 'George, you had a great script and a great cast and we made a good movie. It's not something we should be doing cartwheels over.'"[18]

As the final edit was resolved, the ever-grinding publicity mill continued churning out obligatory press releases and scheduling mandatory interviews with the stars. Typical was Sam Elliott's December 13, 1993, schedule at the Beverly Hill Four Seasons Hotel. After being groomed and made-up by Randi Fallick, Elliott had to sit through the following:

> 1:00–1:15 p.m. *National News Syndicate*
> 1:15–1:30 p.m. CNN
> 1:30–1:45 p.m. HBO
> 1:45–2:00 p.m. TBA
> 2:00–2:15 p.m. *Good Day LA*
> 2:30–3:00 p.m. Roundtable interviews with Drama-Logue, AP Radio, ABC Radio Network, CBS Network Radio, E! Radio, LEG Productions, Premiere Radio, Westwood One, *Entertainment Today,* Interview Factory, KIEV-AM, KBIG/Satellite News, Sheridan Broadcasting, 60-Second Preview, and *USA Overnight.*

Whew!

Russell appeared on *Entertainment Tonight, The Tonight Show, Turner Entertainment Tonight*, MTV, *Good Morning America*, HBO, CNN, while Kilmer hit *Regis & Kathie Lee*, VH-1 and a variety of local stations. Delany appeared on *David Letterman*. The closer the premiere date, which had been pushed back to December 25, the greater the saturation. Jacks had previously stated, "We needed a bit more time in post-production for a movie we wrapped the end of August. Also, the competition on the 17th—when *Pelican Brief* is released—combined with the fact that the weekend before Christmas is one of the worst weekends for movie exhibition—caused Disney to decide Christmas was a better release date."[19]

Typically, film openings deliberately positioned in November and December benefit from the late-game visibility when the Academy picks its nominees the following January, while still meeting the eligibility cut-off for the subsequent awards ceremony in late February or March. And a Christmas opening virtually guarantees a huge box office. In fact, nearly one-third of the top 20 highest-grossing movies of all time were released over the holidays. This practice started in 1947 when Paramount released *Road to Rio*, the fifth installment of the Bob Hope-Bing Crosby-Dorothy Lamour *Road* franchise. *Rio* was the sixth highest grossing movie of the year, and a tradition was born. Disney hoped that lightning would strike once again with quick returns. However, they also had no intention of incurring any additional costs promoting the film for Academy nominations.[20]

But there was an issue on the horizon. Would the expected delivery of 1500 *Tombstone* prints take place before the expected release date? The release had already been pushed back twice; another delay would be a disaster. And it wasn't because the film wasn't ready. Disney had decided to utilize the services of Technicolor Entertainment Services (TES) to deliver the prints, rather than industry stalwart National Film Service (NFS), which had handled prints for all major studios and independents for 47 years. TES is a closed-loop computer system that was designed to constantly track a print during delivery to minimize the risk of piracy. *Tombstone* would be the second major test for the start-up delivery system. Earlier, TES had failed miserably in its attempt to deliver all *Sister Act 2: Back in the Habit* prints to the appropriate theaters; 106 of 2132 prints failed to reach their designated locations. Some prints were delivered to tire stores, restaurants and even a Sears department store. To insure that the *Tombstone* prints arrived on time, each one was scheduled to be received on Friday, December 23. And it worked because except for 15 rural locations with theaters only open on weekends, all prints arrived on time.[21]

Perhaps Disney had wished deliveries of these prints hadn't been so prompt, because the film's initial reviews were less than satisfactory. Though *Tombstone* officially premiered on December 25, several media outlets had previously viewed the film and were just waiting to render their verdicts. (Academy members were invited to preview the film on December 20 at the Magno Sound Review I in New York, New York, and on December 21 at Walt Disney Studios in Burbank, California.) *The Hollywood Reporter* suggested the "ambitious, bloody and touchy-feely rendering of Earp's post–Dodge City days in Tombstone [would] lose most of its audience during its infrequent conversational rides down philosophical box canyons. [Although peppered with] colorful … psychotic killers … in the crazy panorama of a boom town … it shoots itself in the foot with endless big talk as our earnest Earps ponder such queries as 'What do you want out of life?'"[22]

According to Johanna Blume, associate curator of Western art, history and culture at the Eiteljorg Museum of American Indians and Western Art, Westerns "say more about the time that they are created than the time they represent. It's not about what people valued in 1888 but what the filmmaker and the culture valued when the film was made." Stephen Holden of *The New York Times* agreed as he cited the film's "up-to-date … political consciousness," its "contemporary attitude toward alcohol and drug abuse" and its depiction of Josephine Marcus "as the most casually and comfortably liberated woman ever to set foot in 1880s Arizona," played against the opulent and glamorous set of Tombstone. But Holden also suggested that *Tombstone* was actually two films loosely sewn together: one a traditional shoot-'em-up Western, and the other "a self-consciously digressive meditation on the iconography of the Hollywood western," with Val Kilmer chewing up huge chunks of scenery in his portrayal of Holliday as a "prefigurement of a dissolute modern poet, a frontier-era Jim Morrison. Attempting to be at once both traditional and morally ambiguous, the film fails in its harmonic vision."[23]

While Holden recognized the film's underlying themes and the attempt to meld them into a coherent composition, *Entertainment Today*'s Tim Cogshell must have been on location for the entire shoot as he described the film's flaws: Jarre's intent was to make "a serious film and historically correct drama that documented the people and era as accurately as possible." Cosmatos wanted an action-adventure with "gratuitous hyperrealism" and body count. The result fell somewhere in between with an incoherent storyline, unclear motivations, undeveloped characters and wholesale script revisions.[24]

Even local newspapers wanted to get into the act as the *Arizona Republic* claimed in a two-star, so-so review titled, "*Tombstone*: A film too tough to sit through": "[W]hen the mustaches are better than the acting and the scenery tops the story, then you've got a bad Western—or in the case of *Tombstone*, a long bad Western." The *Arizona Daily Star* called the film "dead on arrival," and said it wasted the talent of an impressive cast. In particular, it called Dana Delany's performance a complete washout. But, if one was going, "See it for Val Kilmer … or skip it altogether."[25]

In Los Angeles, most of the reviews weren't any better. The *Los Angeles Times*' Peter Rainer wrote that while the actors slouched well, and spit very convincingly, everything else "in this aggressively overlong Western … seemed posed and facetious…. Mostly it looks like overweening actors playing cowboys." And some critics were downright brutal, such as Tom Long of the *Santa Cruz Sentinel*. After praising Kilmer, Russell and Elliott, and suggesting that the remaining players were standing around waiting for something to do, he took aim at Delany. Long said Dana was "all fresh-faced and full of touchy feely questions and liberated ideas." But he left the best (or worst) for last. Kilmer was the only reason to see the film, Long wrote, despite his "pasty face" and "sweating at least 20 gallons in this movie." However, "You put Olivier in *F Troop*, and you still have *F Troop*. *Tombstone* doesn't deserve Kilmer and Kilmer certainly doesn't deserve *Tombstone*. Neither do you." And *The Inquirer* called it "spasmodically inept."[26]

Variety's Emanuel Levy's review was only slightly less critical: "A decent addition to the current cycle of screen and TV Westerns, *Tombstone* is a tough-talking but soft-hearted tale that is entertaining in a sprawling, old-fashioned manner…. [T]his never-dull oater should do brisker B.O., particularly with younger viewers. Jarre's dialogue is often anachronistic, combining a campy contemporary edge with a more realistic dialect … [resulting in a] fun, if not totally engaging, experience." While praising Fraker's "luminous widescreen lensing" and "accomplished" production values, Levy blasted Broughton for his "bombastic" music. After lambasting the film for coda after coda after coda, ridiculing Powers Boothe as Yosemite Sam, and describing Kilmer's performance as a "fey, fetching, hilarious take on Doc Holliday," Sean O'Neill of the *Los Angeles Village View* admitted that the film knew what the audience wanted and "delivered its thrills with a visceral kick sure to have the audience hooting and hollering."[27]

Many reviewers were waiting with bated breath for the release of Kevin Costner's *Wyatt Earp*, as Desmond Ryan said in the McAllen, Texas, *Monitor*: "[W]e can hope that [Costner's film] is more organized than what's served up in Cosmatos' film. Costner, of course, showed in *Dances with Wolves* that a single picture could revive a genre. Happily, we can remind ourselves as the funeral cortege pulls into Boot Hill in *Tombstone*, one bad western won't kill it." A view repeated by more than just a few critics.[28]

The national reviews weren't nearly as critical and, in fact, some were almost effusive in their praise. *Films in Review*'s Harry Pearson called it "an almost great Western, blessed with an intelligent (though butchered) script. Had it been filmed as written, this would have been an epic Western. Russell had an especially strong performance…. Kilmer [had a] wickedly good take on Doc Holliday." *DramaLogue* said that *Tombstone* crackled with the authentic feel of the Old West.

The farther away some critics were from Los Angeles and Tucson, the better the reviews. The *Ukiah Daily Journal*: "[*Tombstone*] is a worthy adventure." The *Petaluma Argus-Courier* called it "compelling." The Waterloo, Iowa, *Courier*: "*Tombstone* goes out with guns blazin.'" Others called it "very entertaining," "terrific!," "great fun to watch" and "one of the year's ten best." *Screen International* was right on point when it said, "*Tombstone* has its share of cringe-making moments…. [Nevertheless] it is rousing Friday-night entertainment. Although it is unlikely to make much of an impact with the critics, audiences should enjoy the film and help to build solid grosses through word of mouth."[29]

Despite the fact that Buena Vista really didn't promote *Tombstone* all that much and just dumped it on the market … despite the fact that the press really didn't write that much about it … despite the fact that critics sometimes scorn films made by independent production companies outside the mainstream studio domain … despite all that … the film was successful for one simple reason: Audiences liked it. Back in the day when the

Internet wasn't as prevalent as it is today, and nobody had iPhones, word of mouth was a wonderful communications tool. And the word was, *Tombstone* was an entertaining film. Said film critic Roger Ebert, "We didn't review *Tombstone* when it was released late in the holiday season because we couldn't get a screening. [Then] a strange thing started to happen. People started telling me they really liked Val Kilmer's performance in *Tombstone*, and I heard this everywhere I went. When you hear this once or twice, it's interesting, when you hear it a couple of dozen times, it's a trend. And when you read that Bill Clinton loved the performance, you figured you better catch up with the movie." Typical was the letter from a high school student to his local newspaper: "I didn't like *Unforgiven* and I wasn't too big a fan of the film *Posse*. I really don't like westerns all that much. But that all changed when I saw *Tombstone*. Kurt Russell gives the film the gritty, hard-edged performance that it needed. Don't let this tombstone get buried among the other films out there this season. See *Tombstone* at any cost. Grade: A." Journalist and author Allen Barra was correct when he said, "*Tombstone*'s success ... has to do with its skillful action sequences, brilliant cinematography ... and a score of audience-pleasing actors in sharply written roles."[30]

Released over the 1993 Christmas weekend, *Tombstone* earned $14 million in 1504 outlets, and ranked third behind *Mrs. Doubtfire* and *The Pelican Brief*. The following week was just as good: $12 million in 1955 theaters and third again in receipts. *Tombstone*'s original budget (excluding distribution costs) was $23.9 million, but expected overruns increased it to almost $29 million. As a result, in just two weeks, the film's gross receipts almost covered its costs. But that wasn't all. The next week, the film grossed another $8.5 million and the project now was in the black. One industry source claimed "it stands an excellent chance of grossing more than $150 million worldwide and becoming the genuine sleeper of 1993." Not bad results for a film that was almost canceled. In seven weeks, *Tombstone* would go on to gross $50.5 million domestically ($86.7 million adjusted for inflation). Immediately after the Christmas release, Berkley Publishers released Giles Tippette's $4.99 paperback novel based on Jarre's screenplay that included several scenes and expanded dialogue from the film.

Meanwhile, Kevin Costner prepared for the release of his own Earp film. Filming had begun on July 19, 1993, and wrapped up December 15. Obviously, there was no way the film would be ready in time to compete with *Tombstone*, so the release of *Wyatt Earp* was delayed until the summer of 1994. Val Kilmer echoed what Costner must have felt when he said, "[*Tombstone*] came out first and is doing well, so I'm sure they're worried. But our script is so good—why are they bothering!" Why, indeed! Costner took a not-so-subtle shot at *Tombstone* when he said, "[A] lot of crummy Westerns are being made," but his "was crafted with care. It was made thoughtfully and without compromise." Having said that, he also predicted, "*Wyatt Earp* will never be No. 1 this summer. It'll come up third or fourth. *Dances* was never No. 1. We were always behind *Home Alone*, but we ended up making $200 million." Kevin didn't know how prophetic he was when he also stated, "I believe in the freshness of a movie. I think that a movie that is rendered correctly and told in a refreshing way will be popular in any decade, at any time. Westerns don't do very well if the Western is bad. The survival of the genre requires people to make really good, refreshing Westerns." One Warner Bros. source outrageously said, "*Tombstone* was sold to men. *Wyatt Earp* will sell to women. It will be the *Doctor Zhivago* of the Western genre."[31]

In April, exhibitors were underwhelmed at an advance screening of a nearly completed print of Costner's *Earp*. Said one, "It seemed even longer than it was, and the editing was messy. It seemed as if the movie had been rushed." A Warners executive suggested, "It was an incredibly stubborn move not to [shorten the film]." Naturally, Costner was worried. "The opening weekend is a hard one for me," he admits. "Especially when you take a lot of time with a movie. I know how I try to make a movie; I know how I lose sleep over it. And when you work hard on things like that, it's frustrating to me that a movie can be dismissed so easily. It frustrates me when I know that someone's made a really good movie and then there is this instant response. It's frustrating to me when people don't pay attention to detail. I remember when I commissioned this screenplay, the notion was to make it complicated, to make it have layers. To find an original way to get into Wyatt Earp's life. To recognize that the O.K. Corral was a seminal moment in his life but also to ask, 'What kind of boy turned into a man that could walk down that street in that fierce and really special time in our country?'" And Costner was none too happy that *Tombstone* came out first. "I expect people to make movies for the right reason," insists Kevin. "If I was going to make a movie, and I knew somebody else was already making it, I wouldn't do it. [*Tombstone*] was basically rushed out to muddy the waters for us a bit."

Says Michael Biehn, "[*Tombstone*] is a fun movie. It kept people laughing. The quotes were something that a lot people enjoyed. I don't think anyone on our set ever gave that other movie a second thought. We knew it was out there, but I don't think anyone ever cared about it one way or the other." Russell agreed: "*Wyatt Earp* was never a threat to *Tombstone*, but *Tombstone* was always a threat to *Wyatt Earp*. The trouble is that one or the other of these films should have been a great movie, and the other should have been *Tombstone*. As it is, both were made in a rush and both suffered."[32]

If Costner was worried about his film, well, he should have been. Although many thought the critics were tough on *Tombstone*, that was nothing compared to their acerbic opinions about *Wyatt Earp*. Virtually everyone said that with its 192-minute running time, the film was excruciatingly long. (In 1995, a *212*-minute director's cut was released on videocassette and laser disc.) Although some praised Costner's attempt, others called it "somber," "solemn" and "episodic." *Film Reviews'* Anwar Brett wrote, "*Wyatt Earp* is an epic in every sense, a broad, sweeping film that is weighed down rather than invigorated by its excess of detail. Too often we are given a sense of portent and pretension; that this is filmmaking as 'art,' not entertainment. But then there are moments of great satisfaction [and] wonderful cinematic sequences." After one reviewer called it "the longest, prettiest, most spectacularly boring, self-indulgent, 'saddle-sore in your theater seat,' most constipated Western ever made," he suggested that Costner "may bear the dubious distinction of being the man who brought the Western back to life and the same man who killed it." One publication even started a cheeky fund-raising campaign for acting lessons for Costner. Roger Ebert of the *Chicago Sun-Times* gave the film 2 out of 4 stars, saying, "*Wyatt Earp* plays as if they took *Tombstone* and pumped it full of hot air. It involves many of the same characters and much of the same story, but little of the tension and drama. It's a rambling, unfocused biography … that needs better pacing."[33]

After opening to a decent box office ($10.3 million), the bottom dropped out and it was pulled from distribution after only four weeks with a meager $22 million in total receipts. With an estimated $63 million production budget, *Wyatt Earp* was a huge flop. The battle of the dueling Earps was over. At the end of the day, it was *Tombstone* 1, *Wyatt Earp* 0.

To add insult to injury: On June 22, 1994, right before *Earp*'s opening, Disney released 400,000 videocassettes of *Tombstone* to take advantage of the film's popularity and, if it cut into Costner's box office returns, well ... so be it. And it worked, as between the film and video release, *Tombstone* accounted for $15 million revenue in Cinergi's second quarter 1994 financials. Retailers reported a swift rental business. Said James Mulligan of New York's Tower Video, "Everyone who's renting *Tombstone* knew that there were competing films. This one beat *Wyatt Earp* to the theater—and on video." And, by the week ending July 3, *Tombstone* was already the fourth-best video rental in the market. By comparison, *Earp* was a disaster. According to one industry analyst, the film "might just be the worst flop of all time after deductions for profit participants." Explained Barry London, Paramount's worldwide distribution chief, "The pictures that worked found their audiences right from the opening day. The films that missed never showed a flicker of life."[34]

Over the next several years, *Tombstone* was released multiple times in a variety of media formats. On April 15, 1994, a $50, widescreen, letterboxed director's cut laser disc was released with five extra scenes and commentary by George Cosmatos. Three years later, on December 2, 1997, a single-disc, re-purposed (laserdisc) DVD, multi-language edition was brought out, with theatrical and teaser trailers, and on January 15, 2002, a two-disc Vista Series DVD director's cut edition came out, with several documentaries, audio commentary by George Cosmatos, O.K. Corral storyboards, interactive timeline, four pages of the *Tombstone Epitaph*, TV spots, Easter eggs, a collectible Tombstone map, and a DVD-ROM Faro game. Released on April 27, 2010, a two-disc Blu-ray version was almost identical in content to the Vista Series director's cut that excluded the paper collectibles and commentary.[35]

Disney veterans Tony Malanowski and Kevin Reem had the opportunity to work with Cosmatos on the Vista Series release. In the spring of 2001, the duo was asked to be associate producers on the recreation of the *Tombstone* director's cut with additional value material for a new DVD release. Although a VHC copy of the complete version was made available as a check, Tony wanted a Digital BetaCam copy of the cut version of the film, which wasn't readily available, "so I took my laserdisc of the film over to a facility and had them transfer it to Digi-Beta for me!" laughs Tony. "That transfer from laserdisc was used throughout the process as a guide and also to pull clips from for the added value segments." *Tombstone* had sections that easily fit back into the picture, with some minor feathering for sound and a couple of cutaway shots. So, Tony ordered up a workprint off the negative sections, then sent the negative to Technicolor to be spliced. That was the easy part of the project.[36]

Next they had to work with the still-volatile Cosmatos on the commentary. Along with the executive producer from Sparkhill Productions, Reem helped record the audio commentary. "I did most of the research and worked up the questions we would be asking George Cosmatos as he would do the recording while watching the full cut of the movie," Kevin explains. "It took two, three days to record the audio commentary, and also to interview George on camera. Every day, we sent a limo for him, and when George would arrive, he would look at me and bellow, 'Who are you?' And he would do that a few times more over the course of the day. I would explain that I was assigned to the project, and George would nod and then we'd go over the whole thing again a couple of hours later!" Cosmatos would settle into the sound booth and light up a cigar; the smell permeated the entire facility and caused the owner's wife to become so ill she had to leave the building. All the while, Cosmatos kept telling everyone how he had saved *Tombstone*.[37]

Then George sat in on the color correction of the film for a new transfer from the original negative. Malanowski was told he had to be at Telecine Bay to shepherd Cosmatos through the process. The head of Sparkhill was there with the colorist who would program the film's color, shot by shot, to create a new video record of the picture. But then, things got a bit weird. "George kept telling the colorist to add more blue to the picture," remembers Malanowski. "I mean, the movie takes place out west in the desert, for Pete's sake, and George was adding so much blue the sand dunes were looking like rolling ocean waves! The colorist kept looking back at me and George kept bellowing, 'Well, fight me! If it's too blue, you must *fight* me!'" After Malanowski and Cosmatos moved outside to smoke their cigars, the colorist took the opportunity to work on the film undisturbed. Soon, they completed the first color pass and George departed. After Cosmatos left, there was a meeting to decide on what to do with the overabundance of blue that had been programmed in. Malanowski suggested cutting the blue by 30 percent overall and doing a more-involved second pass, which was done. Cosmatos' color records were stored "just in case," but he never returned to the color sessions, and the professional colorist finished the job. That corrected pass is how *Tombstone* was released.

Apparently, there was a reason for Cosmatos' behavior during this color-correcting work. "I can't remember where I read this," recalls Tony, "which obituary it was in—but there was a mention of another health problem that George had around that time. In 2003, Cosmatos lost his sight after surgery to remove cysts over his eyes. The obituary noted that one of the warning signs of that kind of problem would be if you had problems seeing certain colors … like, for example, if you could no longer distinguish the color blue."[38]

Over the years, *Tombstone* has risen in stature to a point where readers' polls consistently rank it as one of the ten best Westerns ever. And rightly so. Over two dozen films have dealt with the events surrounding October 26, 1881, and the aftermath, and this one is among the best. Stripping the Hollywood hokum from previous efforts, it attempts to "make a serious and historically correct drama that documents the people and era as accurately as possible." Many previous films about Wyatt Earp and the O.K. Corral were marvelous pieces of cinema, but terribly inaccurate. Kevin Jarre rectified that with a script that combined crackling dialogue with a well-developed and poetic storyline. When asked if the public needed yet another telling of the O.K. Corral legend, Kurt Russell once replied, "Of course not. But if you're asking me if we need a telling of the story that's based in reality, then I say, 'Yes, yes, yes.' And for my tastes, it's infinitely more entertaining to see a movie like this that is based on the facts. *My Darling Clementine* is great moviemaking but it has nothing to do with the truth."[39]

William Fraker's photography is replete with deliciously filmed sunsets, rugged landscapes and atmospheric richness, counterbalanced against the gritty, newly constructed, bursting-with-life and -energy set designed by Catherine Hardwicke. Again according to Russell, the set wasn't designed to look like the Old West, it was designed the way people saw it in 1879, as the New West. Combine that with costumes designed by Joseph Porro, augmented with the historically correct re-enactors, *Tombstone* is as historically correct a Western as one is likely to see.

No Western is 100 percent accurate. Doc Holliday never killed Johnny Ringo, Virgil and Morgan weren't both ambushed on the same night, and the number of Cowboys killed during Earp's Vendetta ride is highly exaggerated. *Tombstone* is definitely a revisionist take on the historic legend of Earp and the O.K. Corral superimposed on the political and cultural times during which it was made. No longer all black or white, the story is told in shades of gray, with a more realistic and less biased approach toward history. And, despite George Cosmatos' tyrannical, misogynistic and egocentric behavior, credit must be given to this gifted director for taking control of the production and bringing Kevin Jarre's vision to fruition. Were it not for Jarre's brilliant script, and an absolute insistence on authenticity, *Tombstone* would not be half the film that it is.[40]

Kurt Russell doesn't show us a Wyatt Earp who's the traditional, white hat–wearing, one-dimensional lawman, but rather a stoic, dark, somber and, at times, morally ambiguous individual, torn between law and order and happiness. Portraying Earp as both existential and complex, Russell captured the essence of Earp's character: a strong moral fiber with heroic capabilities. In several scenes, Russell's eyes alone give the viewer a clear indication of his character's emotional turmoil. His performance as Earp established Kurt as a Hollywood A-list box-office draw.

The film's supporting cast is a virtual embarrassment of riches, though sadly underutilized. While Billy Bob Thornton's take on the bully Johnny Tyler is effective, and Charlton Heston is his usual larger-than-life self, actresses Lisa Collins and Paula Malcomson as the Earp wives are little more than window dressing. Joanna Pacula, a last-minute replacement, fares well as Holliday's paramour, and although her character wasn't sufficiently developed, her performance made a lasting impression. Dana Wheeler-Nicholson's chararacterization of the drug-addled Mattie was spot-on; it would have been interesting to create the backstory of her addiction. And despite the fact that Dana Delany performs wonderfully as a modern woman of the Old West, the staging of the famous Kaloma photograph seems a bit gratuitous. Billy Zane has a memorable scene as the actor Romulus Fabian, and Sam Elliott, Stephen Lang and Bill Paxton all turn in their usual solid performances. Unfortunately, despite being given significant billing in the film's promotional campaign, Jason Priestley plays a role that is almost non-existent.

Where the film really shines is when Powers Boothe, Michael Biehn and Val Kilmer are on the screen. Boothe's performance as the psychotic Curly Bill Brocius leaves an indelible image. Powers had a unique take on his outlaw character: "Curly Bill was a guy … who everybody liked. He had a lot of dash about him, a lot of panache … tremendous sense of humor. He really lusts for life—he just eats it up." So did Powers, in every scene. From his howling at the moon, to his enthusiastic response to Fabian's theatrical performance, to his humorless reply "Well … 'bye," Boothe brought a certain flamboyance to a traditional outlaw—at times friendly and persuasive, other times vengeful and scheming. Michael Biehn agreed: "There were a lot of great characters in that movie, but Powers—his screen presence just dominates."[41]

Biehn's sociopathic, cold-hearted Johnny Ringo is borderline maniacal. Portrayed as intellectual and cultured, Ringo lacks a conscience, and takes pleasure in killing. Biehn's eyes gleam in intensity during such sequences, which provide a window into his character's insanity. Michael admits he wanted to play Ringo as almost suicidal, and in this he succeeds admirably. In the Making Of documentary, Biehn explains that Ringo "has a lot of problems that stem from his religion, growing up. A really hard-core religious family. He's really a tragic figure." With a flair for the dramatic, Biehn captures the essence of Ringo's personality: the edge, the attitude, a boiling pot waiting to explode. His performance rivals Val Kilmer in passion and impact and is a key reason for the success of the film.[42]

Kilmer's performance as the tubercular, pale, sickly Doc Holliday is nothing less than a tour de force. Blessed with tremendous material to work with, Kilmer applies his own formidable acting skills to a mesmerizing, memorable, scene-stealing signature role. Such descriptions, and many more, have been used to describe his acting in *Tombstone*. Everyone agreed that whoever had the good fortune to land the role of Holliday would steal the movie, and Kilmer did just that. From his dry wit and Southern gentleman manners, to his lightning-fast draw and memorable lines, it seems that "the rest of the movie is happening *around him*."

More than anything, *Tombstone* is a film about the close, "understated but unshakable" relationship between Wyatt and Doc, each on the opposite side of the law, each willing to cross over if required. Loyalty and friendship are keys to their connection. Kilmer observes, "[Doc] had a real respect for Wyatt's morality, even though he didn't live it out, and Wyatt had a real respect for Doc's sense of freedom and experience, so they each possessed a quality … that the other didn't have and they could live vicariously through each other. My feeling about the core of their friendship is that they were different men who found a kinship that each of them was willing to die for. It was a really deep love." Unfortunately, Kilmer never received the credit he deserved for his performance. Said one Disney marketing source, "Look, the film was done through Cinergi Productions, and, by the time it came to us, there were all the stories about the director being fired and bad feeling between him and the producers. It took a while for us to know what kind of film we had, but we're behind it now and pushing as hard as we can."

Really? Russell takes exception to that statement. "The studio was shocked at what they had—they didn't know what to do with the movie. They didn't promote it very much, didn't know what to do with it, didn't know where it was coming from. It was a Western. A Western! They didn't know anything. And it wasn't their baby!" As a result, not only didn't Kilmer win an Academy Award for his performance, he wasn't even nominated.[43]

Tombstone was very much an "actor's picture," with testosterone galloping around the set like rutting studs. Each actor had only a limited number of scenes to show his chops, so to speak, and the tension was thick. But as a result, everyone also brought his "A" game. And sometimes, this tension was even apparent between the actors. According to Powers Boothe, "[Y]our character had his moment to step up to the plate. You had your home run opportunity, and sometimes you'd go up there and hit a single. Nobody was trying to steal scenes." From cast to crew, everyone said that although it was an extremely difficult shoot, projects such as *Tombstone* came along perhaps once in a career, and they were extremely proud to be a part of it.[44]

As Russell said, "The shame about *Tombstone*, that you can't possibly appreciate [is] the movie, what you saw, is that movie. The movie is *The Godfather*—a Western *Godfather*. That's how different that movie is from the one you saw…. [A]ll that stuff is put away in my garage, including an interesting scene that shows a deeper relationship between Wyatt Earp and the Cowboys." Stephen Lang: "I know what's on screen and I also know what we shot and the film that's been made is an excellent film, but I think in the end there was a classic buried in there as well."

As is obvious, there was a tremendous amount of footage that both Jarre and Cosmatos filmed that didn't make it into the final cut: numerous vignettes with the Cowboys both before and after the O.K. Corral shootout; Wyatt's attempt to retrieve his stolen horse and subsequent conversation with McMasters; the killings of Hunt and

Grounds by Breakenridge; Fabian's death and the stagecoach holdup, and on and on. Everyone associated with the film agrees it could be so much better, so much richer, with a well-developed, explainable storyline. Kurt had been given all the footage by Andy Vajna. Perhaps someday, we may see the movie they way Jarre intended ... we can only hope.[45]

Appendix: Tombstone 25th Anniversary Celebration

Tombstone, Arizona. June 30, 2018. It was hot. Damn hot! So hot, you could fry an egg on the sidewalk … if Allen Street had sidewalks. The main venue was a hard-packed, dirt and gravel street, closed to vehicles, compressed by years of foot, horse, and stage-coach traffic, and lined with ten-foot wooden boardwalks, with numerous period correct buildings dotting the façade. Every now and then one could see a closed and abandoned store, awaiting its next tenant. Tourism is the lifeblood of the town and this weekend's activities was a welcome shot in the arm, so to speak. The skies were clear and so blue it hurt you just to look at them. It was a welcome respite from the previous two evenings when thunder boomed and lightning cracked, illuminating the town's buildings as well as the surrounding mountains and desert.

Sponsored by the Tombstone Lions Club and the city of Tombstone, the weekend celebrated Freedom Days with former Florida congressman and radio/TV host, retired Lt. Col. Allen West. It also honored the legendary Buffalo Soldiers along with members of the cast and crew of the film *Tombstone*, who were celebrating the 25th anniversary of the film's release. While West gave a Friday night lecture in historic Schieffelin Hall on the Second Amendment and the importance of the Buffalo Soldiers in American history, *Tombstone* cast and crew members, including Michael Biehn, Billy Zane, Dana Wheeler-Nicholson, Joanna Pacula, Frank Stallone, Catherine Hardwicke, Joseph Porro, Sandy Gibson and Peter Sherayko, enjoyed a dinner at the Longhorn restaurant, renewed old friendships and reminisced about their time on the set. Earlier that day, Sherayko and Stallone sat down with Tina Jennings at KGUN-9 in Tucson as she conducted an interview about the film. When asked why it was such a classic, Sherayko replied, "The script, the cast, and all the stuff in it. It's the only movie that has all the righteous stuff in it—the right saddles, the right guns, the right kind of belts, the right costuming. All that stuff was [attention] to detail by Kevin Jarre, who was the writer and first director. And he insisted on doing it right. He used to tell me, 'There's three things they make wrong with Westerns: hats, guns, and saddles.' He wanted to straighten it out. And if you look at every other Western, and you look at the stuff, you'd say, 'Hey, it's wrong.'" While Stallone and Sherayko were being interviewed, West, and Medal of Honor recipients Drew Dix, and Melvin Morris were given a guided tour of nearby Ft. Huachuca.[1]

The next day, the streets were packed; it was estimated between 7,000 and 9,000 tourists visited the town over the weekend. Naturally, most came to see the film celebrities, but the Buffalo Soldiers exhibit was also well-attended and presented a wonderful static display of their history in the lobby of Schieffelin Hall. As many of the film's stars were scheduled for autograph-signing sessions, people were lined up outside the various venues at 8:00 a.m., well before the events began. Biehn, Zane, and Sherayko were inside Fly's Photographic Studio at the O.K. Corral, Pacula and Wheeler-Nicholson were inside the Crystal Palace, and Stallone and Gibson were located next to the Bird Cage Theater. The lines were long and constant all weekend; Porro and Hardwicke took the opportunity to roam around town and see the various attractions. In fact, on Sunday, Hardwicke even made a five-hour visit to nearby Benson, and later suggested she wanted to return to film a documentary on the area.

After a few hours, all celebrities took a well-deserved break and joined the parade down Allen Street. The grand marshal's spotlight was shared by Allen West, Dix, and Morris. Wheeler-Nicholson became a bit emotional when she gazed at a group of soldiers from Fort Huachuca. As she told *Herald/Review* columnist Dana Cole, "Seeing these soldiers here is extremely moving. Making movies is one thing, but these soldiers are the real deal. They are the true heroes." Pacula seconded the thought: "This is my third time in Tombstone, and it's phenomenal. The weather is perfect, the food is great, and the people here are fabulous. Where else do you see all these Buffalo Soldiers? This is so much fun." After lunch, the actors returned to the various venues for more signing. Zane spoke for everyone when he said, "I've visited Tombstone before, and it's great to be back for the 25th anniversary. The town shows a lot of love and civic pride, and it's nice to see all the improvements the town has made through the years." Stallone, an avid Western historian, said, "Taking a tour of Birdcage was my highlight; it just dripped with history. And walking back to my room at night with no traffic, just imagining what it was like in its heyday." Several celebrities said they enjoyed the weekend so much, they would be more than happy to return the following year![2]

While Tombstone was filled to the brim with visitors, neighboring Mescal, where the majority of the movie was actually filmed, saw its fair share of activity as well. Located about 45 minutes from Tucson, the site is the location for numerous films and Old Tucson Studios, which owns the site, graciously agreed to open the set to tourists over the weekend, allowing them to wander the streets where Kurt Russell, Val Kilmer, Powers Boothe, Dana Delany and many others once walked. To their great delight, over 500 guided tours were conducted on Saturday and Sunday.

Meanwhile, back in Tombstone, in addition to the celebrity signings, there was an abundance of other activities including the obligatory beer tent, hangings and shootouts, actor and performer Will Roberts, the Goose Flats gunfighters, the Tombstone Vigilantes, the Cochise County dance class, and more. A movie memorabilia auction in the city park generated over $3,200 for the local Lions Club and many of the film's stars either autographed or donated items for sale, including scripts, posters, and the duster Sherayko wore as Texas Jack Vermillion. Did you know that Sherayko's long hair in the film was actually a wig? Imagine what that would have gone for! Several Buckaroos including Jeff Dolan, Garrett Roberts, Bill Weddle, Jerry Tarantino and Reggie Byrum set up a tent in the city park where numerous Western items were displayed including an album of Reggie's photos taken on the film's set. Jerry and Judy Crandall also sold several of Jerry's paintings, and *True West* magazine's Bob Boze Bell provided the artwork that Steve Todd used to design a 25th anniversary poster. That evening, many of the film's stars, including Zane and Hardwicke, sat out under the stars as *Tombstone* was shown on a large inflatable screen to the great delight of more than 125 patrons who were in attendance. "I can watch a film like an audience member," explains Zane, "not just an actor who remembers what it was like on that day. I love the movies that I'm in, and I can love them like an audience. And I love this movie." When asked to name his favorite part, he cried, "It was the gunfight at the end! Are you kidding? It was incredible. My speech, please. That was fun, but it was the thunderstorm, the lightning, the laudanum, [Dana] jonesing out on 'H,' Billy Bob getting slapped. That movie was just boss on every level in so many ways!"[3]

Those too tired to celebrity watch could view the Josephine Earp collection on display at the Tombstone Courthouse Historic Park. Donated by Eric Weider, former owner and publisher of *Wild West* magazine, the collection includes handwritten notes and a carbon copy of a proposed Earp biography by John H. Flood, Jr., along with letters to Wyatt from Josephine, telegrams, wills, documents and photos, and Flood's rejection letters.

Saturday afternoon, their wrists sore from signing, and voices raspy from talking to their fans, the celebrities adjourned to Schieffelin Hall where a panel discussion was moderated by Julie-Ann Reams. The audience began to arrive almost two hours before the scheduled start time and the room was quickly filled to capacity. And it was well worth the wait as everyone was entertained by amusing anecdotes shared by all. After opening remarks from Gorden Anderson, and an introduction of each celebrity by Reams, Sherayko kicked off the discussion by explaining how Kevin Jarre, the film's original director and writer, created the script. After a few stories, he began to discuss Jarre's directorial abilities and how they affected the cast; Billy Zane quickly came to his friend's defense: "I'd like to address something Peter mentioned about Kevin, perhaps an alternative view on specificity, and a more nostalgic approach to cinematic direction. Kevin's meticulous, and what makes his script so wonderful, and his vision so acute, is not only his attention to detail as an author, but as a director, he directed like directors did in the 30s and 40s, who were taskmasters, and who were incredibly specific. In our modern age of directing, actors have a lot more freedom to play, a lot more sway and say, and get a little more precious when, God forbid, they're told what to do. Certainly, [that] was not the case back in the day when some of the greatest films of … the pantheon of cinema were produced. And some of the films that clearly informed a great storyteller like Kevin Jarre. So, he entered the space, directing like he, I imagine, dreamt like he could. And was punished for it at every level from every front. And it was a shame."[4]

In an earlier interview given to Michael Mercy at the Genre-con in Guelph (Ontario, Canada), Biehn admitted that George Cosmatos, Jarre's replacement, didn't really know what the film was all about: "The most important thing about any movie is the script. If you have a great story, and then you go out and cast great actors, you really don't have to do very much more. *Tombstone* is a perfect example of a script that was so good, the actors just took it upon themselves to make a good movie out of it. George Cosmatos, who ended up directing it, was more of a sort of visual director. I don't think he knew the beginning from the end of the story. I don't think he had any idea which character was which, but he just wanted to make sure that the picture looked good."[5]

Wheeler-Nicholson then added, "I met [Kevin] through Lisa Zane, the incredibly beautiful, talented actress, who is Billy's sister. She and Kevin were together and he wrote the part of Josephine for her to play. There are a few of us who came onto this movie because of our friendship with Kevin; he believed in us, he wanted us in the film. I would say, certainly myself, Paula Malcomson, Lisa, we were there because he wanted us there, and he fought the studio to get us there. Because they wanted fancier actors, for my part for sure, and he went to the mat about that." As we all know by now, Billy's sister Lisa was initially selected to play the part of Josephine. Billy was extremely gracious when he spoke of her defense of Jarre when Kevin was fired. "It was hard to turn up right at the time that Kevin was fighting," clarified Zane. "Literally, I showed up and two days later he was not there. And then my sister, in solidarity, left the picture. By choice. And that was noble and career suicide at the same time. I was caught in a very … [it was] kind of uncommon. Not many people would have done that. She was braver than I. The girl had moxie. I probably would have, and should have done the same, I think. And, didn't. But she was a little more invested." In a letter to the author, Zane expanded upon those comment: "Kevin wrote *HER*, Lisa as Josie. That is her greatest contribution to the film. She was neither template nor muse. Josie spoke Lisa *verbatim*. Lisa guided Kevin to the shores of a siren's cave, on an Amazon island where the classical female as hero Goddess took the shape of a modern woman in a new frontier, at the end of the 19th century, in a film made nearing the end of the 20th.[6]

"There hasn't been a better, more independent, unapologetic, entirely feminine voice on screen before or since. And that credit is entirely due to Lisa Zane. And certainly Kevin Jarre for being smart enough to capture her attention, hold her interest, and wisely realize he was being invited to assimilate and integrate her into the fabric of his hero's journey. Everything Josie says in the script. Those were Lisa's utterances, her world view, posture, silhouette and stamp. I've heard them. Know them all too well. They helped shape my world view. It was among Lisa's greatest offerings. Perhaps to have actually said them on screen as well would have gilded the lily. Been just too much to bear and distracted the message with the medium. Dana Delaney's turn as Josie was confident and honest and fun loving but those lines, like all in that film, are simply bullet proof. It's one thing to be immortalized in screen legend by another borrowing your moves. Like Slim Keith was to a kid named Lauren Bacall in *To Have and Have Not*, or what Director Guy Hamilton was to Sean Connery before a Scottish lad transformed into James Bond on the set of *Dr. No*, after his tutorial on the finer things found between judo chops and hard kisses. It's quite another thing to be written, cast in typeface, bold as bronze and ageless as marble by the sheer might of Kevin's structure, bookending Lisa's virtual dictation, impervious to all forms of weather damage and hot air any studio executive or movie star could bluster. Lisa Zane, on the page as Josie, was not just the model, nor the sculpture in the stone, but the artist's hand, chisel and inspiration that guided it."[7]

Stallone also talked about how Jarre explained the character Stallone was to play. Kevin "was a very engaging, enthusiastic person, very bright guy," explains Frank. "He goes, 'Now, listen Frank. I want you to play a different character. You're more of a Bowery mug. You're not like a Western guy, you're…' 'Cause, no one is from the West. Everyone came from somewhere. It could have been from Chicago or Boston, kind of urban but still kind of a bully. A mug. He says, 'That's what I want you to do. I don't want you to be Tex Ritter, I want you to be this guy.' The day I got there [was] the day before he was fired. I said, 'I can't wait to see Kevin.' Peter said, 'He's not here anymore.' So, I felt really bad because, as with Billy, it's because of him that it was, vis-à-vis Billy, I'm in the movie. And I really didn't get a chance to work with him, I never got any closure, say hello, call him up, because after that happened, he was MIA for years."[8]

Inevitably, whenever Biehn is in attendance, the question is always asked of him: What about the gun-spinning sequence? And the *Tombstone* panel discussion was no exception. Said Michael of Kevin, "Like most of us, he didn't audition me. I went out to lunch with him, we both read the same book about some psycho killer. We just bonded. I had the Colt and what he would call the rig, and that was what was so great about Kevin's script, the vernacular that he uses in that script. You don't see that in other Westerns: 'lawdog,' 'lunger,' 'I'll be your huckleberry' ... all that stuff was said back then but you don't hear that in other modern Westerns. They used to speak like that. Kevin was a great, great writer, and he was a very stubborn director. He wanted it done his way and only his way, and he was surrounded by some very, very talented people, and he wouldn't listen to anybody. He was going to have it done his way, and his way only. I got the gun and the rig, couldn't call it a holster around him, about two months ahead of time. A guy who was a quick draw artist, his name was Thell Reed. And Thell taught me—the most coolest thing about that routine was that you could actually take a Colt and spin it sideways, I always thought it was [a vertical spin.] And then I started playing around and I think I came up with [the fan movement]. That routine was shot towards the end of the movie, and if you see it in the movie, of course, there's cuts, cuts to Bill Paxton, cuts to Val, cuts to everybody. It's not like I did it all at once. That routine, I could do that routine about once out of every ten tries. I mean perfectly. It was a little bit like a gymnastics routine, 'cause it was tough. You might not even notice but when I pulled my Colt on Val and twisted, as it flips over, I'm cocking it at the same time. And there's stuff like that throughout that sequence that made it what it was. Sometimes I could do it perfectly, but other times it's like falling off the parallel bars. I mean the gun would fly out of my hands. I worked very, very hard on that, and Val worked very, very hard with that cup. I would continually see Val walking around the set practicing with that cup which was not really made to do what he did with it."[9]

Dana agreed: "Val was doing that because the scene didn't happen for a couple of weeks so there was a lead up to when you were going to shoot it. Val was doing that flipping thing the whole time. He'd be talking to you and doing the flipping."[10]

Biehn also explained his relationship with Kilmer: "I don't know Val Kilmer, I never met Val Kilmer, I've never said hello to him. He never said hello to me. We did go out together on my request and practice, figure out how we were going to do the final gun bout. He drove his car, I drove my car. We met. It sounds a little corny, looking back it probably is but ... Bill Paxton was a real good friend of mine at the time and Bill and I didn't really hang out that much on the set or anywhere. I was very into Johnny Ringo and very, very against the Earps and all talk and talk and talk about what really happened down there, what I believed happened. We worked out that and we were basically in character when we worked it out. At no point in the making of that movie did I ever say hello to him or did he say hello to me or join the conversation that he was in. When we went out to do that scene, we decided to do it close. Instead of like from far away like in every other gunfight you've ever seen. The reason that we did that was because they used to have gunfights like that, they draw and fucking shoot and miss, and he would shoot and miss, and shoot again. We decided to make it really intimate and came up with that thing where we're walking around. We had that down to the point to where I knew after I got shot right there, that I was going to stagger forward when he was saying his lines, I was still going to get a gunshot off even thought I had a bullet in my brain." When asked if this behavior was deliberate, Biehn replied, "When you're young, you know you think, 'Fuck 'em.'"[11]

Of course, no *Tombstone* panel discussion would be complete without comments from Val Kilmer but, sadly, he wasn't available. However, Kilmer did explain his preparation for the role at the 2012 Ohio Wizard World Comic-con. "The first thing I did, I called the greatest dialect coach in the world. He used to do lots and lots of theater, and now he does lots of movies. He's really a great guy named Tim Monich. I called him up, I need a southern aristocrat. He said, 'I got it.' I said, 'Let me go on.' He said, 'No I got it.' And he sent me a tape. [His dialect] was soooo slow [and] when you talk that slow, everything is funny. But [Doc] was a socialite from Georgia, and I started listening to this tape all the time. I've got a lot of relatives from the south and I talk to them about what they remembered. I had a lot of horses at the time, and a really good horse trainer, who was oddly a historian about riding. Because a military posture back then … there was a very specific way that they rode. [It was] really strange; they didn't move with the horse so much. They were so rigid because that was the way they were taught to ride. So little tiny things like that that made him different than your average guy out West. And then a lot of things, the role, especially when it's well written, it's all in the writing. Very funny and mean."[12]

Unfortunately for an unknowning audience, Joanna Pacula had been overcome with dehydration and heat exhaustion, and was unable to share any thoughts about her time on location. But later, she told the author, "I had auditioned for George for the movie, 20th Century–Fox, *Leviathan*. I didn't get it; Amanda [Pays] got it. But George really liked me. He wanted me but the studio approved the other girl. Because of this, I think George remembered me and wanted me for *Tombstone*. I tell you, I had no idea what was going on. When I arrived, everybody was very nice. I went to a script meeting and I met everybody. I knew from other people that people were going, being fired, but I completely [had] no clue about what was going on. Everybody was very busy working so I basically waited for my part to be played. I was probably the least involved with the whole hoopla stuff.

"I really did not feel well but I should have said something when Michael Biehn said he does not know Val or doesn't know who he … you remember that? I should have said something. I almost said something but I was getting like goose bumps and shivers from dehydration. So I just didn't say something, but Val is not somebody who is unfriendly or anything. He just stayed in character, and his character is best if he not to interact with Michael. He wanted fresh reactions. So that's why. It's nothing personal whatsoever. He was always in character. If you can imagine, they wanted to look at each other and not know each other because they wanted that surprise, that authentic reaction. Everybody works differently, and you have to respect everyone's way to get there. So, that's how he works. There were script readings and stuff so they did interact a little with each other but they wanted to be real on screen. As good as you can get. Val is very, very smart. Very nice and friendly. We never had one problem, whatsoever, as characters. I like him very much to work with him. He's very intelligent and that's something that not every actor has. He was very much into character. We talked about our scenes. He was absolutely perfectly nice. He was shy."

Joanna also mentioned that several of her scenes with Kilmer were cut out or truncated. The Holliday/Ed Bailey confrontation, for example: "I basically had to grab the money and leave. And we had two horses waiting outside: I'm so sorry it's not in the movie because we did go on those horses and really rode through town. But it probably would have taken too much screen time to leave that. We were good. We both ride horses well, so it would have been fun for us as actors but screen time is screen time. They had to cut a lot of stuff. It would have edited great to the next scene but as actors, we always want more. Just a visual to end that scene with speed. Sort of primal, if I may say. There was one scene in the bar, when Val was leaving and I say, 'It's always Wyatt…' We actually never finished completely that scene, so that's why it probably never ended up in the film. There was not enough time to shoot this movie, there were so many good things going with everybody. It's so hard to judge what you pick and what you do. It's difficult. But we had some really incredible moments. The main relationship was between Kurt and Dana, so that was the romantic relationship. I guess they did not want to compete with other relationships that much. We were secondary, so … there were little moments. We were coming out of the theater, and we had a little exchange with Kurt going to the [Oriental]. Here and there. Like one line, little moments, they had to chop it. But you know what's really weird? Billy Fraker said to me one night, 'Wow, you guys have something really interesting going between you and Val in the movie.' So, I think what he meant was that our relationship was a little bit more interesting, if I may say so."[13]

After the panel discussion was concluded, Catherine Hardwicke gave a presentation on the creation of the movie set. Through photos and sketches, she described the process from ideation to construction while sharing numerous humorous stories about the film and George Cosmatos. "The elegance that Joseph [Porro] brought to this project [through his costumes], we wanted to bring that to this frontier town, too. One thing I thought to show the energy of Tombstone … we also didn't have a lot of money. Remember what other movie was shooting at the same time? *Wyatt Earp*, and they had two or three times our budget, and we thought they were going to kick our ass. But, we kicked their ass. Wooo! We were like the underdog, but we don't hear much about that movie anymore, do we? I thought, let's keep the energy going, so as soon as [construction coordinator] Billy [Holmquist] got the framing up, [I said] don't build it anymore. Let's make it look like it's a work in progress. So it looks like there's always something going on. It's always growing, growing, growing. So, some of these half-built buildings … I thought that was cool. Just the idea of all the cool banners, the fun stuff. The colors. We tried to find out what were the colors, the real paint of that time period. Another building at the end of this street—a church that's not painted so it looks like a work in progress. Here's Fly's studio. Again, we didn't finish painting it, he just put up his backdrops and started opening up the studio before [painting]. He didn't have time. Maybe the paint didn't come in.

"Mescal has been owned for a long time by Old Tucson. So when you say you're going to make a movie in Tucson, you go to Old Tucson and look at that town but that town looked pretty different, though we did use parts of it. We used the train station, we used the inside of the Bird Cage Theater, and then they said we've got this other movie town that you could look at. We went and looked at it and it was falling down. It was crap. Literally, we had to tear some buildings down. We demo'd a lot of buildings because they had been used many years before, and the weather out there in Arizona, it's so extreme with the rain and the wind. Stuff just falls down if you don't take care of it. And we also had a pigeon building. It was like a pigeon infestation, I think one of [our] carpenters went in there, and then he had to go to the hospital. I remember somebody was breathing pigeon shit and the ambulance took him away."[14]

Hardwicke also spoke about the curved bar seen in the Oriental Saloon/Campbell & Hatch Saloon and Billiard parlor that she thought was purchased, but Holmquist quickly corrected her. "We built that beautiful bar that Catherine found in research," said Bill. "[It was a] Brunswick bar from the 1800s. At the end of the show, that bar was going to Aspen. One of the producers was building a big house or cabin [and he wanted it].

Everybody wanted that bar. So we broke it down, crated it and loaded it up on a semi and off it went. We all said we'll never see the bar again. I kind of forgot about it, everybody always wondered what happened to it. I worked on *Deadwood*, the second season in LA. We were scouting there and I was looking around and I walk into this building in this Western town, and part of the bar was there staring back at me. The story is that the bar never made it to Aspen. It was all made out of birch, just a beautiful bar." In a later interview with the author, he also expanded on Hardwicke's construction comments: "When the movie *Tombstone* came in, we bulldozed buildings. The set was in really bad shape. We built the O.K. Corral, Fly's studio, all new construction. All the structures you see in the background. The Oriental and Campbell & Hatch had to be completely rebuilt. We bulldozed the old building that was there because it was falling down, so we started over. Originally we had the Oriental and the Campbell & Hatch separated by a wall that divided the building. Cosmatos looked at the set and decided he wanted the wall out. We started over on the building. We removed sections of roof to crane in a 60-foot I-beam to carry the span of the open space. The Grand Hotel was falling down; the porch was coming off. We built all the [Earp] cottages, those weren't there. There were three of them that we built. We put a façade in front of the barn [for the Bird Cage Theater]. There was just a lot of stuff that was completely gone that we had to come back and rebuild. The Crystal Palace was in really bad shape. They had stuff with porches on it; the roofs all leaked.

"I think we were out there for two and a half months building before shooting began. It wasn't your typical Western where everything is rundown barn wood. I think we touched pretty much every part of that place. Especially, the hospital set. It was just a building on Main Street there. We were just going to straighten it up and paint the whole thing white. It was just a beautiful set, amazing. The drafting department [created the blueprints]. We'd get detailed prints, elevations, floor plans, molding details, everything's to scale. Full-scale, half-scale. Sometimes models. We had to have carpenters on standby when filming began. Three or four guys whatever they need to move or changed."

Holmquist also had his share of amusing stories from the set. "We built Hooker Ranch out of real adobe bricks and it was just a beautiful set at that location," recalls Bill. "They brought cattle out to the ranch and they decided for some reason that the set decorators should build the corrals to keep the cattle in. It wasn't in the shot. At four o'clock in the morning we got a call. They had put the 2 × 12s on the outside of the posts and the cows leaned up against the 2 × 12s and popped them right off. They spent the whole day trying to corral these escaped cows, they finally got them all back. Lesson learned, boards go on the inside of posts."

He also remembered a story about Bill Paxton's "death" scene: "I worked with Bill Paxton on some other movies before he became famous, so I already knew him. In fact, he actually was a set decorator before he became an actor. There is a scene in the film where he gets shot in the Billiard parlor. So, I'm in there with Bill and Cosmatos and I walk in because I have to put a piece of candy-glass in the window where the bullet comes through. When I walk in, Bill is talking to George about how he is going to die. He goes through this whole thing and I'm listening 'cause I'm waiting for Bill to explain it to George. 'Ok, George, the bullet comes through the window, it hits me in the back. I'm going to fall on the pool table and lay here and then I'm going to look up at a spot on the ceiling and my eyes are going to stay open and I'm going to stare at this one spot in the ceiling. That's the way I want to try and do this.' George says ok, so now I get my opportunity to ask about this window. I thought that conversation was over so I go, 'George, excuse me. I need to know what window the bullet's going to come through so I can put a piece of candy glass in there so they can get this thing rigged up.' Bill doesn't realize that I've got George's attention, and Bill goes into this whole acting thing where he acts like he gets shot, then falls on the pool table, laying there, looking up. He does the whole dramatic act. George is trying to figure out the window and I'm looking straight down at Bill; he's staring up at the ceiling, I go, 'Bill. Bill, he's not watching.' He goes, 'What?' 'He didn't see any of that.' He looks up at me, 'Are you kidding me? This shit and he didn't see any of it?' He gets up, he's all pissed off, and walks out of the room. We laughed about it later."[15]

Catherine also shared a funny anecdote about the "snow" in Old Tucson. In the film's final scene, Kurt and Dana dance in the snow outside the "Denver Theater." "Suddenly we found out we had to make a snow scene and it was like about 125 degrees. This was filmed at OTS and they said they weren't going to pay for the snow. But I figured out even if they said they wouldn't, they eventually would. [Bill] found an insulation contractor, and they sprayed that white insulation on the ground and then we had to make snow falling. I remember I was walking along and I thought somebody was using a heat gun because there was so much heat on my legs, but it was a reflection from all that bright light off the insulation. And, it was 120 degrees. At the end, we did it real fast with all the falling potato flakes and then suddenly, it had blown all over Old Tucson. The place was shut down for three days and we had to hire people from the side of the road to clean it all up. Oh, my goodness. It was a mess!"[16]

Porro had the crowd in stitches as he shared memories and answered questions from the audience. "This is really the first period film that I worked on," admitted Porro. "By the way, George was absolutely insane. What he did when he came into me, he went down a line of us. He said, 'You're fired, you're fired.' He came to me. He said, 'I like your stuff. You can stay.' And then he went to the next person. I said this guy's crazy. The only thing he said to me was, 'By the way, all these costumes are mine.'" Porro then spoke to Catherine and said, "Do you know that he shopped your set? When we're done with shooting, he said, 'I want that, I want that.'" Joseph then spoke about the lack of costume availability: "I go out, I'm starting my first Monday, I'm in Hollywood. I start hitting the costume houses. There's nothing left. It's all gone. There's like two cowboy hats from the 1960s in Westerns. I went over to Warner Bros. I hit three other places, same scenario. I said, 'Oh, there's American. American has Western clothing.' I go over to American and I see fabulous Western stuff. We're working on a very small budget so I assuming we're going to rent everything. Lester Bayless, who was John Wayne's personal dresser, looked at me and said, 'So, you see some stuff that you like?' I said, 'Yeah. We can do a big rental here.' He says, 'You'll have to leave right now.' I said, 'Excuse me?' He said, 'When hell freezes over, you can rent my costumes. Please leave the building immediately.' So I left in my car, only to find out that Kevin had hired him and he'd shown up in a meeting drunk. Kevin said, 'I can't go there. The guy's an alcoholic.' So he started interviewing…. [Bayless] owns this costume house and he's just been fired from *Tombstone*. I had no idea. So I called up Kevin and the producers, I said, 'Guys, we're in a lot of trouble. I used to be a fashion designer. The only way I can figure this out is we're going to treat it like a line of clothing. And I've got the research of the period. And we're going to do 100 shirts, and make 40 suits…. For a lot of the fussy women's stuff, I need to take a trip to London.' Back then, designers didn't fly to Europe to rent clothing. It was rather a novelty.

I said, 'For the background people, Victorian hats and all that, you need to send me to London.' I went to London and did the rental. I built all of the men's stuff with a tailor in Hollywood, the principals, downtown to factories to produce a lot of the other things. Maggie McFarland [is here]. She was the dressmaker. She made all of Dana [Delany]'s clothing. Thank god, she was my treasure that I found locally. I didn't know these people, I came in, so this is who you're going to. I'm glad it worked out. Dana was a joy; the ladies were beautiful. The men were a pain in the ass. 'Cause these guys, they all were doing their dream thing. They all had guns and they could play with them. They could ride horses, the guys were in this place. Sometimes they didn't want to come to a fitting because they'd rather be horseback riding. It was a lot of struggle to get them to be disciplined.

"I think I'm going to go there with Val. There's a point with actors when you know to be quiet, but he is a character. He is really a character. There was a lot of political tension on this set with the transformation between the directors. Val Kilmer is the first male actor … I could not control him, on any level. I would show him the sketches, he would like the sketches. Then we made the product. We made all his ties, all his shirts, all his coats. He would take them, he would put them on, but he couldn't decide which one to wear. He took hours, and I had to fit 12 other people today. My fittings are 20 minutes long, they're fast. And Kurt was like, 'Yeah, yeah, OK,' and they were out. Val would preen in front of the mirror and finally I got to the point where I said I need one costume with him. You have to come into his trailer that day, you have to show him what he's worn in other scenes in a photograph. And lay out 30 ties, and lay out shirts. Let him surprise me. I said, 'It's all Doc Holliday clothes so you can pick which one. You just can't repeat to show time has passed.' And that's what we did. It was the weirdest thing I ever did in my career. So every day I had to wait to see what he had on. It was all designed by me, it was just because he could not make up his mind. He would spend sometimes 45 minutes with the ties, going back and forth. I can't deal with that stuff. Everyone else was pretty wonderful, though."

One story he told was particularly funny. Kurt Russell is a pilot and it seems earlier in shooting, he deliberately flew a plane extremely low over the set and ruined a shot. He banked, turned back and with a big shitty grin, did it again as he flipped the bird to everyone. Joseph was standing next to Goldie Hawn as Kurt flew over, and all she could do was to shrug her shoulders as if to say, "What are you gonna do?"[17]

The next day, the celebrities started, once again, to sign autographs. At mid-morning, a 100-person Clanton/McLaury memorial walk began on Allen Street, not only replicating the historic funeral procession but also honoring all those who worked in the movie, now deceased. At 1:30 p.m., the highlight of the day's activities was held—a costume contest judged by Catherine Hardwicke, Joseph Porro and Rene Clothier. With almost 100 contestants, multiple rounds of elimination were necessary but eventually, first and second place winners were announced in five categories.

By 4:00 p.m., for all intents and purposes, the weekend's activities were over. Both celebrities and visitors alike began to filter out of town, heading back from whence they came. But their memories lingered on, and according to the *Tombstone News*, several merchants reported making more money during this weekend than they did on an average *Helldorado* weekend. According to mayor Dusty Escapule, "The event was a success because of everyone working together for the betterment of Tombstone. When we work as a team, everyone benefits."

Particular acknowledgment for the event needs to go to executive producer/local businessowner Gordon Anderson, Lions Club president Bruce Neilson, Jon Donahue, Larry Zeug, Chris Swinney, Old Tucson's Mary Davis, and Julie-Ann Ream, who all ensured the event would happen. Anderson was later named Lions Club "2018 Lion of the Year," and the Film Resource Committee of the Arizona Film Commission named Anderson the film research coordinator for the city of Tombstone. Neilson said that the Lions Club raised a record $10,281 … "money that will go a long, long way to assist children and adults with vision and hearing needs." Sixty-seven Tombstone residents and merchants also graciously volunteered their time and resources, including a generous donation by the O.K. Corral. If I have inadvertently omitted anyone, it wasn't intentional. In addition to the aforementioned individuals, a list of *Tombstone* cast and crew members also in town that weekend, included but not limited to: Mark Balda, Bill Holmquist, Elly McFadden, Maggie McFarland, Lee McKechnie, David Peck, Eddie Perez, Valarie Saunders, Dickie Stanley, John Sundstrom, Mark Tovsen, and Bob Vincent.

Chapter Notes

Prologue

1. *Tucson Citizen*, May 21, 1882; *San Francisco Exchange*, March 17, 1881.

2. *Tombstone Epitaph*, August 14, 1880; *The Law in Tombstone. Ordinances Relevant in the Preliminary Hearing in the Earp/Holliday Case, Heard before Judge Wells Spicer, November 1881;* http://law2.umkc.edu/faculty/projects/trials/earp/ordinances.html.

3. *New York Times*, December 14, 1989; *Los Angeles Times*, January 18, 1994; *Tombstone* publicity kit, Author's collection.

Chapter One

1. *Oregon Historical Quarterly*, Vol. 87, No. 4 (Winter, 1986), 371–72.

2. Lucius Morris Beebe and Charles Clegg, *The American West: The Pictorial Epic of a Continent*; William Henry Bishop, *Mexico, California and Arizona*, 488; Ed Schieffelin, Marilyn F. Butler, ed., *Destination Tombstone: Adventures of a Prospector*, 80–84; www.mininghalloffame.org/inductee/schieffelin.

3. John Myers Myers, *The Last Chance: Tombstone's Early Years*, 18, 29.

4. *Oregon Historical Quarterly*, Vol. 87, No. 4 (Winter, 1986). Moore, 371–72; Casey Tefertiller, *Wyatt Earp: The Life Behind the Legend*, 35; Jeff Guinn, *The Last Gunfight: The Real Story of the Shootout at the O.K. Corral—And How It Changed the American West*, 63; Alice E. Love, *The History of Tombstone to 1887*, unpublished thesis in University of Arizona library, 1933, 9; Myers, 32.

5. *Los Angeles Times*, April 22, 2011; *True West*, October 4, 2011.

6. *True West*, October 4, 2011.

7. Roger Ebert, "Glory," January 12, 1990, www.rogerebert.com; *Los Angeles Times*, January 18, 1990.

8. Duncan Bowles, "Cary Elwes Interview: *Saw 3D, Glory* and *The Princess Bride*," October 25, 2010, www.denofgeek.com/movies/saw/16540/cary-elwes-interview-saw-3d-glory-and-the-princess-bride#ixzz4G7BtG3SV.

9. *Variety*, December 13, 1989.

10. Tom Lisanti, *Dueling Harlows: Race to the Silver*

Screen, 207; *The San Bernardino County Sun*, April 16, 1993; *Variety*, August 22, 1994; *Variety*, May 7, 1997.

11. *Entertainment Weekly*, January 8, 1993, December 24, 1993; "Hannah's Law film review," June 4, 2012, http://henryswesternroundup.blogspot.com/2012/06/hallmarks-hannahs-law-saturday.html; *The Hollywood Reporter*, December 17, 1992; Peter Sherayko interview.

12. Peter Sherayko interview.

13. *Variety*, April 8, 1993; *The Hollywood Reporter*, January 12, 1993.

14. http://elenasandidge.com/2014/01/27/behind-the-scenes-of-tombstone-an-interview-with-peter-sherayko/; Michael F. Blake, *Hollywood and the O.K. Corral: Portrayals of the Gunfight and Wyatt Earp*, 155–56; http://www.angelfire.com/ga/napalousa/tomb.html; Howard Hughes, *Stagecoach to Tombstone: The Filmgoers Guide to the Great Westerns*, 240; Jeff Morey interview.

15. Jim Dunham interview; Jim Dunham letter to author, May 16, 2017.

16. Peter Sherayko interview; Jim Dunham interview; Jeff Morey letter to author, May 10, 2017.

17. www.elenasandidge.com/2014/01/27/behind-the-scenes-of-tombstone-an-interview-with-peter-sherayko/; www.examiner.com/westerns-in-national/making-tombstone-the-movie; http://henryswesternroundup.blogspot.com/2012/06/hallmarks-hannahs-law-saturday.html; Peter Sherayko interview.

18. http://henryswesternroundup.blogspot.com/2012/06/hallmarks-hannahs-law-saturday.html; *Film Review*, October 1994; *Entertainment Weekly*, January 8, 1993; *The Oklahoman*, June 24, 1994; *Los Angeles Times*, August 5, 1994; Robert Palmquist interview; Jeff Morey interview.

19. Meredith Borders, "Showdown at Two O.K. Corrals," March 31, 2016, http://birthmoviesdeath.com/2016/03/31/showdown-at-two-ok-corrals; *The Oklahoman*, June 24, 1994; *Variety*, April 29, 1993; Jeff Morey interview.

20. Kevin Jarre, November 5, 1992, second draft of *Tombstone* script.

21. *Ibid.*

22. Jarre, November 5, 1992, *Tombstone* script, 1–8.

23. *Ibid.*, 11–17.

24. *Ibid.*, 27–29; Lonnie E. Underhill, *The Bird Cage*

Theater, Tombstone, Arizona, 5, 8; Claire E. Willson, *Mimes and Miners*, 9–10, 13; *The Smoke Signal*, Spring 1966, 52.

25. Jarre, November 5, 1992, *Tombstone* script, 38–45; Arizona Historical markers; *The Tombstone Epitaph*, September 9, 1880; Ben Traywick, *This Is Tombstone: The Town Too Tough to Die*, 26.

26. Arizona Historical markers; Jarre, November 5, 1992, *Tombstone* script, 45.

27. Jarre, November 5, 1992, *Tombstone* script, 49–54; www.americancowboychronicles.com.

28. Jarre, November 5, 1992, *Tombstone* script, 54–55.

29. *Ibid.*, 56–62.

30. *Ibid.*, 70–76.

31. *Ibid.*, 76–78.

32. *Ibid.*, 82–83.

33. *Ibid.*, 85.

34. *Ibid.*, 93–98.

35. *Ibid.*, 98–110.

36. *Ibid.*, 110–113.

37. *Ibid.*, 114–115.

38. *Ibid.*, 122.

39. *Ibid.*, 127–130.

40. *Ibid.*, 130–132; Blake, 160.

41. *Ibid.*, 132–135.

42. Blake, 160, 163, 173; *Films in Review*, Vol. XLV, No. ¾, Issue 2; *Los Angeles Times*, December 31, 1993; *Los Angeles Times*, January 18, 1994; *Los Angeles Times*, April 23, 2011; *True West*, October 1, 2006; *True West*, October 4, 2011; cdn2-b.examiner.com/article/making-tombstone-the-movie; Peter Sherayko interview; http://www.armchairgeneral.com/forums/showthread.php?t=109425.

43. *Los Angeles Times*, August 5, 1994; http://birthmoviesdeath.com/2016/03/31/showdown-at-two-ok-corrals.

44. *The Hollywood Reporter*, December 17, 1992; *The Hollywood Reporter*, January 12, 1993; *The Hollywood Reporter*, February 12, 1993; *The Hollywood Reporter*, April 13, 1993; *Variety*, December 7, 17, 1992; Blake, 162n240; Jeff Morey letter to author, December 2, 3, 2016; *Arizona Republic*, July 18, 1993.

45. *Los Angeles Times*, February 4, 1990; *Los Angeles Times*, July 26, 1990; *Variety*, July 12, 1990.

46. *Entertainment Weekly*, July 15, 1994.

47. *Variety*, July 12, 23, 25, 1990; *Los Angeles Times*, July 24, 1990; *Los Angeles Times*, August 7, 1990.

48. *MovieMaker*, December 1, 1996; *People*, May 29, 1995; *Variety*, January 15, 1994.

49. http://birthmoviesdeath.com/2016/03/31/showdown-at-two-ok-corrals; Peter Sherayko interview; *Entertainment Weekly*, January 8, 1993.

50. *Variety*, August 17, 1994.

51. *True West*, October 1, 2006; Blake, 161; *Esquire*, October 25, 2015.

52. *The Hollywood Reporter*, February 12, 1993.

Chapter Two

1. Guinn, 63–64; Alice E. Love, *History of Tombstone to 1887*, unpublished thesis (Tucson: The University of Arizona, 1933), 11; Myers, 35, 69–70, 93.

2. http://www.tombstoneweb.com/history.html; Guinn, 60; Thomas Peterson, "The Tombstone Stagecoach Lines, 1878–1903: A Study in Frontier Transportation," thesis, University of Arizona, Department of History, 1968, 5; Eric Clements, *After the Boom in Tombstone and Jerome, Arizona: Decline in Western Resource Towns*, 25; *Arizona Weekly Citizen*, September 28, 1878; *Arizona Weekly Citizen*, March 7, 1879; *Arizona Weekly Citizen*, July 18, 1879; *Arizona Weekly Citizen*, September 27, 1879.

3. Tombstone historical marker.

4. Jane Eppinga, *Tombstone: Images of America*, 95.

5. *Chicago Tribune*, January 5, 1878; Historic Resources Inventory and Report of Tombstone, Arizona. Johns & Strittmatter Inc., 1996 (tDAR id: 399349); doi:10.6067/XCV8G162MJ; *Arizona Weekly Citizen*, October 26, 1878; *The Arizona Sentinel*, December 14, 1878; *The Arizona Sentinel*, January 11, 1879; *Weekly Republican*, December 21, 1878; *Arizona Weekly Star*, December 9, 1879; *Chicago Daily Tribune*, January 5, 1879; *Los Angeles Herald*, October 29, 1879; *Arizona Daily Star*, January 21, 1879; *Arizona Daily Star*, August 23, 1879; *San Francisco Chronicle*, November 28, 1879; Ben T. Traywick, *1879 Census Tombstone as Taken by Pima County Sheriff Charles A. Shibell on September 18, 19, and 20, 1879*, 19, 21; *Daily Arizona Citizen*, November 3, 1879; Clements, 35.

6. *The Sacramento Daily Record-Union*, March 11, 1880; *The Sacramento Daily Record-Union*, April 21, 1880; *The Sacramento Daily Record-Union*, May 3, 1880; *The Sacramento Daily Record-Union*, July 2, 14, 1880; http://bignosekates.info/history1.html; *Tombstone Epitaph*, September 29, 1880.

7. Ron Fischer, *The Tombstone Business Directory 1880–1884*, 2–5; *Arizona Weekly Citizen*, December 4, 1880.

8. *Cowboys & Indians*, June, 2010; Jeff Morey letter to author December 2, 2016; http://henryswesternroundup.blogspot.com/2012/06/hallmarks-hannahs-law-saturday.html; Peter Sherayko interview; *True West*, October 2006; *Drama-Logue*, January 13–19, 1994; Lisa Zane letter to author, November 22, 2017; http://rheaven.blogspot.com; *Trail Dust*, Winter 1994; letter from Lisa Zane to author, September 12, 2017.

9. Chris Mitchum interview; *Variety*, February 22, 1993; *Variety*, March 1, 1993; *Variety*, May 6, 1993; *Variety*, June 29, 1993; *Tombstone* publicity kit, Author's collection; *Trail Dust*, Fall/Winter 2008, Vol. VII, no. 1; Frank Stallone interview; Stephen Lang letter to author, April 7, 2017; Lisa Zane letter to author, November 22, 2017; Gary Roberts response to *Wild West* letter to editor, June 2017.

10. John Philbin interview.

11. J. Nathan Simmons interview; *Los Angeles Times*, December 25, 1993.

12. Time-Life, *100 Years of Hollywood*, Our American Century, 109.

13. www.collider.com.

14. *Tombstone* press book, Author's collection; Paul Lawton, *Images of America, Old Tucson Studios*, 99–101; Matt Marich interview; Catherine Hardwicke interview, "The Making of Tombstone ... Making an Authentic Western," Buena Vista, 2002; Chris Swinney interview; Catherine Hardwicke interview; Production Cost Report, 09/18/93, BFC.

15. Catherine Hardwicke interview, "The Making of Tombstone...."; Matt Marich interview; letter from Mark Worthington, Catherine Hardwicke, Tombstone Productions to Dan Aylward, Nicola Hartmann, Old Tucson, April 27, 1993; Jeff Morey interview.

16. Catherine Hardwicke interview.

17. *Tucson Daily Citizen*, July 7, 1967; *Tucson Daily Citizen*, October 19, 1967; *Tombstone* Art Department memo, April 26, 1993.

18. *Tombstone* Art Department memo, April 26, 1993.

19. Contract between Tombstone Productions and Old Tucson studios; draft letter between Daniel Aylward and Terry Collis, BFC; Paul, Allen, Paul. "Earps ride into Tucson: Filming on the movie 'Tombstone' will begin May 17 in southern Arizona," Undated; *Tombstone* Production Cost Report, 05/29/93, BFC; *Tombstone* Art Department memo, April 26, 1993.

20. Old Tucson/Cinergi rental agreement, Various, May–July 1993; Joanne Gammon interview; Brian Stewart letter to author, December 15, 2016.

21. Joanne Gammon interview; Matt Marich letter to author, February 18, 2017.

22. Kasdan, 18–19; Matt Marich interview.

23. *Los Angeles Times*, January 18, 1994; John Peel interview.

24. Robert Burke interview.

25. Blake, 165; Joseph Porro interview.

26. Peter Sherayko interview; Peter Sherayko, *Tombstone: The Guns and Gear*, 145; Blake, 163.

27. Peter Sherayko interview; Sherayko, 105–6; *True West*, July 9, 2013.

28. Joseph Porro interview; Peter Sherayko letter to author, June 6, 2017; *Trail Dust*, Winter 1994.

29. Joseph Porro interview; Tombstone History Discussion Forum, Jeff Morey, February 2, 2011; Paula Mitchell Marks, *And Die in the West: The Story of the O.K. Corral Gunfight*, 139; Dickie Stanley interview.

30. Old Tucson/Cinerig rental agreement, Various, May–July 1993.

31. Rick Terry interview.

32. Tom Hirt interview; Tom Hirt Facebook page, "The hats of Tombstone."

33. Tom Hirt interview.

34. *Ibid*.

35. Peter Sherayko interview.

36. Renee Clothier interview.

Chapter Three

1. Jeff Guinn, *The Last Gunfight, The Real Story of the Showdown at the O.K. Corral—And How It Changed the American West*, 10–12.

2. Louis L'Amour, *How the West Was Won*, 14; *American Experience, Wyatt Earp: Hero, Outlaw, Legend*, Paul Hutton, historian, PBS, 2010; Roger Lax and Frederick Smith, *The Great Song Thesaurus*, 377; Margaret Bradford Boni, ed., *The Fireside Book of Favorite American Songs*, 307.

3. Guinn, 89.

4. Glenn Frankel, *The Searchers: The Making of an American Legend*, 31–2; www.dps.texas.gov/Texas Rangers/HistoricalDevelopment.htm; Handbook of Texas Online, Ben Procter, "Texas Rangers." www.tsha online.org/handbook/nline/articles/met04; Christina Claridy, *Indians and Rangers in 19th Century Texas*.

5. Marshall Trimble, *Arizona Outlaws and Lawmen: Gunslingers, Bandits, Heroes and Peacekeepers*, 10.

6. http://online.nmartmuseum.org/nmhistory/growing-new-mexico/tourism/history-tourism.html; *Arizoniana*, Vol. 2, No. 1 (Spring 1961).

7. *Arizoniana*, Vol. 2, No. 1 (Spring 1961); *Rangelands*, 14(5), October 1992.

8. *Arizona Daily Star*, January 20, 2008; Eddie Perez interview; Charles Schneider interview; Glen Gold interview.

9. John Peel interview; Jerry Crandall interview; Kane Rubalcaba interview; Tom Ward interview.

10. Forrie Smith interview; Jerry Crandall interview; Judy Crandall letter to author, February 1, 2017; Judy Crandall letter to author, May 15, 2017; Peter Sherayko letter to all Buckaroos, April 21, 1993; John Peel interview; Reggie Byrum interview; Tom Ward Facebook post, October 31, 2017; Tom Ward interview; Chris Ramirez interview; Charley Ward interview.

11. *Arizona Republic*, May 12, 1993; *Variety*, April 29, 1993; *Variety*, May 6, 1993; *Variety*, May 12, 1993.

12. Tony Bill, *Movie Speak: How to Talk Like You Belong on a Film Set*, 23.

13. Karie Lord interview; Robert Palmquist interview; Nancy Sosa interview; Catherine Hardwicke interview.

14. *Arizona Daily Star*, December 25, 1993.

15. Bill Getzwiler interview.

16. Larry Zeug interview; July 14, 1993, list of motel rooms/housing accommodations; Elly McFadden interview.

17. John Peel interview.

18. Chris Ramierez interview; Jerry Tarantino interview.

19. May 8, 1993, *Tombstone* final budget #2, BFC; May 14, 1993, memo from Tombstone AD's to cast and crew, BFC.

20. *True West*, August 25, 2017.

21. Robert Burke interview.

22. John Philbin interview.

23. Ben Traywick interview; Stephen Lang letter to author, April 7, 2017.

24. www.bradleydpettit.blogspot.com/2011/06/my interview with actor Michael Biehn.

25. Gary Gang interview; Robert Burke interview; Larry Zeug interview.

26. Gary Gang interview; Robert Burke interview; Gary Gang letter to author, November 18, 2017; Lisa Zane letter to author, November 22, 2017.

27. Red Wolverton interview; *Western Horseman*, November 2004; *The Morgan Horse*, July 2014; Tom Ward, Facebook post, November 16, 2017.

28. Bobby Vincent interview; Larry Zeug interview.

29. May 10, 1993, master shooting schedule, BFC; *Tombstone* maps given to cast and crew.

30. Larry Zeug interview.

31. www.armchairgeneral.com; wn.com; Dave Cox letter to author, March 30, 2017; *Drama-Logue*, January 13–19, 1994.

32. Tom Ward interview.

33. Charley Ward interview.

34. Nikki Pelley interview.

35. *Arizona Republic*, June 13, 1993; Forrie Smith interview.

36. Dana Loraine Goodge interview.

37. Terry Leonard interview.

38. Jerry Crandall interview.

39. *Ibid*.

40. Terry Leonard interview.

41. Chris Swinney letter to author, June 22, 2017.

42. Letter to author from Billy Lang, January 9, 2018.

43. Kane Rubalcaba interview; James Danicic interview; Tom Hirt interview.

44. Forrie Smith interview; Chris Ramirez interview.

45. *Drama-Logue*, January 13–19, 1994.

46. Jennifer Van Sijll, *Cinematic Storytelling: The 100 Most Powerful Film Conventions Every Filmmaker Must Know*, 154; Matt Marich interview; Larry Zeug interview.

47. Jeff Dolan interview.

48. Chris Mitchum interview.

49. Jeff Dolan interview; Sam Dolan letter to author, May 22, 2017.

50. B. Alan Orange, "Michael Biehn Revisits Johnny Ringo in Tombstone," https://movieweb.com/exclusive-michael-biehn-revisits-johnny-ringo-in-tombstone/

51. Eddie Perez interview; Matt Marich interview; Grant James interview; Victor Vizcarra interview; *Tombstone* memorandum, July 31, 1993; *Arizona Republic*, July 16, 1993; *True West*, August 25, 2017; Chris Swinney interview.

52. Victor Vizcarra interview; James Brooks interview; Elly McFadden interview.

53. Robert Burke interview; Elly McFadden interview; Donna Cline interview.

54. Chris Ramirez interview; Kane Rubalcaba interview.

55. Chris Swinney interview.

56. Peter Sherayko interview.

57. Greg Poulos interview.

58. Forrie Smith interview.

59. www.deadline.com; Anne Taylor interview.

60. Anne Taylor interview.

Chapter Four

1. Paula Mitchell Marks, *And Die in the West: The Story of the O.K. Corral Gunfight*, 25–29.

2. *Arizoniana*, Vol. 2, No.1 (Spring 1961).

3. Joyce Aros, *Murdered on the Streets of Tombstone*, 12–13, 48.

4. About William "Curly Bill" Brocius, *Eagle Free Enterprises*, http://www.pictures.eaglefreeenterprises.com/william_brocius.htm, retrieved October 17, 2011.

5. *True West*, September 2017.

6. https://tshaonline.org/handbook/online/articles/fri51; *Arizona Capital Times*, March 23, 2012; David Johnson, "Johnny Ringo: King of the Cowboys. www.johnnyringo.com.

7. Bob Boze Bell, *The Illustrated Life & Times of Wyatt Earp*, 12–23; Tom Clavin, *Dodge City: Wyatt Earp, Bat Masterson, and the Wickedest Town in the American West*, 32, 56–7, 73–4.

8. Ephraim Katz, *The Film Encyclopedia*, 490; Joseph Musso interview; John Peel interview; www.jwayne.com.

9. www.digitalwriting101.net, "Guide—Composing Shots and Scenes for Cinematic Storytelling."

10. http://dictionary.tdf.org/line-reading/; *True West*, August 2013; Lisa Zane to author, November 22, 2017.

11. Peter Sherayko interview.

12. www.computerstories.net; Blake, 194.

13. Letter from Bob Misiorowski to Andy Vajna, June 7, 1993, BFC; undated letter from Andy Vajna and Buss Feitshans to Kevin Jarre, BFC; www.informit.com.

14. *Tombstone script*, March 18, 1993, fourth draft.

15. Michael Blake letter to author, July 19, 2017; *Entertainment Weekly*, December 24, 1993; James Danicic interview; Michael Walker interview; Peter Sherayko interview.

16. www.movieweb.com; Grant James interview; *Entertainment Weekly*, December 24, 1993; Chris Mitchum interview; *True West*, October 2006.

17. Stephen Lang letter to author, April 7, 2017; Catherine Hardwicke interview.

18. Jake Johnson interview.

19. Bob Boze Bell interview; *True West*, October, 2006; Jeff Dolan interview; Mark Rainsford interview.

20. Billy Lang interview.

21. Jeff Dolan interview.

22. *Entertainment Weekly*, December 24, 1993; avclub.com; Bob Boze Bell interview; *True West*, October 2006.

23. Bob Palmquist interview.

24. Jerry Tarantino interview; Kathy Tarantino interview.

25. Reggie Byrum interview.

26. Rick Terry interview.

27. Jeff Dolan interview; Michael Blake letter to author, July 19, 2017; www.rheaven.blogspot.com.

28. Bob Boze Bell interview; Jeff Morey letter to author, January 7, 2017.

29. Bob Boze Bell interview.

30. www.starpulse.com; Peter Sherayko, *Tombstone: The Guns and Gear,* 8; *Drama-Logue,* January 13–19, 1994; www.northhollywoodfilms.com; www.slashfilm.com; August 24, 1994, letter from Guy McElwaine to John Fasano; *Quad-City Times,* January 2, 1994; Edie Fasano interview; John Fasano letter to Andy Vajna, July 16, 1994.

31. Tombstone call-sheets June 10–15, 1993, BFC; Daily production report, June 15, 1993, BFC; Michael Blake letter to author, July 21, 2017; Peter Sherayko letter to author July 21, 2017.

32. Interoffice memorandum from Erick Feitshans to Andrew Vajna, June 22, 1993, BFC; Feitshans to Terry Collis, June 15, 1993, BFC; Revised overage calculation, Bob Misorowski, June 16, 1993, BFC.

33. Reggie Byrum interview; Michael Blake letter to author, October 13, 2017; Anne Taylor letter to author, October 5, 2017; Tom Ward interview.

34. Sherayko, *The Guns and Gear,* 8; *Los Angeles Times,* January 18, 1994; *Drama-Logue,* January 13–19, 1994.

35. *Quad-City Times,* January 2, 1994.

36. *Drama-Logue,* January 13–19, 1994; www.aintit cool.com.

37. *Quad-City Times,* January 2, 1994.

38. www.movieweb.com.

39. Michael Walker interview.

40. *Los Angeles Times,* April 27, 2005; *The Guardian,* April 26, 2005.

41. *True West,* October 2006; Glen Gold interview; John Peel interview; Hamilton, 62; Tomas Arana interview; *Entertainment Today,* December 24–30, 1993; *The Age,* January 27, 1994.

42. Val Kilmer blog, posted August 10, 2017.

43. *Drama-Logue,* January 13–19, 1994; Val Kilmer blog, posted August 10, 2017; Sherayko, *The Guns and Gear,* 8; *American Cowboy,* January 19, 2015; John Philbin interview.

44. Robert Burke interview.

45. Sherayko, *The Guns and Gear,* 9; www.movieweb.com; *True West,* August 1, 2008; Edie Fasano interview.

46. John Philbin interview; Larry Zeug interview; Peter Sherayko interview; Forrie Smith interview; Tomas Arana interview.

47. Matt Marich interview; Lisa Zane letter to author, November 22, 2017.

48. *American Cowboy,* January 19, 2015; www.star pulse.com; Frank Stallone interview; *Drama-Logue,* January 13–19, 1994; *The New Yorker,* January 14, 2008; *The New York Review of Books,* November 6, 2008; Billy Lang interview.

49. Steven Melton interview.

50. Catherine Hardwicke interview.

51. Chris Swinney interview.

52. Bo Gray interview; John Philbin interview.

53. Jeff Dolan interview.

54. Lee McKechnie interview.

55. Robert Burke interview.

56. John Philbin interview; James Danicic interview.

57. Blake, 172; Sabino Canyon recreation area brochure, September 2016, RG-R3-05-21; Blumes Tracy interview.

58. Dickie Stanley letter to author, December 12, 2017; Dickie Stanley interview; Director's commentary, Vista *Tombstone* DVD.

59. Larry Zug interview; Jeff Dolan letter to author, October 11, 2017.

60. John Pell interview; Peter Sherayko Facebook post, November 2, 2017.

61. Rick Terry interview.

62. Jerry Tarantino interview; Garrett Roberts Facebook post, November 3, 2017.

63. Larry Zeug interview; Blake, 173.

64. Rick Terry interview.

65. Letters from Jeff Morey to author, January 5, 7, 2017.

66. Larry Zeug interview.

67. Jake Johnson, Peter Sherakyo, Samuel Kilborn Facebook post, October 10, 2017.

Chapter Five

1. Robert Vincent Facebook post, March 13, 2018.

2. Kane Rubalcaba interview; Larry Zeug letter to author, June 2, 2017.

3. *Arizona Capital Times,* May 2, 2014; *Tombstone Epitaph,* December 28, 1881.

4. Charles Schneider interview.

5. *Ibid.*

6. Lisa Zane letter to author, November 22, 2017; Director's commentary, Vista *Tombstone* DVD.

7. *Tombstone* script, June 24, 1993, fifth draft; Cindy Wykes interview; Matt Marich interview; J. Nathan Simmons interview.

8. Charles Schneider interview.

9. Larry Zeug interview.

10. Donna Cline interview.

11. Donna Cline interview; James Danicic interview; Billy Getzwiler interview.

12. Sam Dolan interview.

13. Michael Walker interview; Getzwiller interview; Blake, 174; www.fdtimes.com/2011/02/15william-a-fraker; Anne Taylor letter to author, November 6, 2016.

14. James Danicic interview; Dickie Stanley letter to author, December 12, 2017.

15. Lee McKechnie interview.

16. Glen Gold interview.

17. Steve Melton interview; Jan Robinson interview.

18. Bobby Vincent interview.

19. Paul Lawton letter to author, October 19, 2017; Jake Johnson letter to author, October 19, 2017; Larry Jensen Facebook post, October 19, 2017; Larry Jensen,

Hollywood's Railroads: Volume one, Virginia & Truckee, 67; Sam Dolan Facebook message, October 18, 2017.

20. Sam Dolan interview.

21. Gary Gang interview; Greg Poulos interview; Dana Loraine Goodge interview.

22. Frank Magill, *Magill's Cinema Annual 1994,* 370–73; *Tombstone* press booklet, 17; *The New York Times,* December 24, 1993.

23. Kane Rubalcaba interview.

24. Walter Noble Burns, *Tombstone: An Iliad of the Southwest,* 138; www.trend-chaser.com.

25. Mark Tovsen interview.

26. Sam Dolan letter to author, May 22, 2017; *Santa Cruz Sentinel,* September 12, 1995.

27. Catherine Hardwicke interview.

28. *Ibid.*

29. Matt Marich interview.

30. www.angelfire.com.

31. Frank Stallone interview; Eddy McFadden interview; Chris Mitchum interview.

32. John Peel interview; Greg Poulos interview; Chris Swinney interview; Catherine Hardwicke interview.

33. Peter Sherayko interview; Frank Stallone interview, John Peel interview; Blake, 175; Letter from Terry Collis to Randy Paul, September 20, 1993. BFC.

34. www.Lebeau'sLeBlog.com; www.denofgeek.com; The Ultimate Michael Biehn interview, Duncan Bowles, August 31, 2011; www.hollywoodnews.com; Exclusive: Michael Biehn Digs Up Details about the Making of "Tombstone," Todd Gilchrist, April 23, 2010; Bo Gray interview; Steve Melton interview.

35. Greg Poulos interview.

36. Lawton, *Old Tucson Studios,* 76; Nicola Hartmann memorandum to all OTS departments, July 8, 1993; American King James Version bible, Revelation 6: 7–8; www.slackerwod.com/node/2929; www.movieweb.com/person/Michael-biehn; www.ign.com/articles/201/05/01; Stephen Lang letter to author, April 15, 2017.

37. *Variety,* June 29, 1993; James Danicic interview; Blake 194; Steve Melton interview; John Peel interview; Blumes Tracy interview.

38. Jeff Ramsey interview.

39. Jeff Dolan interview.

40. Sam Dolan interview; letter from Sam Dolan to author, May 18, 2017; J. Nathan Simmons interview.

41. Donna Cline interview.

42. Steve Melton interview.

43. Sam Dolan interview; Stephen Lang letter to author, April 15, 2017; Greg Poulos interview; David Russell letter to author, January 4, 2017; Larry Zeug interview.

44. James Danicic interview.

45. Peter Sherayko interview; Chris Ramirez interview.

46. Jeff Dolan interview; Steve Melton interview; www.angelfire.com; John Peel interview; Bobby Vincent interview; Michael Walker interview; Mark Rainsford interview.

47. James Danicic interview; Tombstone shooting schedule, BFC.

48. Chris Swinney interview.

49. Tombstone Daily Production Reports, BFC; August 21, 1993, letter to Andy Vajna from George Cosmatos, BFC; August 21, 1993, letter from Bob Misiorowski to Andy Vajna, BFC; Greg Poulos interview.

50. Catherine Hardwicke interview.

51. Reggie Byrum interview; John Peel interview.

52. Chris Swinney interview; Josh Swinney interview.

53. Rick Terry interview; http://www.angelfire.com/ga/napalousa/val.html.

Chapter Six

1. Emily Blanton interview; Billy Lang interview.

2. Director's commentary, Vista *Tombstone* DVD.

3. Terry Leonard interview.

4. Reggie Byrum interview.

5. Reggie Byrum interview; Blake, 179; Chris Ramierez interview.

6. John Peel interview; Billy Lang interview; Reggie Byrum interview.

7. Chris Swinney interview; Josh Swinney interview; Michael Walker interview; Larry Zeug interview; James Brooks interview.

8. John Philbin interview.

9. Rick Terry interview; Reggie Byrum interview.

10. James Danicic interview.

11. Lee McKechnie interview.

12. Dana Loraine Goodge interview.

13. Glen Gold interview.

14. Sam Elliott interview, "Dobe and a Company of Heroes," SCHOT Productions, Inc., 2002.

15. Terry McGahey interview.

16. Director's commentary, Vista *Tombstone* DVD.

17. Terry McGahey interview; Dickie Stanley interview.

18. Jim Dunham letter to author, May 16, 2017.

19. https://ncxtooze.com/peter-sherayko-takes-us-behind-the-scenes-of-the-movie-tombstone/.

20. Red Wolverton interview; *The Morgan Horse,* July 2014; E-mail from Kip Wolverton to author, March 2, 2018.

21. *American Cowboy,* January 19, 2015; Director's commentary Vista *Tombstone* DVD.

22. Chris Swimmey letter to author, January 7, 2018.

23. Rick Terry interview.

24. John Philbin interview; Sam Dolan interview; letter from Jeff Morey to author, April 4, 2017.

25. *The San Bernardino County Sun,* January 5, 1994.

26. Sam Dolan interview; John Peel interview; Robert Burke interview.

27. Jay Gammons interview; John Peel interview; *Washington Times,* December 19, 1993; Director's commentary, Vista *Tombstone* DVD.

28. Eddie Perez interview; *Los Angeles Times,* August 11, 1993.

29. David Russell letters to author, December 15, 2016, January 4, 2017; Larry Zeug interview.

30. Jake Johnson interview; *The Washington Times*, December 19, 1993; *Tombstone* publicity kit, author's collection; Director's commentary, Vista *Tombstone* DVD.

31. Eddie Perez interview; Director's commentary, Vista *Tombstone* DVD.

32. Lee McKechnie interview.

33. Donna Cline interview; *The Washington Times*, December 19, 1993.

34. Josh Swinney interview.

35. Rick Terry interview; American Humane Association movie review, November 24, 1993, BFC.

36. Robert Burke interview.

37. Dickie Stanley interview.

38. *Guns & Ammo*, December, 1997; www.therpf. com.

39. Jake Johnson interview.

40. Bo Gray interview.

41. *American Cowboy*, Jan 19, 2015.

42. Peter Sherayko, John Peel, Facebook posts.

43. *American Cowboy*, January 19, 2015; Sherayko, *Tombstone: The Guns and Gear*, 17, 22; Forrie Smith interview; *The Westerner*, Vol I, No. I; *Trail Dust*, Winter 1994; *True West*, July 9, 2013; www.bradleydpettit. blogspot.com/2011/06/my interview with actor Michael Biehn.

44. Jake Johnson interview.

45. Dana Loraine Goodge interview.

46. Frank Stallone interview.

47. Katie Lord interview; *Tombstone*, George Cosmatos commentary, Vista Series, Director's cut, 2002.

48. John Peel interview; Stephen Lang letter to author, April 7, 2017; Sam Dolan letter to author, December 27, 2017.

49. J. Nathan Simmons interview.

50. Grant James interview.

51. John Philbin interview; Stephen Lang letter to author, April 7, 2017; Jeff Morey letter to author, January 5, 2017; William Hamilton, *Blessed, Life and Films of Val Kilmer*, 64; *Tombstone*, George Cosmatos commentary, Vista Series, 2002.

52. Greg Poulos interview; Elly McFadden interview.

53. Eddie Perez interview.

54. Greg Poulos interview.

55. Sam Dolan Facebook post, June 24, 1993, fifth draft *Tombstone* script.

56. *Ibid.*

57. *Ibid.*

58. Donna Cline interview.

59. Sam Dolan letter to author, May 22, 2017.

60. Emily Blanton interview.

61. Facebook message from John Peel to author, February 2, 2018.

62. Tom Ward interview; Mark Rainsford interview.

63. Charley Ward interview.

64. Kathy Tarantino interview.

65. Michael Walker interview.

66. Kathy Tarantino interview; August 11, 1993, letter from Terry Collis to Buzz Feitshans, BFC; Director's commentary, Vista *Tombstone* DVD.

67. Kathy Tarantino interview; Jerry Tarantino interview.

68. Peter Sherayko interview; Blake, 181–2.

69. Letter from Sam Dolan to author, May 22, 2017; Larry Zeug Facebook post, December 29, 2017; Sam Dolan Facebook post.

Chapter Seven

1. *True West*, July 2003, August 2005, September 2005, May 2010; www.policeone.com; www.legendsof america.com; https://archive.is/20120713003618; *Arizona Daily Star*, May 30, 1882; www.pbs.org/wgh/ americanexperience; Paula Mitchell Marks, *And Die in the West: The Story of the O.K. Corral Gunfight*; Casey Tefertiller, *Wyatt Earp: The Life Behind the Legend*; Tom Clavin, *Dodge City: Wyatt Earp, Bat Masterson, and the Wickedest Town in the American West*; Bob Boze Bell, *The Illustrated Life and Times of Doc Holliday*; Bob Boze Bell, *The Illustrated Life and Times of Wyatt Earp*; Gary L. Roberts, *Doc Holliday: The Life Behind the Legend*; www.confederateamericanpride. com/OldWest/DocHolliday; Victoria Wilcox, *Gone West, The Last Decision, The Saga of Doc Holliday, Books two and three*; William Brechenridge, *Helldorado*; John Richard Stephens, *Wyatt Earp Speaks.*

2. John Philbin interview; Larry Zeug interview.

3. www.express.co.uk/dayandnight/69210.

4. *Cowboy Legends: Outlaws & Lawmen*, August 2013.

5. Reggie Byrum interview; Larry Zeug interview; Blake, 175.

6. Larry Zeug interview; Sam Dolan interview; Mark Rainsford interview; Larry Zeug letter to author, February 23, 2018.

7. www.moveiweb.com; Robert Burke interview; *The San Bernardino County Sun*, December 30, 1993.

8. Hamilton, 65; *Arizona Republic*, November 7, 1993.

9. August 18–November 4, 1993, post-production schedule and notes, post production schedule, August 30, 1993, December 21 release, February delivery, Tombstone 09/18/93 Production Cost Report, BFC; *The Lincoln Star*, January 16, 1994; *Entertainment Today*, December 24–30, 1993.

10. www.indiewire.com/2015/04/attention-film-makers-heres-why-you-should-make-medium-length-films-62586/; *True West*, September 2017; *Trail Dust*, Winter 1994.

11. November 5, 1993, letter from Sean Daniel to Andy Vajna.

12. *Trail Dust*, Winter 1995; Bo Gay interview.

13. Bo Gray interview.

14. June 18, 1993, letter from Tania Steele to Andy Vajna, BFC; June 28, 1993, letter from Michael Werner to Andy Vajna, BFC; undated from Patti Hawn to all cast and crew, BFC; August 26, 1993, letter from Cirina

Kay to Nancy Griffen, BFC; September 14, 1993, letter from Patt/Mory Hobin to Janet Stoudt, BFC.

15. Bruce Broughton letter to author, February 22, 2018; liner notes, *Tombstone* CD, Intrada, 2006.

16. R. Sadoff, "The Role of the Music Editor and the 'Temp Track' as Blueprint for the Score and Source Music of Films," *Popular Music*, 25(2) (2006), 165–183, doi:10.1017/S0261143006000845.

17. Broughton letter to author, February 23, 2018.

18. American Humane Association film review, November 24, 1993, BFC; Buena Vista Marketing memorandum, from Denise Greenawalt to all concerned, November 30, 1993, BFC; *Arizona Republic*, December 22, 1993; *Entertainment Weekly*, December 24, 1993; *Los Angeles Times*, February 6, 1994.

19. Sam Elliott interview schedule, December 13, 1993, BFC; letter from Denise Greenawalt to Esme Chandlee, December 9, 1993, BFC; Buena Vista Pictures Marketing memorandum, from Denise Greenawalt to those concerned, December 15, 1993, BFC; letter from Denise Greenawalt to Arlene Ludwig/Terry Greenberg, December 17, 21, 29, 1993, BFC; *The Hollywood Reporter*, November 24, 1993.

20. www.minyanville.com.

21. *Daily Variety*, December 23, 27, 1993.

22. *The Hollywood Reporter*, December 23, 1993.

23. *The New York Times*, December 24, 1993; www.ibj.com.

24. *Entertainment Today*, December 24, 1993.

25. *Arizona Republic*, December 24, 25, 1993; *Arizona Daily Star*, December 25, 1993.

26. *Los Angeles Times*, December 25, 1993; *Los Angeles Village View*, December 31, 1993–January 6, 1994; *Santa Cruz Sentinel*, December 31, 1993.

27. *Variety*, December 22, 1993.

28. *The Monitor*, December 31, 1993.

29. *Films in Review*, Vol XLV, No. 3/4, issue 2; *Drama-Logue*, January 13–19, 1994; *The Courier*, December 31, 1993; *Ukiah Daily Journal*, January 7, 1994; *The Petaluma Argus-Courier*, January 7, 1994; *Screen International*, January 23, 1994.

30. *The Orlando Sentinel*, January 14, 1994; *The Philadelphia Inquirer*, February 5, 1994; Siskel and Ebert review of *Tombstone*, undated.

31. *Film Review*, March 1994; *The Desert Sun*, June 24, 1994; Kasdan, 107; *Entertainment Weekly*, June 17, 1994.

32. *The Press Democrat*, June 26, 1994; *Entertainment Weekly*, June 17, July 15, 1994; *Film Review*, October 1994; *Virginian-Pilot*, October 29, 1994; *The Oklahoman*, June 24, 1994; https://movieweb.com/exclusive-michael-biehn-revisits-johnny-ringo-in-tombstone/.

33. *The Los Angeles Times*, July 2, 1995; *The Desert Sun*, June 24, 1994; *Film Reviews*, October 1994; *The Signal*, June 24, 1994; www.rogerebert.com/reviews/wyatt-earp-1994.

34. *Variety*, August 16, 1994; *Entertainment Weekly*, July 15, 1994; *Statesman Journal*, June 3, 1994; *Asheville Citizen-Times*, July 6, 1994.

35. *The Dispatch*, July 20, 1994.

36. Tony Malanowski interview.

37. Kevin Reems interview.

38. Tony Malanowski interview.

39. *Arizona Daily Star*, December 31, 1993.

40. *Los Angeles Times*, January 18, 1994.

41. *True West*, September 2017.

42. Vista Series, *Tombstone*, Director's Cut, "Making of" featurette, Michael Biehn, 2002.

43. https://cinapse.co/i-am-legend-tombstone-the-cinematic-perfection-of-wyatt-earp-and-doc-holliday-490267f15acc; www.angelfire.com; *Los Angeles Times*, January 18, 1994; *True West*, October 2006.

44. http://www.aintitcool.com/node/44840; *American Cowboy*, January 19, 2015.

45. *True West*, August, 2013; http://northhollywoodfilms.com/2016/06/14/interview-gridlocked-villain-stephen-lang-talks-cable-via-deadpool-2-avatar-sequels-and-one-long-career-in-film/.

Appendix

1. *KGUN* interview, June 29, 2018; *Tombstone News*, July 6, 2018.

2. Frank Stallone letter to author, June 13, 2018; https://www.myheraldreview.com/news/community/tombstone-actors-help-community-celebrate-th-anniversary-of-popular-movie/article_e367ae02-7cc5-11e8-bef5-b7826b972e7b.html.

3. Tombstone panel discussion, June 30, 2018.

4. *Ibid.*

5. You Tube, Interview: Michael Biehn (*Aliens, The Terminator, Tombstone*), August 6, 2017.

6. Tombstone panel discussion, June 30, 2018; letter from Billy Zane to author, July 15, 2018.

7. Zane letter to author, July 15, 2018.

8. Tombstone panel discussion, June 30, 2018.

9. *Ibid.*

10. *Ibid.*

11. *Ibid.*

12. You Tube, interview, Val Kilmer.

13. Joanna Pacula interview.

14. Tombstone, Hardwicke Q&A.

15. Bill Holmquist interview.

16. Tombstone, Porro Q&A.

17. Conversation with Joseph Porro, June 30, 2018.

Bibliography

Books

Aros, Joyce. *Murdered on the Streets of Tombstone.* Tombstone, AZ: Goose Flats Publishing, 2013.

Bailey, Lynn R. *A Tenderfoot in Tombstone: The Private Journal of George Whitwell Parsons: The Turbulent Years: 1880–82.* Tucson, AZ: Westernlore Press, 1996.

Bechdolt, Frederick R. *When the West Was Young.* Roselle, NJ: Howard Press, 2008.

Beebe, Lucius Morris, and Charles Clegg. *The American West: The Pictorial Epic of a Continent.* New York: Random House, 1989.

Bell, Bob Boze. *The Illustrated Life and Times of Doc Holliday.* Phoenix, AZ: Tri Star, 1995.

_____. *The Illustrated Life & Times of Wyatt Earp.* Peoria, AZ: Tri Star, 2008.

Bifulco, Michael. *Image of Old Tucson: Western Feature Filmmaking in the Desert.* Lexington, KY: CreateSpace, 2011.

Bill, Tony. *Movie Speak: How to Talk Like You Belong on a Film Set.* New York: Workman Publishing, 2008.

Bishop, William Henry. *Mexico, California and Arizona; Being a New and Revised Edition of Old Mexico and Her Lost Provinces.* New York: Harper & Brothers, 1900.

Blake, Michael F. *Hollywood and the O.K. Corral: Portrayals of the Gunfight and Wyatt Earp.* Jefferson, NC: McFarland, 2007.

Boni, Margaret Bradford, ed. *The Fireside Book of Favorite American Songs.* New York: Simon & Schuster, 1952.

Breakenridge, William M. *Helldorado: Bringing Law to the Mesquite.* Lincoln: University of Nebraska Press, 1992.

Burns, Walter Noble. *Tombstone: An Iliad of the Southwest.* Garden City, NY: Grosset & Dunlap, 1929.

_____. *Tombstone: Gun-Toting, Cattle Rustling Days in Old Arizona.* Garden City, NY: Grosset & Dunlap, 1929.

Clavin, Tom. *Dodge City: Wyatt Earp, Bat Masterson and the Wickedest Town in the American West.* New York: St. Martin's, 2017.

Clements, Eric L. *After the Boom in Tombstone and Jerome, Arizona. Decline in Western Resource Towns.* Reno: University of Nevada Press, 2003.

Cunningham, Doug. *Tombstone & Beyond: Guide to Movie Locations in Arizona.* Gilbert, AZ: Faraway Productions, 2004.

DeMille, Cecilia, and Mark Alan Vieira. *Cecil B. DeMille: The Art of the Hollywood Epic.* Philadelphia, PA: Running Press, 2014.

Eppings, Jane. *Around Tombstone: Ghost Towns and Gunfights.* Charleston, SC: Arcadia, 2009.

_____. *Tombstone.* Charleston, SC: Arcadia, 2003.

Fischer, Ron. *The Tombstone Business Directory 1880–1884.* Tombstone, AZ: Ron Fischer Enterprises, 2002.

Frankel, Glenn. *The Searchers: The Making of an American Legend.* New York: Bloomsbury, 2013.

Guinn, Jeff. *The Last Gunfight: The Real Story of the Shootout at the O.K. Corral—And How It Changed the American West.* New York: Simon & Schuster, 2011.

Hamilton, William. *Blessed, Life and Films of Val Kilmer.* Middletown, DE: POD, 2016.

Hughes, Howard. *Stagecoach to Tombstone: The Filmgoer's Guide to the Great Westerns.* New York: I.B. Tauris, 2008.

Jensen, Larry. *Hollywood's Railroads: Volume One, Virginia & Truckee.* Tucson, AZ: Cochetopa Press, 2015.

Johnson, David. *Johnny Ringo: King of the Cowboys.* Denton: University of North Texas Press, 2008.

Kasdan, Lawrence, and Jake Kasdan. *Wyatt Earp: The Film and the Filmmakers.* New York: Newmarket Press, 1994.

Katz, Ephraim. *The Film Encyclopedia.* New York: HarperCollins, 2005.

L'Amour, Louis. *How the West Was Won.* New York: Bantam Books, 1978.

Lawton, Paul L. *Hollywood in the Desert: The Films of Old Tucson Studios.* Tucson, AZ: Old Tucson Studios, 2009.

_____. *Old Tucson Studios.* Tucson, AZ: Old Tucson Studios, 2008.

_____. *Old Tucson Studios: Film History/Then and Now.* Tucson, AZ: Old Tucson Studios, 2009.

Lax, Roger, and Frederick Smith. *The Great Song Thesaurus.* Oxford: Oxford University Press, 1984.

Lisanti, Tom. *Dueling Harlows: Race to the Silver Screen.* Lexington, KY: CreateSpace, 2011.

Marks, Paula Mitchell. *And Die in the West: The Story of the O.K. Corral Gunfight.* Norman: University of Oklahoma Press, 1989.

Myers, John Myers. *The Last Chance: Tombstone's Early Years.* Lincoln: University of Nebraska Press, 1973.

Old Tucson Famous Movie Location: 12 Miles and 100 Years from Town. Phoenix, AZ: Petley Studios, 1980.

Rizzo, Michael. *The Art Direction Handbook for Film.* Burlington, MA: Focal Press, 2005.

Roberts, Gary L. *Doc Holliday: The Life and Legend.* Hoboken, NJ: John Wiley & Son, 2006.

Rothel, David. *An Ambush of Ghosts: A Personal Guide to Favorite Western Film Locations.* Madison, NC: Empire Publishing, 1990.

Russell, Mary Doria. *Doc.* New York: Ballantine Books, 2011.

Schieffelin, Ed. *Destination Tombstone: Adventures of a Prospector.* Meza, AZ: Royal Spectrum Publishing, 1996.

Sherayko, Peter. *The Fringe of Hollywood: The Art of Making a Western.* Aqua Dulce, CA: Caravan West Productions, 2011.

_____. *Tombstone: The Guns and Gear.* Aqua Dulce, CA: Caravan West Productions, 2010.

Stephens, John Richard. *Wyatt Earp Speaks! Written by Wyatt Earp and Others.* New York: Fall River Press, 2009.

Taylor, Don. *Tombstone: The First Fifty Years, 1879 to 1929.* Tucson, AZ: Old West Research & Publishing, 2010.

Tefertiller, Casey. *Wyatt Earp: The Life Behind the Legend.* New York: John Wiley & Sons, 1997.

Time-Life. *100 Years of Hollywood.* Our American Century. Richmond, VA: Time-Life, 1999.

Tippette, Giles. *Tombstone.* New York: Berkley Books, 1994.

Traywick, Ben T. *1879 Census Tombstone as Taken by Pima County Sheriff Charles A. Shibell on September 18, 19, and 20, 1879.* Tombstone, AZ: Red Marie's Books, 1999.

_____. *This Is Tombstone: The Town Too Tough to Die.* Tombstone, AZ: Red Marie's Books.

Trimble, Marshall. *Arizona Outlaws and Lawmen: Gunslingers, Bandits, Heroes and Peacekeepers.* Charleston, SC: The History Press, 2015.

Underhill, Lonnie E. *The Bird Cage Theater, Tombstone, Arizona.* Gilbert, AZ: Roan Horse Press, 2016.

Van Sijll, Jennifer. *Cinematic Storytelling: The 100 Most Powerful Film Conventions Every Filmmaker Must Know.* San Francisco: Michael Wiese Productions, 2005.

Wilcox, Victoria. *Gone West: The Saga of Doc Holliday, Book Two.* Atlanta, GA: Knox Robinson Publishing, 2016.

_____. *Inheritance: The Saga of Doc Holliday, Book One.* Atlanta, GA: Knox Robinson Publishing, 2016.

_____. *The Last Decision: The Saga of Doc Holliday, Book Three.* Atlanta, GA: Knox Robinson Publishing, 2016.

Willson, Claire E. *Mimes and Miners: A Historical Study of the Theater in Tombstone.* Tucson: University of Arizona Press, 1935.

Articles in Newspapers, Magazines, Periodicals

Alderidge, David. "Going West: David Alderidge Meets Kurt Russell and Val Kilmer—Riding into Town to Promote *Tombstone.*" *Film Review,* March 1994.

Allen, Paul. "Earps Ride into Tucson: Filming on the Movie 'Tombstone' Will Begin May 17 in Southern Arizona." Undated.

Anderson, Janette. "'Alright Lunger … Let's Do It!'" *Trail Dust,* Winter 1994, Vol. II, No. 3.

_____. "A Powerful Performance." *Trail Dust,* Winter 1994, Vol. II. No. 3.

_____. "Stallone: Rides Alone … By Request." *Trail Dust,* Fall/Winter 2008, Vol. VII, No. 1.

Arar, Yardena, "Getting Back in the Saddle Tough for Russell." *The Lincoln Star,* January 16, 1994.

Archerd, Army. "Just for Variety." *Variety,* February 22, 1993.

_____. "Just for Variety." *Variety,* May 12, 1993.

Armstrong, Gene. "Here Lies Tombstone; Residents Look Forward to a Boost from Movie." *Arizona Daily Star,* December 25, 1993.

Ayscough, Suzan. "Costner, Kasdan Link on Earp Pic." *Variety,* December 17, 1992.

_____. "Tig Prods. Has Films, TV in Works." *Variety,* April 29, 1993.

Ayscough, Suzan, and Christian Moerk. "Wild West: Dueling Earp Pix Ink Stars." *Variety,* May 6, 1993.

Baller, Bryn. "Old Tucson: How the West Was Redone." *Arizona Daily Star,* January 3, 1997.

Barra, Allen. "'Tombstone' Full of Box-Office Life Movies: The Surprise Hit about the Bustling Western Frontier Town Soon Will Reach $40 Million in Domestic Grosses, Despite a Troubled Start." *Los Angeles Times,* January 18, 1994.

_____. "'Tombstone' Is Still a Draw." *The Philadelphia Inquirer,* February 5, 1994.

_____. "Tributes to Kevin Jarre (1954–2011): The Story of Tombstone's Creator, Told by Those Who Know Him." *True West,* October 4, 2011.

Beaks, Mr. "Mr. Beaks Takes a Trip Back to Tombstone with Curley Bill Brocius Himself, Powers Boothe!" April 27, 2010. www.aintitcool.com.

Beck, Henry Cabot. "Farewell to Curly Bill." *True West,* September 2017.

_____. "The Tombstone that Might Have Been." *True West,* October 4, 2011.

_____. "Val Kilmer Returns." *True West,* August 1, 2008.

_____. "The 'Western' Godfather." *True West,* October 1, 2006.

Bell, Bob Boze. "Behind the Eight Ball." *True West,* September 2005.

_____. "50 Things You Don't Know about Wyatt Earp." *True West,* July 2003.

_____. "The Fight Scene That Kills Off Kevin." *True West,* October 2006.

_____. "The Mysterious Death of Johnny Ringo." *True West,* August 2005.

_____. "Wyatt Goes Rogue." *True West,* May 2010.

Boessenecker, John. "The Rise of the Cow-boys." *True West,* September 2017.

Borders, Meredith. "Showdown at Two O.K. Corrals." March 31, 2016. http://birthmoviesdeath.com/2016/03/31/showdown-at-two-ok-corrals.

Boston, John. "'Wyatt Earp.' (Long Pause). The Saddlesore of Westerns." *The Signal,* June 24, 1994.

Bowles, Duncan. "Cary Elwes Interview: Saw 3D, Glory and The Princess Bride." October 25, 2010. http://www.denofgeek.com/us/movies/saw/16540/cary-elwes-interview-saw-3d-glory-and-the-princess-bride.

Brett, Anwar. "Wyatt Earp." *Films Review,* October 1994.

Brodie, John. "Studios Seeing Double." *Variety,* August 22, 1994.

Brodine, John, and Jay Greene. "Jilted Hits Haunt H'Wood." *Variety,* August 17, 1994.

Brown, A.K. "'Old Tucson' Nearly Beyond Repair Stage." *Tucson Daily Citizen,* December 21, 1945.

Brown, J.P.S. "Where Legends Strode." *American Cowboy,* May-June 2004.

Bullock. Diane. "Why Is Christmas Day a Go-To for Movie Releases?" www.minyanville.com/business-news/editors-pick/articles/why-christmas-day-movie-releases-the/12/20/2013/id/53117.

Busch, Anita M. "Cinergi Carves 'Tombstone.'" *The Hollywood Reporter,* February 12, 1993.

Byrge, Duane. "'Tombstone.'" *The Hollywood Reporter,* December 23, 1993.

Canby, Vincent. "Black Combat Bravey in the Civil War." *New York Times,* December 14, 1989.

Champlin, Charles. "Threads That Led to the Making of 'Glory': Movies: Screenwriter Kevin Jarre Recalls the 'Unbelievable Odyssey' in Getting the Tale of a Black Civil War Regiment Made." *Los Angeles Times,* January 18, 1990.

Christopher, James. "Texas Frightmare 2012: Tales from 'Tombstone.'" www.slackerwood.com/node/2929.

Clancy, Michael, and Dolores Tropiano. "Geraldo Mines Mother Lode of Local Angst." *Arizona Republic,* May 12, 1993.

_____. "Jan D'Atri Cast as Star Angler on Travel Show." *Arizona Republic,* June 13, 1993.

Claridy, Christina. "Indians and Rangers in 19th Century Texas." Texas Ranger Research Center. www.texasranger.org.

Cogshell, Tim. "Entertainment? Yes. History Lesson? No." *Entertainment Today,* December 24, 1993.

_____. "No Complaints." *Entertainment Today,* December 24–30, 1993.

Coleman, Jason. "Interview: 'Gridlocked' Villain Stephen Lang Talks Cable Via Deadpool 2, Avatar Sequels and One Long Career in Film." June 14, 2016. www.northhollywoodfilms.com.

"A Computer-Generated Imagery (CGI) History." May 11, 2001. www.computerstories.net.

Corella, Hipolito, and Joe Burchell. "Old Tucson Studios Set to Reopen Thursday." *Arizona Daily Star,* December 31, 1996.

Cosulich, Bernice. "Huge Construction Task Preceded Film Making." *Arizona Daily Star,* November 15, 1940.

Cowan, Ron. "'Tombstone' Oozes Blood, Shootouts." *Statesman Journal,* December 31, 1993.

"Cowboy Christmas." *The Hollywood Reporter,* November 24, 1993.

Davidson, Miriam, and Richard F. Casey. "Fire Burns Old Tucson: Movie Location Nearly Gutted: Cause Unknown." *Arizona Republic,* April 25, 1995.

Demsey, Paul. "Tombstone." *Screen International,* January 23, 1994.

Denby, David. "Balance of Terror." *The New Yorker,* January 14, 2008.

DeWeese, G. Daniel. "The Tombstone Legacy." *True West,* July 9, 2013.

Duarte, Carmen. "After 20 Years, Firefighters Recall Old Tucson Inferno." *Arizona Daily Star,* April 23, 2015.

_____. "Arson Suspected as Cause of Fire at Old Tucson." *Arizona Daily Star,* April 27, 1995.

_____. "'A Great History … Suddenly It's Gone': Former Restorer Laments Loss as Fire Clues Sought." *Arizona Daily Star,* April 26, 1995.

_____. "Steady Signs of Life at Old Tucson." *Arizona Daily Star,* June 10, 1995.

Dutka, Elanie. "Hollywood Habits: Leave 'Wyatt Earp' off his Tombstone." *Los Angeles Times,* August 5, 1994.

Easton, Nina. "Costner May Put Morgan Creek Ahead of Robin Hood Pack." *Los Angeles Times,* July 24, 1990.

_____. "A Flock of Robins." *Los Angeles Times,* July 26, 1990.

Ebert, Roger. "Costner Faces Another Showdown." *The Press Democrat,* June 26, 1994.

_____. "Glory." January 12, 1990. www.rogerebert. com.

_____. "Wyatt Earp." June 24, 1994. www.roger ebert.com/reviews/wyatt-earp-1994.

Eller, Claudia. "Costner Nears 'Prince' Deal; Fox, Tri-Star up a Creek." *Variety,* July 23, 1990.

_____. "Roth Feels Robbed on 'Robin.'" *Variety,* July 12, 1990.

Elson, Jerry W. "Tri Cultures of New Mexico." *Rangelands* 14(5), October 1992.

Eppinga, Jane. "Tombstone's Bird Cage Theater." *Arizona Capital Times,* May 2, 2014.

_____. "Tombstone's Deadliest Gunfighter." *Arizona Capital Times,* March 23, 2012.

Fedunak, Steffannie, and Steve Meissner. "Blaze Destroys Old Tucson: Landmark Is Engulfed in Minutes." *Arizona Daily Star,* April 25, 1995.

Fenster, Bob. "'Tombstone': A film Too Tough to Sit Through." *Arizona Republic,* December 25, 1993.

Fine, Marshall. "What 'Wyatt Earp' Really Needs Is Some Action Scenes." *The Desert Sun,* June 24, 1994.

Fleming, Michael. "Costner and Kasdan Heading West Again." *Variety,* December 7, 1992.

_____. "Did Russell Muscle Megapic Payday?" *Variety,* February 15, 1993.

Friedman, Roger D. "Kilmer's Quiet Success: Val Kilmer, Who's Starring in 'Tombstone, Prefers not to Make Too Much of His Popularity." *Los Angeles Times,* December 31, 1993.

Frook, John Evan. "Pre-Xmas Exhib Anxiety: Delivery Snafus on BV's 'Tombstone' Feared." *Daily Variety,* December 23, 1993.

_____. "'Tombstone' Delivery Confirmed." *Daily Variety,* December 27, 1993.

Galbraith, Jane. "Wait, There's More: Didn't Get Your Fill of Oaters Last Week? Read on." *Los Angeles Times,* December 12, 1993.

Gallant, Kathryn. "Morgans Making Magic in Movies." *The Morgan Horse,* July 2014.

Goldstein, Patrick. "Previews—How Early Is Too Early?" *The Los Angeles Times,* February 6, 1994.

Grant, James. "Wyatt Earp's Fifth Cousin Takes His Best Shot Movies: With Two Films Due out on His Famous Relative, Glen Wyatt Earp Figured There Had to be a Part for Him." *Los Angeles Times,* December 25, 1993.

Hall, Jacob. "Kurt Russell on the American Tough Guy and His New Cannibal Western." *Esquire,* October 25, 2015.

"Hanging Out with Ol' Dobe—The Interview." www.jwayne.com.

Henry, Bonnie. "'46 Ruins Salvaged." *Arizona Daily Star,* August 1, 1990.

Herdy, Amy. "Tombstone Rides On: The Cast of 'Tombstone' Shares Their Stories from the Set." *American Cowboy,* January 19, 2015.

Holden, Stephen. "A Fractious Old West in a Modern Moral Universe." *The New York Times,* December 24, 1993.

Honeycutt, Kirk. "Dueling Earps at Uni, Warners." *The Hollywood Reporter,* December 17, 1992.

_____. "Kennedy Rides 'Savage Land.'" *The Hollywood Reporter,* January 12, 1993.

"Johnny Ringo Remembers Tombstone." www.ign. com/articles.

Joyner, J Courtney. "10 Questions for Michael Biehn." *True West,* July 9, 2013.

_____. "Tombstone at 20: The Movie Too Tough to Die." *True West,* August 2013.

Keating, Micheline. "Facelifting Old Tucson." *Tucson Daily Citizen,* April 4, 1958.

_____. "The New Old Tucson." *Tucson Daily Citizen,* July 20, 1968.

_____. "What Became of Old Tucson." *Tucson Daily Citizen,* February 19, 1966.

Kimmey, Bill. "Million Dollar Project." *Tucson Daily Star,* May 8, 1959.

Kiss, Tony. "Val Kilmer Rescues 'Tombstone' as Doc Holliday." *Asheville Citizen-Times,* December 31, 1993.

Kit, Zorianna. "Producing Features." *MovieMaker,* December 1, 1996.

Klady, Cinefile. "Jarre off 'Tombstone.'" *Variety,* June 14, 1993.

_____. "Pigs, Ducks, Geese and Lassie on Comeback Trail." *Variety,* June 29, 1993.

Knight, Jacob. "I Am Legend: Tombstone & the Cinematic Perfection of Wyatt Earp and Doc Holliday." https://cinapse.co/i-am-legend-tombstone-the-cinematic-perfection-of-wyatt-earp-and-doc-holliday-490267f15acc.

Koltnow, Barry. "Russell Entranced by Real Story Behind the O.K. Corral." *Arizona Daily Star,* December 31, 1993.

Kreutz, Douglas. "Flames Took Irreplaceable Sets, Props." *Arizona Daily Star,* April 26, 1995.

Levitt, Shelly. "Kevin Costner's Hawaii Uh-Oh." *People,* May 29, 1995.

Levy, Emanuel. "Review: 'Tombstone.'" *Variety,* December 22, 1993.

Long, Tom. "Val Kilmer Gets Buried Beneath 'Tombstone.'" *Santa Cruz Sentinel,* December 31, 1993.

Loose, Duane. "Introduction to the DCC Pre-Production Process." www.informit.com.

Mal, Vincent. "A Dune Deal. MGM Breaks the

Banks and Heads to Outer Space with Stargate." *Virginian-Pilot*, October 29, 1994.

Marx, Andy. "Studios Fast to Corral Western Pix." *Variety*, April 8, 1993.

Mattern, Hal. "Earp 'Family' Western." *Arizona Republic*, December 22, 1993.

McGahey, Terry. "Galeyville and Curly Bill." *The American Cowboy Chronicles*, August 22, 2016.

Moore, Richard. "The Silver King: Ed Schieffelin, Prospector." *Oregon Historical Quarterly*, Vol. 87, No. 4 (Winter, 1986): 367–387.

Namiotka, Jim. "Famed V&T Locomotive in Tucson Fire." *Reno Gazette-Journal*, April 28, 1995.

Nelson, Valarie J. "Kevin Jarre Dies at 56; Screenwriter of 'Glory' and 'Tombstone.'" *Los Angeles Times*, April 22, 2011.

Noglows, Paul. "Cinergi Financial Picture Rosy." *Variety*, August 16, 1994.

Noon, Adolphus Henry. "A Visit to Tombstone City." *Chicago Tribune*, January 5, 1878.

Oliver, Myrna. "George P. Cosmatos, 64; Director Was Known for Saving Troubled Projects." *Los Angeles Times*, April 27, 2005.

O'Neill, Sean. "Dumb Fun: Tombstone Succeeds with a Bang." *Los Angeles Village View*, December 31–January 6, 1994.

Orange, B. Alan. "Michael Biehn Revisits Johnny Ringo in Tombstone." www.movieweb.com.

O'Steen, Kathleen. "Gordon Leaves Largo." *Variety*, January 15, 1994.

Parke, Henry C. "Farewell to Curly Bill." *True West*, August 25, 2017.

Parker, Melody. "'Tombstone' Goes Out with Guns Blazin'." *The Courier*, December 31, 1993.

Pavillard, Dan. "More than $1 Million Spent in Tucson on 'The High Chaparral." *Tucson Daily Citizen*, October 9, 1967.

_____. "Old Tucson Gets 'Alamo' Props." *Tucson Daily Citizen*, November 26, 1966.

Pearson, Ben. "Kurt Russell on His Approach to Ego in 'Guardians Vol. 2' and the Most Surprising Thing About 'Tombstone.'" www.slashfilm.com.

Pearson, Harry. "Tombstone." *Films in Review*, Vol XLV, no. 3/4, issue 2.

Pedersen, Ann-Eve. "Fire Marshal's Office Failed to Inspect Park." *Arizona Daily Star*, April 26, 1995.

_____. "Old Tucson's Fire Readiness Found Lacking." *Arizona Daily Star*, May 14, 1995.

Perry, Vern. "'Tombstone' Laser Disc Isn't Worth the Price." *The Dispatch*, July 20, 1994.

Prentice, Melissa. "Summertime Arson Spree Still Frustrates Authorities." *Arizona Daily Star*, October 17, 1995.

Pristin, Terry. "Brandon Lee's Mother Claims Negligence Caused His Death." *Los Angeles Times*, August 11, 1993.

Rainer, Peter. "Gunfight at the *Auteur's* Corral." *The Los Angeles Times*, July 2, 1995.

_____. "'Tombstone' Latest in a New Line of Designer Westerns." *Los Angeles Times*, December 25, 1993.

Rawlinson, John. "$100,000 Fire at Old Tucson Destroys Set." *Arizona Daily Star*, June 7, 1969.

Rich, Nathaniel. "The Deceptive Director." *The New York Review of Books*, November 6, 2008.

Riley, Tim. "'Tombstone' Goes for Authentic Western Look." *Ukiah Daily Journal*, January 7, 1994.

Rodd, David. "DGA & WGA Members Use Fake Names to Work Nonunion Reality Shows." www.deadline.com.

Ryan, Desmond. "'Tombstone' Film Arrives D.O.A." *The Monitor*, December 31, 1993.

Ryan, James. "Kurt Russell Carves His Name on 'Tombstone.'" *Quad-City Times*, January 2, 1994.

_____. "Studios Are Poised to Stampede with More Westerns." *The San Bernardino County Sun*, April 16, 1993.

Ryan, Pat M. "Tombstone Theater Tonight! A Chronicle of Entertainment on the Southwestern Mining Frontier." *The Smoke Signal*, Spring 1966.

"Sam Elliott on George Clooney's Eyes, Jeff Bridges' Dudeness, and Working with Ron Swanson." October 10, 2013. www.avclub.com.

Schuldt, Scott. "Costner Calls His Film Epic." *The Oklahoman*, June 24, 1994.

Scott, Walter. "Personality Parade." *Arizona Republic*, July 18, 1993.

Simon, Stephanie. "Fire Ravages Old Tucson Film Studio Blaze: Three-fourths of Facility's Wooden Buildings, Seen in Hundreds of TV and Movie Westerns, Are Destroyed or Damaged. Priceless Artifacts Are Also Lost." *Los Angeles Times*, April 26, 1995.

Skinner, M. Scot. "'Lackluster' Fitting Epitaph for New Movie." *Arizona Daily Star*, December 25, 1993.

Staff Writer. *Arizona Daily Star*, August 23, 1879.

_____. "Arizona Letters." *Los Angeles Herald*, March 7, July 18, September 27–28, October 29, 1879.

_____. *Arizona Weekly Citizen*, December 4, 1880.

_____. *Arizona Weekly Star*, December 9, 1879.

_____. "Balm for the Burn." *Arizona Daily Star*, May 19, 1995.

_____. "Cast in the Shadows." *Arizona Republic*, July 16, 1993.

_____. *Chicago Daily Tribune*, January 5, 1879.

_____. "'China Beach' Star Stays Busy." *Sun Sentinel*, October 1, 1993.

_____. "Cinergi Will Be Carving 'Tombstone' in May." *The Hollywood Reporter*, April 13, 1993.

_____. "Coast News Clippings." *The Sacramento Daily Record-Union*, March 11, 1880.

_____. "County Acquires State Land Title." *Arizona Daily Star,* May 5, 1942.

_____. *Daily Arizona Citizen,* November 3, 1879.

_____. "Early Buzz on Hot AFM Titles." *Variety,* March 1, 1993.

_____. "Early Replica of Tucson Will Be Built here." *Arizona Daily Star,* July 22, 1939.

_____. "Film Maker Cites Wide Opportunities in Tucson." *Arizona Daily Star,* June 10, 1966.

_____. "Film Men Ponder 'Arizona' Locale." *Arizona Daily Star,* July 20, 1939.

_____. "A Flourishing Mining Town." *The Sacramento Daily Record-Union,* May 3, 1880.

_____. "For Sale: One Unit Nearby Movie Unit." *Arizona Daily Star,* April 22, 1942.

_____. "Fort to Be Constructed at Old Tucson Site." *Arizona Daily Star,* February 23, 1960.

_____. "Fox Changes Its 'Robin Hood,'" *Los Angeles Times,* August 7, 1990.

_____. "Gambling in the Old West." *The Westerner,* Vol. I, No. I.

_____. "Glory." *Variety,* December 13, 1989.

_____. "Group Lease 'Old Tucson.'" *Arizona Daily Star,* Jul 21, 1959.

_____. "Hollywood Pictures Welcomes Audiences Back to the Old West in 'Tombstone.'" *Drama-Logue,* January 13–19, 1994.

_____. "In Brief: Tombstone Director George Cosmatos Dies." *The Guardian,* April 26, 2005.

_____. "Inferno Claims Old Tucson." *Tucson Citizen,* April 25, 1995.

_____. "Interview with Virgil Earp." *Arizona Daily Star,* May 30, 1882.

_____. "Items from Tucson." *The Sacramento Daily Record-Union,* July 14, 1880.

_____. "Jaycees Lease Old Tucson Set." *Arizona Daily Star,* June 6, 1946.

_____. "Jaycees May Operate Set at Old Tucson." *Tucson Daily Star,* March 7, 1946.

_____. "Jaycees Name Group to run 'Old Tucson.'" *Arizona Daily Star,* April 26, 1946.

_____. "Jaycees Plan Operation of 'Old Tucson.'" *Tucson Daily Star,* March 21, 1946.

_____. "Jaycees to Stage 'Old Tucson 4 Color Days.'" *Arizona Daily Star,* November 14, 1956.

_____. "Jaycees Vote to Take Over 'Old Tucson.'" *Tucson Daily Star,* April 11, 1946.

_____. "Jaycees Will Hear Report on Rodeo Sales." *Tucson Daily Star,* February 20, 1946.

_____. "Kelland Picture 'Set' Is Leased." *Arizona Republic,* July 22, 1939.

_____. "Kinship." *Variety,* June 28, 1993.

_____. "Lease on Old Tucson Replica for 5 Years Is Given to Jaycees." *The Arizona Daily Star,* April 12, 1946.

_____. "Letter from Tombstone." *Arizona Daily Star,* January 21, 1879.

_____. "Local Matters." *The Arizona Sentinel,* December 14, 1878.

_____. "Local Matters." *The Arizona Sentinel,* January 11, 1879.

_____. "Local Splinters." *Tombstone Daily Epitaph,* December 28, 1881.

_____. "Male Lead of 'Arizona' Named." *Arizona Daily Star,* March 16, 1940.

_____. "Mining News." *Weekly Republican,* December 21, 1878.

_____. "Old Tucson Acquires Historic Locomotive." *Tucson Daily Citizen,* July 31, 1970.

_____. "Old Tucson Amusement Center Is Dedicated." *Arizona Daily Star,* January 30, 1960.

_____. "Old Tucson Expansion Plan Will Give More of the Past." *Tucson Daily Citizen,* December 13, 1976.

_____. "Old Tucson Fire Probably Arson-Caused." *Arizona Republic,* April 27, 1995.

_____. "Old Tucson Gets Kansas 'Town.'" *Arizona Daily Star,* September 8, 1960.

_____. "Old Tucson Given Jaycees." *Tucson Daily Star,* June 6, 1946.

_____. "Old Tucson Is Appraised for Pima Purchase." *Tucson Daily Citizen,* February 20, 1942.

_____. "Old Tucson Is to Be Repaired by Supervisors." *Tucson Daily Citizen,* February 12, 1946.

_____. "Old Tucson Set May Go to JC's." *Tucson Daily Star,* April 2, 1946.

_____. "Old Tucson Set Offered J'Cees." *Arizona Daily Star,* February 13, 1946.

_____. "Old Tucson Set to Be Kept in Repair." *Tucson Daily Citizen,* February 16, 1946.

_____. "Old Tucson Spending $100,000." *Tucson Daily Citizen,* November 15, 1960.

_____. "Old Tucson Studio Movie Set Goes up in Flames." *Sheboygan Press,* April 25, 1995.

_____. "Old Tucson to Dedicate Sound Stage Next Month." *Tucson Daily Citizen,* October 19, 1967.

_____. "'Old Tucson' Will Live Again; to Be Rebuilt for New Movie." *Arizona Daily Star,* November 17, 1946.

_____. "'Old West' Town Planned as New Tourist Showcase." *Arizona Daily Star,* May 6, 1959.

_____. "Opening of Old Tucson to Be a Colorful Affair." *Tucson Daily Citizen,* January 15, 1960.

_____. "Outtakes." *Los Angeles Times,* February 4, 1990.

_____. "Pacific Coast Items." *The Sacramento Daily Record-Union,* April 21, 1880.

_____. "Pacific Coast Items." *The Sacramento Daily Union,* July 2, 1880.

_____. "Patent Is Issued for 'Old Tucson.'" *Arizona Daily Star,* May 27, 1942.

_____. "Peter Sherayko Takes us Behind the Scenes of the Movie Tombstone." March 23, 2012.

_____. "Pima Buys Half of Old Tucson Land." *Tucson Daily Citizen,* April 23, 1942.

_____. "Russell, Actor for Hire, Rides Shotgun to Save 'Tombstone.'" *The Age,* January 27, 1994.

_____. *San Francisco Chronicle,* November 28, 1879.

_____. "Sound Stage Contract Signed." *Tucson Daily Citizen,* July 7, 1967.

_____. "Southern Arizona Wood and Timber." *Arizona Weekly Citizen,* October 26, 1878.

_____. "Stars Have Roles in Arizona Film and Land Plots." *Arizona Republic,* November 7, 1993.

_____. "Tombstone." *Arizona Republic,* December 24, 1993.

_____. *Tombstone Epitaph,* September 14, 1880.

_____. *Tombstone Epitaph,* September 29, 1880.

_____. "Tombstoned!" *Film Review,* October 1994.

_____. "Video Hot Sheet." *Statesman Journal,* June 3, 1994.

_____. "Western Is Heavy-Handed." *The Paris News,* January 16, 1994.

_____. "Wyatt Earp Gang: 3 Films and 1 Actor." *Arizona Republic,* August 4, 1993.

Starl, Susan. "Costner Takes a Break from Filming." *The Desert Sun,* June 24, 1994.

Stimac, Elias. "Hollywood Pictures Welcomes Audiences Back to the Old West in 'Tombstone.'" *Drama-Logue,* January 13–19, 1994.

Thompson, Anne. "Quiet Earp." *Entertainment Weekly,* July 15, 1994.

_____. "Two Wyatt Earp Films in Production." *Entertainment Weekly,* January 8, 1993.

_____. "'Wyatt Earp' Trampled by 'Tombstone.'" *Entertainment Weekly,* July 15, 1994.

Vervier, Catherine. "How the West Was Won—by the Old Latin Tongue." *Independent,* January 30, 1994.

Villarreal, Phil. "Tucson on Television." *Arizona Daily Star,* January 20, 2008.

Wagoner, J.J. "Overstocking of the Ranges in Southern Arizona During the 1870's and 1880's." *Arizoniana,* Vol. 2, No. 1 (Spring 1961).

Weeks, Janet. "'90210's' Jason Priestly Sheds His Nice Guy Image in 'Coldblooded.'" *Santa Cruz Sentinel,* September 12, 1995.

Weintraub, Steve. "Director Catherine Hardwicke Says There Are 12 Deleted Scenes on the TWILIGHT DVD!" http://collider.com/director-catherine-hardwicke-says-there-are-12-deleted-scenes-on-the-twilight-dvd/.

Wilkinson, Wendy. "Thomas Haden Church." *Cowboys & Indians,* June 2010.

Wolf, Jeanne. "The Earp Story Is Hot as Kurt Russell and Kevin Costner Tackle the Role." *The San Bernardino County Sun,* December 30, 1993.

Newspapers

The Age (Melbourne, Victoria, Australia)
Arizona Daily Star (Tucson, Arizona)
Arizona Republic (Phoenix, Arizona)
The Arizona Sentinel (Yuma, Arizona)
Arizona Weekly Citizen (Tucson, Arizona)
Arizona Weekly Star (Tucson, Arizona)
Asheville Citizen-Times (Asheville, North Carolina)
Chicago Daily Tribune (Chicago, Illinois)
Chicago Times (Chicago, Illinois)
The Courier (Waterloo, Iowa)
Daily Arizona Citizen (Tucson, Arizona)
The Desert Sun (Palm Springs, California)
The Dispatch (Moline, Illinois)
The Hollywood Reporter (Hollywood, California)
Independent (London, England)
The Lincoln Star (Lincoln, Nebraska)
The Los Angeles Times (Los Angeles, California)
The Monitor (McAllen, Texas)
New York Times (New York City)
The Oklahoman (Oklahoma City, Oklahoma)
The Paris News (Paris, Texas)
The Petaluma Argus-Courier (Petaluma, California)
The Philadelphia Inquirer (Philadelphia, Pennsylvania)
The Press Democrat (Santa Rosa, California)
Quad-City Times (Davenport, Iowa)
Reno Gazette-Journal (Reno, Nevada)
Sacramento Daily Record-Union (Sacramento, California)
The San Bernardino County Sun (San Bernardino, California)
San Francisco Chronicle (San Francisco, California)
The San Francisco Exchange (San Francisco, California)
Santa Cruz Sentinel (Santa Cruz, California)
The Sheboygan Press (Sheboygan, Wisconsin)
The Signal (Santa Clara, California)
Statesman Journal (Salem, Oregon)
Sun Sentinel (Broward County, Florida)
Tombstone Epitaph (Tombstone, Arizona)
Tucson Citizen (Tucson, Arizona)
Ukiah Daily Journal (Ukiah, California)
Variety (Los Angeles, California)
Virginian-Pilot (Norfolk, Virginia)
Weekly Republican (Phoenix, Arizona)

Interviews

All interviews were conducted by the author, except the ones indicated by an asterisk. Those were found online or in newspapers and magazines, among other sources.

Tomas Arana—Frank Stillwell
Allen Barra—Journalist/author
Bob Boze Bell—Executive editor, *True West* magazine
Michael Biehn*—Johnny Ringo
Michael Blake—Author
Emily Blanton—Saloon girl
Powers Boothe*—Curly Bill Brocius
James Brooks—Holiday Inn room service waiter
Bruce Broughton—Composer and arranger
Frank Brown—Mescal set caretaker
Robert Burke—Frank McLaury
Reggie Byrum—Buckaroo
Harry Carey, Jr.*—Marshal Fred White
Donna Cline—Storyboard artist and Illustrator
Renee Clothier—Wardrobe Manager/Art/Prop/ Scenic department at Old Tucson Studio
George Cosmatos*—Director
Dave Cox—Davis Leather Company
Jerry Crandall—Buckaroo
James Danicic—Hot Head Technician
Dana Delany*—Josephine Marcus
Jeff Dolan—Buckaroo
Samuel Dolan—Buckaroo/Young boy with Earp horse
Jim Dunham—Miner/historian
Sam Elliott*—Virgil Earp
Edie Fasano—Wife of screenwriter John Fasano
John Fasano*—Associate producer/screenwriter
Jay Gammons—Owner Gammon's Gulch
Joanne Gammons—Owner Gammon's Gulch
Gary Gang—Wrangler
Billy Getzwiler—Tucson transportation captain
Glen Gold—Town person
Dana Loraine Goodge—Stand-in/featured extra
Bo Gray (Greigh)—Wes Fuller
Catherine Hardwicke—Production designer
Charlton Heston*—Henry Hooker
Tom Hirt—Hat maker
James Jacks*—Producer
Grant James—Dr. Goodfellow
Kevin Jarre*—Director/screenwriter
Rob Jensen—Head of entertainment, Old Tucson Studios
Jake Johnson—Buckaroo
Courtney Joyner—Author/journalist
Val Kilmer*—Doc Holliday
Billy Lang—Buckaroo
Stephen Lang—Ike Clanton
Paul Lawton—Old Tucson historian
Dianne Lebovitz—Cinergi executive
Terry Leonard—2nd unit director/stunts
Karie Lord—Mother Bobby Stevens—Buckaroo
Tony Malanowski—Associate Producer *Tombstone* DVD restoration
Matt Marich—Set dresser
Elly McFadden—Manager, marketing and sales, Tucson Holiday Inn/co-owner Bobby Joe's Irish Pub, Mescal

Terry McGahey—Cowboy in saloon
Lee McKechnie—Buckaroo/wrangler/stand-in
Steve Melton—Property master
Christopher Mitchum—Hooker Ranch foreman
Jeffrey Morey—Historian/consultant
Joseph Musso—Storyboard artist/Production illustrator
Joanna Pacula—Big Nose Kate
Robert Palmquist—Historian/consultant
Bill Paxton*—Morgan Earp
John Peel—Buckaroo
Nikki Pelley—Emigrant woman wagon train
Eddie Perez—Cowboy in saloon
John Philbin—Tom McLaury
Joseph Porro—Costume Designer
Gregory Poulos—Assistant prop master
Mark Rainfield—Key Grip
Christian Ramirez—Buckaroo
Jeff Ramsey—Mexican Rurale/stuntman
Thell Reed*—Armorer
Kevin Reem—Associate Producer *Tombstone* DVD restoration
Garrett Roberts—Buckaroo
Jan Robinson—Townsperson
Michael Rooker*—Sherm McMasters
Kane Rubalcaba—Buckaroo
David Russell—Storyboard artist/Illustrator
Kurt Russell*—Wyatt Earp
Valerie Saunders—Lighting and prop crew member
Charles Schneider—Professor Gillman
Peter Sherayko—Texas Jack Vermillion
J. Nathan Simmons—Town person
Forrie Smith—Pony Deal
Frank Stallone—Ed Bailey
Dickie Stanley—Stuntman/ Drunken miner
Brian Stewart—Propmaker
Chris Swinney—Set medic
Josh Swinney—Child actor
Jerry Tarantino—Buckaroo
Kathy Tarantino—Stand-in
Ann Lockhart Taylor—Wife of Adam Taylor, 1st assistant director
Buck Taylor*—Turkey Creek Jack Johnson
Don Taylor—Tombstone historian
Rick Terry—Buckaroo
R.L. Tolbert—Stuntman
Mark Tovsen—Undertaker/Funeral supplies
Blumes Tracy—Special effects
Ben Traywick—Tombstone historian/author
Bobby Vincent—Buckaroo
Victor Vizcarra—Holiday Inn, Tucson waiter/busboy/room service
Michael Walker—B camera focus puller
Charley Ward—Buckaroo
Tom Ward—Buckaroo
Kip Wolverton—Wrangler/stagecoach driver

Red Wolverton—Owner of/stagecoach driver
Wendy Wolverton—Wrangler
Cindy Wykes—1st Monkey Faust sequence
Billy Zane*—Romulus Fabian
Lisa Zane—Josephine Marcus/Kate Horony/Choreographer
Larry Zeug—Buckaroo/gunsmith

Other Sources

Scripts

John Fasano: June 24, 1993; July 1, 1993; July 2, 1993; July 3, 1993; July 6, 1993.
Kevin Jarre: June 25, 1992; November 5, 1992; January 30, 1993; March 15, 1993; March 18, 1993.

Television

American Experience. Wyatt Earp: Hero, Outlaw, Legend. Paul Hutton, historian. PBS, 2010.

Special Collections

Buzz Feitshans collection (abbrev. BFC). Margaret Herrick Library, Academy of Motion Picture Arts and Sciences.
Love, Alice E. *History of Tombstone to 1887.* Unpublished thesis. Tucson: The University of Arizona, 1933.
Peterson, Thomas H. "The Tombstone Stagecoach Lines, 1878–1903: A Study in Frontier Transportation." Thesis, University of Arizona, 1968.

Websites

aintitcool.com.
americancowboychronicles.com/2016/08/galey ville-and-curly-bill.
angelfire.com/ga/napalousa/tomb.html.
archive.is/20120713003618.
archive.org/web/20090428084917.
armchairgeneral.com/forums/showthread.php?t= 109425.
avclub.com.
bignosekates.info/history1.html.
birthmoviesdeath.com/2016/03/31/showdown-at-two-ok-corrals.
bradleydpettit.blogspot.com/2011/06/my-inter view-with-actor-michael-biehn.html.
cdn2-b.examiner.com/article/making-tombstone-the-movie.
cinapse.co/i-am-legend-tombstone-the-cinematic-perfection-of-wyatt-earp-and-doc-holliday-490 267f15acc
collider.com/director-catherine-hardwicke-says-there-are-12-deleted-scenes-on-the-twilight-dvd/.
computerstories.net.
confederateamericanpride.com/OldWest/DocHolli day.

deadline.com/2014/6/dga-wga-mkekmbers-use-fake-names.
denofgeek.com/movies/saw/16540/cary-elwes-inter view-saw-3d-glory-and-the-princess-bride#ixzz 4G7BtG3SV.
Denofgeek.com. The Ultimate Michael Biehn interview.
dictionary.tdf.org/line-reading.
Digitalwriting101.net.
Disc.yourwebapps.com/Indices/39627.html.
dps.texas.gov/TexasRangers/HistoricalDevelop ment.htm.
elenasandidge.com/2014/01/27/behind-the-scenes-of-tombstone-an-interview-with-peter-sherayko/.
examiner.com/article/making-tombstone-the-movie.
express.co.uk/dayandnight/69210.
fdtimes.com/2011/02/15william-a-fraker.
henryswesternroundup.blogspot.com/2012/06/hall marks-hannahs-law-saturday.html.
hollywoodnews.com. exclusive: Michael Biehn digs up details about the making of "Tombstone."
ibj.com/articles/67784-eiteljorg-show-looks-at-the-good-the-bad-and-the-ugly-of-hollywood-westerns
ign.com/articles/2010/05/01.
indiewire.com/2015/04/attention-filmmakers-heres-why-you-should-make-medium-length-films-62586.
informit.com/article.
Johnnyringo.com.
Jwayne.com.
law2.umkc.edu/faculty/projects/trials/earp/ordi nances.html.
Lebeau'sLeBlog.com.
legendsofamerica.com.
mininghalloffame.org/inductee/schieffelin.
minyanville.com/business-news/editors-pick/art icles/why-christmas-day-movie-releases-the/12/ 20/2013/id/53117
movieweb.com.
nextooze.com.
northhollywoodfilms.com.
online.nmartmuseum.org/nmhistory/growing-new-mexico/tourism/history-tourism.
Pbs.org/wgbh/americoanexperience/features/tran script/wyatt-transcript.
policeone.com.
Rheavcn.blogspot/com.
Rogerebert.com.
Slackerwood.com/node/2929.
Slashfilm.com.
starpulse.com.
texasranger.org.
therpf.com.
tshaonline.org/handbook/nline/articles/met04.
tombstoneweb.com/history.html.
trend-chaser.com.
wn.com.

Index

Numbers in *bold italics* indicate pages with illustrations.